Complete Italian

Lydia Vellaccio
and Maurice Elston

Advisory editor
Paul Coggle

For UK order enquiries: please contact Bookpoint Ltd, 130 Milton Park, Abingdon, Oxon OX14 4SB. *Telephone*: +44 (0) 1235 827720. Fax: +44 (0) 1235 400454. Lines are open 09.00–17.00, Monday to Saturday, with a 24-hour message answering service. Details about our titles and how to order are available at www.teachyourself.com

For USA order enquiries: please contact McGraw-Hill Customer Services, PO Box 545, Blacklick, OH 43004-0545, USA. *Telephone*: 1-800-722-4726. Fax: 1-614-755-5645.

For Canada order enquiries: please contact McGraw-Hill Ryerson Ltd, 300 Water St, Whitby, Ontario L1N 9B6, Canada. *Telephone*: 905 430 5000. Fax: 905 430 5020.

Long renowned as the authoritative source for self-guided learning – with more than 50 million copies sold worldwide – the *Teach Yourself* series includes over 500 titles in the fields of languages, crafts, hobbies, business, computing and education.

British Library Cataloguing in Publication Data: a catalogue record for this title is available from the British Library.

Library of Congress Catalog Card Number: on file.

First published in UK 1998 as *Teach Yourself Italian* by Hodder Education, part of Hachette UK, 338 Euston Road, London NW1 3BH.

First published in US 1998 by The McGraw-Hill Companies, Inc.

This edition published 2010.

The *Teach Yourself* name is a registered trade mark of Hodder Headline.

Typeset by Julie Martin. Illustrated by Barking Dog Art, Sally Elford, Oxford Designers and Illustrators.

Printed in Italy for Hodder Education, an Hachette UK Company, 338 Euston Road, London NW1 3BH.

The publisher has used its best endeavours to ensure that the URLs for external websites referred to in this book are correct and active at the time of going to press. However, the publisher has no responsibility for the websites and can give no guarantee that a site will remain live or that the content is or will remain appropriate.

Hachette UK's policy is to use papers that are natural, renewable and recyclable products and made from wood grown in sustainable forests. The logging and manufacturing processes are expected to conform to the environmental regulations of the country of origin.

Impression number 10 9 8 7 6 5 4 3

Year 2014 2013 2012 2011 2010

Contents

Meet the authors

Our experience of teaching Italian to English-speaking students from all sorts of social and educational backgrounds has convinced us that although ability and intelligence do play a significant role, the most important contributory factor to your successful language acquisition is likely to be your need to learn.

We have produced this course with your needs in mind. Our dialogues represent the sort of everyday situations and exchanges you are likely to come across in your daily life in Italy. The explanation of the grammar points and practice sections are there to enable you to begin to adapt the language you learn to your particular requirements. At first you will find that you are simply repeating what you see, and, if you have the recording, what you hear. Then, little by little, you will acquire the skills to modify the language to a point where you will be confident enough to deal with a variety of specific situations. By the end of the course you will be surprised by how much you have learnt. Your perseverance will be rewarded: you will be able to adapt what you have acquired to cope with whatever situations you are likely to encounter. You will also find when you have the opportunity to meet Italians face to face, that you will be guided by their body language, and will even end up imitating it yourself. At this point our course will have served its purpose, and you will be able to continue your journey unaided. Then, as Italians say: **In bocca al lupo!** *Good luck!*

Only got a minute?

First of all, a little background knowledge: Italian is spoken by over sixty million people. Apart from in Italy (which, by the way, includes the islands of Sicily and Sardinia), Italian is spoken in Corsica, parts of Istria and Dalmatia in the former Yugoslavia, and the Ticino canton in Switzerland. Massive emigration over the past hundred years has led to the establishment of Italian-speaking communities all over the world, including in the United States, Brazil, Argentina, Australia and (to a lesser extent) New Zealand.

For centuries, Italian has been the language of art, music, design and fashion. Tourists have flocked to Italy, attracted by the climate, art and architecture, opera houses and the people. Many, as a result of their visit, have decided to stay and learn the language. What is it about Italian that makes it so attractive to listen to? Is it because so many of us associate it with singing and music? One reason why singers love singing in Italian is that once they see it on the printed page, it is relatively easy to pronounce: in Italian what you see is what you hear, and every syllable counts. Once you have mastered the basic sounds you are well on the way to understanding. You probably know quite a lot already: **pizza**, **maestro**, **spaghetti** and **ciao** have all become part of English.

Whatever your reasons for studying Italian, this course will provide you with an excellent introduction to mastering this beautiful language and acquainting yourself with its wonderful people.

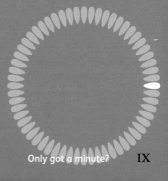

5 Only got five minutes?

Italian, French, Portuguese and Spanish are grouped together under the heading of Romance Languages. Romance in this particular context has nothing to do with romantic novels. It means that all these languages have a close relationship with Rome and the Romans: they all derive to a greater or lesser extent from Latin. If you are only vaguely familiar with one of these languages, you will notice many similarities if you decide to learn another in this group: it will be rather like meeting old friends under a different guise. If, on the other hand, Italian is the very first foreign language you are learning, you are in for a very pleasant surprise, because, unlike English, where many of us find ourselves constantly consulting the dictionary to check our spelling, Italian sounds match the spelling or written language to a remarkable degree.

Take for instance this group of five words: **prima donna**, **viola**, **concerto** and **virtuoso**. They are, so to speak, direct imports from Italy: they have come unchanged straight into English. An Italian hearing an English speaker pronounce them would recognise them instantly. The one exception is perhaps **concerto**: try pronouncing it for yourself once or twice and you will realise that the 'r' sound has mysteriously disappeared when you say it in English. We will come back to that in a moment. What we, as English speakers, have done is to take over these words (we have in a way 'borrowed' them) and pronounced them as closely as we can to the original Italian. If we said them aloud to an Italian, he would certainly understand what we were saying but they would sound slightly odd to his ear. These words are in fact 'specialist' words: they belong to a particular trade or profession, and in this case it is the world of music and opera (another 'specialist' word), where the Italians reigned supreme for a long time: although opera is now performed internationally, much of the vocabulary has retained more or less its original Italian pronunciation. The same may be said of Italian food. Italian chefs have spread their culinary skills worldwide, and so we tend to pronounce words such as **pizza**, **spaghetti** and **pasta** much in the same way as Italians do. Remember though; it is not quite the same.

Now take a look at this second group of words: *concert*, *intelligent*, *romantic* and *nation*. An Italian hearing us say these words for the first time might not have the slightest idea what they meant, although if he saw them written down he would recognise them instantly. So, why the difference? They are still very close to their Italian equivalents *concerto*, *intelligente*, *romantico* and *nazione*, but they reached our language by a different route, probably across the Alps via France. Time, travel and long widespread usage have 'customised' these words and absorbed them into our everyday speech. There are lots of words like this that you will recognise instantly once you see them written in Italian – this will be a great help in learning. But if we want a guide to pronunciation we must go back to that 'specialist' word **concerto**. Try pronouncing it two or three times. What do you notice about that letter 'c'? It is pronounced in two different ways. The first 'c' is very close to our English *cat*, but the second one is pronounced more like the 'ch' in *church*. The reason is very simple: that's the way the Italians always pronounce 'c' when it comes before the letters *e* and *i*. No exceptions! As for the letter 'r' , which has mysteriously disappeared when the word is pronounced in English, it is *always* pronounced in Italian. Again – no exceptions! It is this consistency that makes Italian such an attractive language to learn.

And so, after our first lesson in pronouncing Italian, let's consider the grammar. For some reason, when some students hear this word, it's enough to turn them off completely. Of course, we would like to think that life would be much simpler if there were no grammar at all. Many foreigners think English is virtually grammar-free. What they really mean is that English grammar is not at all like theirs, even though it *does* exist, all the same. It's just that it works in a different way. If we go back to our group of Romance Languages, all of them show remarkable similarities grammar-wise. So what distinguishes them from English?

Let's return briefly to Latin. The Latin that developed into these languages is known today by a special label: Vulgar Latin (not because it was considered cheap and nasty, but simply because it was the Latin spoken by ordinary people going about their daily lives, picking up what bits of Latin they could from their Roman conquerors, who were, after all, mainly soldiers by trade). Classical Latin, on the other hand, was the language of the great Roman orators, statesmen, poets and historians, and judged by today's standards, it is all rather artificial.

In Latin, you have to focus particularly on the endings of words to make any sense of them within a sentence. These endings have remained in Italian to some extent, as we shall see now.

The most striking difference between Italian and English is a structural one. If we take a very common verb or activity such as the English to put, if you think about it, the word can only exist in three forms, namely: *put, puts, putting*. Once you know these three forms you can describe something that is happening now, (*he puts* or *he is putting*), something that happened in the past (*he put* or *has put*), or something that will happen in the future (*he will put*). Italian expresses present, past and future in a rather different but more concise way: it sticks endings onto the verb or activity. *He puts* or *is putting* therefore becomes **mette**, *he put* or *he has put* becomes **ha messo**, and *he will put* becomes **metterà**. What you need to bear in mind and remember for the moment is not the words themselves, but why the ending matters – it tells you who is doing what and when they are doing it. Your first thought may be how on earth are you going to remember all these different endings. You will find that because they have meaning and significance you will do so almost unconsciously. You will be meeting them all the time in relevant and meaningful situations. You will most likely find the opposite: you won't be able to forget them! In English we often swallow our final syllables or vowels, but in Italian every syllable counts, especially the vowel at the end (you will notice that nearly all Italian words end in a vowel). This has to ring out loud and clear, and this is one of the reasons why international singers love singing in Italian. It is also why you too will have far less trouble spelling Italian words than you ever had (and may still have!) spelling English ones. Because the end of the word in Italian tells you who is performing the activity, the words for *I*, *you*, *he* etc. are generally only used for emphasis, contrast or in case of ambiguity, and are very often not used at all. You will soon get accustomed to this too.

The other big difference between Italian and English concerns names: names for things, and names for people and places. You may have heard them called nouns, but the important thing is to be able to recognise them.

You may be familiar with some Italian names. Men's forenames for example often end in –o: **Romeo**, **Mario**, **Roberto**, etc., whereas women's ones tend to end in –a: **Maria**, **Lucia**, **Vera**, **Ida** etc. What about if we are talking about things instead? In Italian, nouns are divided by gender in the same way. To those of us who know only English this may seem slightly strange, until we realise that *all* the Romance Languages (and many others too) divide names for things in this way. Why? Because Latin did, and so did Sanskrit before it, the origin of most European languages. What makes this way of going about things simpler to manage in Italian is that in most cases these endings (which are always clearly heard) are pointers not only to putting phrases and sentences together, but to understanding them too. We explain through simple dialogues in everyday situations not only why this is important in Italian, but how you too can use this knowledge to build on a solid foundation that will, if you persevere with this course, enable you to speak and understand Italian with confidence.

For most beginners learning Italian is an exciting and exhilarating experience. This is probably because they have met or heard Italians discussing, arguing, and gesticulating amongst themselves: whether they are angry or contented they seem to us Anglo-Saxons to be living life to the full. Learning Italian may yet add another dimension to your life too!

10 Only got ten minutes?

Early pre-eminence in European architecture, banking, painting, literature and music has enriched the English language with many words of Italian origin: dome, cupola, bank, fresco, sonnet, piano, opera and concerto are a few of the more obvious examples.

The great appeal of Italy has long been its landscape, its literary and artistic heritage, and of course its great operatic tradition. More recently it has seen itself as a great rival to France in its culinary skills and fashion and design know-how. However, it is equally important to note that like Great Britain and the USA, it is a great manufacturing and trading nation. It still supports too a substantial amount of agriculture. **Agriturismo**, the combination of farming with tourist resorts, and **arteturismo**, the combination of tourism with the local arts and crafts of a particular region, are both more recent developments that combine new ideas with traditional skills: wherever you go in Italy, you are struck by the skilful way in which Italians manage to achieve this blend of ancient and modern. A glance at its long history may provide some clues to this rich heritage.

Long before the foundation of Rome by the legendary Romulus and Remus, Greek civilisation had reached the coasts of the Italian mainland and the island of Sicily in the shape of colonial settlements. Pythagoras, for instance, had migrated to Crotone on the southern coast of Italy, and Archimedes lived in **Siracusa** or Syracuse, a Greek colony in Sicily. The dialects in those regions still retain remnants of Greek vocabulary, and the coastal city of Naples, or **Napoli**, is a shortened form of its Greek name **Neapolis**, meaning 'The New City'. Meanwhile, inland, Etruscan tribes were warring amongst thenselves: they left many traces of their culture, in the form of tombs and mysterious inscriptions. However, up until now, unfortunately, no one has been able to decipher or make much sense of them.

The remains of the Greek temples and theatres are still there. Excavations are continuously revealing more and more antiquities every year. Their design and structure was revered by the Romans, who, by superior organisation and military supremacy, managed to conquer most of the Italian peninsula and the Mediterranean countries surrounding it. They were most scrupulous in imitating Greek art and architecture, but unfortunately became more and more unscrupulous in plundering their conquered territories. As Rome grew richer and more powerful, ultimately developing into a vast empire, colonial resentment grew ever more bitter. Ultimately, the Empire the Romans had created declined, but as a result of the Emperor Constantine's conversion from paganism to Christianity, this became the state religion. Constantine moved his capital from Rome to a city he gave his name to: Constantinople, now known as Istanbul. Rome became the capital of Christianity, known ever since (except for a brief spell in Avignon in the 13th century) as the Eternal City of the Papacy.

Since then, European rulers were anxious to obtain the divine seal of approval from the Pope before coming to the throne. The papacy therefore grew in power and prestige, and artists from all over Europe flocked to Rome to obtain papal commissions for works of sacred art, music and architecture. But while countries such as England, France and Spain were coalescing into nationhood and growing more and more united, Italy, or rather the country we now call Italy, was developing in a much more fragmented way along the lines of autonomous republics and kingdoms. The Pope developed his own army. Other states soon followed suit. So it came to pass that Rome, Venice, Florence and many other cities in the peninsula had their own rulers, armies, and more significantly, their own languages or dialects. These were a mixture of Latin acquired from the long occupation and administation of Roman military personnel, and whatever language was spoken by the local tribe. Each city occupied as much land as it could in the surrounding area, and so became a city-state. The Latin in everyday use at the time was not the literary language that the great Roman poets and orators had employed at the height of the Empire, but Vulgar Latin, the everyday language of the common people. As each state isolated itself from its neighbours, so individual dialects began to develop and diverge, until, in the process, separate dialects developed for each region. These dialects still exist. However, side by side with this development, since most of the educated classes had close links with the Catholic Church, and since the official language amongst the priesthood was Latin (a form of it that was closer to, but simpler than Classical Latin), this was the language in which all European diplomacy was carried out, and this was the language any serious treatise would be written in, whether in mathematics, astronomy, medicine or topography.

To understand how modern Italian came into being, we have to focus not on Rome, but on Florence in Tuscany, which, even in mediaeval times was a rich and beautiful city-state: the Florentines elected their own rulers and had their own army. These rulers, mainly from the merchant class, grew rich through commerce and trade. They became famous all over Europe through their patronage of the arts. Artists, musicians and poets gathered there, just as they had and continued to do in Rome. All of them were well versed in Church and Classical Latin, the language of the educated. One of its citizens, at first well-respected, but subsequently banished from the city, had the then revolutionary idea of writing a long epic poem not in Latin but in his native Tuscan dialect: his name was Dante (1265—1321) and his long epic poem **La Divina Commedia** describes his imaginary journey through Hell, Purgatory and Paradise. This poem became so famous not only in Tuscany but throughout the whole of the Italian peninsula, and subsquently all over Europe, that the Tuscan dialect became the standard against which most subsequent Italian literary works were judged, and it gradually became the dominant written language. Italian as we know it today was gradually replacing Church Latin, even in diplomatic circles.

Centuries later, while most of Europe was growing rapidly into a community of nation states, a Scottish writer, Walter Scott (1771—1832) began writing historical novels: stirring events, at first of Scottish history, woven into long novels, put the mountains and lakes of Scotland onto the European literary map.

Just as **La Divina Commedia** had stirred the imagination of mediaeval Europe, so the novels of Sir Walter Scott gripped the romantic imagination of the European public of the nineteenth century. In Italy, his novels were widely read and one of them was turned into an opera by Donizetti (**Lucia di Lammermoor**). But for one Italian writer in particular Scott's works were a source of remarkable literary inspiration. Alessandro Manzoni, stirred by the rising tide of public opinion demanding the unification of Italy, decided to write a novel set in the period of Spanish domination in the sixteenth century. He was especially concerned with style and decided, just as Dante had done before him, to choose as his standard model the Tuscan dialect (or the written form of it). He was writing at a time of particular ferment in national politics: Napoleon, who was at first looked upon as the great liberator after freeing Northern Italy from Austrian domination, was later reviled as a tyrant, and dead by the time Manzoni's novel (**I Promessi Sposi** – *The Betrothed*) was completed. This work, looked upon as a classic, helped establish once and for all the supremacy of Tuscan in the written language. At the time Manzoni was born,

Italy was still a conglomeration of independent states. By the time he had died in 1873, through the efforts of Garibaldi, Mazzini and Cavour, Italy had become one nation with Rome its capital once more. The Papacy continued to enjoy prestige, power and independence: in fact, even when Rome succumbed, the Pope and his retinue continued to lead a life apart, the vestiges of which still remain today in the Vatican City, which is technically still an independent state. Tuscan was increasingly becoming the one language not only read but also spoken all over Italy by the educated classes (bear in mind however that the educated classes were still a minority in this agrarian society). The Tuscan language was gradually becoming what we now call Italian. There still remained one or two local variations but they were were mainly ones of accent.

Italian as we know it today was still mainly confined to the towns. It was the arrival of universal education in the form of compulsory schooling in the late nineteenth and early twentieth centuries that enabled Italian to become widely accepted even in the remotest communities. Consequently, anyone who consistently spoke in dialect began to be regarded as uneducated.

Over the past ten or fifteen years there has been official encouragement in Italy to reverse this trend and revive the study and use of dialect. The general trend, however, continues to move towards their disappearance, except in the case of Neapolitan, where most popular singers include in their repertoire a selection of songs old and new in dialect. This is a pity, because the dialects have certainly added a touch of disinctivenes and individuality to the various regions. From your point of view however, as a prospective beginner, it is obviously an advantage, since you can be sure that the Italian you will now be learning will be understood throughout the country.

Are you ready now to take that first plunge and discover a whole new world, just as Cristoforo Colombo, that great Italian navigator, did, when he set sail from Genova in search of other unknown lands, just over six centuries ago?

Introduction

Welcome to Complete Italian!

Is this the right course for you? If you are an adult learner with no previous knowledge of Italian and studying on your own, then this is the course for you. Perhaps you are taking up Italian again after a break from it, or you are intending to learn with the support of a class? Again, you will find this course very well suited to your purposes.

DEVELOPING YOUR SKILLS

The language introduced in this course is centred around realistic everyday situations. The emphasis is first and foremost on **using** Italian, but we also aim to give you an idea of how the language works, so that you can create sentences of your own.

The course covers all four of the basic skills – listening and speaking, reading and writing. If you are working on your own, the recording will be all the more important, as it will provide you with the essential opportunity to listen to Italian and to speak it within a controlled framework. You should therefore try to obtain a copy of the recording if you haven't already got one.

Use it or lose it!

Language learning is a bit like jogging – you need to do it regularly for it to do any good! Ideally, you should find a 'study buddy' to work through the course with you. This way you will have someone to try out your Italian on. And when the going gets tough, you will have someone to chivvy you on until you reach your target.

The structure of this course

The course book contains **25 course units** plus a **reference section** at the back of the book. There are also **two recordings** which you really do need to have if you are going to get maximum benefit from the course.

THE COURSE UNITS

The course units can be divided roughly into the following categories, although of course there is a certain amount of overlap from one category to another.

Statement of aims
You will be told what you can expect to learn, mostly in terms of what you will be able to do in Italian by the end of the unit.

Presentation of new language
Usually in the form of dialogues which are recorded and also printed in the book. Some assistance with vocabulary is also given. The language is presented in manageable chunks, building carefully on what you have learned in earlier units.

Practice of the new language
Practice is graded, so that activities which require mainly *recognition* come first. As you grow in confidence in manipulating the language forms, you will be encouraged to produce both in writing and in speech.

Description of language forms
In these sections you learn about the *forms* of the language, thus enabling you to construct your own sentences correctly. For those who are daunted by grammar, assistance is given in various ways.

Pronunciation and intonation
The best way to acquire good pronunciation and intonation is to listen to native speakers and try to imitate them. But most people

do not actually notice that certain sounds in Italian are pronounced differently from their English counterparts, until this is pointed out to them. For this reason we include specific advice within the course units.

Information on Italy and Italian life
Here you will find information on Italy and various aspects of Italian life – from the level of formality that is appropriate when you talk to strangers, to how the health service works if you should fall ill.

REFERENCE SECTION

The reference section includes:

- ▶ *a glossary of grammar terms*
- ▶ *a key to the exercises*
- ▶ *Italian–English and English–Italian vocabularies.*

How to use this course

At the beginning of each course unit make sure that you are clear about what you can expect to learn.

Read any background information that is provided. Then listen to the dialogues on the recording. Try to get the gist of what is being said before you look at the printed text in the book. Refer to the printed text and the key words and phrases in order to study the dialogues in more detail.

KEEP LISTENING!

Don't fall into the trap of thinking you have 'done that' when you have listened to the recording a couple of times and worked through the dialogues in the book. You may *recognise* what you hear and read, but you almost certainly still have some way to go before you can *produce* the language of the dialogues correctly and fluently. This is why we recommend that you keep listening to the recording at every opportunity – sitting on the tube or bus, waiting at the dentist's or stuck in a traffic jam in the car, using what would otherwise be 'dead' time. Of course, you must also be internalizing what you hear and making sense of it – just playing it in the background without really paying attention is not enough!

CHECK YOUR PROGRESS

As you work your way through the exercises, check your answers carefully in the back of the book. It is easy to overlook your own mistakes. If you have a study buddy, it's a good idea to check each other's answers. Most of the exercises have fixed answers, but some are a bit more open-ended, especially when we are asking you to talk about yourself. We then, in most cases, give you a model answer which you can adapt for your own purposes.

Before you move on to a new unit always make sure that you know all the new words and phrases in the current unit. Try covering up the English side of the page and producing the English equivalents of the Italian. If you find that relatively easy, go on to cover up the Italian side of the page and produce the Italian equivalents of the English. You will probably find this more difficult. Trying to recall the context in which words and phrases were used may help you learn them better. After Units 6, 12, 18 and 25, check your progress in the *Test your Italian* section towards the end of the book.

GRAMMAR

We have tried to make the grammar explanations as user-friendly as possible, because we recognize that many people find grammar daunting. But in the end, it is up to you just how much time you spend on studying and sorting out the grammar points. Some people find that they can do better by getting an ear for what sounds right, others need to know in detail how the language is put together.

Sources of real Italian

See Unit 25 and the *Taking it further* section for information about the Italian media. The Italian Cultural Institute is also a useful resource – there are branches throughout the world, for example in London, at 39 Belgrave Square, SW1X 8NX (tel. 020 7235 1461); in New York, at 686 Park Avenue, NY 10021 (tel. 212 879 4242).

1

Scusi!
Excuse me!

In this unit you will learn:
- *how to attract someone's attention*
- *how to say what languages you speak*
- *how to make and respond to simple enquiries or requests*
- *how to say you don't know*
- *how to exchange greetings formally*
- *how to accept or refuse what is offered to you.*

1 Parla inglese?
Do you speak English?

Il portiere (*the porter*) of a small hotel in Rome is having difficulties communicating with his foreign guests. He is looking for an Italian who speaks English and German to help out. He addresses **la signorina Anna Muti** (*Miss Anna Muti*).

If you have the recording listen to the following dialogue carefully, and without looking at the text, answer the following questions orally:

  a *How does the porter ask her: 'Do you speak English?'*

Portiere	Scusi, signorina!
Sig.na M.	Sì ...? Prego?
Portiere	Parla inglese?
Sig.na M.	Sì. Parlo inglese e francese.
Portiere	Ah, benissimo! Parla anche tedesco, vero?
Sig.na M.	No. Mi dispiace. Non parlo tedesco.

Insight

Attenzione! In this book we use a line under a vowel to show the stressed syllable. So we say **benissimo**, with the stress on the second syllable. See the Pronunciation section later in this unit for more information.

QUICK VOCAB

Sì ...? Prego? *Yes ...? Can I help you?*
Benissimo! *Splendid! Great!*
Parla anche tedesco, vero? *You speak German, too, don't you?*
No. Mi dispiace. *No. I'm sorry (I don't).*
e *and*

   b *How does Anna say: 'I speak English and French'?*
   c *How does she say: 'I don't speak German'?*

◀) **CD 1, TR 1, 01:29**

Listen to the following list of languages. Tick the ones that have appeared in the dialogue. Can you guess the others? If in doubt, check them in the vocabulary at the back of the book.

italiano ☐   russo ☐   tedesco ☐   cinese ☐   giapponese ☐
spagnolo ☐   greco ☐   francese ☐   inglese ☐   portoghese ☐

   d *How would you say that you speak the following languages?*
      __ inglese. __ francese. __ tedesco.
   e *How would you say that you don't speak the following?*
      __ cinese. __ giapponese. __ russo.

f *Now ask someone: 'Do you speak Italian?'* __

Parla also means *he/she speaks* or *he/she is speaking*.

Pablo Serra parla spagnolo.	*Pablo Serra is speaking Spanish.*
Anna Muti parla italiano.	*Anna Muti is speaking Italian.*

g *Match each picture with the correct caption (the first one is done for you), and complete the captions for* **Gérard Dupont** *and* **Helga Weil.**

Pablo Serra parla spagnolo.
Anna Muti parla italiano.   *Betty Warren parla inglese.*
Gérard Dupont _____ .   *Helga Weil* _____ .

---

2 Sì, è lì
Yes, it's (over) there

Two guests ask the porter for information. The first guest, **una signora** (*a woman*), asks him where the lift and telephone are.

a *How does she attract the porter's attention and ask where the lift is?*

Signora	Scusi, l'ascensore, per favore?
Portiere	L'ascensore? Sì, è lì.
Signora	E il telefono?
Portiere	È qui, a sinistra.
Signora	Grazie.
Portiere	Prego.

QUICK VOCAB

l'ascensore *the lift*
per favore *please*
è qui, a sinistra *it's here on the left*
prego *don't mention it, you're welcome*

b *How does she say: 'Thank you'?*
c *How would* **you** *attract someone's attention and ask where the telephone is?*

---

3 Non lo so
I don't know

The second guest, **un signore** (*a man*), asks him where the station and the bank are. Being new to Rome, **il portiere** doesn't know all the answers.

◆) **CD 1, TR 1, 02:30**

a *There is another way of saying please in this dialogue: what is it?*

Signore	Scusi, la stazione, per piacere?
Portiere	Sempre dritto, poi a destra. Dopo il semaforo.
Signore	E la banca?
Portiere	Mi dispiace. Non lo so.

sempre dritto *straight on*
poi *then*
a destra *on the right*
dopo *after*
il semaforo *the traffic lights*

b *How does the porter say: 'I'm sorry'?*
c *How would you attract someone's attention and ask where the bank is?*
d *If you were asked the same question how would you reply: 'I don't know'?*
e *Listen to the above dialogues and mark where the stress falls in the following words:*
   Esempio (example): **scusi**
   sinistra, stazione, ascensore, grazie, telefono

Look at the following town signs. Are the statements underneath each one *true or false* (**vero o falso**)? Correct the false statements.

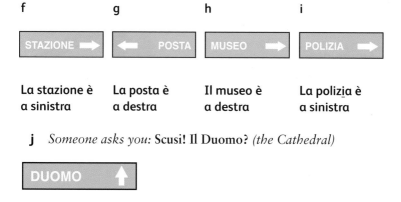

f

STAZIONE ➡

La stazione è
a sinistra

g

⬅ POSTA

La posta è
a destra

h

MUSEO ➡

Il museo è
a destra

i

POLIZIA ➡

La polizia è
a sinistra

j *Someone asks you:* **Scusi! Il Duomo?** *(the Cathedral)*

DUOMO ⬆

Look at the sign. What do you answer?

k **La posta** *is the post-office. Can you guess what* **il museo** *and* **la polizia** *are?*

4 Buongiorno. Come sta?
Good morning. How are you?

Un professore (*a teacher*) meets **Giulia**, one of his students. They exchange greetings. How does the teacher greet **Giulia**? What does **Giulia** say when she leaves?

CD 1, TR 1, 02:56

Professore	Buongiorno, signorina Giulia.
Giulia	Buongiorno, professore. Come sta?
Professore	Bene, grazie. E lei?
Giulia	Molto bene, grazie.
Professore	Ci vediamo domani! Arrivederci!
Giulia	Arrivederci, professore!

VOCAB

E lei? *And you?*
(molto) bene *(very) well*
Ci vediamo domani. *See you tomorrow!*

5 Un gelato?
An ice cream?

Il professore goes into a café where un dottore (*a doctor*) and other friends of his are waiting for him. He offers them something to drink.

a *What does the teacher say to offer an ice cream to the young woman?*

CD 1, TR 1, 03:28

Professore	Un tè, signora?
Signora	No, grazie.
Professore	Un gelato, signorina?
Signorina	Sì, grazie.
Professore	E per lei, dottore? Un caffè o una birra?
Dottore	Un espresso e una pasta, grazie.

Sources of real Italian

See Unit 25 and the *Taking it further* section for information about the Italian media. The Italian Cultural Institute is also a useful resource – there are branches throughout the world, for example in London, at 39 Belgrave Square, SW1X 8NX (tel. 020 7235 1461); in New York, at 686 Park Avenue, NY 10021 (tel. 212 879 4242).

per *for*
o *or*
una pasta *a cake*

Bar Italia

acqua
minerale
tè
caffè
birra
espresso
limonata
cioccolata

b *What expressions are used for no, thank you and yes, please?*

c *Guess what the drinks in the dialogue are. If necessary, check your answers in the vocabulary at the back of the book.*

d *If you have the recording, you will hear a list of drinks. Listen carefully and see which ones you can recognize. Tick them off on the Bar Italia board above as you hear them. Look up those you don't understand. There should be one left over: which is it?*

Respond to the pictures as in the example. ✔ = you accept.
✗ = you refuse.

e	**f**	**g**
✗	✔	✗	✔

Esempio: Un espresso? No, grazie.

Pronunciation

🔊 **CD 1, TR 2**

VOWELS

Italian has five vowels: **a, e, i, o, u**. The vowels **a, i** and **u** each represent one sound only. When the vowel is stressed it is slightly longer.

a is pronounced as in *bat*: listen to the following words: p**a**sta,
limon**a**ta, parla, banana. Notice particularly how, in the Italian
word **banana**, the vowel **a** has exactly the same sound throughout,
even though the second **a** is longer because of the stress: **ba-na-na**.

i is pronounced as in English *machine*: sì, sinistra, scusi, birra.

u is pronounced as in English *rule*: **u**n, **u**na, mus**e**o, scusi,
cappucc**i**no

Insight

Attenzione! Beware! Pronounce *u* as in *rule* NOT as in *tune*.
e has two sounds:
   as in English *get*: è, pr**e**go, tel**e**fono, d**e**stra, caffè.
   as in English *they*: e, franc**e**se, piac**e**re, s**e**ra, arrived**e**rci.
o has two sounds:
   as in English *got*: no, po', posta.
   as in English *ought*: Roma, come, parlo.

STRESS: BENISSIMO

1 *Stress usually falls on the last syllable but one:* pr**e**go,
stazi**o**ne, limon**a**ta.
2 *An accent on the final vowel of a word must be stressed:* caffè.
3 *Occasionally, the stress falls on the last syllable but two:*
ben**i**ssimo, tel**e**fono, **u**tile, sem**a**foro.
In all such cases, and especially where any doubts or confusion
may arise, we mark the stress with a line under the stressed vowel
(or vowels, in the case of diphthongs): **Gi**u**lia, poli**z**ia**.

ACCENTS

There are two accents in Italian: the grave (`) for open vowels
(verità, caffè, così, andrò, gioventù) and the acute (´) for closed
vowels (perché, ventitré). In this book we follow normal everyday
practice in using the grave accent even on vowels that are
considered to be closed. Apart from showing final stress, the accent
distinguishes between two words that would otherwise be written
the same: e *and*; è *is*; la *the*; là *there*.

Grammar

1 SAYING 'PLEASE' AND 'THANK YOU'

grazie	*thank you*
prego	*not at all, don't mention it*
per favore ⎤	
per piacere ⎦	*please*

Although **grazie** normally means *thank you* and **per piacere** or **per favore** *please*, care must be taken to use only **sì, grazie/no, grazie** when someone is offering you something:

Un caffè, dottore?	*A coffee (Doctor)?*
Sì, grazie.	*Yes, please.*
Una cioccolata, signora?	*A hot chocolate (Madam)?*
No, grazie.	*No, thank you.*

In response to thanks Italians instinctively reply **prego**:

Grazie.	*Thank you.*
Prego.	*Not at all, you're welcome, don't mention it.*

When **Prego?** is used as a question it means *Can I help you?* or *Pardon?*

2 PARLO, PARLA *(I SPEAK, YOU SPEAK)*

(Io) parlo	*I speak, I am speaking.*
(Lei) parla	*You speak, you are speaking.*

Parla can also mean *he/she speaks* or *he/she is speaking*, as explained above.

The pronouns (**io** *I*, **lei** *you*, etc.) are only used for emphasis, contrast, or to avoid ambiguity. The context will usually make it clear whether **parla** refers to you, *he* or *she*. Notice also that the verb 'to be' is not used. Therefore in Italian *I am speaking* is the same as *I speak*: **parlo**.

3 DOMANDE E RISPOSTE *QUESTIONS AND ANSWERS*

To ask a question, Italians simply change the intonation of their voice. Listen to all the questions on the recording very carefully and compare the intonation with that of statements.

Parla italiano?	*Do you speak Italian?*
Sì. Parlo italiano e inglese.	*Yes. I speak Italian and English.*
Parla inglese?	*Does he/she speak English?*

Vero (literally *true*) added to the end of a question is the equivalent of the English *don't you? isn't it? aren't they?* etc.

Maria parla tedesco, vero?	*Maria speaks German, doesn't she?*
No. Parla spagnolo.	*No. She speaks Spanish.*
È lì, vero?	*It's (over) there, isn't it?*
Sì. È lì.	*Yes. It's (over) there.*

In answer to questions such as *Do you speak Italian?* we would normally answer in English: *Yes, I do* or *No, I don't*. Italians simply answer: **Sì** or **No,** or they repeat the whole sentence: **Sì. Parlo italiano** or **No. Non parlo italiano.** They do *not* express *do* or *don't*.

4 THE NEGATIVE

In negative sentences use **non** before the verb:

parlo; non parlo	*I speak; I don't speak*
Anna parla inglese, ma non parla tedesco.	*Anna speaks English, but she doesn't speak German.*

Non è qui Roberto? *Isn't Robert here?*

5 GREETINGS AND TITLES

Buongiorno (lit: *good day*) *hello, good morning, goodbye*

Buonasera (lit: *good evening*) is used for the late afternoon and evening.

Buonanotte *goodnight*

Arrivederci *goodbye* (at any time of day)

Note the various meanings of the following words and their abbreviated forms from the dialogues:

signore (sig.)	*(gentle)man, Mr, sir*
signora (sig.ra)	*lady, Mrs, madam*
signorina (sig.na)	*young lady/woman, Miss*
professore (prof.)	*any professor or teacher*
dottore (dott.)	*any university graduate; not restricted to the medical profession*

Italians normally use titles when addressing each other formally:

Buongiorno, signora.	*Good morning (madam).*
Buonasera, signorina.	*Good evening (miss).*
Grazie, dottore. Arrivederci!	*Thank you (doctor). Goodbye.*

6 NOUNS AND ARTICLES – SINGULAR

In Italian most words end in a vowel.

Names for men usually end in -o: Carlo *Charles*, Franco *Frank*, amico *friend* (male).

Names for women usually end in -a: Anna *Anne*, Maria *Mary*, amica *friend* (female).

Names for things usually end in -o or -a: gelato, posta.

If they end in -o they are called masculine nouns.

If they end in -a they are called feminine nouns.

Masculine		Feminine	
il **gelato**	*the ice cream*	la **birra**	*the beer*
il **museo**	*the museum*	la **polizia**	*the police*
il **dottore**	*the doctor*	la **lezione**	*the lesson*
l'**amico**	*the friend (male)*	l'**amica**	*the friend (female)*
un **espresso**	*an expresso*	una **pasta**	*a cake*
un **aperitivo**	*an aperitif*	una **parola**	*a word*
un **tè**	*a tea*	una **stazione**	*a station*

Come si dice in italiano?
How do you say it in Italian?

◀) **CD 1, TR 3**

How to:

1 *attract someone's attention*   **Scusi!**
*reply to someone attracting your
    attention*   **Prego?**

2 *ask someone whether they speak*   **Parla inglese?**
*   English*

say that you speak English and   **Parlo inglese e
    Italian*   italiano.**

3 *say that you don't speak Spanish*   **Non parlo spagnolo.**

4 *make a simple enquiry (buildings*   **Il museo, per favore?**
*   you know)*

say whether something is: here/   **È qui/lì**
*   (over) there*

on the right/on the left/ straight   **a destra/a sinistra/sempre
*   ahead*   dritto.**

make a simple request (in a café)   **Una birra, un tè per piacere/
    per favore.**

5 *greet someone:*
*   (morning/early afternoon)*   **Buongiorno!**
*   (later afternoon/evening)*   **Buonasera!**
*   (before going to bed)*   **Buonanotte!**
*   (on departure)*   **Arrivederci!**

| **6** | *offer someone a coffee* | **Un caffè?** |
| | *accept/refuse what you are offered* | **Sì, gr<u>a</u>zie./No, gr<u>a</u>zie.** |

| **7** | *say you don't know* | **Non lo so.** |

| **8** | *say 'thank you'* | **Gr<u>a</u>zie.** |
| | *respond to thanks* | **Prego.** |

Now cover up the right-hand side and try to give the Italian.

Insight

This procedure will help you to learn fast by doing this in every **Come si dice** section.

Practice

1

Olga · Franco · Anna · Alfredo · Carlo · Rita · Roberto · Maria

Coca-cola · Caffè · Gelato · Cioccolata · Birra · Granita di limone* · Cappuccino · Tè

crushed ice flavoured with lemon

Look at this group of friends sitting round a café table; go round clockwise and write down what drink each person is asking for. Choose carefully between **un** and **una**.

Esempio: **a** Franco: 'Un caffè, per favore.'; **b** Anna: __ ;
c Alfredo: __ ; **d** Maria: __; **e** Roberto: ___ ; **f** Rita: __ ;
g Carlo: __ ; **h** Olga: __

2 *Now help the waiter when he returns by telling him which drink is for which person. Choose carefully between* il *and* la.
Esempio: Il caffè è per Franco.

3 *Look at the following table which tells you what language(s) Olga and her friends speak. If you were talking about Olga you would write:* Olga parla inglese, francese e spagnolo. *What would you write about* **a** *Franco,* **b** *Rita,* **c** *Carlo?* **d** *How would you write that Carlo speaks German but (*ma*) doesn't speak French?*

	inglese	francese	tedesco	spagnolo
Olga	✔	✔		✔
Franco	✔			
Rita		✔		✔
Carlo			✔	✔

e *How would you say: 'I don't speak Spanish'?*

f *How would you ask someone: 'Do you speak French?'*

g *Pretend you are Olga and say which languages you speak; which languages you don't speak.*

Note that capital letters are not used for languages in Italian.

4 Ora tocca a te! *Now it's your turn.*

A tourist stops you in the street and asks you the way. Complete your side of the following conversation:

(If you are using the recording, use the pause button to give you time to answer.)

Turista	Scusi!
You	(*Respond to him*).
Turista	La posta, per favore?
You	(*It's over there on the left*).
Turista	E la stazione?
You	(*Straight ahead*).
Turista	Grazie.
You	(*Don't mention it*).

Check your responses against those of the model dialogue in the *Key to the exercises* at the end of the book, then use that dialogue so that you take the part of the tourist.

Coffee

The general word for coffee in Italian is **caffè**. Espresso (*black*) coffee is served in very small cups as it is quite strong. A **cappuccino** is a frothy white coffee given a distinctive flavour by a sprinkling of chocolate. **Caffè macchiato** is coffee with a dash of milk.

TEST YOURSELF

Match the column on the left with the appropriate continuation on the right.

1 Un caffè, signorina?

2 Francesca parla inglese?

3 Scusi, l'ascensore, per piacere?

4 Una birra per la signorina!

5 Sandra parla tedesco e russo, ma ...

6 Come sta?

7 Ci vediamo

8 Scusi, il museo è a destra?

9 Il Bar Italia, per favore?

10 Grazie.

a ... non parla francese.

b No, è a sinistra.

c Anche per lei, dottore?

d domani.

e Sempre dritto, poi a destra dopo il semaforo.

f Sì, grazie.

g Prego!

h Sì, parla inglese e greco.

i Molto bene, grazie.

j Mi dispiace, non lo so.

2

In giro per la città
Out and about in town

In this unit you will learn:
- *how to identify things and places*
- *how to ask and say where people and places are*
- *how to order a snack or drink and ask for the bill.*

___

1 Cos'è?
What is it?

Franco is showing **Roberta** round the town.

a *What are the words he uses to point out the Cathedral?*

Franco	Ecco il Duomo!
Roberta	E cos'è questo?
Franco	Questo è il Museo Nazionale.
Roberta	Bello! E questo palazzo? Cos'è? È una banca?
Franco	Sì. Questa è la Banca Commerciale.

CD 1, TR 5

questo/questa *this*
bello/bella *beautiful, nice*
palazzo *building*

VOCAB

b *How does he say: 'The National Museum' and 'the Commercial Bank'?*

c *How would you say: 'This is the museum'?*

---

2 Dov'è?

Where is it?

Roberta now wants to know where the Europa Hotel is and where the shops are.

a *How does Franco say: 'After the American Consulate'?*

b *There are two words for street in this dialogue. What are they? What is the word for main?*

CD 1, TR 5, 00:36

Roberta	Dov'è l'Albergo Europa? Non è qui?
Franco	No. È più avanti. Dopo il Consolato Americano.
Roberta	Ma dove sono i negozi?
Franco	I grandi magazzini sono in Via Roma: la strada principale.
Roberta	Ah, sì! Vicino a Villa Millefiori.
Franco	No, no. Sono vicino a Piazza Municipio.

QUICK VOCAB

più avanti *further on*
i negozi *the shops*
i grandi magazzini *the department stores*
vicino a *next to, near*
Piazza Municipio *the Town Hall Square*
è *(it) is, it's*
sono *(they) are*

c *How would you ask: 'Where is the Town Hall Square, please?'*

d *How would you say: 'It's near Via Roma?'*

e *How would you ask: 'Where are the shops, please?'*

3 Cosa prende?
What are you having?

Franco and **Roberta** are now at the **Bar-Ristorante Roma.** They say in turn what they are having. Then Franco calls the waiter (**cameriere**).

a *How does Franco say: 'I'm having a pizza and a glass of wine'?*

b *How does he ask Roberta: 'What are you having?'*

c *What is 'red wine' in Italian?*

Franco	Io prendo una pizza e un bicchiere di vino. Lei, Roberta, cosa prende?
Roberta	Un panino con formaggio.
Franco	Cameriere! Un panino con formaggio e una pizza.
Cameriere	Va bene. E da bere?
Roberta	Un'acqua minerale con limone e senza gas.
Franco	E per me, vino, vino rosso. E poi, due caffè.

CD 1, TR 5, 01:16

un bicchier(e) di vino *a glass of wine*
cosa prende? *What are you having?*
un panino con formaggio *a cheese roll*
va bene *all right*
e da bere? *and to drink?*
un'acqua minerale *a mineral water*
con/senza *with/without*
poi, due ... *then, two ...*

QUICK VOCAB

d *How would you ask for a sparkling mineral water?*

e *How would you ask for a glass of red wine?*

4 Il conto, per favore!
The bill, please!

a *How does the waiter ask whether they want anything else?*

Cameriere	Ecco: Il panino e l'acqua minerale per la signorina, e il vino e la pizza per lei. Altro?
Franco	No, grazie. Il conto, per favore.
Roberta	E lo zucchero ...!
Cameriere	Subito, signorina.

lo zucchero *the sugar*
subito *straight away*

b *How does Roberta ask for the sugar?*
c *How would you say: 'The sugar, please'?*

Listen to the numbers in Italian from 0 to 10:

0 1 2 3 4 5 6 7 8 9 10
zero uno, una due tre quattro cinque sei sette otto nove dieci

---

5 Un tavolo per dieci persone
A table for ten

Una guida (*a guide*) enters the **bar-ristorante** with a group of tourists and orders for all of them.

a *How many beers, how many sandwiches and how many ice creams are ordered?*

Guida	Un tavolo per dieci persone.
Cameriere	Va bene qui?
Guida	Sì. Va bene. Sette birre e cinque tramezzini con prosciutto crudo.
Cameriere	E per i bambini? I gelati sono molto buoni.
Guida	Allora: un gelato misto e un'aranciata fresca.
Cameriere	Ecco: le birre, i tramezzini, il gelato e l'aranciata.

Va bene qui? *Is it all right here?*
tramezzini *sandwiches*
prosciutto crudo *Parma ham (lit. raw ham)*
i bambini *the children*
allora *then*
i gelati sono molto buoni *the ice creams are very good*
misto/a *mixed*
fresco/a *cool, fresh*

Pronunciation

◀) **CD 1, TR 6**

CONSONANTS

Most consonants in Italian correspond roughly to their English equivalents, but double consonants (**mm, gg, cc,** etc.) must be heard: they are more deliberately pronounced than in English.

c and **g** need particular care before **e** and **i**:

c followed by **e** or **i** is pronounced with a soft sound, as in English *child*: vicino, cinque, dieci, dice, cento, ufficio, farmacia.

c followed by **a, o, u** or a consonant is pronounced with a hard sound, as in *cat*: banca, con, cameriere, cosa, come.

ch is as in *architect*: che, bicchiere, zucchero, macchina.

g followed by **e** or **i** is pronounced with a soft sound, as in *general*: gelati, formaggio, angela, giro.

g followed by **a, o, u** or a consonant is pronounced with a hard sound, as in *gun*: granita, negozio, guida, albergo.

g followed by **h** is pronounced with a hard sound, as in *gherkin*: alberghi.

gn as *ni* in *onion*: signore, signora, signorina.

Grammar

1 *WHAT? WHERE?*

Cosa, che cosa and che can all be used to mean *what* in English.

Cos'è stands for cosa + è; the final -a is dropped for ease of pronunciation.

Che cos'è? ⎫
Cos'è? ⎭   *What is it?*

Cosa ⎫
Che cosa ⎬ **prende?**   *What are you having?*
Che ⎭

Dov'è stands for dove (where) + è. The final -e of dove is dropped for the same reason.

Dov'è?	*Where is it/he/she? Where are you?*
Dov'è la stazione?	*Where's the station?*
Dov'è Roberto?	*Where's Robert?*
Dove sono i negozi?	*Where are the shops?*

2 *VERBS*

Parlo and parla (Unit 1) are parts of the verb parlare (infinitive) *to speak.* Prendo and prende are parts of the verb prendere, *to have, to take*:

prend -o *I have, I take*; prend -e *you have/you take*; *he/she has, he/she takes*

È *you are, he/she/it is/it's,* and sono *they are,* are parts of the verb essere *to be* (Unit 3, Section 2).

3 NOUNS: FORMATION OF PLURAL

Nouns ending in -o (masc.) change the final -o to -i:

muse*o* – muse*i*   *(museums)*

Nouns ending in -a (fem.) change the final -a to -e:

birr*a* – birr*e*   *(beers)*

Nouns ending in -e (masc. or fem.) change the final -e to -i:

masc: **ristorant*e* – ristorant*i*** *(restaurants)*
fem: **stazion*e* – stazion*i*** *(stations)*

Nouns ending in a consonant or in an accented vowel do not change:

caffè – due caffè   *(two coffees)*
bar – tre bar   *(three cafés)*

4 ARTICLES *(CONTINUED)*

un' (*a/an*) is used only before feminine words beginning with a vowel: **un'**acqua minerale.

But **un** (masc.) (*a/an*) is used before consonants and vowels: **un** albergo (*a hotel, inn*), **un** ascensore (*a lift*), **un** gelato.

Notice: **un** amico (without an apostrophe) but **un'**amica (with an apostrophe because it is feminine).

lo (*the*) and **uno** (*a/an*) are used before masculine singular nouns beginning with **z** or **s** + consonant:

uno **scontrino** *a ticket/receipt*   *uno* **studente** *a student*
lo **scontrino** *the ticket/receipt*   *lo* **studente** *the student*
lo **zucchero** *the sugar*

il becomes i before masculine plural nouns: *il* **museo**, *i* **musei**; *il* **duomo**, *i* **duomi**.

la becomes le before feminine plural nouns: *la* **birra**, *le* **birre**; *la* **parola** *the word*, *le* **parole**; *la* **stazione**, *le* **stazioni**.

5 ARTICLES WITH PIAZZA, VIA

La piazza *the square*, **la via** *the road*; but when the square or the road is named, omit the article: **Piazza Municipio, Via Roma.**

6 ADJECTIVES

Adjectives agree in number and gender with the nouns they qualify:

il vino rosso   *the red wine*
la mela rossa   *the red apple*
un panino fresco   *a fresh roll*
un'aranciata fresca *a cool orangeade*

Questo/questa must also agree:

Questo palazzo è bello.   *This building is beautiful.*
Questa piazza è bella.   *This square is beautiful.*

Unlike English, adjectives in Italian often follow the noun they refer to: **vino** *rosso*, **acqua** *minerale*, **aranciata** *fresca*, **prosciutto** *crudo*. However, one or two very common ones such as **bello/bella** *beautiful, nice*; **piccolo/piccola** *small* tend to come before: **una bella città** *a beautiful town*; **un piccolo albergo** *a small hotel*.

7 NUMBERS: UN, UNO, UNA

un, una, besides meaning *a* or *an*, also
mean *one*. It is the only number which
agrees with the noun following it. The
others do not change. When there is no
noun following, use **uno, una: un museo**
but (**numero**) **uno** (*number*) *one*. For 0–10
see earlier in this unit.

Quanti caffè ...? Uno!
> *How many coffees ...? One!*

Quante pizze ...? Una!
> *How many pizzas ...? One!*

8 CON *WITH;* SENZA *WITHOUT*

Un panino *con* formaggio	*a cheese roll (literally means 'a roll with cheese')*
un'acqua minerale *con* gas	*sparkling mineral water*
un'acqua minerale *senza* gas	*still or natural mineral water*
***con/senza*: limone, zucchero, latte, burro**	*with/without lemon, sugar, milk, butter*

Come si dice?
How do you say it?

🔊 **CD 1, TR 7**

1 *How to ask what something is*   **Cos'è?/Cos'è questo/questa?**

    How to say what it is   **È un museo. È una banca.**

2 *How to ask what things are*   **Cosa sono?/Cosa sono Standa e Upim?**

    How to say what they are   **Sono grandi magazzini.**

3 *How to ask where a thing or person is*

Dov'è?/Dov'è la posta?
Dov'è Franco?

Say where he, she or it is

È qui, è lì, ecc.
(ecc. is the Italian abbreviation for etcetera, etc. in English.)

4 *How to ask where things or people are*

Dove sono i negozi? Dove sono Anna e Roberta?

5 *How to ask what someone is having*

Cosa prende?

How to say what you are having

(Io) prendo un tè …

6 *How to say that you are having … with …*

Prendo un tè con latte.

7 *How to say that you are having … without …*

Prendo un caffè senza zucchero.

8 *How to ask for the bill*

Il conto, per favore!

Practice

◀) CD 1, TR 8

1 *Listen to this list of towns, then to the list of famous places that follows:* **Milano, Firenze, Londra, Parigi, Pisa, Napoli, Roma, Venezia.**

Il Colosseo, Piazza San Marco, il Vesuvio, il Ponte Vecchio, la Torre Eiffel, il Palazzo del Parlamento, la Torre Pendente, La Scala.

Try repeating them.

2 *Look at the illustrations below. Match the name of the place with the name of the town, as in the example* **a.**

   a *La Scala, Milano.*

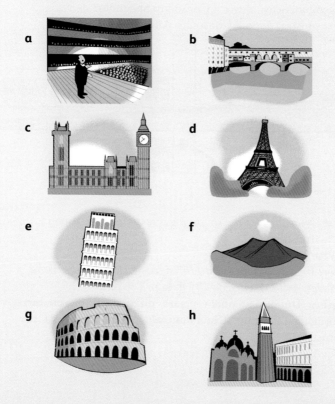

3 *To say in Rome, in Venice, etc. use* **a**: **a Roma, a Venezia.**
Dov'è La Scala? A Milano. *Where is La Scala? In Milan.*
Form similar questions and answers for **il Colosseo, il Vesuvio** *and* **la Torre Eiffel.**
Now make statements about where the rest are. Start with: **La Scala è …**

4 *Use the diagram to form questions and answers about these places as in the example:*

   a *il Consolato Americano*
   b *Piazza Garibaldi*
   c *il Duomo*
   d *l'Albergo Miramare*

Esempio: Scusi, dov'è il Consolato Spagnolo?
È a sinistra, dopo il Consolato Americano.

   e *Now answer the following question:* **Dove sono i consolati?**

5 *What are they?*
Sort this list of words into three categories, Drinks, Food, Places, and precede each by **il, la** *or* **l'**:
banca Duomo limonata piazza pizza pasta museo birra formaggio albergo acqua minerale panino aranciata tè prosciutto

6 *With or without?* **Con** *or* **senza?**
How do they take their tea? With or without sugar, etc.?

Look at the table and make two statements, one about **Marta** and one about **Filippo**. Start with: **Marta prende il tè ...**

	limone	latte	zucchero
Marta		✔	✔
Filippo	✔		✘

Ora tocca a te! *How do you take your tea?*

7 *What's this?* **Cos'è questo/questa?**

Look at the illustrations in Unit 1, after Dialogue 5d, and form a question and answer for each using **Cos'è questo?** or **Cos'è questa?** depending on whether the nouns are masculine or feminine.

◄) **CD 1, TR 8, 01:00**

8 *Here are some more Italian town signs: how many can you guess? Look up those you don't know in the vocabulary at the back of the book:*

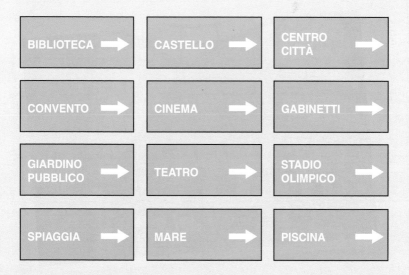

BIBLIOTECA ➡   CASTELLO ➡   CENTRO CITTÀ ➡

CONVENTO ➡   CINEMA ➡   GABINETTI ➡

GIARDINO PUBBLICO ➡   TEATRO ➡   STADIO OLIMPICO ➡

SPIAGGIA ➡   MARE ➡   PISCINA ➡

Italian city life

Attenzione! Strictly speaking, **palazzo** means *palace*, but it is generally used to describe any large building or block of flats/apartment block. Although **strada** means *road* or *street* it is never used in naming any particular one. **Via** is used for this. **Via** may also mean *way* or *route*.

The many restaurants and cafés you will see in squares and on pavements in any Italian town are a reminder that Italy is a country where life goes on mainly out of doors.

In Italian towns **la piazza** is the centre of social life where everyone meets for a date, a coffee or a chat.

One of the most famous is **Piazza San Marco** (St Mark's Square) in Venice.

Il bar is the normal name for an Italian café. Both alcoholic (**alcolici**) and soft/non-alcoholic (**analcolici**) drinks are served there. In most you have to pay at the cashier's desk first, obtain the ticket/receipt (**lo scontrino**) and present it at the counter to get your drink. If you sit at a table, you pay more.

Don't throw away any receipts you are given (especially in cafés or restaurants) while you are in the vicinity. The police may want to see them: to check not on you, but on the vendors for tax purposes!

The most popular department stores are **Upim**, **Standa**, **La Rinascente** and **Coin**. They can be found in most Italian towns. **Upim** and **Standa** especially are reasonably priced and there are large food departments in some of them. Shop opening hours vary between regions. Most of them are open from 8.30/9.30 a.m. to 12.30/1.00 p.m., and from 3.30/4.00 p.m. until 7.00/8.00 p.m. Many of them observe half-day closing during the week, usually Monday morning, others one whole day. The latter, such as tobacconist's, chemist's, hairdresser's and some restaurants, may close on a rota system. However, there is an increasing tendency for the big stores to be open throughout the day (**orario continuato**), especially in the major cities.

Pizza is a speciality of Naples and the **Campania** region. It can be bought in a variety of sizes either in a **pizzeria**, which is like a restaurant but cheaper, or in a **rosticceria**, a take-away which often has limited seating space for customers.

You may also have a pizza cut from a large slab in which case it is called **pizza al metro** or **al taglio**. You may ask for your **taglio** (*cut*) by weight, size or value.

All the Italian cities mentioned in this unit have websites:

Firenze	http://www.firenze.turismo.toscana.it
Milano	http://www.traveleurope.it/milano
Napoli	http://www.ept.napoli.it
Pisa	http://www.pisa.turismo.toscana.it
Roma	http://www.romaturismo.it
Venezia	http://www.provincia.venezia.it

TEST YOURSELF

Fill in the gaps as appropriate, using each word in the box below once only.

1 *L'Albergo Miramare e l'Albergo Paradiso __ più avanti.*

2 *__ il Duomo per piacere?*

3 *La stazione è vicino __ Piazza Garibaldi.*

4 *Cosa __ ? Un gelato o un caffè?*

5 *Roberto è __ un'amica.*

6 *I gelati sono molto __ .*

7 *Il museo __ vicino a Via Roma.*

8 *Firenze è una __ città.*

9 *Piazza Vittoria è qui __ .*

10 *__ sono Milano e Napoli?*

....

a – bella – con – a destra – dove – è – prende – buoni – dov'è –
sono
....

3

Come si chiama?

What's your name?

In this unit you will learn:
- *how to exchange personal details formally and informally*
- *how to introduce yourself and others*
- *how to respond to introductions.*

🔊 **CD 1, TR 9**

Listen to the following ordinal numbers:

1st	2nd	3rd	4th
primo, prima	**secondo, seconda**	**terzo, terza**	**quarto, quarta**

---

1 A che piano ...?
On what floor ...?

Il signor Russo asks **il portiere** on what floor **i signori Nuzzo** (*Mr & Mrs Nuzzo*) live: he has been invited to a party at their home.

a *How does he ask on what floor they live?*

> **Sig. Russo** A che piano abitano i signori Nuzzo, per favore?
> **Portiere** Terzo piano, numero 20. Quarta porta a destra.
> **Sig. Russo** Grazie mille.
> **Portiere** Prego.

porta *door*
grazie mille *many thanks*

---

2 Come si chiama? (formal)
What's your name?

Il sig. Russo meets **la sig.na Finzi** for the first time.

a *How does he ask: 'What's your name?' How does he give his own name?*

b *How does she ask: 'Where are you from?' How does he answer?*

> **Sig. Russo** Come si chiama?
> **Sig.na Finzi** Sandra Finzi. E lei?
> **Sig. Russo** Mi chiamo Marco Russo.
> **Sig.na Finzi** Di dov'è?
> **Sig. Russo** Sono di Napoli.
> **Sig.na Finzi** Io sono di Torino.

---

3 Di dove sei? (informal)
Where are you from?

In another part of the room **Elena** (*Helen*) and **Massimo** (*Max*), two younger people, meet on a more informal basis. Compare this dialogue (which is informal) with the second dialogue (which is formal).

a *How does* Elena *ask: 'What's your name?' Compare it with the same question that il Sig. Russo asked in the second dialogue.*

b *How does she say: 'I'm from Milan'?*

c *How does he ask what she does and how does she answer: 'I'm a secretary'?*

CD 1, TR 9, 01:26

Elena	Come ti chiami?
Massimo	Massimo. E tu?
Elena	Elena. Sei di Milano?
Massimo	No. Sono di Firenze. E tu, di dove sei?
Elena	Io sono di Milano.
Massimo	Che cosa fai?
Elena	Sono segretaria.
Massimo	Io sono ragioniere. Lavoro in banca.

Che cosa fai? *What do you do?*
ragioniere (m) *accountant*
Lavoro in banca. *I work in a bank.*

VOCAB

4 Di che nazionalità è? (formal)
What's your nationality?

Il sig. Russo is now talking to **la sig.na Galli**.

a *How does he ask her nationality and how does she answer: 'I'm Italian'?*

b *How does he say: 'I'm Italian too'?*

c *How does la sig.na Galli say: 'She's Greek'?*

Sig. Russo Di che nazionalità è, signorina?
Sig.na Galli Sono italiana. Sono di Palermo.
Sig. Russo Anch'io sono italiano. Chi è questa bella ragazza?
Sig.na Galli Maria Toffalis. È greca. Non parla italiano.
Sig. Russo Ho capito. È qui in vacanza?
Sig.na Galli Chi, io? Sono a Roma per studiare l'informatica.

QUICK VOCAB

Chi è …? *Who is …?*
ragazza *girl*
Ho capito. *I understand (lit. I have understood).*
per studiare *to study*
l'informatica *information technology*

---

5 Quanti anni hai? (informal)
How old are you?

Elena and Massimo are interrupted in mid-conversation by Ugo.
Massimo introduces first himself, then Elena, to him.

  a *How does Massimo introduce himself to Ugo (Hugh)?*
  b *How does he introduce Elena to Ugo? How does she respond?*
  c *How does Massimo ask how old Elena is and how does she answer?*

Massimo	Io sono Massimo, e questa è Elena.
Elena	Piacere.
Ugo	Piacere, Ugo.
Massimo	Dunque … Elena, quanti anni hai?
Elena	Ho diciotto anni.
Massimo	Beata te! Io sono vecchio: ho ventisei anni.

At this point **Sandra,** in a hurry to be off, spots **M<u>a</u>ssimo,** who is a friend of hers, and greets him.

Sandra	Ciao, M<u>a</u>ssimo!
M<u>a</u>ssimo	Ciao! Come stai?
Sandra	Non c'è male, gr<u>a</u>zie. E tu?
M<u>a</u>ssimo	Abbastanza bene, gr<u>a</u>zie. Ci vediamo più tardi. Ciao!
Sandra	Ciao!

piacere *how do you do?*
dunque ... *well, where was I ...?*
Beata te! *Lucky you!*
Ciao! Come stai? *Hi! How are you?*
non c'è male *not too bad*
abbastanza bene *quite well*
ci vediamo più tardi *see you later*

QUICK VOCAB

---

6 Quanti figli ha? (formal)
How many children have you got?

Finally, in another group, **Ugo** talks to **la sig.ra Dini.**

a *How does* **la sig.ra Dini** *say she's married?*
b *How does* **Ugo** *ask how many children she has?*
c *How does he ask their age?*
d *How does* **la sig.ra Dini** *say the little girl is only four?*
e *Now look at the picture on the right and answer the question about the Busi family.*

Famiglia Busi

Nino

Quanti fratelli e quante sorelle ha Nino?

Ugo	È sposata?
Sig.ra Dini	Sì. Sono sposata.
Ugo	Quanti figli ha, signora?
Sig.ra Dini	Due: Luisa e Paolo.
Ugo	Quanti anni hanno?
Sig.ra Dini	Il ragazzo ha undici anni e va a scuola. La bambina ha solo quattro anni.
Ugo	Ah, sono piccoli! Io sono single: non sono sposato. Mio fratello invece è sposato. Ma è separato.
Sig.ra Dini	Quanti fratelli e quante sorelle ha?
Ugo	Ho un fratello e una sorella. Io sono il secondo.

QUICK VOCAB

figli *children*
ragazzo *boy*
va a scuola *goes to school*
piccolo/a *young, small*
invece *but, on the other hand*
fratello, sorella *brother, sister*

Pronunciation

◀) **CD 1, TR 10**

CONSONANTS (CONTINUED)

s has two sounds:
s as in English *song*: secondo, solo, Massimo, sono, suo, inglese
s as in *toes* (usually between vowels): musica, scusi, sposato
sc followed by e or i is pronounced as in English *she*: ascensore
z has two sounds:
ts as in *cats*: stazione, grazie, ragazza
ds as in *odds*: zero, zucchero, gorgonzola

Grammar

1 SUBJECT PRONOUNS

singular		plural	
io	*I*	noi	*we*
tu	*you* (informal)	voi*	*you* (plural)
lei	*you* (formal)		
lui, lei	*he, she*	loro	*they*

*When talking directly to more than one person the plural of both **tu** and **lei** is **voi**.

Use the familiar form **tu** (2nd person singular) to a relative, friend or children. Young people also use it among themselves. Use **Ciao!** to say *hello* or *goodbye* when you are on **tu** terms with someone (as in Dialogue 5, above). **Lei** means both *you* and *she* and is used whether you are talking directly to a man or a woman formally, or talking about a girl or woman. The context should make it clear. From now on 'informal' will be abbreviated to (inf); 'formal' to (form).

2 VERBS

Present tense (irregular) of **essere** *and* **avere**

Present tense **essere** *to be*			**avere** *to have*	
(io)	sono	*I am*	ho	*I have*
(tu)	sei	*you are* (inf)	hai	*you have* (inf)
(lei)	è	*you are* (form)	ha	*you have* (form)
(lui, lei)	è	*he, she, (it) is*	ha	*he, she, (it) has*
(noi)	siamo	*we are*	abbiamo	*we have*
(voi)	siete	*you* (plural) *are*	avete	*you* (plural) *have*
(loro)	sono	*they are*	hanno	*they have*

Present tense (regular) of -are verbs

The infinitives of regular verbs end in **-are, -ere** or **-ire.** For the present tense of **-are** verbs add the endings written in bold characters to the stem (**parl-**), as shown in the box below.

Notice that *the first person singular* of the present tense of a verb always ends in **-o**, and the second person **tu** in **-i.**

Present **tense**	**parl-are** *to speak (regular* **-are** *verb)*	
(io)	parl **-o**	*I speak, I am speaking*
(tu)	parl **-i**	*you* (inf) *speak, you are speaking*
(lei)	parl **-a**	*you* (form) *speak, you are speaking*
(lui, lei)	parl **-a**	*he, she, (it) speaks, he, she, (it) is speaking*
(noi)	parl **-iamo**	*we speak, we are speaking*
(voi)	parl **-ate**	*you* (plural) *speak, you are speaking*
(loro)	parl **-ano**	*they speak, they are speaking*

In this unit you have met **abitano** (from **abitare**), **lavoro** (from **lavorare**) and **studiare** which are all conjugated like **parlare**. But verbs ending in **-iare** do not double the final **-i** in the second person singular **tu** form: **tu studi.**

3 TITLES

Signore (*Mr*), **Signora** (*Mrs*), **Signorina** (*Miss*), **Signori** (*Mr & Mrs*)

Titles ending in -ore, such as **signore**, **dottore** and **professore**, drop the final -e when followed by a proper name: **Buongiorno, dottore!** becomes **Buongiorno, dott_or_ Nuzzo! Buongiorno, professore!** becomes **Buongiorno, profess_or_ Salviati!**

When you are not addressing people directly, but talking about them, you must use the definite article before the title: **il signore, la signora**, etc.

Dov'è il dottore?	*Where is the doctor?*
Dov'è il dott_or_ Nuzzo?	*Where is Doctor Nuzzo?*

Although **signori** is masculine plural it can refer to both men and women:

I signori Spada *Mr and Mrs Spada*

Similarly, **i ragazzi** can mean *boys* or *boys and girls*; **i figli**, *sons*, or *sons and daughters*, etc.

4 NUMBERS (CONTINUED)

First, second, third, etc., are adjectives in Italian:

il primo piano	*the 1st floor*
la terza porta	*the 3rd door*
il secondo di_a_logo	*the 2nd dialogue*
la quarta strada a destra	*the 4th road on the right*

5 WHAT'S YOUR NAME?

(**lei**) **Come si chiama?** literally *How do you call yourself?* is the normal way of asking someone's name. (**Come** means *how*.)

(io) Mi chiamo Ant_o_nia.	*My name is Antonia.*
(lei) Come si chiama?	*What's your name? (form)*
(tu) Come ti chiami?	*What's your name? (inf)*

Like nouns there are two types of adjectives: those ending in -o/-a: piccolo/a *small*; ricco/a *rich*; those ending in -e (m & f): intelligente *intelligent*; interessante *interesting*.

As we have seen in Unit 2, Section 6, adjectives agree with the nouns they qualify. In the following examples notice the endings:

Masculine singular	Feminine singular
un edificio moderno	una casa moderna
a modern building	*a modern house*
un uomo ricco *a rich man*	una donna ricca *a rich woman*
un ragazzo intelligente	una ragazza intelligente
an intelligent boy	*an intelligent girl*
un dottore inglese	una ragioniera inglese
an English doctor	*an English accountant*

The plural of adjectives corresponds to the plural of nouns (again see Unit 2, Section 6). For mixed genders use masculine adjectives.
Franco e Ida sono italiani.

Masculine plural	Feminine plural
i gelati **italiani**	le pizze italiane
i dottori **inglesi**	le ragioniere inglesi
i ristoranti **francesi**	le lezioni interessanti

Quanti, quante are also adjectives and must agree with the noun they qualify:

Quanti fratelli e quante sorelle ha?   *How many brothers and sisters have you?*

7 I ALSO/ME TOO

Notice how subject pronouns (**io, tu, lui, ecc.**) are used after **anche** for emphasis:

Mangia anche lei?	*Are you eating too?*
Sì. **Mangio anch'io!**	*Yes, I'm eating too.*
Aspettate anche voi?	*Are you waiting too?*
Sì. **Aspettiamo anche noi.**	*Yes, we are (waiting) too.*

8 WHO/WHOM?

Chi? is used to refer to people:

Chi è questa ragazza? (È) Maria.	*Who is this girl? (It's) Maria.*

Notice how Italians answer this question when a pronoun is involved:

Chi è? Sono io.	*Who is it? It's me.*
È lui, è lei.	*It's him, it's her/you.*

9 ETÀ AGE

To express **età** *age* in Italian, use the verb **avere** (*to have*):

Quanti anni ha Bruno?	*How old is Bruno?*
Ha trentaquattro anni.	*He's thirty-four (years old).*

10 POSSESSIVES WITH FAMILY RELATIONS

Mio/mia *my*, **tuo/tua** *your*, **suo/sua** *your* are adjectives and must therefore agree with the nouns they qualify. Say **tuo/tua** when using the informal **tu**, and **suo/sua** when using **lei**. Take special care with **suo/sua**, which apart from *your* can each mean *his* or *her*, depending on the context.

mio fratello *my brother*
sua sorella *his sister, her sister, your sister*
suo padre *his father, her father, your father*

Come si dice?
How do you say it?

◀) **CD 1, TR 11**

1 *How to ask someone's name* **Come si chiama?** *(form)*
  a *formally* **b** *informally* **Come ti chiami** *(inf)?*

  How to give your name **Mi chiamo …/Sono …**

2 *How to ask where someone* **Di dov'è?** *(form)*
  is from **a** *formally* **b** *informally* **Di dove sei?** *(inf)*

  How to say where you are **Sono di Londra, sono di Parigi,**
  from (referring to town) **ecc.**

3 *How to ask what someone's* **Che cosa fa?** *(form)*
  job is **a** *formally* **b** *informally* **Che cosa fai?** *(inf)*

4 *How to ask someone's* **Di che nazionalità è?** *(form)*
  nationality **a** *formally* **Di che nazionalità sei?** *(inf)*
  b *informally*

  How to give your nationality **Sono inglese** *(m/f)*,
  sono americano/a, ecc.

5 *How to ask someone's age* **Quanti anni ha?** *(form)*
  a *formally* **b** *informally* **Quanti anni hai?** *(inf)*

  How to give your age **Ho venticinque anni, ho**
  ventotto anni, ecc.

6	*How to ask who someone is*	**Chi è questa ragazza?**
	How to say who someone is	**È Maria.**
7	*How to introduce yourself*	**Io sono …**
	How to introduce others	**Questo è/questa è …**
	How to respond to an introduction	**Piacere.**

Practice

◀) CD 1, TR 12

1 *Repeat the numbers from 11 to 50 as you hear them. Listen carefully to 21, 28, 31, 38, 41 and 48. What difference do you notice between these six numbers and the other numbers from 20 to 50?*

11 undici	**12** dodici	**13** tredici	**14** quattordici
15 quindici	**16** sedici	**17** diciassette	**18** diciotto
19 diciannove	**20** venti	**21** ventuno	**22** ventidue
23 ventitrè	**24** ventiquattro	**25** venticinque	**26** ventisei
27 ventisette	**28** ventotto	**29** ventinove	**30** trenta
31 trentuno	**32** trentadue	**33** trentatrè	**34** trentaquattro
35 trentacinque	**36** trentasei	**37** trentasette	**38** trentotto
39 trentanove	**40** quaranta	**41** quarantuno	**42** quarantadue
43 quarantatré	**44** quarantaquattro	**45** quarantacinque	**46** quarantasei
47 quarantasette	**48** quarantotto	**49** quarantanove	**50** cinquanta

2 *You will hear the names of five people on the recording with the number of the floor they live on and their door number. Fill them in as in the example. (The Roman numerals I, II, III, IV denote the floor.)*

Esempio   a   b

| DOTT. COLOMBO PROFESSORE II 21 | PROF. P. RUSSO ARCHITETTO | CARLO PINI RAGIONIERE |

Secondo piano
numero ventuno.

Primo piano,
numero dodici.

Quarto piano,
numero
quarantasette.

c   d

| OLGA FULVI DENTISTA | ANNA BIONDI GIORNALISTA |

Primo piano,
numero tredici.

Terzo piano,
numero trentotto.

3 *Using the information from the nameplates on the previous page, write down what each person's occupation is.* **Esempio: Il dottor Colombo è professore.**

4 *Languages are masculine and don't change:* **greco, russo, ecc.** *(Unit 1). The same words are used for nationalities except that in this case they are adjectives and must agree with the nouns they qualify:* **Pippa non è italiana, ma parla italiano.** *Here is a list of countries and people. Can you tell from the countries what nationality these people are? Remember that 'German' is* **tedesco, tedesca.**
Esempio: L'Inghilterra: Rita e Olga. Rita e Olga sono inglesi.

a *la Germania: Helga.*
b *la Francia: Gérard e Philippe.*
c *la Spagna: Juanita.*
d *la Russia: Ivan e Natasha.*
e *l'Italia: Anna e Pina.*

5 *Now say what town they are from. Esempio: Londra. Rita e Olga sono di Londra.*
a *Bonn* **b** *Nizza* **c** *Barcellona* **d** *Omsk* **e** *Trento.*

6 *Finally, say what town they live in. Esempio: Rita e Olga abitano a Londra.*

7 *Here is the beginning of a letter from Luisa, who is writing to her new pen-pal Anna.*

Roma, 3 novembre
Cara Anna,
mi chiamo Luisa. Ho quindici anni. Sono di Trento, ma abito a Roma. Ho una sorella. Si chiama Vittoria e ha tredici anni. Mio padre è francese e mia madre è italiana ...

Write the beginning of **Anna's** letter to **Luisa** in which she gives the following information. Start your letter: **Cara Luisa,**

Age 17
Town she comes from: Siena
Town she lives in: Lucca

Father: Italian
Mother: German
Brother: Luigi, 18 years old

Social niceties

Il sig. Russo said (Dialogue 4 above): **Chi è questa bella ragazza?** Making and receiving compliments is an essential feature of Italian daily life. They are not meant to be offensive or patronizing. They are linked to another aspect of Italian culture: **fare bella figura** – that is, 'creating a good impression'; it is important to make the right impression, in dress, bearing and general attitude. Perhaps equally important, if not more so, is not 'to create a bad impression': **fare brutta figura**.

Dress, in particular, figures prominently as a priority (It has even been said that Italians would rather starve than dress badly!). A great deal of media time and press space is devoted to trends in style. During the summer months many fashion shows take place in the open air. Italian dress designers have a flair for presenting the latest styles against the background of a Greek temple (in Sicily for instance), or of a Roman amphitheatre, thus combining the very latest trends in fashion with the classical elegance of the past.

TEST YOURSELF

Unscramble the following to make meaningful sentences:

1 *a anch' abito Milano io.*

2 *a il piano abita che Marini signor?*

3 *Piazza Mazzini vediamo ci a tardi più.*

4 *il si di figlio Roberto come chiama?*

5 *parla cinese ragazza questa molto bene greca.*

6 *di e sei dove, Anna, tu?*

7 *per non qui lavorare sono.*

8 *chiami tu ti e come?*

9 *bambina ha anni la sette.*

10 *padre madre mia mio tedesca italiano è è e.*

4

Quant'è?
How much is it?

In this unit you will learn:
- *how to ask for opening and closing times*
- *the days of the week*
- *how to ask the price and pay for purchases*
- *how to talk about colour and size (shoes and clothing).*

◆) **CD 1, TR 13**

Listen to the main divisions of the clock:

alle due *at 2.00*; alle tre *at 3.00*; alle due e un quarto *at 2.15*; alle tre e un quarto *at 3.15*; alle quattro e mezza *at 4.30*; alle cinque e mezza *at 5.30*; alle sei meno un quarto *at 5.45*; alle sette meno un quarto *at 6.45*; all'una *at 1.00*; all'una e un quarto *at 1.15*; all'una e mezza *at 1.30*

1 A che ora apre il tabaccaio?
At what time does the tobacconist's open?

a *How does* **B** *say: 'At eight o'clock'?*

> **A** Scusi, signore, a che ora apre il tabaccaio?
> **B** Alle otto.
> **A** E a che ora chiude?
> **B** Alle dodici.

The days of the week

lunedì, martedì, mercoledì, giovedì, venerdì, sabato, domenica.

Insight
Attenzione! When you listened to the days of the week **i giorni della settimana**, did you notice the stress? Except for **sabato** and **domenica** the stress falls on the final vowel. In Italy the week starts on Monday and the days are written without capitals.

2 Che giorno parte?
What day are you leaving?

Il tabaccaio (*the tobacconist*) asks **il dottore** (*the doctor*), a regular customer of his, on what day he is leaving for Paris.

a *What are the words for 'morning' and 'evening' in this conversation?*

> **Tabaccaio** Che giorno parte per Parigi? Giovedì o venerdì?
> **Dottore** Giovedì.
> **Tabaccaio** Quando ritorna?
> **Dottore** Parto giovedì mattina e ritorno domenica sera.

Now listen to these numbers and repeat them.

🔊 **CD 1, TR 13, 02:18**

1,000 2,000 20,000 120,000 220,000

mille duemila ventimila centoventimila duecentoventimila

Insight

Attenzione! The plural of **mille** (1,000) is **mila**, but the noun that follows is always plural. **Cento** (100) is invariable: **duecento** (200); **seicento** (600) etc. (see Section 10 below).

Although the conversion to **euro** was in 2002, many Italians continue to think and count in **lire**, (**mille**, **centomila lire** ecc.) when dealing with money: this involves thinking in thousands rather than in tens and hundreds. Rightly or wrongly the conversion is still blamed for many price rises.

For the numbers from 60 to 100 see Unit 5. However, if you have the recording, try to understand the prices in Dialogue 3 first.

Insight

The euro is divided into 100 **centesimi**; these are shown after the comma: €10,20 is **dieci euro e venti centesimi**, or commonly expressed as **dieci euro e venti**. 'Euro' is invariable. (The comma in Italian = the decimal point in English.)

---

3 Vorrei tre francobolli
I'd like three stamps

The doctor then buys some stamps, postcards and newspapers.

a *How much did the three stamps cost?*

b *How does* **il tabaccaio** *ask: 'Do you want these?'*

c *How many postcards and how many newspapers does* **il dottore** *want to buy?*

Dottore	Vorrei tre francobolli.
Tobaccaio	Per l'estero?
Dottore	Sì. Per l'Inghilterra. E tre cartoline.
Tobaccaio	Queste sono belle. Vuole queste?
Dottore	Sì. E questi due giornali.
Tobaccaio	E poi …?
Dottore	Nient'altro, grazie. Quant'è?
Tobaccaio	I giornali, €1,76; le cartoline, €1,20; i francobolli, €1,23.
Dottore	Mi dispiace, non ho spiccioli. Ho solo un biglietto da cinquanta.
Tobaccaio	Non importa. Ecco il resto.
Dottore	Grazie. Buonasera.

per l'estero *for abroad*
la cartolina *postcard*
il giornale *the newspaper*
nient'altro *nothing else*
non ho spiccioli *I haven't any change*
solo *only*
un biglietto *a (bank) note*
non importa *it doesn't matter*

d *Look at the bank notes below. Which one did* **il dottore** *pay with:* i, ii, iii *or* iv?

i    **ii**

56

iii
20 EURO

iv
50 EURO

e *È una cartolina di Londra o di Roma?*

Fontana di Trevi

4 A che ora aprono i negozi?
At what time do the shops open?

a *How does A say: 'Very kind of you'?*
b *Write down in figures at what time the shops open in the morning and at what time they close at night.*

A	Scusi, a che ora aprono i negozi la mattina?
B	Alle nove.
A	E a che ora chiudono?
B	All'una.
A	E di pomeriggio?
B	Aprono alle quattro e chiudono alle otto.
A	Grazie. Molto gentile.
B	Prego. Si figuri!

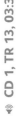
CD 1, TR 13, 03:38

di pomeriggio *in the afternoon*
si figuri! *not at all*
molto gentile *very kind of you*

QV

5 Vorrei un vestito
I would like a dress

a *How does* **la commessa** *(shop assistant) ask: 'Can I help you?'*
b *How does* **la cliente** *ask: 'How much does it cost?'*
c *How does she say: 'The blouse is too dear'?*

CD 1, TR 13, 04:09

Commessa	Buongiorno, signora. Desidera?
Cliente	Vorrei un vestito e una camicetta.
Commessa	Di che colore, signora?
Cliente	Il vestito? Bianco o nero.
Commessa	Che taglia?
Cliente	La quaranta.
Commessa	Ecco: questo nero è semplice, ma elegante.
Cliente	Infatti. È molto carino. Lo posso provare?
Commessa	Certo, signora. Di qua, prego.
Cliente	Sì. Questo va bene. Quanto costa?
Commessa	Cinquantanove euro. Non costa molto.
Cliente	No. Non è caro.
Commessa	E la camicetta, signora? Non vuole la camicetta?
Cliente	No. La camicetta è troppo cara.

QUICK VOCAB

vestito *dress*
camicetta *blouse*
bianco/a, nero/a *white, black*
che taglia? *what size?*
carino/a *pretty, nice*
Lo posso provare? *Can I try it on?*
Di qua, prego. *This way, please.*
Questo va bene. *This one is (fits) all right.*

6 Quanto costano queste scarpe?
How much do these shoes cost?

a *How does* **il cliente** *say: 'I'll take a pair of brown sandals'?*
b *How does* **il commesso** *ask: 'What size?'(for the sandals)?*

Cliente	Scusi, quanto costano queste scarpe?
Commesso	Centosessanta euro.
Cliente	Sono bellissime! Ma sono troppo care. Prendo un paio di sandali marroni e un paio di calzini beige.
Commesso	D'accordo. Che numero?
Cliente	Il quarantuno.
Commesso	Ecco …
Cliente	Sì. Sono proprio comodi.
Commesso	Desidera altro, signore?
Cliente	No, grazie. Quant'è?
Commesso	Non paga qui. Paga alla cassa.

d'accordo *fine*
proprio comodo/a *really comfortable*
Paga alla cassa. *You pay at the desk.*

QV

Pronunciation

🔊 **CD 1, TR 14**

CONSONANTS (CONTINUED)

gu before a vowel is like *gu* in *linguist*: lingua, guida, guanto

qu before a vowel is like *qu* in *quite*: qui, acqua, quarto, quaranta

Mark the stress in these words: **lunedì, sabato, domenica, aprono, chiudono.**

Grammar

1 *PRESENT TENSE (REGULAR* **-ERE** *AND* **-IRE** *VERBS)*

As with **-are** verbs, the endings in bold are added to the stem which is obtained by taking off -ere and -ire, respectively. Compare the **lei, voi** and **loro** endings with those of -**are** verbs (Unit 3, Section 2).

Prendere to take, to have is conjugated like **chiudere**. **Sentire** to hear or to feel and **partire** to leave behave like **aprire**.

Present tense **chiud-ere** *to close (regular* -**ere** *verb)*

(io)	chiud-**o**	*I close, I am closing*
(tu)	chiud-**i**	*you* (inf) *close, you are closing*
(lei)	chiud-**e**	*you* (form) *close, you are closing*
(lui, lei)	chiud-**e**	*he, she, (it) closes, is closing*
(noi)	chiud-**iamo**	*we close, we are closing*
(voi)	chiud-**ete**	*you close, you are closing*
(loro)	chiud-**ono**	*they close, they are closing*

Present tense **apr-ire** *to open (regular* -**ire** *verb)*

(io)	apr-**o**	*I open, I am opening*
(tu)	apr-**i**	*you open* (inf), *you are opening*
(lei)	apr-**e**	*you* (form) *open, you are opening*
(lui, lei)	apr-**e**	*he, she (it) opens, is opening*
(noi)	apr-**iamo**	*we open, we are opening*
(voi)	apr-**ite**	*you open, you are opening*
(loro)	apr-**ono**	*they open, they are opening*

---

2 A CHE ORA ...? *AT WHAT TIME ...?*

To say *at 2 o'clock, 3 o'clock, 4 o'clock*, etc. up to *12 o'clock*, use **alle** for *at*: **alle due, alle tre, alle quattro, alle dodici**. Instead of **alle dodici** *at twelve* you can also say **a mezzogiorno** *at midday*, **a mezzanotte** at midnight. For *at 1 o'clock* use **all'una**; *at about 1 o'clock* **verso l'una**.

Ci vediamo verso l'una, verso le due, ecc.	*See you at about one, at about two etc.*

However, when not referring to the time use **circa** instead: see Section 9 below.

see Section 9 below.

3 DI CHE COLORE? *WHAT COLOUR?*

Colours are adjectives and
therefore agree with the noun they qualify.
Like most adjectives they follow the noun.

azzurro *blue*; **bianco** *white*; **giallo** *yellow*; **grigio** *grey*; **nero** *black*;
rosso *red*

il vestito giallo	*the yellow dress*
i vestiti gialli	*the yellow dresses*
la gonna rossa	*the red skirt*
le gonne rosse	*the red skirts*

To ask what colour a thing is/things are: **Di che colore è?/Di che colore sono?**

Di che colore è la giacca?	*What colour is the jacket?*
Di che colore sono i guanti?	*What colour are the gloves?*
La giacca è grigia e i guanti sono neri.	*The jacket is grey and the gloves are black.*

Colours that end in **-e** in the singular (m & f), such as **verde** *green*
and **marrone** *brown*, end in **-i** in the plural (m & f):

Singular		Plural	
il vestit**o**	*dress, suit*	**i** vestit**i**	
	verd**e**/marron**e**		verd**i**/marron**i**
la magliett**a**	*T shirt*	**le** magliett**e**	

The following colours never change their endings: **beige** *beige* **blu** *navy blue* and **rosa** *pink*: **il** vestit**o** rosa, **la** giacc**a** beige, **i** pantaloni bl**u**, **le** gonne rosa.

4 QUANT'È? *HOW MUCH IS IT?*

Quant'è stands for **quanto è**. **Quant'è** is especially used when you are buying more than one thing and want to know what the total comes to:

Quant'è (in tutto)?	*How much is it (altogether)?*

5 UN PAIO, DUE PAIA *ONE PAIR, TWO PAIRS*

The plural of **paio** (m) *pair* is **paia** (f): **un paio** but **due paia**.

un paio di guanti	*a pair of gloves*
due paia di scarpe	*two pairs of shoes*

6 *HOW MUCH DOES IT COST? HOW MUCH DO THEY COST?*

Make sure to use the plural **costano** when asking the price of more than one article:

Quanto costa il vestito?	*How much does the dress/suit cost?*
Quanto costano queste scarpe?	*How much do these shoes cost?*

7 *VERY*

To give the idea of very, subtract the final vowel from an adjective and add **-issimo/a** for the singular or **-issimi/e** for the plural:

bello/a → bell- → bellissimo/a	*very beautiful*
caro/a → car- → carissimo/a	*very dear*
una camicia bellissima	*a very beautiful shirt*
due quadri carissimi	*two very expensive pictures*

8 *I HAVEN'T ANY …*

In negative sentences in the plural, such as *I haven't any change*, *I haven't any brothers*, *any* remains unexpressed in Italian:

Non ho spiccioli	*I haven't/don't have any (small) change*
Non ho soldi.	*I haven't/don't have any money.*

Similarly, *any* is omitted when negative questions are in the plural:

Non ha amici italiani?	*Haven't you got/don't you have any Italian friends?*

9 COUNTRIES

Countries are normally preceded by the definite article in Italian:

L'Italia ha circa 60 milioni di abitanti.	*Italy has about 60 million inhabitants.*
Vorrei due francobolli per la Svizzera.	*I'd like two stamps for Switzerland.*

Notice how in the first example approximate numbers are expressed by **circa**.

10 WRITING NUMBERS

Numbers are all written in one word, however long:

Quant'è? Centoventisei euro.	*How much is it? 126 euros.*

Cento *a/one hundred* and **mille** *a/one thousand* are used without **un** (*a/one*). The noun following is always plural:

cento sterline; mille euro	*a hundred pounds; a thousand euros*
mille baci	*a/one thousand kisses*
centomila persone	*one hundred thousand people*

but *1 million* is **un** milione **di**:

un milione di dollari	*a million dollars*
due milioni di anni	*2 million years*

11 SEE YOU!

Ci vediamo literally means *We see each other*.

Ci vediamo	stamattina dopo oggi stasera	See you	this morning later today this evening/tonight

Other ways of using **ci vediamo**:

Ci vediamo	domani dopodomani lunedì martedì	mattina pomeriggio sera	See you	tomorrow the day after tomorrow on Monday on Tuesday	morning afternoon / evening/ night

12 PREPOSITIONS

Here is a list of some Italian prepositions. Their English equivalents are very approximate but they can be a useful guide to understanding:

di *of*	**a** *at, to*	**da** *from, by*
in *in*	**con** *with*	**su** *on*
per *for*	**tra/fra** *between or among*	**senza** *without*

It must be emphasized, however, that their meanings vary enormously according to the context.

Come si dice?
How do you say it?

🔊 **CD 1, TR 15**

1 *How to ask at what time a place opens/closes*

A che ora apre/chiude?

 How to say at what time it opens/closes

Apre/chiude alle …/all'…/a …

2 *How to ask on what day someone is leaving*

Che giorno parti (inf)/parte (form)?

 How to say on what day you are leaving

Parto lunedì/giovedì, ecc.

3 *How to say what you would like (to buy)*

Vorrei una cartolina, un francobollo, ecc.

4 *How to ask about … colour*
   size: **a** *clothes in general*
        b *footwear*

Di che colore è/sono?
Che taglia?
Che numero?/misura?

5 *How to ask how much a thing/things cost*

Quanto costa?/Quanto costano?

 How to ask what the price comes to

Quant'è?

Practice

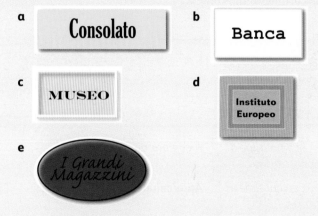

a **Consolato**

b **Banca**

c **MUSEO**

d **Instituto Europeo**

e *I Grandi Magazzini*

◀) CD 1, TR 16

1 *Listen to the recording and write down in figures the opening and closing times of the above places.*

    a *La mattina il consolato apre alle nove e mezza e chiude all'una.*

    b *Il pomeriggio la banca apre alle tre e chiude alle quattro.*

    c *Il museo apre alle nove e chiude alle due.*

    d *L'Istituto Europeo apre alle nove e chiude all'una e mezza.*

    e *I grandi magazzini aprono alle nove e chiudono alle sette e mezza.*

2 *Match the words below with the correct pictures. Look up those you don't know.*

i jeans; la cam<u>i</u>cia; i pantaloni; le scarpe; la gonna; i s<u>a</u>ndali; la camicetta; la cravatta; la giacca; la maglietta; i guanti; il vestito

3 *Form questions to ask* **a** *how much the T shirt costs;* **b** *how much the trousers cost;* **c** *how much the shoes cost. Write down in words the price of each.*

Insight

Remember to distinguish between **costa** and **c<u>o</u>stano**.

4 a *Write down what* **Carlo** *buys, using the information in the table overleaf. On the left-hand side you see the clothes he buys. The figures refer to the number he buys of each, and at the top of the table you will see what colours he chooses* (**comprare** *to buy*).

	rosso	giallo	nero	verde
maglietta	1	3		
cravatta		1		1
p<u>ai</u>o di scarpe			2	
p<u>ai</u>o di pantaloni		1		1

Start: **Carlo compra una …**

b *Assuming* **Carlo** *pays the prices given in the illustration above, how much does he pay in total?*

5 **Ora tocca a te!** *Now it's your turn.*

Add your side to the dialogue.

> **Tabacc<u>ai</u>o** Des<u>i</u>dera?
> **You** *Two stamps.*
> **Tabacc<u>ai</u>o** Per l'<u>e</u>stero?
> **You** *Yes. For France.*
> **Tabacc<u>ai</u>o** Altro?
> **You** *A postcard of Rome and this newspaper.*
> **Tabacc<u>ai</u>o** Poi …
> **You** *Nothing else. How much does it come to?*
> **Tabacc<u>ai</u>o** Due <u>e</u>uro e dieci.
> **You** *Here you are.*

6 *What do you think CHIUSO, APERTO and SALDI mean in the signs below? Check the meanings in the vocabulary.*

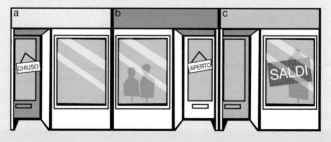

7 *Look up the words you don't know in this advert. What are they offering a discount for? When?*

Prices

In markets and small shops you can often bargain for the price of an article or ask for a discount (**uno sconto**) unless, that is, the sign **prezzi fissi** *fixed prices* is displayed.

Tabaccaio *Tobacconist*

In Italy tobacco and salt are state monopolies. They are both sold in tobacconists' shops, **Sale e Tabacchi**, which also sell stamps. **Carta bollata** and **marche da bollo** are also obtainable there. The first is government stamped paper: it is used for a variety of official purposes such as drawing up contracts and making statements to the police. The second are revenue stamps used for, among other things, official receipts.

Cigarettes are relatively cheap in Italy, and the cheapest brand, **le nazionali** are manufactured by the state which holds the monopoly and uses **il tabaccaio** as an outlet for its products. Italy has also been a tobacco producing country. However, it has had to conform to European Union legislation regarding cigarette advertising, and in common with other European countries, has enacted legislation prohibiting smoking in public places. In compensation, it receives an annually diminishing EU subsidy, to facilitate the gradual replacement of tobacco crops by more acceptable agricultural produce. Although there has been a marked decrease in smoking amongst the older members of the population (even if a recent statistic suggests that Italian women find it much harder than men to give up smoking for good), this has been accompanied by a worrying increase in the number of teenagers and university students who have adopted the habit.

TEST YOURSELF

Write meaningful sentences by putting the words in the correct order.

1 a chiude che questo negozio ora?

2 costano queste quanto scusi scarpe?

3 i di colore che pantaloni sono?

4 che a banca la apre ora?

5 nera la quanto gonna costa?

6 è questo semplice troppo vestito.

7 un di per sandali paio piacere rossi.

8 Parigi abitano a Franco Roberta e.

9 una di vorrei cartolina Torino.

10 verso dottore per il le parte domani otto Venezia sera.

5

Il coll**o**quio
The interview

In this unit you will learn:
- *how to exchange information about where you are going (country, town)*
- *how to ask why … and say because …*
- *how to ask and say how something is spelt*
- *how to ask and tell the time*
- *how to ask for someone's address and phone number*
- *how to say you do/don't understand.*

1 Dove vai?
Where are you going?

B**a**rbara tells her friend **Beatrice** that she is going to Bologna for her job interview (**il coll**o**quio**).

a *How does B**a**rbara say: 'I'm going to Bologna'?*
b *How does B**a**rbara say: 'By train'?*
c *How does Beatrice say: 'Only for ten days'?*

Beatrice	Dove vai?
Barbara	Vado a Bologna per il colloquio.
Beatrice	Come vai? In macchina?
Barbara	In treno. Ma anche tu parti, no?
Beatrice	Sì. Vado in Inghilterra con la mia amica francese. Andiamo a Londra.
Barbara	Per quanto tempo?
Beatrice	Oh! Solo per dieci giorni.
Barbara	Andate in albergo o a casa di amici?
Beatrice	Andiamo in una piccola pensione. Gli alberghi sono cari.

QUICK VOCAB

in macchina *by car*
in treno *by train*
andiamo *we are going*
per quanto tempo? *how long for?*
a casa di amici *to a friends' house*
una pensione *a guest house*

2 Quanto tempo ci vuole?
How long does it take?

Barbara asks **un passante** *a passer-by* if he knows where the shoe factory is.

a *She asks where the shoe factory is in a slightly different way from the one you have already learnt: can you spot the difference and repeat the question?*

b *How does* **il passante** *say: 'It's not far'?*

Barbara	Scusi, sa dov'è la fabbrica di scarpe?
Passante	Certo, signora. Sempre dritto dopo la chiesa.
Barbara	È lontano da qui?
Passante	No. Non è lontano. È vicino.
Barbara	Quanto tempo ci vuole?

Passante	A piedi, mezz'ora.
Barbara	E in autobus?
Passante	Solo cinque minuti.
Barbara	Ho capito. Che ore sono adesso, per piacere?
Passante	Sono le dieci.
Barbara	Già le dieci? Allora prendo l'autobus.

QUICK VOCAB

lontano *far*
a piedi *on foot*
mezz'ora *half an hour*
Che ore sono? *What time is it?*
adesso *now*
già *already*
chiesa *church*

   c *What is* **una fermata?**

3 Il suo nome?
Your name?

Barbara is being interviewed by **il dottor Verga, Direttore del Personale** *the Personnel Manager.*

   a *What expression does he use to ask her to spell her name?*
   b *How does* **Barbara** *say: 'My husband is Swiss'?*
   c *How does she say: 'I understand everything'?*

Dottor Verga	Il suo nome, signora?
Barbara	Barbara Setzler.
Dottor Verga	Setzler? … Come si scrive?
Barbara	Dunque: S come Salerno, E come Empoli, T come Torino, Z come Zara, L come Livorno, E come Empoli, R come Roma.
Dottor Verga	Non è italiana?
Barbara	Sì. Sono italiana. Mio marito è svizzero.
Dottor Verga	Capisce l'inglese?
Barbara	Capisco tutto, ma non parlo bene.

Q. VOCAB

Come si scrive? *How do you spell it/how is it spelt?*
marito *husband*
tutto *everything*

4 Qual è il suo indirizzo?
What's your address?

The interview continues. **Barbara** says where she was born.

a *How does she say: 'I was born in Lucca, but I live in Siena'?*
b *How does* il dott. Verga *ask: 'How many languages do you speak?'*

Dottor Verga	Dove abita?
Barbara	Sono nata a Lucca, ma abito a Siena.
Dottor Verga	Dove lavora?
Barbara	A Firenze: in uno studio legale.
Dottor Verga	Perchè vuole cambiare il suo lavoro attuale?
Barbara	Perchè vorrei usare le lingue che conosco.
Dottor Verga	Quante lingue parla?
Barbara	Quattro. Tre abbastanza bene.
Dottor Verga	Qual è il suo indirizzo?
Barbara	Via Lazio 68.
Dottor Verga	E il numero di telefono?
Barbara	Il mio numero di telefono è 33 55 541.

studio legale *lawyer's office*
Perchè vuole cambiare ...? *Why do you want to change ...?*
cambiare *to change*
attuale *present/current*
le lingue che conosco *the languages that I know*
abbastanza bene *quite well*

Pronunciation

🔊 **CD 1, TR 18**

The Italian alphabet has 21 letters: **a, b, c, d, e, f, g, h, i , l, m, n, o, p, q, r, s, t, u, v, z.** For spelling names, the town alphabet is normally used:

a	A come Ancona	n	Enne come Napoli
b	Bi come Bari	o	O come Otranto
c	Ci come Capri	p	Pi come Palermo
d	Di come Domodossola	q	Cu come Quebec
e	E come Empoli	r	Erre come Roma
f	Effe come Firenze	s	Esse come Salerno
g	Gi come Genova	t	Ti come Torino
h	Acca come Hotel	u	U come Udine
I	I come Imola	v	Vu come Venezia
l	Elle come Livorno	z	Zeta come Zara
m	Emme come Modena		

The following are not part of the Italian alphabet but may be required for spelling foreign names:

j	I lunga come Jazz	w	Doppia vu come Washington
k	Kappa come Kaiser		
y	Ipsilon come York	x	Ix come raggi X

Grammar

1 VERBS

In Dialogue 1 above **vai** *you* (informal) *are going* is part of the irregular verb **andare** *to go*.

Present tense	**andare** *to go*		
(io) vado	*I go, am going*	**(noi) andiamo**	*we go, are going*
(tu) vai	*you* (inf) *go, are going*	**(voi) andate**	*you* (pl) *go, are going*
(lei) va	*you* (form) *go, are going*		
(lui, lei) va	*he/she/it goes, is going*	**(loro) vanno**	*they go, are going*

Capisce is part of **capire** *to understand*, another type of -ire verb. The endings in bold are added to the stem **cap-**.

Present tense	**capire** *to understand*		
(io) cap-**isco**	*I understand*	**(noi)** cap-**iamo**	*we understand*
(tu) cap-**isci**	*you* (inf) *understand*	**(voi)** cap-**ite**	*you* (pl) *understand*
(lei) cap-**isce**	*you* (form) *understand*		
(lui, lei) cap-**isce**	*he/she/it understands*	**(loro)** cap-**iscono**	*they understand*

The most common verbs like **capire** are: **finire** *to finish*, **preferire** *to prefer* and **pulire** *to clean*.

fin-**isco**, fin-**isci**, fin-**isce**, fin-**iamo**, fin-**ite**, fin-**iscono**;
prefer-**isco**, prefer-**isci**, prefer-**isce**, prefer-**iamo**, prefer-**ite**, prefer-**iscono**;
pul-**isco**, pul-**isci**, pul-**isce**, pul-**iamo**, pul-**ite**, pul-**iscono**.

Insight

Ho capito (lit: *I have understood*) is what Italians usually say to show that they understand what has been said to them: **'Ripeto? – No, no. Va bene. Ho capito.'** (*Shall I repeat? No, no. That's all right. I understand.*)

When **capire** is used with the name of a language, it is preceded by the article: **'Capisce l'inglese? Sì. Capisco l'inglese e il tedesco.'**

2 ANDARE A/IN ... *TO GO TO ...*

With towns, use **andare a ...**; with countries, use **andare in ...**

Vado a Nizza, a Pisa ...
  I'm going to Nice, to Pisa ...
Andiamo in Italia, in Francia ...
  We're going to Italy, to France ...

3 *ARTICLES:* **GLI** *THE*

Gli, plural of **lo** and **l'** (Unit 2, Section 4) is used before masculine plural words beginning with a vowel, **s** + consonant, or **z**:

	Singular		Plural	
l' + vowel	**l'ascensore**		**ascensori**	*the lifts*
	l'amico		**amici**	*the friends*
	l'albergo		**alberghi**	*the hotels*
	l'ufficio	**gli**	**uffici**	*the offices*
lo + s + cons.	**lo studente**		**studenti**	*the students*
	lo straniero		**stranieri**	*the foreigners*
lo + z	**lo zio**		**zii**	*the uncles*

Note: **amico** *(male) friend* plural: **amici** but **amica** *(female) friend* plural: **amiche**.

Take care with words ending in -co, -ca, -go, -ga. They often insert an h in the plural to preserve the same c or g sound (see Pronunciation, Unit 2): la banca, le banche (*the banks*); il lago, i laghi (*the lakes*).

4 PERCHÈ...? PERCHÈ... *WHY ...? BECAUSE ...*

Perchè means both *why* and *because*:

Perchè non vai in albergo?	*Why don't you go to a hotel?*
Perchè gli alberghi sono cari.	*Because hotels are expensive.*

5 SCUSI, SA DOV'È ...? *EXCUSE ME, DO YOU KNOW WHERE ... IS?*

As in English, the expression **Scusi, sa dov'è ...?** is frequently used as another way of asking **Dov'è ...?**

6 QUANTO TEMPO CI VUOLE? *HOW LONG DOES IT TAKE?*

Use the expression **Quanto tempo ci vuole?** to ask or say how long something takes:

Quanto tempo ci vuole per andare a casa di Maria?	*How long does it take to go to Mary's house?*
Ci vuole un'ora.	*It takes an hour.*
Ci vuole un quarto d'ora.	*It takes a quarter of an hour.*

For plural nouns: **ore** *hours*, **minuti** *minutes*, **giorni** *days*, etc., ci vuole becomes ci vogliono.

Quanto tempo ci vuole per ritornare?	*How long does it take to return/get back?*
Ci vogliono cinque minuti.	*It takes five minutes.*

7 WHAT TIME IS IT?

To ask the time, either **Che ora è?** or **Che ore sono?** may be used, but the answer will depend on whether the time is singular or plural. Always use **sono le ...** in your answer unless talking about *one o'clock*, *midday* or *midnight*. **Sono le due, sono le cinque, sono le sei, but è l'una, è l'una e mezza, è mezzogiorno, è mezzanotte.**

The clocks (**gli orologi**) below show how e is used to say '*past*', and **meno** (*less*) on the left to say '*to*'.

meno   **e**

11.40	12.00	12.05
Sono le dodici meno venti	Sono le dodici È mezzogiorno / mezzanotte	Sone le dodici e cinque

12.45	1.00	1.15
È l'una meno un quarto	È l'una	È l'una e un quarto

2.45	3.00	5.30
Sono le tre meno un quarto	Sono le tre	Sono le cinque e mezza

5.50	11.00	4.20
Sono le sei meno dieci	Sono le undici	Sono le quattro e venti

andare in/a ... *to go by/on ...*		
	aereo	*air*
	autobus	*bus*
	bicicletta	*bike*
Vado in	macchina	*I'm going by*	*car*
	metropolitana	*underground*
	treno	*train*
	vaporetto	*boat*
but **Vado a piedi**		*I'm going on foot/I'm walking*

9 POSSESSIVE ADJECTIVES

When referring to *one member* of the family *only* (**mio fratello, sua sorella ecc.**; see Unit 3, Section 10) the article is not used before **mio, tuo, ecc.** In other cases, however, the definite article is required and must precede the possessive:

Le mie sorelle e i tuoi fratelli vanno a casa.   *My brothers and your sisters are going home.*

(Notice **vanno** from **andare**: Unit 5, Section 1.)

Here are the possessive adjectives for *my, your, his, her*.

Singular			Plural		
	m	f	m	f	
(io)	il mio	la mia	i miei	le mie	*my*
(tu)	il tuo	la tua	i tuoi	le tue	*your* (inf)
(lui/lei)	il suo	la sua	i suoi	le sue	*his, her; your* (form)

il mio orologio; il suo orologio	my watch/clock; his/her/your watch/clock
la mia città; la sua città	my town; his/her/your town
i miei amici; i suoi amici	my friends; your/his/her friends (m)
le mie amiche; le sue amiche	my friends; your/his/her friends (f)

10 I WAS BORN IN ...

It is important to use the present tense of <u>essere</u>, not the past, when saying when or where you were born:

| Dov'è nato/a? | Where were you born? |
| Sono nato/a a Roma. | I was born in Rome. |

11 HOW DO YOU SPELL (WRITE) IT?

To ask 'How do you spell ...?' Italians say 'How do you write ...?'
Come si scrive?

Si means *one, you* (i.e. *people in general*), and is used frequently in Italian. It is always used with the third person of the verb, and precedes it:

Come si fa?	How do you do it?
Come si dice in italiano?	How do you say it in Italian?
Qui si parla italiano.	Italian is spoken here. (lit: here one speaks Italian.)
In questo ristorante si mangia bene.	You can eat well in this restaurant.

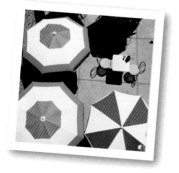

Come si dice?
How do you say it?

1 *How to ask where someone is going* — **Dove va?** *(form)*/**Dove vai?** *(inf)*

How to say where you are going (country, town) — **Vado in Italia, a Genova.**

2 *How to ask why … and say … because* — **Perchè …?**
Perchè …

3 *How to ask how something is spelt* — **Come si scrive?**

4 *How to ask and tell the time* — **Che ora è?/Che ore sono? È l'una …/Sono le due …**

5 *How to ask for someone's address/phone number* — **Qual è il suo** *(form)*/**il tuo** *(inf)* **indirizzo? Qual è il suo (form)/il tuo (inf) numero di telefono?**

6 *How to say you understand/ don't understand (what you have been told)* — **Ho capito./Non ho capito.**

After this unit only the **lei** form (formal *you*) will be used in the *How do you say it?* section unless **tu** is more appropriate.

Practice

1 *Numbers (continued)*

First repeat the round numbers from 60–100 as you hear them.

60	70	80	90	100
sessanta	settanta	ottanta	novanta	cento

Now use your pause button so that you can say the following numbers before you hear them:

61	68	82	88
sessantuno	sessantotto	ottantadue	ottantotto

91	97	98	99	100
novantuno	novantasette	novantotto	novantanove	cento

Finally, listen to the ordinal numbers 5th to 10th and repeat them:

5th	6th	7th	8th	9th	10th
quinto/a	sesto/a	settimo/a	ottavo/a	nono/a	decimo/a

2 *In the eight addresses below, the house numbers are written out in full. See if you can recognize what they are by listening to the recording. Write them down in figures.*

a *Via Nazionale settantasei*
b *Via Quattro Novembre ottantacinque*
c *Via Cavour sessantotto*
d *Via Martelli settantanove*
e *Via Romolo centosettanta*
f *Via Mercuri centonovantotto*
g *Via Vittorio Emanuele centosettantasette*
h *Via Terni centodue*

3 *Say where Carlo, Roberto, etc. are going, and how they get there (using the words given in Sections 2 and 8 above).*

Insight
Remember that the plural of **va** is **vanno**.

a *Carlo __ in* **ufficio** __.

b *Roberto __* **Parigi** __.

c *Franco __* **Roma** ___.

d *Anna __ a* **casa** __.

e *I bambini ____ a* **scuola** __.

f *Francesca __* **Milano** __.

4 *Now imagine a conversation with* **Carlo**: *the information given in* **Exercise 3** *could be rendered in question-and-answer form:*

– Dove vai, Carlo? – Vado in ufficio.
– Come vai? – In bicicletta.

Write similar conversations with **Franco**, **Anna** *and* **Francesca**.

5 *Write these times out in words starting with* È ... *or* Sono ... *(see Section 7 above):*
a 10.05 b 12.45 c 2.50 d 3.20 e 5.45 f 6.30 g 12.00 (noon) h 12.00 (midnight)

6 *Ora tocca a te!*

You have a short interview with **un dirigente** *a Manager*. You are
Pat Brown, 33 years old and American. You work in **un'agenzia di
viaggi** *a travel agency*. Use the pause button to complete your side
of the interview.

CD 1, TR 20, 02:36

Dirigente	Il suo nome?
You	*Pat Brown.*
Dirigente	Brown? Come si scrive?
You	*Spell it for him.*
Dirigente	È inglese, vero?
You	*No. I'm American, but I live in London.*
Dirigente	Quanti anni ha?
You	*I am 33.*
Dirigente	Che lavoro fa?
You	*I work in a travel agency.*
Dirigente	Parla francese e tedesco?
You	*I understand everything but I don't speak well.*

7 *What is this handbook for?*

Guida alle Carriere Professionali

Guida Alle Carriere Professionali

Interviews and exams

In Italy most examinations have an oral component, whatever the subject: many will see job interviews as an extension of this practice. Since job security is still considered by many to be the ultimate goal, and since traditionally, state funded posts in schools, universities and government departments are considered to offer jobs for life, they are hotly contested in competitive examinations (**i concorsi**), even though they are not considered to be particularly well paid. Alongside this there continues to exist the system of **raccomandazioni**, that is, gaining a cherished post by obtaining the recommendation of someone who hopefully has some influence. It is interesting to note from a recent poll, that whereas the majority of students in the North of Italy considered that one could and should succeed by one's own efforts, most students from the South assumed that without these **raccomandazioni** one could get nowhere. All that remained for them was unemployment or **la precarietà** (**lavoro precario** *temporary employment*).

Public transport

Buses are the most usual form of **public transport** in Italian towns, though trams and trolley buses still exist. You must buy your ticket before boarding the bus, otherwise you are liable to a fine (**la multa**). You normally buy **un blocchetto** *a carnet* of ten before the journey, at the tobacconist's, at the newsagent's or in bars.

More websites

http://www./lucca.turismo.toscana.it
http://www./siena.turismo.toscana.it

TEST YOURSELF

Match up each question on the left with the most suitable answer on the right.

1 Dove andate?

a Certo signore: dopo l'agenzia di viaggi.

2 Non è lontano?

b Sono le tre.

3 È tardi. Allora, andiamo?

c Perchè non capisco tutto.

4 Scusi, che ora è?

d Andiamo in Francia.

5 Quanto tempo ci vuole?

e Sono professore.

6 Non è italiano?

f In aereo.

7 Sa dov'è la fermata?

g Vanno a piedi.

8 Che lavoro fa?

h Ci vogliono solo cinque minuti.

9 Come va in Italia?

i Sì, andiamo!

10 Perchè non parla?

j No. Non sono italiano. Sono tedesco.

Now, fill in the gaps using each word in the box once only.

11 ___ sua amica è italiana.

12 Le ___ amiche abitano a Roma.

13 La ___ macchina è bella.

14 I ___ genitori sono di Torino.

15 Il ___ orologio è svizzero.

> tua - mie - la - mio - suoi

6

Alla stazione
At the station

In this unit you will learn:
- *how to buy a rail ticket and book a seat*
- *how to ask about train times*
- *how to enquire about other travel details.*

_____

1 A che ora parte il prossimo treno?
At what time does the next train leave?

At the railway station **un viaggiatore** *a traveller* is buying a ticket to Turin.

  a *How does* **l'impiegato** *the (booking) clerk say 'at 3.25 p.m.'?*
  b *How does* **il viaggiatore** *ask: 'From what platform?'*

> **Viaggiatore** Vorrei un biglietto per Torino.
> **Impiegato** Prima o seconda classe?
> **Viaggiatore** Prima classe. A che ora parte il prossimo treno?
> **Impiegato** Alle quindici e venticinque. Fra dieci minuti.
> **Viaggiatore** Da che binario?
> **Impiegato** Dal binario diciotto.
> **Viaggiatore** A che ora arriva a Torino?
> **Impiegato** Alle venti e cinquanta.

CD 1, TR 21

> **Viaggiatore** Devo cambiare?
> **Impiegato** No. È diretto. Guardi, signore, l'orario dei treni è là in fondo.

QUICK VOCAB

prossimo/a *next*
fra dieci minuti *in ten minutes*
Da che/quale binario? *From what platform?*
Guardi... *Look...*
Devo cambiare? *Do I have to change?*
l'orario dei treni *the train timetable*
là in fondo *down there*

2 Vorrei prenotare ...
I'd like to book ...

At the railway station a man is trying to book three seats for tomorrow morning, but there will be a strike (**sciopero**) on.

a *How does A say: 'Three seats for tomorrow morning'?*

b *You have now learnt two meanings for* **espresso** *and two for* **biglietto**: *what are they?*

CD 1, TR 21, 00:57

> **A** Vorrei prenotare tre posti per domani mattina.
> **B** Domani? Impossibile!
> **A** Perchè impossibile?
> **B** Perchè domani c'è lo sciopero.
> **A** Un altro sciopero? Ci sono sempre scioperi. Tre posti per dopodomani, allora.
> **B** C'è l'Eurostar alle otto e trenta e un espresso alle dieci e quaranta.
> **A** Meglio l'Eurostar. Tre biglietti, andata e ritorno.

ci sono sempre ... there *are always ...*
meglio *better*
dopodomani *the day after tomorrow*
andata e ritorno *return ticket*
andata *single, one way ticket (US)*

---

3 C'è un treno diretto ...?
Is there a through train ...?

A traveller wants to go to Florence
and asks for the times of the trains
(**l'orario dei treni**) at the enquiry desk
(**Ufficio Informazioni**).

a *How does* **l'impiegato** *say: 'It's
two minutes late'?*
b *'The train is leaving from platform 9.' What is the Italian
equivalent?*

Viaggiatore	C'è un treno diretto per Firenze o devo cambiare?
Impiegato	Se vuole prendere l'espresso, deve aspettare tre ore, fino alle diciotto e quarantacinque.
Viaggiatore	Non c'è un treno prima delle sette meno un quarto?
Impiegato	L'Eurostar. Ma deve cambiare a Bologna.
Viaggiatore	È in orario l'Eurostar?
Impiegato	No. È in ritardo di due minuti.
Viaggiatore	Meno male! Da quale binario parte?
Impiegato	È in partenza dal binario nove. Se ha già il biglietto, può pagare il supplemento in treno.

Se vuole prendere … *If you want to take …*
aspettare *to wait for*
fino a *until*
prima di *before*
in orario/in ritardo *on time/late*
meno male! *thank goodness!*
può pagare *you can pay*

4 Si scende dall'altra parte
You get off on the other side

Il signor Neri asks a passenger whether the bus (**l'autobus**) on which they are travelling goes to the main line station.

a *How does* il sig. Neri *ask: 'Where's the 68 bus stop?'*
b *How does* il passeggero *say: 'I'm getting off at the next stop too'?*
c *What are the three expressions you have met for 'please' up to now?*

Sig. Neri	Va alla stazione centrale quest'autobus, per favore?
Passeggero	No, signore. Deve prendere il 68.
Sig. Neri	E dov'è la fermata del 68, per cortesia?
Passeggero	Davanti all'università. Dopo il municipio.
Sig. Neri	Grazie. Può dirmi quando devo scendere?
Passeggero	Certamente. Alla prossima fermata.
Sig. Neri	Ho capito. Scendo e vado davanti all'università.
Passeggero	Guardi, alla prossima fermata scendo anch'io.
Sig. Neri	Allora scendiamo insieme. Si scende da qui?
Passeggero	No. Si scende dall'altra parte. Da qui si sale solamente.

per cortesia	*please*
davanti a	*in front of*
Può dirmi …?	*Can you tell me …?*
insieme	*together*
da qui	*over here*
si sale (salire irr)	*you get on*
solamente	*only*

Pronunciation

◀) **CD 1, TR 22**

a + i   vai, stai, ai binari

e + u   l'Albergo Europa, l'Istituto Europeo, la Comunità Europea

i + e   le mie amiche, i miei amici, l'impiegato

u + o   può, vuoi andare, i suoi fratelli.

Grammar

1 L'ORARIO DEI TRENI *THE TRAIN TIMETABLE*

The 24-hour clock is normally used for all official purposes: **dodici e quindici** *12.15*; **quindici e quarantacinque** *15.45*; **diciotto e trenta** *18.30*; **venti e cinquanta** *20.50*.

2 *NEXT*

To ask when the first, second, next, or last train leaves:

	il primo treno?		the first train	
A che ora parte	**il secondo treno?**	*At what time does*	*the second train*	*leave?*
	il prossimo treno?		*the next train*	
	l'ultimo treno?		*the last train*	

3 *TO THE, FROM THE:* **A, DA** *+ DEFINITE ARTICLE*

When the above prepositions combine with the article they are called contracted prepositions. We have already seen **alle** (**a** + **le**) used with times (Unit 4, Section 2). Always place the definite article before the noun first, as in column 1 below. Then remember that **a** + **il** at the contracts to **al**. In all other cases you put **a** before the article and double the 'l' if there is one. Note that **il cinema** is masculine.

il cinema	**a + il = al**		**al** cinema	*at*	*the cinema*
lo sportello	**a + lo = allo**		**allo** sportello		*the counter*
l'entrata	**a + l' = all'**		**all'**entrata	*(in*	*the entrance*
la biglietteria	**a + la = alla**	(davanti)	**alla** biglietteria	*front*	*the ticket office*
i bambini	**a + i = ai**		**ai** bambini	*of)*	*the children*
gli studenti	**a + gli = agli**		**agli** studenti		*the students*
le ragazze	**a + le = alle**		**alle** ragazze	*to*	*the girls*

A + definite article appears in many idiomatic expressions:

al sole	*in the sun*	**all'aperto**	*in the open air*
al mare	*at/to the seaside*	**all'ombra**	*in the shade*
al fresco	*in the cool*		

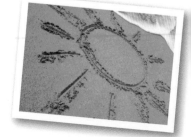

Like **davanti a, vicino a** *near*:

Ci vediamo vicino alla fontana! *See you near the fountain!*
Il cinema è vicino all'albergo. *The cinema is near the hotel.*

Da + definite article behaves in exactly the same way. Don't forget that **da + il** becomes **dal**:

Il ristorante è lontano dal centro. *The restaurant is far from the centre.*

L'albergo è lontano dall'aeroporto. *The hotel is far from the airport.*

4 *OF THE:* **DI** + *DEFINITE ARTICLE*

When **di** combines with the definite article it becomes **de**. Once this change is made, and you remember that **di + il** becomes **del**, you will see that the same pattern as **a + definite article** holds good.

In the following examples notice where the English differs from the Italian rendering: whereas we say 'the station clock', Italians say 'the clock of the station'.

il mare	**di + il = del**	l'acqua **del** mare	*seawater*
lo sport	**di + lo = dello**	La Gazzetta **dello** Sport	*The Sports Gazette*
l'autobus	**di + l' = dell'**	la fermata **dell'au**tobus	*the bus stop*
la stazione	**di + la = della**	l'orologio **della** stazione	*the station clock*
i negozi	**di + i = dei**	le vetrine **dei** negozi	*the shop windows*
gli affari	**di + gli = degli**	il mondo **degli** affari	*the business world*
le vacanze	**di + le = delle**	la fine **delle** vacanze	*the end of the holidays*

5 DEVO ...? *DO I HAVE TO ...?*

Devo comes from **dovere** *to have to*. It means *I have to* or *I must*. **Vuol**(e) and **vorrei** come from **volere** *to wish* or *to want*. Both **dovere** and **volere** are irregular (for **vuol** see Unit 14).

(io)	devo	*I have to, I must*	(noi) dobbiamo	*we have to, we must*
(tu)	devi	*you* (inf) *have to, you must*	(voi) dovete	*you* (pl) *have to, you must*
(lei)	deve	*you* (form) *have to, must*		
(lui, lei)	deve	*he, she has to, must*	(loro) d<u>e</u>vono	*they have to, they must*

(io)	v<u>o</u>glio	*I want*	(noi) vogliamo	*we want*
(tu)	vu<u>oi</u>	*you* (inf) *want*	(voi) volete	*you* (pl) *want*
(lei)	vuole	*you* (form) *want*		
(lui, lei)	vuole	*he/she wants*	(loro) v<u>o</u>gliono	*they want*

From now on the second person singular **lei** (*you*) form will be omitted in verb tables as it is always the same as the third person singular.

Insight

Attenzione! Verbs immediately after **volere** and **dovere** must be in the infinitive.

V<u>o</u>glio ⎤	partire	*I want* ⎤	*leave*
Vorr<u>ei</u> ⎬	telefonare	*I would like* ⎬ *to*	*phone*
Devo ⎦	mangiare	*I have* ⎦	*eat*
	andare in banca		*go to the bank*

Perchè non vu<u>oi</u> andare alla discoteca con i tu<u>oi</u> amici?
Why don't you want to go to the discotheque with your friends?

Perchè devo studiare. *Because I have to/must study.*

6 C'È, CI SONO *THERE IS, THERE ARE*

C'è = ci + è.

Use **c'è** to say *there is, is there?* Use **ci sono** to say *there are, are there?* For the negative, use **non c'è** *there isn't*, **non ci sono** *there aren't*.

(Non) c'è un espresso per Firenze?	*Is(n't) there an express to Florence?*
No, perchè c'è lo sciopero.	*No, because there's a strike.*
(Non) ci sono treni la domenica?	*Are(n't) there any trains on Sundays?*

7 ASPETTARE *TO WAIT FOR,* ASCOLTARE *TO LISTEN TO,* GUARDARE *TO LOOK AT*

The above verbs are followed by a direct object in Italian. The prepositions **for, to** and **at** are not expressed:

Aspetta l'autobus?	*Are you waiting for the bus?*
Aspetto un mio amico.	*I'm waiting for a friend of mine.*
Guardo spesso la televisione.	*I often look at (watch) television.*
Ascoltiamo la radio.	*We listen to the radio.*

8 PRIMA DI, DOPO *BEFORE, AFTER*

Note how **prima di** is used with times. **Di** combines with **l'** and **le** to become **dell'** and **delle**:

prima dell'una, prima delle due, prima delle sei, ecc.	*before 1 o'clock, before 2 o'clock, before 6 o'clock, etc.*

but

prima di mezzogiorno,   *before midday, before midnight.*
   prima di mezzanotte

For *after* simply use **dopo: dopo le due; dopo mezzanotte**

9 BUYING A TICKET

Although **comprare** means *to buy*, the normal way of saying *to buy
a ticket* is **fare il biglietto** (lit: *to make the ticket*).

10 IN 10 MINUTES

Fra always refers to the future:

Fra dieci minuti.   *In 10 minutes.*
Fra mezz'ora.   *In half an hour's time.*
Fra un paio di settimane.   *In a couple of weeks' time.*

11 LATE, ON TIME

Il treno è in	{	ritardo orario anticipo arrivo partenza	The train is	{	late on time early arriving leaving

---

Come si dice?
How do you say it?

◄ CD 1, TR 22, 00:36

1 *How to buy … a second class   **Vorrei … un biglietto di
   ticket*   seconda classe**

... a single/return ticket	... **(un biglietto) andata/andata e ritorno.**
2 How to ask the time of departure of the next train, etc.	**A che ora parte il prossimo treno, ecc.?**
3 How to ask from what platform it leaves	**Da che binario parte?**
4 How to ask whether you have to change ...	**Devo cambiare?**
... and where	**Dove?**
How to ask if there's a through train	**C'è un treno diretto?**
5 How to ask to book a seat	**Vorrei prenotare un posto.**

Practice

◀) CD 1, TR 22, 01:09

1 *Listen to the four dialogues below, which all take place at a booking-office. For each conversation in turn fill in the details on the grid opposite.*

a A *Un biglietto per Siena.*
B *Andata?*
A *Sì. Andata. Seconda classe.*
B *Quindici euro e cinquanta.*
A *A che ora parte il treno?*
B *Alle sedici e venti dal binario tre.*

b A *Buongiorno. Vorrei due biglietti per Roma.*
B *Seconda classe?*
A *Prima classe. Quando parte il treno?*
B *Parte alle dieci e quaranta e arriva a Roma alle quindici e venti.*
A *Da che binario parte?*
B *Dal binario quindici.*

c A *A che ora parte l'ultimo treno per Genova?*
B *Alle ventitrè e cinquantacinque.*
A *Dal binario dodici?*
B *No. L'ultimo treno parte dal binario sette.*
A *Un biglietto, allora. Seconda classe.*

d A *Uno per Novara. Prima classe.*
B *Solo andata?*
A *Andata e ritorno. Quant'è?*
B *Trentaquattro euro e quarantacinque.*
A *A che ora parte il treno?*
B *Alle diciotto e trenta. Primo binario. Buon viaggio!*

	Destinazione	Numero di biglietti	Classe	Ora di partenza	Binario
a					
b					
c					
d					

2 *Using each contracted preposition from the box below once only, fill in the gaps.*

  a *Non so il prezzo __ orologio.*
  b *Il professore parla __ studenti.*
  c *L'appartamento __ ragazze italiane è molto bello.*
  d *Vuoi comprare la macchina __ zio di Giulia?*
  e *Vuole accompagnare Mario __ stadio domenica prossima?*
  f *L'orario __ autobus è lì.*
  g *A che ora va __ istituto?*
  h *Il treno parte __ diciotto e quindici.*
  i *Il dirigente __ fabbrica è occupato.*
  j *Aspettiamo Massimo davanti __ bar.*

> dell' dello della degli delle
> al allo all' agli alle

3 *Which line from the right-hand column fits with i? You can see that e makes most sense. Fit the others together in the same way.*

i Voglio comprare le scarpe	**a** Perchè non ho il suo numero di telefono.
ii Lucia deve andare alla biglietteria	**b** perchè è disoccupato (unemployed).
iii Devo prendere l'autobus	**c** perchè voglio andare a lavorare in Italia.

iv	Perchè non telefoni a Mario?	**d**	perchè ho un messaggio importante per lei (for her).
v	Giorgio non ha soldi	**e**	perchè ci sono i saldi.
vi	Studio l'italiano	**f**	perchè è troppo caro.
vii	Devo vedere Francesca	**g**	perchè c'è lo sciopero dei treni.
viii	Non compro il vestito	**h**	Perchè non ho il suo indirizzo.
ix	Perchè non scrivi a Fabrizio?	**i**	perchè vuole fare il biglietto per Livorno.

4 *Here is a list of buildings (**edifici**) and monuments (**monumenti**) in various places. Using c'è or ci sono as appropriate, make a statement about each, modelling it on the first example which is done for you:*
Esempio: In Via Rossini ci sono due banche.
Via Rossini: La Banca Commerciale, La Banca Nazionale del Lavoro.
Via Terni: L'Albergo Alba, l'Albergo Luxor, l'Albergo Rialto.
Piazza Dante: Il Palazzo Visconti.
Piazza Cavour: Il Bar Parini, il Bar Stella, il Bar Verdi, il Bar Marotta.
Roma: (L'Aeroporto) Ciampino, (l'Aeroporto) Fiumicino.

5 *From the two sentences provided, make a statement using **fra** as in the example:*
Esempio: Sono le nove meno un quarto. Adriano va a scuola all nove.
Adriano va a scuola fra un quarto d'ora.
  a *Sono le dieci. Pina va in banca alle undici.*
  b *È mezzogiorno. Giorgio va al colloquio alle tre.*
  c *Sono le sei e mezza. Enrico ritorna a casa alle sette meno un quarto.*
  d *Sono le undici e venti. Carlo va alla discoteca alle undici e mezza.*
  e *Sono le sette e mezza. Il treno arriva alle sette e trentacinque.*

6 *Ora tocca a te!*

You would like to book three seats to Florence. Complete your side of the conversation.

CD 1, TR 22, 02:50

Impiegato	Sì … Prego?
You	*I would like to book three seats for the day after tomorrow, Thursday.*
Impiegato	Destinazione?
You	*Florence.*
Impiegato	Vuole partire la mattina o la sera?
You	*Isn't there a through train at 11 o'clock?*
Impiegato	No, ma c'è un espresso che parte a mezzogiorno.
You	*All right. Three seats for Thursday, then. Second class.*

7 *Look at the two flyers (adverts) and answer the questions.*

Viaggi meglio e spendi meno, con la Carta Amicotreno.

Nuova Carta Amicotreno. Il viaggiare intelligente che diventa conveniente.

FERROVIE DELLO STATO

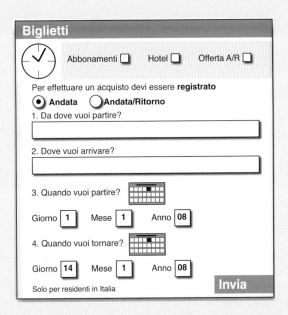

Biglietti

Abbonamenti ☐   Hotel ☐   Offerta A/R ☐

Per effettuare un acquisto devi essere **registrato**

⦿ Andata   ◯ Andata/Ritorno

1. Da dove vuoi partire?

2. Dove vuoi arrivare?

3. Quando vuoi partire?

Giorno 1   Mese 1   Anno 08

4. Quando vuoi tornare?

Giorno 14   Mese 1   Anno 08

Solo per residenti in Italia

Invia

---

a What are the two advantages claimed for the Amicotreno railcard?

b What is the Italian for: 'When do you want to leave?'

c Can anyone buy a ticket on-line? If not, why not?

Italian trains

Before boarding your train you must validate your ticket (**convalidare il biglietto**) in a machine which stamps the time and date on it.

Ferrovie dello stato, *State railways* have now been partially privatized. **Trenitalia** is in charge of bookings, ticket sales and timetables. Luxury high-speed trains link the main cities in the peninsula to the rest of Europe.

However, when Italians refer to **Eurostar**, they are usually referring to **Eurostar Italia**, and not to the Channel Link. A new tunnel is in the course of construction under the Alps which will ultimately provide a rapid service between **Torino** Turin, and **Lyon** in France. In spite of many environmental protests on the Italian side in the **Val de Susa** area, it is likely that work will be completed on time. Another project, a bridge linking the mainland to Sicily has had to be shelved through lack of funding.

There are two websites for the Italian railway system:
Ferrovie dello Stato: http://www.fs-on-line.it
Trenitalia: http://www.trenitalia.com

Now turn to *Test your Italian I*.

TEST YOURSELF

Using *di* or each contracted preposition from the box below once only, fill in the gaps.

1 *Voglio partire prima __ una.*

2 *Scusi! Dov'è l'orario __ autobus?*

3 *Andiamo __ Stadio Olimpico.*

4 *Dov'è il dirigente __ fabbrica, per piacere?*

5 *Perchè non andiamo __ centro?*

6 *Dov'è la biglietteria? Vorrei un biglietto __ prima classe.*

7 *Devo telefonare __ miei figli.*

8 *Perchè non andate __ discoteca?*

9 *Oggi lavoro __ ufficio informazioni.*

10 *Partiamo __ sette.*

11 *Il professore parla __ studenti.*

12 *Scusi, dov'è la fermata __ ventidue?*

13 *La casa __ mie amiche è a destra.*

14 *Oggi c'è lo sciopero __ treni.*

15 *Compriamo la Gazzetta __ Sport.*

al - alla - allo - all' - ai - alle - agli - del -
della - dello - dell' - dei - delle - degli -di

7

Al ristorante
At the restaurant

In this unit you will learn:
* *how to ask/say whether a place is open/closed*
* *how to order a meal*
* *how to ask for more bread/wine, etc.*
* *how to say that it's enough*
* *how to ask the waiter what he recommends*
* *how to say that it doesn't matter.*

1 Buon appetito!
Enjoy your meal!

◄)) **CD 1, TR 23**

Listen to these snippets of conversation and circle the appropriate letter for the correct situation. Try making a guess before looking anything up!

  A Buon appetito! Grazie altrettanto!
    This is taking place:
      a *just before a meal.*
      b *immediately after a meal.*
      c *at the cash desk.*
      d *just before the end of the meal.*

B Un altro po' di vino? No. Basta così.
The second speaker:
  a *wants some more wine.*
  b *doesn't like the wine.*
  c *is refusing more wine.*
  d *wants a glass of red wine.*

C Scusi, è occupato questo posto? No. È libero. Prego, si accomodi!
The second speaker says that:
  a *the seat is clean.*
  b *the seat is taken.*
  c *the seat is dangerous.*
  d *the seat is free.*

D Il menù è a prezzo fisso? No. Alla carta.
The second speaker wants:
  a *to pick and choose from the menu.*
  b *the set meal.*
  c *the wine list.*
  d *the meal of the day.*

---

2 Che facciamo?

What shall we do?

A couple are deciding whether to eat in the hotel or to have a meal out.

a *How does* **il marito** *say: 'Excellent idea'?*

CD 1, TR 23, 00:41

Marito	Dunque. Che facciamo oggi? Mangiamo qui in albergo?
Moglie	No. Usciamo! Andiamo a pranzo fuori! Magari, stasera torniamo qui per la cena.
Marito	ottima idea!

Usciamo! *Let's go out!*
pranzo *lunch*
magari *perhaps*
tornare = ritornare *to return*
cena *dinner*
ottima idea *excellent idea*

3 'Da Peppino' è aperto
'Da Peppino' is open

Having decided to go out they make enquiries.

  a *How does* il signore *say: 'But it's closed today'?*
  b *How does* il marito *ask: 'Is there a good restaurant nearby?'*

Marito	Scusi, signore, c'è un buon ristorante qui vicino?
Signore	Sì. Il ristorante 'Da Peppino'. È buono e non è caro. Ma oggi è chiuso.
Signora	No. La trattoria è chiusa. 'Da Peppino' è aperto.
Marito	Allora, andiamo lì, no ...?
Moglie	Come vuoi!

trattoria *modest restaurant (see 'Eating out in Italy' at the end of this unit)*
Come vuoi! *As you wish!*

4 Conosco un ristorante vicino al mare
I know a restaurant by the sea

Listen to another person giving information about a restaurant.

  a *How does the first speaker say: 'Every day except Monday'?*

A	Conosco un ristorante vicino al mare dove si mangia molto bene.
B	Quando è aperto?
A	Tutti i giorni, eccetto il lunedì.

5 Vogliono ordinare?
Do you wish to order?

Before reading this dialogue look at 'Eating out in Italy' at the end of this unit, where you will find out about meals in restaurants and see some of the vocabulary for food.

The waiter tells **Anna** and **Silvia** that if they prefer to lunch outside, **all'aperto**, they'll have to wait. They decide to remain where they are.

   a *How does* **il cameriere** *say: 'There are a lot of people today'?*
   b *How does he say: 'It's a speciality of the house'?*

Cameriere	Ecco il menù. Vogliono ordinare subito? Se preferiscono pranzare all'aperto, devono aspettare un po'. C'è molta gente oggi.
Anna	No. Non fa niente. Pranziamo qui. Per antipasto io prendo melone con prosciutto.
Silvia	Io, coppa di gamberetti. E per primo, risotto alla milanese.
Anna	Risotto anche per me.
Cameriere	Mi dispiace, ma il risotto non c'è. È finito.
Silvia	Allora, spaghetti alle vongole.
Anna	E per me, lasagne al forno.
Cameriere	Benissimo. E per secondo piatto: carne o pesce?
Anna	Carne: bistecca ai ferri. E per contorno patatine fritte e fagiolini.
Cameriere	Bene. Bistecca anche per lei, signorina?
Silvia	No, no. Non mangio carne. Che cosa mi consiglia?

Cameriere	Il fritto misto di pesce. È una specialità della casa. E il pesce è freschissimo.
Silvia	Beh … no. Preferisco sogliola alla griglia con insalata verde.
Cameriere	D'accordo. E da bere? Vino rosso o vino bianco?
Anna	Rosso. Una bottiglia di Barolo. E ci porti un po' di ghiaccio per l'acqua, per piacere.
Silvia	E un po' di vino bianco … locale.

VOCAB

non fa niente *it doesn't matter*
Che cosa mi consiglia? *What do you recommend (me)?*
E da bere? *Anything to drink?*
ci porti *bring us*
un po' di ghiaccio *some ice*

---

6 Tutto bene?
Is everything all right?

Il **cameriere** asks whether they want dessert.

   a *How does* il **cameriere** *ask: 'A little more wine?'*
   b *How does* Silvia *say: 'Nothing for me'?*

CD 1, TR 23, 03:56

Cameriere	Tutto bene …? Un altro po' di vino?
Silvia	No. Va bene. Basta così. Grazie.
Cameriere	Dolce o frutta?
Anna	Formaggio, e una macedonia.
Silvia	Per me niente. Solo un caffè e un amaro.

VOCAB

Un altro po' …? *A little more …?*
Va bene. *That's OK.*
Basta così. *That's enough.*
Per me niente. *Nothing for me.*
un amaro *a bitter after-dinner liqueur*

Pronunciation

◆) **CD 1, TR 24**

DOPPIE CONSONANTI *DOUBLE CONSONANTS*

Primo piatto, patatine fritte, spaghetti, un po' di ghiaccio, una bottiglia di latte, birra, frutta, formaggio, bistecca, eccetto.

Grammar

1 VERBS

Present tense (irregular) of **fare** *to do, make* and **uscire** *to go out.*

Present tense	**fare** *to do, make*
(io) faccio	*I do, am doing, make, etc.*
(tu) fai	*you do, are doing, make, etc.*
(lui, lei)* fa	*he/she does, is doing, makes, etc.*
(noi) facciamo	*we do, are doing, make, etc.*
(voi) fate	*you* (pl) *do, are doing, make, etc.*
(loro) fanno	*they do, are doing, make, etc.*

Present tense	**uscire** *to go out*
(io) esco	*I go out, am going out*
(tu) esci	*you go out, are going out*
(lui, lei) esce	*he/she goes out, is going out*
(noi) usciamo	*we go out, are going out*
(voi) uscite	*you* (pl) *go out, are going out*
(loro) escono	*they go out, are going out*

*As explained in Unit 6, the **lei** form 2nd person singular (formal 'you') is omitted from now on because it is exactly the same as the 3rd person singular: **lei fa** = *you do, make,* etc.

Insight

Attenzione! Note the difference between **uscire** *to go out* and **andare** *to go*.

Esci ...?	*Are you going out?*
Dove vai?	*Where are you going?*

Uscire used with **da** means *to leave, to come out of, to go out of*:

Escono dall'ufficio alle due.	*They leave the office at two.*
Usciamo dalla banca a mezzogiorno.	*We leave the bank at midday.*

But

La mattina esco di casa alle otto.	*In the morning I leave home at eight.*

2 PRESENT TENSE AS IMMEDIATE FUTURE

The present tense is also used in Italian to express an intention or a suggestion where we would use the future in English:

Mangiamo qui stasera?	*Shall we eat here this evening/ tonight?*
Oggi prendo l'autobus.	*Today I'll take the bus.*

The first person plural present ending **-iamo** also denotes the imperative: *let us ...*

Andiamo! *Let's go!*   **Usciamo!** *Let's go out!*

The context and the tone of voice will make the meaning clear (see Unit 14, Section 4).

3 HOW TO USE **BUONO/A**

Buono/a is nearly always shortened to **buon** before a masculine singular noun. It follows the pattern of the indefinite article **un/uno/una**. It is often heard in expressions where Italians wish each other something:

Buon divertimento! *Have a good time!*
Buona giornata! *Have a good day!*
Buon appetito! *Enjoy your meal!*
Buon Natale! *Merry Christmas!*
Buon Anno! *Happy New Year!*
Buon viaggio! *Have a good journey!*

4 TUTTO/A *ALL, EVERYTHING*

In the singular **tutto/a** means *whole, all, everything*:

Tutta la famiglia è in vacanza. *The whole family is on holiday.*
Mangia tutto. *He eats everything.*
È tutto per me. *It's all for me.*

In the plural **tutti/e** means *all, every*:

Tutti i negozi sono aperti. *All the shops are open.*
Usciamo tutti i giorni. *We go out every day.*

5 ON MONDAYS

When the definite article precedes the day it gives the idea of *every*:

È chiuso il lunedì. *It's closed on Mondays/every Monday.*
È aperto la domenica. *It's open on Sundays/every Sunday.*

6 PEOPLE

La gente is singular in Italian:

La gente parla.	*People talk.*
In piazza c'è poca gente.	*There are few people in the square.*

7 VERY, MANY, TOO

Molto may be used either as an adverb (*very*) or as an adjective (*a lot of*, *many*). When used as an adverb it is invariable.

È molto brava. *(adverb)*	*She's very good/clever.*
Questi musei sono molto interessanti. *(adverb)*	*These museums are very interesting.*
Il negozio all'angolo ha molta roba. *(adj)*	*The corner shop has a lot of stuff.*
In Italia ci sono molti mercati. *(adj)*	*There are many markets in Italy.*

Troppo behaves in the same way:

La camicetta è troppo cara. *(adverb)*	*The blouse is too dear.*
In classe ci sono troppi studenti. *(adj)*	*There are too many students in class.*

8 DO YOU WISH TO ORDER?

The plural of **tu** and **lei** is **voi**. But in Dialogue 5 the waiter asks: '**Vogliono ordinare?**' This third person plural **loro** form is very much used instead of **voi** by waiters, hotel staff and shop assistants when addressing more than one person.

9 NON FA NIENTE *IT DOESN'T MATTER*

When Italian uses a negative word such as **niente** *nothing*, unlike English, **non** must still be used: **Non voglio niente** literally means

I don't want nothing. The main negative expressions are: **non ... niente** *nothing*; **non ... mai** *never*; **non ... nessuno** *no one*.

Lino non mangia niente.	*Lino is not eating anything.*
Non bevo mai a quest'ora.	*I never drink at this time.*
Non c'è nessuno a casa.	*There isn't anyone at home.*
Non capisce niente!	*He doesn't understand anything!*

10 AL, ALLA *MEANING 'IN THE STYLE OF, WITH'*

a + definite article is used to show that food or drink is cooked, served or prepared in a particular style. **Risotto alla milanese** is therefore a rice dish cooked in the Milanese style (see 'Eating out in Italy', at the end of this unit). **Un tè al limone** is tea served with lemon, i.e. lemon tea. This is why you often hear **un tè al limone** instead of *con* **limone**, and **un panino al formaggio** instead of **con formaggio**.

11 DA *MEANING 'TO'*

There are many expressions where **da** followed by an infinitive means *to*:

Cosa c'è da bere?	*What is there to drink?*
Ho molto da fare.	*I've a lot to do.*
Non c'è niente da mangiare.	*There's nothing to eat.*

You should note examples as you come across them throughout the book.

12 A BIT OF (SOME) ...

The easiest way to express 'some' when it means 'a little of something' is to use **un po' di** (lit: *a bit of*):

Vorrei: un po' di formaggio,	*I'd like: some cheese, some*
un po' di pane, un	*bread, some wine, some water.*
po' di vino, un po' d'acqua.	

13 BASTA COSÌ *THAT'S ENOUGH*

As with **costa, costano** (Unit 4, Section 6) it is important to distinguish between singular and plural when using **basta:**

Mezza bottiglia basta.	*Half a bottle is enough.*
Due sterline bastano.	*Two pounds is enough.*

Come si dice?
How do you say it?

🔊 **CD 1, TR 24, 00:32**

1 *How to ask if a place is open/closed*

È aperto/a? È chiuso/a?

How to say a place is open/closed

È aperto/a. È chiuso/a.

2 *How to order a meal*

Per antipasto, per primo, per secondo, per contorno, prendo …

3 *How to ask for some (more) bread/wine, etc.*

Un (altro) po' di pane / di vino, ecc.

How to say that it's enough

Basta così.

4 *How to ask the waiter what he recommends*

Che cosa mi consiglia?

5 *How to say that it doesn't matter*

Non fa niente / Non importa.

Practice

1 *Opposite there are some examples of Italian food and drink, many of which are explained in the section. Which section of the menu on the right does each one belong to?*

Menu

ANTIPASTI

PRIMI PIATTI

SECONDI PIATTI

CONTORNI

FRUTTA – DOLCI

DA BERE

acqua minerale
antipasto misto
coppa di gamberetti
bistecca alla griglia
fagiolini
fritto misto di pesce
frutta fresca
gelati misti
insalata mista
lasagne al forno
macedonia di frutta
sogliola alla griglia
spaghetti alle vongole
vino bianco
vino rosso

melone con prosciutto
patatine fritte
pollo arrosto
risotto alla milanese

2 *Which of the phrases on the right complete the sentences on the left?*

> **Insight**
> To do this exercise you need to look at the verb endings carefully.

i *E tu Mario,*

ii *Anche noi*

iii *Anche voi*

iv *Maria è vegetariana:*

v *Anch'io*

a *non mangia carne.*

b *restare a casa stasera.*

c *vanno sempre al ristorante la domenica.*

d *cosa vuoi?*

e *mangiate fuori stasera?*

vi *Tutta la famiglia Ferni*   **f** *vado 'Da Peppino' oggi.*
vii *Giovanni e Antonella*   **g** *va in pizzeria.*
viii *I miei amici vogliono*   **h** *preferiamo la cucina italiana.*

TRATTORIA MEZZA LUNA
DI AVERINO BAFFO
Ubic. Eser. Via Ripa Serancia, 3 - Tel. 0763 341234
ORVIETO
Dom. Fisc. Via Ripa Serancia, 1

RICEVUTA N. 16

	EURO	
PANE E COPERTO	2×1,05	2,10
PRIMO PIATTO	1×4,70	4,70
SECONDO PIATTO	1×5,16	5,16
CONTORNO	1×2,10	2,10
CAFFÈ	2×0,80	1,60
SERVIZIO	10%	1,57

TOT. EURO IVA INCLUSA **17,3**
TOTALE DOCUMENTO 17,23
13-34 03/01/03 6865362

3 *Here are four restaurant advertisements. Make sure you understand them, then answer the questions below.*

a

LA TORINESE

Ristorante Caratteristico

Vasto Parcheggio

Giochi per bambini

(Chiuso il mercoledì)

b

La Bella Napoli

Ristorante
e
Pizzeria

Aperto solo la sera

<table>
<tr>
<td>

c

TEMPIO di DIANA

Hotel Ristorante
con cucina francese
Vasto parco nel bosco

MARTEDÌ CHIUSO

</td>
<td>

d

VILLA TOTÒ
RISTORANTE

*specialità marinare
Si mangia bene e si
mantiene la linea*

DOMENICA SERA E
LUNEDÌ RIPOSO

</td>
</tr>
</table>

   i *It's Monday lunch time: are there any restaurants that you couldn't go to?*

  ii *Where would you go if you liked seafood?*

 iii *Which one of these restaurants is unlikely to be in the town centre? Why?*

  iv *Which one would you consider if you were on a diet?*

   v *Which two would probably offer better parking facilities?*

4 *Ora tocca a te!*

You are ordering a meal in a restaurant.

CD 1, TR 25

Cameriere	Cosa prende?
You	*I'd like a selection of appetizers.*
Cameriere	E per primo?
You	*Vegetable soup.*
Cameriere	Vuole ordinare il secondo adesso?
You	*Why not? What do you recommend (me)?*
Cameriere	Oggi il pesce è buonissimo.
You	*I don't eat fish. Grilled steak.*
Cameriere	Certo. E per contorno, cosa desidera?
You	*I'll have a mixed salad and french fries.*
Cameriere	E da bere?
You	*Half a bottle of local wine.*
Cameriere	Bianco o rosso?
You	*Better the red wine with the steak.*
Cameriere	Subito!
	...

Cameriere	Tutto bene?
You	*Yes. Fine. A bit more bread, please.*
Cameriere	Ecco. Desidera altro?
You	*No, thank you. That's enough.*

5 *Can you label each of these using the words from the box? Look up the words you don't know in the vocabulary at the back.*

aceto bicchiere coltello cucchiaio forchetta
olio pepe piatto sale tovagliolo

Eating out in Italy

Before starting your meal it is customary to say: **Buon appetito!** The response is **Grazie, altrettanto!** (*Thank you*) *the same to you!*

La cucina italiana *Italian cooking* is regional: names of dishes vary from one part of the country to another.

Antipasti starters or hors d'oeuvres. Among other things, these appetizers consist of a variety of cooked or cured meats such as **prosciutto crudo** (this is often served with melon), **mortadella**, **salame**; seafood such as **coppa di gamberetti** *prawn cocktail*, and various vegetables, raw or preserved in oil such as **carciofi** *artichokes* and **funghi** *mushrooms*. **Antipasto misto** is a selection of appetizers: ham, salami, mortadella, olives (**olive**), etc.

I primi (**il primo piatto** *the first course*) would offer **minestra** soup, **minestrone** *vegetable soup* or a choice of **pasta** dishes e.g: **spaghetti alle vongole** *spaghetti with clams*, **lasagne al forno** *layers of pasta slices with meat sauce and mozzarella cheese baked in the oven,* **tagliatelle al pomodoro** *pasta strips in tomato sauce*, etc. **Risotto alla milanese** *is rice cooked in broth with onions.*

I secondi (**il secondo piatto** *the second course*) consist of (**la) carne** *meat* or (**il) pesce** *fish*. **Alla griglia** or **ai ferri** both mean *grilled*. **Bistecca** is *steak*, **pollo arrosto** is *roast chicken*, **sogliola** is *sole*, **fritto misto di pesce** *mixed fry* of smaller Mediterranean fish.

I contorni *side dishes* could be **insalata (mista)** *(mixed) salad* or a selection of vegetables such as **fagiolini** *green beans*, **melanzane** *aubergines*, **peperoni** *peppers*, **zucchini** *courgettes*, **patatine fritte** *chips/french fries*.

Frutta *fruit*: this is often eaten at mealtimes instead of **dolci** *desserts*; **macedonia di frutta** *fruit salad*; **gelati** *ice cream*.

Barolo is a famous red wine from the Piedmont region in Northern Italy. Most regions produce their own local wine, **vino locale**, which is usually excellent value.

Mineral water, both fizzy (**gassata**) and still (**non gassata**), is very popular in Italy.

Your restaurant bill will probably include a cover charge: **pane e coperto**. Where the service charge is included in the price, you will see **servizio compreso** *service included*. You yourself may ask: '**È compreso il servizio?**' *'Is service included?'* However, even when it is, it is customary to leave a tip (**la mancia**) on top of this. **(La) tavola calda** and **la trattoria** are normally cheaper than a restaurant but in some places **la trattoria** may have a sort of snob value and be quite expensive, i.e. **Trattoria del Vecchio Pozzo** Restaurant of the Old Well would be fully decorated to give an 'Olde Worlde' atmosphere.

TEST YOURSELF

Match up the column on the left with the appropriate continuation on the right.

1 Allora, cosa facciamo?   **a** Lo pago io.

2 Perchè non andiamo a ...   **b** È occupato. Mi dispiace.

3 Dopo andiamo al cinema: **c** Perchè non mangio carne.

4 Conosco una buona   **d** No. È aperta fino a mezzanotte.
trattoria ...

5 Non è troppo cara e   **e** Restiamo a casa o usciamo?

6 Non è chiusa oggi?   **f** il servizio è ottimo.

7 Scusi, è libero questo   **g** mangiare al ristorante?
posto?

8 Perchè non prendi la   **h** vicino al mare: 'La Gondola'.
bistecca?

9 Cosa prendiamo da bere?   **i** ghiaccio.

10 E dell'acqua con ...   **j** Una bottiglia di vino locale.

11 Altro? Dolce, frutta,   **k** al 'Rivoli' c'è un bel film.
formaggio?

12 Chi paga il conto?   **l** Nient'altro, grazie.

In albergo
At the hotel

In this unit you will learn:
- *how to ask for a room*
- *how to give the dates you require it for*
- *how to ask for full or half-board*
- *how to ask for and give details of mealtimes*
- *how to respond to a request for means of identification.*

---

1 Ha una c<u>a</u>mera, per favore?
Have you got a room, please?

Roberto asks **il direttore** for a room with a shower (**d<u>o</u>ccia**).

a *How does* il direttore *ask: 'Single or double?'*
b *How does Roberto ask: 'Is breakfast included in the price?'*

Direttore	Buonasera. Dica!
Roberto	Ha una c<u>a</u>mera, per favore?
Direttore	Come la vuole? S<u>i</u>ngola o d<u>o</u>ppia?
Roberto	S<u>i</u>ngola con d<u>o</u>ccia.
Direttore	Per quanto tempo?
Roberto	Per una notte.
Direttore	Sì. Ha un documento?
Roberto	Ho il passaporto. La colazione è compresa nel prezzo?
Direttore	No. È a parte.

⏺ CD 1, TR 26

Dica! (from dire to say) *Yes? Can I help you?*
Come la vuole? *How would you like it?*
notte (f) *night*
mezza pensione *half board*
a parte *not included*

---

2 Abbiamo due camere all'ultimo piano
We have two rooms on the top floor

Il sig. Conti is booking in advance: he wants a room with a double bed and private bath.

a *How does he say: 'From the 26th of July to the 9th of August'?*

b *What are the words for breakfast, lunch and dinner in Italian?*

Direttore	Una camera a un letto o una camera a due letti?
Sig. Conti	Una camera matrimoniale con bagno: dal 26 luglio al 9 agosto.
Direttore	Vediamo un po'… Abbiamo due camere all'ultimo piano. Una piccola con balcone, e una grande.
Sig. Conti	La camera grande è tranquilla?
Direttore	Molto tranquilla e dà sul mare.
Sig. Conti	La camera grande, allora. A che ora è il pranzo?
Direttore	La colazione è dalle 7.00 alle 9.30. Il pranzo dalle 12.00 alle 2.00 e la cena dalle 7.30 alle 10.00.

camera a un letto *single room*
camera a due letti *twin-bedded room*
camera matrimoniale *double bedroom*
dà (from dare) *looks out over*
vedere *to see*
vediamo un po' *let's have a look*
tranquillo/a *quiet*

3 Mezza pensione o pensione completa?
Full or half board?

a *How long does* **la signora Marini** *want the room for?*
b *How does she say: 'We have a driving licence. Here it is'?*

Direttore	Mezza pensione o pensione completa?
Sig.ra Marini	Mezza pensione per due persone per una settimana.
Direttore	Sì, va bene. Avete il passaporto?
Sig.ra Marini	No. Non l'abbiamo. Abbiamo la patente di guida.
Direttore	La patente va benissimo.
Sig.ra Marini	La vuole ora …? Un attimo … Ah …! eccola!
Direttore	Ed ecco le chiavi, signora. Camera 408. Gli ascensori e i gabinetti sono là in fondo. Il parcheggio è dietro l'albergo.

CD 1, TR 26, 01:47

pensione completa *full board*
una settimana *a week*
la patente di guida *driving licence*
ora *now*
la chiave *key*
gabinetto *toilet*
dietro *behind*

VOCAB

4 C'è l'acqua calda e l'acqua fredda
There's hot and cold water

a *How does* **il signor Marini** *say: 'The luggage is in the car'?*
b *How does* **il direttore** *say: 'I'll call him immediately'?*

Sig. Marini	C'è l'acqua anche in camera?
Direttore	Certo, signore. In tutte le camere, c'è l'acqua calda e l'acqua fredda.
Sig. Marini	I bagagli sono nella macchina. Li porto sopra.
Direttore	Non si preoccupi! Li prende il ragazzo. Lo chiamo subito.
Sig. Marini	Grazie.
Direttore	Se qualche volta non volete fare il bagno nella piscina, c'è la nostra spiaggia privata con gli ombrelloni e le sedie a sdraio.

Insight

Attenzione! Notice that **i bagagli** *luggage* is plural in Italian.

Li porto sopra. *I'll take them upstairs.*
Non si preoccupi! *Don't worry.*
qualche volta *sometimes*
fare il bagno *to bathe, go swimming*
la nostra spiaggia privata *our private beach*
ombrellone (m) *beach umbrella*
sedia a sdraio *deck-chair*

5 Può svegliarmi?
Can you wake me up?

a *How does* la segretaria *say: 'At 6 o'clock on the dot'?*
b *How does Pippa say: 'The room that looks out over the terrace'?*

Pippa	Può svegliarmi domani mattina alle sei?
Segretaria	Certamente, signorina. Camera 307, vero?
Pippa	Sì. La camera che dà sulla terrazza.
Segretaria	Va bene. Domani mattina alle sei in punto la chiamo io personalmente. Non si preoccupi!
Pippa	Grazie, molto gentile.

6 Lavoro solo d'estate
I only work in the summer

Il **cameriere** explains that tourists come in the month of August especially.

a *How does* il **cliente** *say: 'So many tourists'?*
b *How does* il **cameriere** *say: 'I begin at six and finish at about one'?*

CD 1, TR 26, 03:49

Cliente	Impossibile parcheggiare! Vengono sempre tanti turisti qui?
Cameriere	Sempre. Specialmente nel mese di agosto.
Cliente	Lavora molto, allora!
Cameriere	D'estate, sì. Moltissimo! Ma si guadagna bene!
Cliente	A che ora incomincia a lavorare la mattina?
Cameriere	Presto. Comincio alle sei e finisco verso l'una, le due di notte.
Cliente	Però, d'inverno è tutto chiuso!
Cameriere	Esatto. Lavoro solo d'estate da maggio a ottobre.
Cliente	Già. D'inverno non viene nessuno da queste parti!

Vengono (from **venire**) ... **tanti turisti?** *Do so many tourists come ...?*
guadagnare *to earn*
(in)cominciare a *to start, begin to*
presto *early*
però *however, but*
d'inverno, d'estate *in winter, in summer*
esatto *that's right, precisely*
da queste parti *to these parts*

QUICK VOCAB

Pronunciation *Months and Seasons*

◀ CD 1, TR 27

I mesi dell'anno: gennaio, febbraio, marzo, aprile, maggio, giugno, luglio, agosto, settembre, ottobre, novembre, dicembre

Le stagioni dell'anno: l'inverno, la primavera, l'estate, l'autunno

Grammar

1 *I'VE GOT A PASSPORT*

> **Insight**
>
> **Attenzione!** Notice the use of **il/la**, the definite article, where in English we say *a/an*:
>
> **Ha il passaporto, la carta d'identità, la patente di guida, la macchina?** *Do you have a passport, an identity card, a driving licence, a car?*

2 DATA E STAGIONI *DATE AND SEASONS*

Like the days, the months start with lower-case letters: **ottobre, novembre, dicembre**, ecc.

Quanti ne abbiamo (oggi)?	*What's the date (today)?*
(Ne abbiamo) 10.	*(It's) the 10th.*

Ordinary numbers are used for the date:

il due marzo, il cinque luglio   *2nd of March, 5th of July*

However, for the first of the month you must use **il primo** (*first*):

Oggi è il primo giugno;	*Today is the first of June;*
il primo maggio.	*the first of May.*

Note that *on* is not expressed, as in the following examples:

Ci vediamo il tre agosto.	*See you **on** the 3rd of August.*
Lo vedo sabato.	*I'll see him **on** Saturday.*

With months **in** or **a** is used:

in/a giugno, in/a settembre, ecc.	*in June, in September, etc.*

But with months beginning with a vowel, only **in** is used: **in aprile, in agosto**.

Note in the table below how *in spring*, *in summer*, etc. is expressed and how **di** often becomes **d'** before words beginning with a vowel: **d'estate, d'inverno**.

	d'inverno		*winter*
	d'estate	*in*	*summer*
in	**autunno**		*autumn*
	primavera		*spring*

In primavera andiamo in campagna.	*In spring we go to the country.*
D'estate va al mare o in montagna.	*In summer he goes to the seaside or the mountains.*
In autunno ricomincia a lavorare.	*In autumn he starts working again.*

3 DARE *TO GIVE;* VENIRE *TO COME*

Both these verbs are irregular:

Present tense **dare** *to give*		
(io)	**do**	*I give, am giving*
(tu)	**dai**	*you give, are giving*
(lui, lei)	**dà**	*he/she gives, is giving*
(noi)	**diamo**	*we give, are giving*
(voi)	**date**	*you* (pl) *give, are giving*
(loro)	**danno**	*they give, are giving*

Present tense **venire** *to come*		
(io)	**vengo**	*I come, am coming*
(tu)	**vieni**	*you come, are coming*
(lui, lei)	**viene**	*he/she comes, is coming*
(noi)	**veniamo**	*we come, are coming*
(voi)	**venite**	*you* (pl) *come, are coming*
(loro)	**vengono**	*they come, are coming*

4 NEL, NELLA, *IN THE;* SUL, SULLA *ON THE*

In *in* also combines with the definite article (**il, la, ecc.**) to mean *in the*. When this happens **in** becomes **ne**. **Nel** is therefore the contracted form of **in + il**, and **nella** of **in + la**. The pattern is then exactly the same as **del, della**, etc. (Unit 6, Section 4): **nel, nello, nella, nell', nei, negli, nelle**.

La macchina è nel garage.	*The car is in the garage.*
Le chiavi sono nella borsa.	*The keys are in the bag.*

Su *on* contracts in the same ways as **a** *at, to.* Just as **a + il** becomes **al**, **su + il** becomes **sul**:

| La camera dà sul mare. | The room looks out over the sea. |
| I guanti sono sulla sedia. | The gloves are on the chair. |

5 OBJECT PRONOUNS

....

| **lo** *him, it* | **li** *them* (m pl) |
| **la** *you, her, it* | **le** *them* (f pl) |

....

Lo, la, li, le, are called object pronouns and usually precede the verb.

Insight

Attenzione! At first they seem very similar to the definite article, but unlike the article, they replace the noun. The following examples make this clear.

Compro il libro. Lo compro.	*I'll buy the book. I'll buy **it**.*
Compro i libri. Li compro.	*I'll buy the books. I'll buy **them**.*
Compro la rivista. La compro.	*I'll buy the magazine. I'll buy **it**.*
Compro le riviste. Le compro.	*I'll buy the magazines. I'll buy **them**.*

Look at the first two examples above and see how the following question and answer are based on them:

| Quando compra il libro? | *When will you buy the book?* |
| Lo compro domani. | *I'll buy **it** tomorrow.* |

Ora tocca a te! See if you can fill in the blanks for the rest on your own (the answers are in the *Key to the exercises*):

a Quando compra __ libri? __ compro stasera.

b Quando compra __ riviste? __ compro dopo.

c Quando compra __ rivista? __ compro stamattina.

d Quando paga __ conto? __ pago adesso.

In negative sentences put **non** before the pronoun.

Conosci Gino? No. Non lo conosco.	*Do you know Gino? No, I don't (know him).*

Lo, la (singular only) become **l'** before a vowel or '**h**':

Dove aspetti Anna?	*Where are you waiting for Anna?*
L'aspetto a casa.	*I'm waiting for **her** at home.*

But (plural) Apro le finestre. Le apro. *I'll open the windows. I'll open **them**.*

When addressing a man or woman formally, the direct object pronoun for *you* is **la**:

La ringrazio, dottor Bertini, del suo gentile pensiero.	*I thank **you**, Dr Bertini, for your kind thought.*
La disturbo, signora?	*Am I disturbing **you**, Madam?*
Mi conosce?	*Do you know **me**?*
Sì. La conosco.	*Yes. I know **you**.*

6 ECCOLA! *HERE IT IS!*

Ecco combines with object pronouns to mean *here he/she/it is, here they are.*

Dov'è Maria? Eccola!	*Where is Mary? Here **she** is!*
Dov'è Pietro? Eccolo!	*Where is Peter? Here **he** is!*
Dove sono le valigie? Eccole!	*Where are the suitcases? Here **they** are!*

7 SOME, SOMETIMES, OCCASIONALLY

Qualche means *a few* or *some* and is always followed by a singular noun, which must be countable (compare to **un po' di**, Unit 7, Section 12).

Vengo con qualche amico.	*I'll come along with some friends.*
Ho qualche libro sull'Italia.	*I've got some books on Italy.*
Usa spesso l'internet?	*Do you often use the internet?*
L'uso qualche volta.	*I use it occasionally.*

8 TO START TO …

When a verb follows **incominciare**, use **a** + infinitive.

Incominciare and **cominciare** both mean *to start* or *to begin*.

Incomincio *a capire*.	*I'm beginning to understand.*
Il bambino comincia *a parlare*.	*The baby is beginning to speak.*
Quando incominci *a fare i bagagli*?	*When do you start packing?*

Come si dice?
How do you say it?

◀) **CD 1, TR 27, 00:50**

1	*How to ask for a room*	**Ha una camera/singola/doppia/ matrimoniale?**
2	*How to give the dates you require it for*	**Dal primo … al dieci, ecc. Da lunedì a giovedì, ecc.**
3	*How to ask for full or half-board*	**Pensione completa/mezza pensione.**
4	*How to ask for and give details about mealtimes*	**A che ora è la colazione/il pranzo/ la cena? Dalle … alle …**
5	*How to ask and respond to a request for means of identification*	**Ha un documento? Ho il passaporto/la patente di guida.**

Practice

1 *What sort of hotel accommodation are the three people overleaf asking for? Tick the appropriate places on the grid, and fill in the days or dates in English.*

a **Direttore** Prego?
    Signore Ha una camera singola?
    Direttore Con bagno?
    Signore La preferisco con doccia.
    Direttore Per quanto tempo?
    Signore Da giovedì a lunedì. Pensione completa.

b **Direttore** Sì?
    Signora Vorrei una camera dal venticinque giugno al quattro luglio.
    Direttore Singola o doppia?
    Signora Una camera matrimoniale con bagno. Pensione completa.

c **Direttore** Dica!
    Signorina Ha una camera a due letti dal nove maggio?
    Direttore Per quante notti?
    Signorina Per dieci notti. Mezza pensione.
    Direttore Fino al diciannove?
    Signorina Sì. Esatto.
    Direttore Con bagno?
    Signorina No, con doccia.

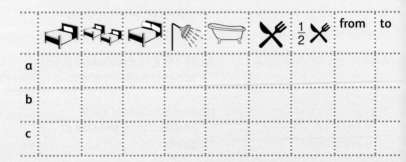

camera singola camera doppia

 camera matrimoniale

 doccia bagno

X pensione completa $\frac{1}{2}$ X mezza pensione

2 *In a frenzy of last-minute packing, your friend asks you where one or two items are. Find them for him and answer with the appropriate pronoun as in the example:*

Esempio: Dov'è la patente di guida? Dove sono i libri?
You   Eccola! Eccoli!

   a *Dov'è il passaporto?*
   b *Dov'è la borsa?*
   c *Dov'è l'indirizzo dell'albergo?*
   d *Dove sono i biglietti?*
   e *Dove sono le chiavi?*
   f *Dov'è la pianta (map)?*
   g *Dov'è il giornale?*
   h *Dov'è l'orologio?*

3 *Answer these questions, using pronouns and translating the English as in the example.*

Esempio: Conosce Pietro? Sì. __*well*.
Sì. Lo conosco bene.

   a *Conosce Luisa? Sì. ____ very well.*
   b *Conosce le mie cugine? Sì. ____ fairly well.*
   c *Quando vede Anna? ____ at about 8 o'clock.*
   d *Quando invita Luigi? ____ today.*
   e *Invita qualche volta i suoi amici? ____ often.*
   f *Quando guarda la televisione? ____ after dinner.*
   g *Conosce l'Albergo Cesare? Sì. ____ well.*
   h *Vede Carlo domani? No. ____ this evening.*

4 *Select each contracted preposition from the box below once only and fill in the gaps (see Section 4 above)*

   a *I passaporti sono __ studio.*
   b *Il ghiaccio è __ acqua.*
   c *I pigiami sono __ letto.*
   d *Gli ombrelloni sono __ spiaggia.*
   e *Il vino è __ bicchiere.*
   f *Le chiavi sono __ borsa.*
   g *I vestiti sono __ valigie.*
   h *Non c'è sale __ spaghetti.*

> nel nello nella nell' nelle negli sul sulla

5 *Answer the questions using the first person of* **venire**. *If the question is addressed to more than one person, as in the 2nd example, answer with the 1st person plural.*
Esempio: Viene in macchina? ... autobus.
No. Vengo in autobus.
Venite in autobus? ... piedi.
No. Veniamo a piedi.

   a *Viene in aereo? ... macchina.*
   b *Viene in metropolitana? ... piedi.*
   c *Viene in macchina? ... aereo.*
   d *Venite in autobus? ... metropolitana.*
   e *Venite a piedi? ... bicicletta.*

6 *Read the following passage in which Anna is talking about herself and note how all the information can be extracted from the table below:*

Abito a Milano. Lavoro in una banca commerciale. La mattina esco alle otto meno un quarto. Incomincio a lavorare alle otto e mezza. Finisco di lavorare alle cinque. Torno a casa alle sei meno un quarto. Il sabato non lavoro. Vado al mare con mia sorella.

Dove abita?	Dove lavora?	A che ora esce la mattina?	A che ora incomincia a lavorare?	A che ora finisce?	A che ora torna a casa?	Dove va il sabato? Con chi?
Anna: Milano	banca commerciale	7.45	8.30	5.00	5.45	al mare sorella
Maria: Terni	agenzia di viaggi	8.15	9.00	6.00	6.45	in montagna marito
I sig.ri Spada: Napoli	istituto di lingue	7.20	8.00	1.00	1.40	in campagna genitori*

* **i nostri/loro genitori** *our/their parents*

a *Write similar passages, first saying what* **Maria** *would say about herself, and then what* **i signori Spada** *would say about themselves* (**Abitiamo, ecc. ...**)

b *Write contrasting statements about* **Anna** *on the one hand and* **i signori Spada** *on the other. Start like this:* **Anna abita a Milano, ma i signori Spada abitano a Napoli.**

7 **Ora tocca a te!**

You are booking rooms in a hotel.

Direttore	Buongiorno.	
You	*Good morning. Do you have two rooms for ten days?*	
Direttore	Per quante persone?	
You	*For four people.*	
Direttore	Abbiamo due camere al terzo piano.	
You	*With private bath?*	
Direttore	Una con bagno, l'altra con doccia.	
You	*Yes. That's fine. Is there a restaurant in this hotel?*	

CD 1, TR 27, 02:43

Direttore	No. C'è solo il bar.
You	*Is there a restaurant nearby?*
Direttore	C'è la 'Trattoria Monti' in piazza.

8 Look at this table from a hotel guide and find out how to say in Italian:
   a *Credit cards are accepted.*
   b *Pets are accepted.*
   c *tennis court*

 Parco giardino dell'esercizio

 Si accettano piccoli animali domestici

 Sala congressi

 Accettazione gruppi

 Baby sitting

 Accettazione carta di credito

 Parcheggio custodito

 Autorimessa dell'esercizio

 Trasporto clienti

 Campo da tennis

What do these signs mean?

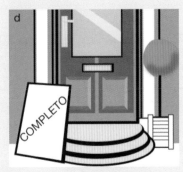

Hotels and guest houses

The Italian hotel industry as a whole has been rather slow in adopting internet booking, but recent government initiatives have done everything to remedy this by promoting modernization in an area that is vital to Italy's economy: the tourist trade. Indeed, one innovation, **la chiave magnetica**, is claimed to have been originally manufactured by an Italian firm. You are now more likely to be given your key (**chiave**) in the form of a swipe card.

Although **pensioni** have the reputation of being more modest establishments than **alberghi**, there is no clearcut dividing line. Many pensioni offer excellent value and are often family run. In regional brochures both **alberghi** and **pensioni** are now listed together, according to price and the facilities they offer. Remember however that the star rating applies to the number of facilities offered, not necessarily to the quality of service.

Other accommodation

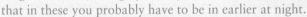

Ostelli per la gioventù *Youth hostels*, **Campeggi** or **Camping** *Campsites*, **Villaggi turistici** *Holiday villages* and **Agriturismo** *Farm holidays* offer a variety of accommodation to suit all pockets. There are also **Case religiose di ospitalità**, hospitality offered by religious bodies, though you may find that in these you probably have to be in earlier at night.

The Italian State Tourist Office (**ENIT**) provides information about travel and accommodation in Italy. Regional brochures are available there. Address: 1 Princes St, London W1B 2AY (Tel: 020 7408 1254).

Tourism–related websites:
http://www.enit.it
http://www.alitalia/co.uk

TEST YOURSELF

Fill in the gaps as appropriate, using each word or expression in the box below once only.

1 *Sì, la camera è molto tranquilla. Non si ___!*

2 *Ha ___ passaporto?*

3 *D'inverno è ___chiuso.*

4 *Quanti ___abbiamo oggi?*

5 *Ha una camera a ___letti al___piano?*

6 *D'estate andiamo ___mare.*

7 *___sempre___turisti qui?*

8 *Lavoro molto ___guadagno bene.*

9 *Vengo con ___amico.*

10 *___tutte le sere.*

11 *___con la carta di credito.*

12 *Dov'è la ___?*

....

due - preoccupi - il - ne - tutto - vengono - un - spiaggia - terzo - al - ma - esco - tanti - pago

....

Al telefono
On the phone

In this unit you will learn:
- *how to ask to speak to someone on the phone*
- *how to ask someone to repeat/speak louder*
- *how to ask whether you have the wrong number*
- *how to ask whether someone is in and answer accordingly*
- *how to ask whether you can leave a message or call back later*
- *how to ask and grant permission to enter a room.*

---

1 Pronto? Chi parla?
  Hello, who's speaking?

The secretary is on the phone with **l'avvocato** (lawyer) **Ferri,** who wishes to speak to **il dottor Fini.**

- **a** *How does* **la segretaria** *ask: 'Have you got an appointment?'*
- **b** *How does* **la segretaria** *say: 'I'll pass you to Dr Fini'?*

Segretaria	Pronto? Chi parla?
Avvocato	Sono l'avvocato Ferri. Vorrei parlare con il dottor Fini.
Segretaria	Io sono la segretaria. Il dottore è occupato: è in riunione. Ha un appuntamento?
Avvocato	No, signorina. Ma è urgente. Urgentissimo.
Segretaria	Un momento, avvocato … Le passo il dottor Fini.
Avvocato	Grazie.
Segretaria	Prego.

QV **in riunione** *in a meeting*

2 In un ufficio
In an office

Sig. Cioffi asks to speak to the firm's Director, but on being told by the Secretary that he is at the Head Office (**la sede centrale**), he decides to wait until the director comes back.

  a *How does* **la segretaria** *say: 'Come in'?*
  b *How does* **la segretaria** *say: 'Can I offer you a coffee?'*

Sig. Cioffi	Permesso?
Segretaria	Avanti!
Sig. Cioffi	(*not hearing her*) Permesso … Posso entrare?
Segretaria	Avanti! Avanti! Prego, si accomodi!
Sig. Cioffi	Vorrei parlare con il direttore.
Segretaria	Mi dispiace, il direttore non c'è. È alla sede centrale. Se vuole, può parlare con me.
Sig. Cioffi	No. Devo parlare con lui personalmente.
Segretaria	Allora, deve tornare più tardi.
Sig. Cioffi	Più tardi non posso. Devo andare a Milano per affari. A che ora ritorna il direttore?
Segretaria	Fra venti minuti. Vuole aspettare qui? Prego, si accomodi! Posso offrirle un caffè?
Sig. Cioffi	Grazie. Molto gentile.
Segretaria	Prego. Si figuri!

Permesso? Posso entrare? *May I come in?*
il direttore non c'è *the director is out*
Prego, si accomodi! *Please sit down.*
per affari *on business*
Prego. Si figuri! *No trouble at all!*

3 C'è Luisa?
Is Luisa in?

a *How does Roberto say: 'I'm afraid she's out'?*
b *How does Roberto say: 'Just a minute. I'll call her'?*
c *How does Ida say: 'It's me'?*

Ida	Pronto? C'è Luisa?
Roberto	No. Mi dispiace, non c'è.
Ida	C'è Carla?
Roberto	Sì. C'è. Un attimo. La chiamo.
Carla	Pronto ...!
Ida	Ciao, Carla! Sono io, Ida.
Carla	Ciao, Ida!

CD 1, TR 28, 01:51

4 La segreteria telefonica
The answer-phone

◄) **CD 1, TR 28, 02:25**

Il nostro ufficio è chiuso. Dopo il
segnale acustico, si prega di lasciare
il nome, il numero di telefono e un
breve messaggio. Sarete contattati al
più presto. Grazie.

il segnale acustico *the beep, tone*
si prega di lasciare il nome *please leave your name*
sarete contattati *you will be contacted*
si prega di … *please …*
al più presto *as soon as possible*

Pronunciation

🔊 **CD 1, TR 29**

Listen to the sound of '**puoi**', '**può**' and '**vuol**'.

Puoi venire più tardi? Non può partire? Vuol ripetere il suo nome?

Grammar

1 *THE IRREGULAR VERB* **POTERE** *TO BE ABLE*

Present tense **potere** *to be able*		
(io)	**posso**	*I am able, I can*
(tu)	**puoi**	*you are able, you can*
(lui, lei)	**può**	*he/she is able, he/she can*
(noi)	**possiamo**	*we are able, we can*
(voi)	**potete**	*you* (pl) *are able, you can*
(loro)	**possono**	*they are able, they can*

Verbs that follow **potere** must be in the infinitive.

Use **potere** to:

i ask for or give permission (this could take the form of a polite request):

148

Posso fumare?	*Can/may I smoke?*
Le posso fare una domanda?	*Can/may I ask you a question?*
Può assaggiare il vino se vuole.	*You can taste the wine if you like.*

ii say whether you are able or unable to do something:

(Non) possiamo venire domenica.	*We are (un)able to come on Sunday.*
(Non) posso arrivare prima delle undici.	*I'm (un)able to arrive before eleven.*

2 OBJECT PRONOUNS

'*I'll pass you Dr Fini*' means *I'll pass Dr Fini to you*. **To you** in this case is the indirect object and is expressed by **le** (m or f) in Italian. Both object pronouns and indirect object pronouns (see Unit 18) usually precede the verb. However, with **potere**, **dovere**, **volere** and **sapere** you have a choice. You may put the pronouns before these verbs, or attach them to the infinitive that follows, from which you take off the final -e: **Posso offrirle = posso offrir(e) + le**. Some other common verbs that take an indirect object are: **dare** *to give*, **parlare** *to speak*, **scrivere** *to write*, **presentare** *to introduce* and **telefonare** *to phone*.

Insight

Bear in mind then that infinitives end in **-ar(e)**, **-er(e)** or **-ir(e)**, then you should have little difficulty in seeing if a pronoun has been added to it or not.

Le telefono dopo.	*I'll phone you later.*
Un momento! Le do il numero di telefono di Anna.	*One moment! I'll give you Anna's phone number.*
Le posso offrire qualcosa da bere? **Posso offrirle qualcosa da bere?**	*Can I offer you something to drink?*

Notice how in the last example **le** can either precede **posso** or follow the infinitive.

3 PERMESSO ...? *MAY I ...?* **AVANTI!** *COME IN!*

In the second dialogue **il sign_or Cioffi** says **Permesso?** to ask whether he may come in. **Avanti!** *Come in!* is the normal response. **Permesso** is also used when you wish someone to move aside to let you pass – in crowded places, buses, etc: **Permesso!** *Excuse me, please.* In this case the response is **Prego!**

4 C'È/NON C'È *HE/SHE'S IN, HE/SHE'S OUT*

A frequent use of **c'è**, **non c'è** is to indicate whether someone is in or not. Notice how it is used in the negative and in questions:

C'è il dott_or Bassani?	*Is Dr Bassani in?*
Mi dispiace. Non c'è.	*No. I'm afraid he's out.*

5 CON ME, CON TE *WITH ME, WITH HIM*

Notice the use of **me** and **te** with prepositions. The other subject pronouns remain unchanged:

P_aolo viene con te o con me?	*Is Paul coming with you or me?*
Perchè non vieni con noi?	*Why don't you come with us?*
Andiamo con lui, con loro!	*Let's go with him, with them!*

6 PIÙ *+ ADJECTIVES/ADVERBS*

To say *later, earlier, dearer, bigger*, use **più** with adjectives or adverbs:

più presto *earlier*, **più tardi** *later* (adverbs)
più caro/a *dearer*, **più grande** *bigger* (adjectives).

7 *FORMING ADVERBS:* **PERSONALMENTE** *PERSONALLY*

To form an adverb add -**mente** to the end of an adjective:

evidente *evident* → **evidentemente** *evidently*

adjectives ending in -**o** add -mente to the feminine form:

vero, vera *true* → **veramente** *truly, really*
chiaro, chiara *clear* → **chiaramente** *clearly*
pratico, pratica *practical* → **praticamente** *practically*

adjectives ending in -**le** or -**re** drop their final -e:

facile *easy* → **facilmente** *easily*
generale *general* → **generalmente** *generally*
regolare *regular* → **regolarmente** *regularly*

8 ARRIVEDERLA *GOODBYE*

Arrivederla is a more formal way of saying **arrivederci,** but it can only be used when addressing one person. **La** is the object pronoun for *you* that we met in Unit 8.

Come si dice?
How do you say it?

◄) **CD 1, TR 29**

1 *How to ask to speak to someone on the phone*
   Vorrei/Posso parlare con …

2 *How to ask someone to repeat/ speak louder*
   Può ripetere per favore/parlare più forte?

3 *How to ask whether you have the wrong number and apologize if you have*

Ho sbagliato n_umero? Mi scusi!

4 *How to ask whether someone is in*

C'è …?

How to answer accordingly

Sì. C'è./No. Non c'è.

5 *How to ask whether you can leave a message*

Posso lasciare un mess_aggio?

How to ask if you can call back later

Posso richiamare più tardi?

6 *How to ask and grant permission to enter a room*

Permesso? Avanti!

Practice

1 *Listen to these two conversations and answer the questions on them.*

◀ CD 1, TR 30

Ho sbagliato numero? *Have I got the wrong number?*

Gianna	Pronto! Ho sbagliato numero …? No? … Pu<u>o</u>i parlare più forte, Sandro? Non sento niente. Vorr<u>e</u>i parlare con Vincenzo.
Sandro	Vincenzo non c'è. Pu<u>o</u>i richiamare più tardi?
Gianna	D'accordo. Richiamo fra mezz'ora. Ciao!
Sandro	Ciao!

    a *Is Vincenzo in or out?*
    b *What does the man (Sandro) ask the woman (Gianna)?*
    c *What does she say she will do?*

Tutto a posto *Everything is in order*

Dott. Cervi	Non c'è? … Posso lasciare un mess<u>a</u>ggio?
Segret<u>a</u>ria	Sì, certo. Dica!
Dott. Cervi	Tutto a posto. La conferenza è il dieci giugno.
Segret<u>a</u>ria	Vuole rip<u>e</u>tere il suo nome, per cortes<u>i</u>a?
Dott. Cervi	Cervi. Il dott<u>o</u>r Cervi. C come Capri, E come <u>E</u>mpoli, R come Roma, V come Ven<u>e</u>zia, I come <u>I</u>mola.
Segret<u>a</u>ria	La ringr<u>a</u>zio, dott<u>o</u>r Cervi. Arrivederla.
Dott. Cervi	Buongiorno.

    d *When is the conference?*
    e *What does the woman ask the man to repeat?*

2 *Fill in the blanks in the following dialogue, using* **lo, la** *or* **le***.*

Signore	Posso parlare con il dott<u>o</u>r Dolci?
Segret<u>a</u>ria	Mi dispiace, il dottore non c'è. Oggi non è in uff<u>i</u>cio.
Signore	Dove ___ posso contattare?

Segretaria	__ chiamo io domani mattina quando il dottore è qui.
Signore	Grazie, ma non posso aspettare fino a domani. È urgente.
Segretaria	In questo caso __ do il suo numero telefonico privato.
Signore	Grazie. Molto gentile.
Segretaria	E se il dottore telefona qui oggi, __ richiamo io. Va bene?
Signore	D'accordo. __ ringrazio molto, signorina.

3 *Match the phrases on the right with those on the left.*

i	*Posso lasciare*	**a**	*Può telefonare verso le dieci?*
ii	*Non possiamo venire adesso,*	**b**	*un messaggio?*
		c	*il suo nome, per favore?*
iii	*Non vogliamo disturbare Luisa*	**d**	*perchè è molto occupata.*
		e	*perchè non ho la chiave.*
iv	*Non posso uscire stasera*	**f**	*perchè devo lavorare fino a tardi.*
v	*Vuol ripetere*		
vi	*Scusi, le posso*	**g**	*ma possiamo venire più tardi.*
vii	*Le lascio il mio numero telefonico.*	**h**	*fare una domanda?*
viii	*Non posso aprire la porta*		

4 *In the table below:*
   ✔ = *what Elena wants to do.*
   ! = *what Elena has to do.*
   ✘ = *what Elena can't do.*
   Write nine complete statements about her. Start: **Vuole ...**

(volere) ✔	(dovere) !	(potere) ✘
a telefonare ad Anna	d lavorare fino a tardi	g fumare
b vedere un film	e uscire con i suoi genitori	h comprare un altro vestito
c uscire con Carla	f scrivere una lettera a suo zio	i venire a pranzo con noi

5 *Imagine you are making the following requests to your friend: how would you make them in Italian? (Use the **tu** form.)*

a *Can you wait here?*

b *Can you phone for (per) me?*

c *Can you pass the salt and pepper?*

d *Can you book another room?*

e *Can you open the door please?*

6 **Ora tocca a te!** *Add your side of this phone conversation (you are **Pat Iles**):*

Segretaria	Pronto!
You	*Hello! May I speak to Lisa please?*
Segretaria	Lisa è in riunione.
You	*Can I leave a message?*
Segretaria	Certo. Chi parla?
You	*Pat Iles.*
Segretaria	Come si scrive?
You	*Spell out your whole name (see the town alphabet, Unit 5).*
Segretaria	E qual è il messaggio?
You	*Pat Iles cannot go to the meeting tomorrow.*

7 *Label the items in the picture with the words from the box. Look up those you don't know.*

l'agenda – il calend*a*rio – la carta – il cassetto – il computer – la matita – l'or*o*logio – la penna – il quadro – la scrivan*i*a – la s*e*dia – la segreter*i*a telef*o*nica – la tastiera – il tel*e*fono – il telefonino/il cellulare

8 *Quanto costa questa segreter*i*a telef*o*nica, e per quanto tempo è garantita?*

Facile

- colore bianco
- testo di annuncio su memoria digitale
- registrazione su microcassetta delle chiamate entranti
- funzione "memo" per lasciare messaggi anche da un altro telefono
- accensione e controllo a distanza

in vendita a €55,78 IVA inclusa (garanzia 6 mesi)

9 *Per chi è il telefono azzurro e quanto costa per telefonare?*

**Telefono Azzurro
Linea gratuita   19696
per i bambini**

Mobile phones **I cellulari**
In a country where intercommunication on every level is paramount, it is not surprising that the mobile phone has had such instant success amongst Italians of every class. Now, with the break-up of the **Telecom Italia** monopoly on telecommunication systems, the amount of television advertising time devoted to mobile sales suggests that competition to own the latest model with the most number of innovative components is going to grow even fiercer. Now **i videofonini** are becoming more and more prevalent. Their use by pupils in schools, however, has provoked a national scandal, caused serious discipline problems, and raised doubts as to whether they should be allowed at all in such institutions.

Phonecard **La scheda (tessera) telefonica**
In a few places it is still possible to use money when making outside calls, but in most cases you need **la scheda telefonica**, which you can buy **all'edicola** *at the news-stand* or **dal tabaccaio**.

TEST YOURSELF

Here are some short sentences you should be able by now to translate into Italian.

1 *Hello! Who's speaking?*

2 *I'm sorry. I've got the wrong number.*

3 *Can I speak to Pietro?*

4 *I'm sorry. He's not in.*

5 *I'd like to see the secretary.*

6 *I have to leave tomorrow morning.*

7 *Can I leave a message for Dr Bini?*

8 *Can you wait a moment, please?*

9 *He's not here. I'll call him.*

10 *I have to go to a conference.*

10

Lavoro e tempo libero
Work and spare time

In this unit you will learn:
- *how to say in what part of town you live*
- *how to talk about the type of work you do*
- *how to say what you do in your spare time*
- *how to talk about your family*
- *how to invite someone out.*

---

1 Leggo, scrivo, ascolto la radio
I read, write and listen to the radio

Marisa interviews **Carmela** in the town square. **Carmela** explains that she comes from Palermo but that she lives and works in Naples. Then **Marisa** asks her in what part of Naples she lives, what her work is and what she does in her spare time.

a *How does* **Carmela** *say: 'I live and work in Naples'?*

b *How does* **Carmela** *say: 'I play tennis'?*

Carmela	Sono di Palermo, vivo e lavoro a Napoli.
Marisa	In che parte di Napoli abita?
Carmela	Al centro. Vicino all'università.
Marisa	Che lavoro fa?
Carmela	Insegno matematica in un istituto tecnico.
Marisa	Cosa fa nel pomeriggio?
Carmela	Se ho una riunione rimango a scuola, altrimenti torno a casa. Quando ho un po' di tempo libero, gioco a tennis o esco con qualche amica.
Marisa	E la sera?
Carmela	Dipende … Leggo, scrivo, ascolto la radio, guardo la televisione, oppure se c'è un bel film, vado al cinema.

insegnare *to teach*
rimango (from **rimanere** irr) *I remain, stay*
altrimenti *otherwise*
dipendere *to depend*
leggo (from **leggere**) *I read*

2 Io e la mia famiglia
My family and I

Marisa looks at a family photo of **Pietro, Carmela**'s colleague.

a *How does* **Marisa** *ask: 'Are they your parents?'*
b *How does* **Pietro** *say: 'And these are my grandparents (here)'?*

Marisa	Che bella fotografia! Chi è quel signore lì vicino alla sedia?
Pietro	Sono io.
Marisa	E quei signori davanti a lei, sono i suoi genitori?
Pietro	Sì. Questi sono i miei genitori: mio padre, mia madre, e questi qui sono i miei nonni.
Marisa	È sua sorella la signora dietro ai nonni?
Pietro	No. È mia moglie, e il bambino seduto per terra è nostro figlio Alessandro.

quel *that*
sedia *chair*
quei *those*
i genitori *parents*

i nonni *grandparents*
moglie (f) *wife*
seduto/a *sitting*
per terra *on the floor*

Pronunciation

◄) **CD 1, TR 32**

The order of the present tense of **conoscere** and **leggere** has been changed to focus on the 'k' sound in **conosco, conoscono** and the hard 'g' sound in **leggo, leggono** (see the Pronunciation section in Unit 2 and Unit 12, Section 8).

Conoscere: conosco, conoscono; conosci, conosce, conosciamo, conoscete
Leggere: leggo, leggono; leggi, legge, leggiamo, leggete

Grammar

1 RIMANERE *TO REMAIN, TO STAY*

Both **rimanere** and **restare** mean *to stay* or *to remain*. **Rimanere**, however, is irregular:

Present tense **rimanere** *to stay or remain*		
(io)	**rimango**	*I stay, I am staying*
(tu)	**rimani**	*you stay, you are staying*
(lui, lei)	**rimane**	*he/she stays, is staying*
(noi)	**rimaniamo**	*we stay, we are staying*
(voi)	**rimanete**	*you* (pl) *stay, you are staying*
(loro)	**rimangono**	*they stay, they are staying*

2 AL CENTRO *IN THE CENTRE*

You may either say **al centro** or **in centro**. We have already met expressions where **in** is used without the definite article. A few more examples are grouped here:

in {
città
periferia
piazza
campagna
montagna
}
in {
town
the suburbs
the square
the country
the mountains
}

But remember to say **al mare** *by the sea, at/to the seaside*.

3 GIOCARE A *TO PLAY*

To play a game is **giocare a:**

giocare a { **tennis** **c_alcio/pallone*** **rugby** **carte** } *to play* { *tennis* *football* *rugby* *cards* }

*un c_alcio (lit: *a kick*) **un pallone** *a football*

4 CHE …! *WHAT A …!*

Che in exclamations can be used with nouns or adjectives:

Che bello/a!
Che belli/e! } *How lovely! How nice!*
Che bella m_acchina! *What a lovely car!*
Che peccato! *What a pity!*
Che gu_aio! *What a nuisance!*

5 BELLO/A *AND* QUELLO/A *PRECEDING THE NOUN*

Insight
When **bello** *beautiful, lovely* and **quello** *that* precede the noun they qualify, they behave like **nel, nello, nella, nell', n_ei, negli, nelle** (Unit 8, Section 4).

È un bel bambino. *He's a lovely child.*
Che bello scaffale! *What a nice book-case/shelf!*
Quei libri sono interessanti. *Those books are interesting.*
Quell'uomo è p_overo. *That man is poor.*
Quegli appartamenti sono belli. *Those flats are nice.*

6 RELATIVES (FAMILY)

Here are some members of the family you may have already met or may have forgotten:

		(i) nonni *grandparents*			
		(i) genitori *parents*			
(il)	**nonno**	*grandfather*	(la)	**nonna**	*grandmother*
(il)	**padre**	*father*	(la)	**madre**	*mother*
(il)	**figlio**	*son*	(la)	**figlia**	*daughter*
(il)	**marito**	*husband*	(la)	**moglie**	*wife*
(lo)	**zio**	*uncle*	(la)	**zia**	*aunt*
(il)	**cugino**	*cousin (male)*	(la)	**cugina**	*cousin (female)*
(il)	**nipote**	*nephew or grandson*	(la)	**nipote**	*niece or grand-daughter*

Insight

Possessive adjectives ('my', 'your' etc.) must always
be preceded by 'the', unless you are talking about one
member of the family only (see examples in Unit 3): **mio
fratello** *my brother*, BUT **i miei fratelli** *my brothers*; **vostra
figlia** *your daughter*, BUT **le vostre figlie** *your daughters*.

7 POSSESSIVE ADJECTIVES

The table sets out all the remaining forms of the possessive
adjectives *'our'*, *'your'*, *'their'*. They are always preceded by the
definite article, unless you are talking about a singular member of
the family. Note that **loro** their never changes and that it is always
preceded by the definite article, whether the noun is singular or
plural: **il loro cugino** *their cousin*, **i loro cugini** *their cousins*.

noi	il nostro	la nostra	i nostri	le nostre	*our*
voi	il vostro	la vostra	i vostri	le vostre	*your* (pl)

loro	il la i le	loro	albergo camera bagagli chiavi	*their*	*hotel* *room* *luggage* *keys*

La loro cugina ha una villa in montagna.	*Their cousin has a villa in the mountains.*
I vostri colleghi sono in ufficio.	*Your colleagues are in the office.*
I loro amici vengono da Roma.	*Their friends come from Rome.*

Come si dice?
How do you say it?

◀)) **CD 1, TR 33**

1 *How to say you live and work in a particular town*

Vivo e lavoro a …

2 *How to ask in what part of a town someone lives*

In che parte di … abita?

How to say in what part of a town you live

Abito al/in centro/in periferia.

3 *How to say what you do in your spare time*

**Leggo, scrivo, ascolto la radio …
Gioco a tennis/a pallone/a carte …**

4 *How to identify members of your family (from a photo)*

**Questo qui è mio marito …
Questi sono i miei genitori …**

5 *How to invite someone out (informally)*

Vuoi venire con me?

Practice

1 Insert the correct form of **quel, quello, quella, quell', quei, quegli, quelle** in the following sentences:

    a Chi è __ signore?
    b __ orologio è giapponese.
    c __ camicia costa poco.
    d __ istituto è grande.
    e __ studente è australiano.
    f __ appartamenti sono moderni.
    g __ libri sono belli.
    h Non sono buoni __ pomodori?
    i __ cartoline sono di Roma?
    j Sono di cristallo __ bicchieri?

2 Insert the correct form of **bel, bello, ecc.** in the following sentences:

    a Che __ macchina!
    b Che __ studio!
    c Che __ posto!
    d Che __ bambini!
    e Che __ albero!
    f Che __ spiaggia!
    g Che __ camere!
    h Che __ uccelli!

3 This is Lucia's account of what she does every day of the week. Fill in the blanks, using each of the words in the box below once only.

....

ballare - esco - guardo - giocare - gioco - mangio - rimango - vado

....

    a Lunedì __ a casa e __ la televisione.
    b Martedì vado a __ in discoteca.
    c Mercoledì __ al cinema con Cesare.
    d Giovedì resto a casa a __ a bridge.
    e Venerdì __ a tennis con Enrico.
    f Sabato sera __ di casa alle otto e vado in piazza.
    g Domenica __ al ristorante con i miei genitori.

4 *Match the phrases on the right with the sentences on the left:*

i	Non posso giocare a bridge	**a**	perchè non ho la racchetta.
ii	Non posso giocare a calcio	**b**	perchè non ho le carte.
iii	Non posso giocare a tennis	**c**	perchè non ho il costume.
iv	Non posso fare il bagno	**d**	perchè non ho il pallone.

5 **Cosa *facciamo* quando non *lavoriamo*?**
What would the people below say if asked what they do in their spare time? Answer for **Adamo e Ida,** *and* **Enzo e Rina** *together (1st person plural) but* **Guido** *speaking just for himself, would start:* **Vado al cinema, …**

	🎥	📺	🎾	📚	💃	🎭	📻
Guido	✔			✔			✔
Carla		✔	✔	✔			
Adamo e Ida	✔			✔		✔	✔
Enzo e Rina		✔	✔	✔	✔		

 = *andare al cinema*   = *andare a ballare*

 = *guardare la televisione*   = *andare a teatro*

 = *giocare a tennis*   = *ascoltare la radio*

 = *leggere*

6 *Marco is explaining who is who in his family*

  I *Continue for him, using the details from his family tree below.*

    a *Io sono Marco.*   **f** __

    b *Anna è mia moglie.*   **g** __

    c *Enzo è* __   **h** __

    d __   **i** __

    e __

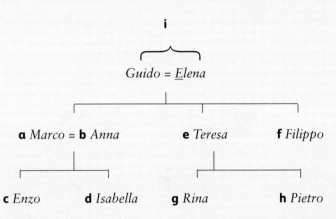

  II *Now imagine that Enzo and Isabella are explaining the same family tree to someone else. They would start:*

    a   *Marco è nostro padre.*   **f** __

    b   *Anna è* __   **g** __

    c, d *Noi siamo i*   **h** __

    e   *Teresa è*   **i** __

7 *Laura would like to go on an exchange (**fare uno scambio di ospitalità***) with Gloria, who lives in England. In this letter she gives Gloria details about herself and her family. Look up any words you don't know, then imagine you are Gloria and write an answer along the guidelines provided below.*

Cara Gloria,

mi chiamo Laura Valli. Ho sedici anni e vorrei studiare l'arte culinaria all'Istituto Carlo Porta di Milano. Vorrei poi continuare i miei studi negli Stati Uniti. Le lingue straniere sono molto importanti per la mia carriera, ma non conosco bene l'inglese. Leggo discretamente e capisco tutto, però non so parlare.

Ho un fratello e due sorelle. Mio fratello Mario studia medicina a Bologna. Fa il terzo anno. Le mie sorelle sono sposate. Io vivo a casa con mio padre che lavora per la ferrovia, e mia madre che è parrucchiera. Anche mia nonna vive con noi. È simpaticissima e passa molto tempo a parlare con il nostro pappagallo messicano Pancita. Abbiamo anche un bel cane Rex, e un piccolo gatto Fifì.

Vorrei fare uno scambio di ospitalità con te, se è possibile, per qualche mese. So che vuoi venire in Italia per imparare l'italiano. Il nostro paese non è lontano da Firenze. In Italia ci sono molte scuole e università per stranieri.

Puoi venire quando vuoi. Aspetto una tua risposta.

Un caro saluto,

Laura

*Before answering Laura's letter to Gloria, look at the suggested reply, then go back to her letter and underline any words or expressions that you could use or adapt. Use the **tu** form.*

Start: **Cara Laura,**
   grazie della tua lettera.
   Say that you are 17 and that one day you would like to work in Italy. This year you are studying Italian and French. They are two very interesting languages.

   You live in a village (**un piccolo paese**) near Brighton which is not too far from London.

   Your father is an electrician (**elettricista**) and your mother works at home for an advertising agency (**agenzia pubblicitaria**).

   You have a brother who works in London and a little sister who is 7 years old. Her name is Sandra and she spends a lot of time playing with your dog Rover.

   You would like to go (use **venire**) to Italy in July.

   End your letter: **A presto** (*see you soon*). **Un caro saluto** (*love*),

   Gloria

---

8 **Ora tocca a te!** *You are* **Isa,** *and* **Angelo** *is asking you to go out dancing. Add your side of the conversation.*

CD 1, TR 34

Angelo	Ciao, Isa!
You	*Hello!*
Angelo	Vuoi venire con me?
You	*Where?*
Angelo	A ballare.
You	*When? Now?*
Angelo	Stasera alle nove.
You	*No. This evening I can't. I have to go to the cinema with a friend.*
Angelo	Puoi venire domani? O devi uscire anche domani?
You	*Tomorrow evening I have to go to the theatre with my parents.*
Angelo	Peccato! Domenica alle otto?
You	*Sunday is fine. But I can't come before nine.*
Angelo	Alle nove va bene. Ciao, allora!
You	*Goodbye.*

Schools

In Italy the normal school timetable starts at about 8.00/8.30 a.m. and ends at around 2.00 p.m.

The family

La famiglia *the family* is still a very important unit in Italy. As food also plays a significant role in Italian life, mealtimes form an integral part of Italian culture, where everyone is free to join in and discuss decisions that may affect any of the individual family members. A recent European survey established that in Italy 93% of teenagers eat regularly with their parents and it is still the custom for children to remain in the family home until they get married, unless work takes them to another town or they go away to live with their partner (**compagno/compagna**): only 15 per cent of under 25s live away from home.

Italy, at least in an official capacity, has been slow in adopting alternatives to conventional marriage, though there is now some prospect of legalizing the position of partners living together (**coppie di fatto**). The birth-rate too has given some cause for concern: at an average of 1.5 children per couple, it is now the lowest in Europe, though there are still plenty of large families in the south.

It is not unusual for Italians you have just met, especially on long train journeys, to show you their family snapshots and ask personal questions. They don't mean to be indiscreet: they are generally interested in you, your family and your children.

Soccer

For soccer enthusiasts or supporters (**i tifosi**) here is the **Lazio** website:
http://www.sslazio.it

TEST YOURSELF

Fill in the gaps as appropriate using each word in the box below once only.

1 *I miei genitori giocano spesso __ carte.*

2 *Abitano in __ ma __ al centro di Milano.*

3 *In treno, Lino e Paolo __ sempre.*

4 *Se vuoi io __ a casa e tu esci.*

5 *Che __ palazzo! Mi piace moltissimo.*

6 *Per arrivare al centro ci __ dieci minuti.*

7 *Non è __ la fotografia __ zio?*

8 *Che __ stadio! È stupendo!*

9 *Questa è mia moglie e queste sono le __ sorelle.*

10 *Prima __ la radio.*

---

a - ascoltiamo - leggono - quella - mie - bello - bel - rimango - periferia - dello - lavorano - vogliono

---

11

Necessità quotidiane e preferenze
Daily necessities and preferences

In this unit you will learn:
- *how to say you are hungry or thirsty*
- *how to say what provisions you want to buy and ask for specific quantities*
- *how to talk about your likes and dislikes*
- *how to identify what something is made of*
- *how to ask for and state preferences.*

1 Ho sete
I'm thirsty

Marcello and **Pippa** have been out all morning. As one of them is thirsty and the other hungry, they decide to go shopping (**fare la spesa**) and return home for lunch.

a *How does Pippa say: 'I'm hungry'?*
b *How does Pippa say: 'I'd like to eat something'?*

Marcello	Senti, ho sete. Vorrei bere.
Pippa	Io, invece, ho fame. Vorrei mangiare qualcosa.
Marcello	Sai se c'è una salumeria da queste parti?
Pippa	C'è un negozio di generi alimentari a due passi da qui.
Marcello	Allora facciamo la spesa e poi torniamo subito a casa per il pranzo. Che ne dici?

QUICK VOCAB

senti *listen*
qualcosa = qualche cosa *something*
sai se ...? *do you know whether ...?*
salumeria *delicatessen*
da queste parti *round here*
negozio di generi alimentari *grocer's*
a due passi da qui *very near here*
Che ne dici? (from **dire irr)** *How about it? (lit: what do you say about it?)*

2 Al negozio di generi alimentari
At the grocer's

Marcello and **Pippa** are buying provisions from the **salumiere** *grocer.*

  a *How does Pippa ask for some rolls?*
  b *How does Pippa ask for half a kilo of spaghetti?*

Salumiere	Cosa desidera, signora?
Pippa	Vorrei dei panini, del formaggio, del burro e della mortadella.
Salumiere	Quanto formaggio, e quanta mortadella, signora?
Pippa	Un etto di formaggio, due etti di burro, sei fette di mortadella, e sei panini.
Salumiere	Ecco, signora.
Pippa	Vorrei anche degli spaghetti e dello zucchero.

Salumiere	Quanto zucchero?
Pippa	Mezzo chilo di spaghetti e un chilo di zucchero. Poi vorrei delle uova fresche e dell'olio.
Marcello	Anche un chilo di mele e mezzo chilo di uva.
Salumiere	Subito, signore. Ecco. Desidera altro?
Marcello	No. Basta così.

dei panini *some rolls*
del burro *some butter*
un etto di *100 grams of*
fetta *slice*
un chilo di *a kilo of*
delle uova fresche *some fresh eggs*
mele, uva *apples, grapes*

_____

3 Pelletteria: le piace?
Leather goods shop: do you like it?

Ada and Simona are choosing some leather goods. First Simona
buys a leather handbag, **una borsa di pelle.**

a *How does Ada exclaim: 'How nice this handbag is!'?*
b *How does Simona say: 'I don't like it'?*

Ada	Com'è bella questa borsa! Le piace?
Simona	No. Non mi piace. È troppo grande.
Ada	Questa qui è più piccola. Va bene con i guanti.
Simona	Sì, però è troppo chiara. Non ce n'è una più scura?
Ada	Lì ce n'è una. È meno cara, ma è di plastica. Preferisce quella?
Simona	No. Preferisco questa di pelle. Quanto costa?
Ada	Costa molto.
Simona	Non importa. La compro lo stesso.

CD 2, TR 1, 01:47

a due passi da qui	*a couple of paces from here = very near here*
a dieci chilometri da Roma	*ten kilometres away from Rome*
a due chilometri dall'autostrada	*two kilometres (away) from the motorway*

4 SOME, ANY

Di + the definite article (see Unit 6) is also used to express the idea of *some* or *any*: **del burro** *some butter*; **della marmellata** *some jam*; **dei panini** *some rolls*; **dell'uva** *some grapes* (notice that **uva** is always singular).

5 UN UOVO, DELLE UOVA AN EGG, SOME EGGS

Un uovo *an egg* is masculine, but the plural **uova** is feminine: **delle uova fresche**. It behaves in the same way as **un paio, due paia** (see Unit 4). The plural of **l'uovo** is therefore **le uova**.

6 COM'È ...! HOW ...!

Com'è = come + è. Like **che** (Unit 10, Section 4) **come** can be used in exclamations, but must be followed by a verb:

Com'è grande!	*It's big, isn't it? (lit: How big it is!)*
Come sono eleganti!	*They're elegant, aren't they?*
Com'è bella questa borsa!	*How nice this (hand)bag is!*

> **Insight**
>
> **Come** can also be used to introduce questions asking what someone or something is like (literally *how* something or someone is):
>
> | **Com'è la sua casa?** | *What's your/his/her house like?* |
> | **Com'è l'amico di Pietro?** | *What is Peter's friend like?* |

7 LE PIACE? LE PIACCIONO? *DO YOU LIKE IT? DO YOU LIKE THEM?*

Insight

Attenzione! Mi piace is used to translate 'I like', but in fact it means 'To me pleases'. This is why you use it with an indirect object pronoun ('to me'), and why the verb changes if you like plural things – it is they that are doing the pleasing!

Piacere (lit: *to please*, *be pleasing to*) is used to express the idea of liking in Italian; it requires an indirect object pronoun (Unit 18):

Mi piace.	*I like … or I like it. (lit: It is pleasing to me.)*
Le (*form*)/ti (*inf*) piace.	*You/she likes (it). (lit: It is pleasing to you/to her.)*
Gli piace.	*He likes (it). (lit: It is pleasing to him.)*
Mi piace tanto questo cd! **Questo cd mi piace tanto!**	*I like this CD very much.*

Use the third person plural of **piacere** when more than one thing or person is liked:

Le piacciono queste pesche?	*Do you like these peaches?*
Queste pesche le piacciono?	*(lit: Are these peaches pleasing to you?)*

To express dislikes use **non** before **mi piace, le piace,** ecc:

Le olive non mi piacciono.	*I don't like olives.*

To emphasize **non** you can use **non … mica** or **non … affatto** *not … at all*:

Questa borsa non mi piace mica/affatto.	*I don't like this bag at all.*

Note that the preposition **a** is required:

a when a name is used:

A Carlo non piace l'arte moderna.	*Charles doesn't like modern art.*

b with pronouns when emphasis or contrast occurs:

Piace a me, ma non piace a te.	*I like it, but you don't.*

8 SOME (OF IT)

Ne meaning *some, any, of it, (some) of it, (some) of them* replaces a noun or phrase where numbers or quantities are involved; like the pronouns **lo, la, li, le** it usually precedes the verb:

Quanto burro compra?	*How much butter are you buying?*
Ne compro un etto.	*I'm buying 100 grams (of it).*
Ha degli spiccioli?	*Have you got any small change?*
Non ne ho.	*I haven't (got any).*

9 DI *MEANING 'MADE OF'*

To show what something is made of, use **di**:

un portaf<u>o</u>glio *di cu<u>o</u>io/di pelle*	*a leather wallet*
dei calzini *di cotone*	*(some) cotton socks*
una cam<u>i</u>cia *di pura seta*	*a pure silk shirt*
un golf *di pura lana*	*a pure woollen cardigan/jumper*
un anello *d'oro*	*a gold ring*
un bracciale *d'argento*	*a silver bracelet*

10 PIÙ … DELLA … *MORE … THAN …*

Di (or **di** + article) can also mean *than*. In Italian, you don't say *larger* or *smaller* but *more large*, *more small*, etc. Use **più … di** (with names of people or towns, cities, etc.) or **di** + article to say *more … than*, **meno … di** (or **di** + article) to *say less … than*:

Londra è *più grande di* Roma.	*London is larger than Rome.*
Mar<u>i</u>a è *meno alta di* Rita.	*Mary is not as tall as Rita.*
L'a<u>e</u>reo è *più veloce del* treno.	*The plane is faster than the train.*

Il/la più means *the most*:

***Il più* bel giorno della mia vita.**	*The most beautiful day of my life.*

11 *BOTH (OF THEM)*

We have seen that **tutti/e** means *all, every*:

Tutti noi.	*All of us.*
Tutti i giorni.	*Every day.*

Note also **tutti/e e** when used with numbers:

Sono tutti e due italiani.	*They are both Italian.*
Tutte e tre (le ragazze) vanno a Roma.	*All three (girls) are going to Rome.*

12 *NEGATIVE PLURAL EXPRESSIONS*

The partitive article (**del, della, dei, ecc.**) is not used in negative plural expressions (see Unit 4, Section 8).

Non ha mai soldi.	*He never has any money.*
Non bevo liquori.	*I don't drink liqueurs.*
Non ho più soldi.	*I haven't any more money.*

Come si dice?
How do you say it?

◄) **CD 2, TR 2**

1	*How to say you are hungry or thirsty*	**Ho fame. Ho sete.**
2	*How to say what provisions you want to buy*	**Vorrei del burro, dell'olio, ecc.**
	How to ask for specific quantities	**Vorrei un etto di burro, un litro di olio, ecc.**
3	*How to talk about your likes and dislikes*	**Le/ti piace? Mi piace. Non mi piace. Le/ti piacciono? Mi piacciono. Non mi piacciono.**
4	*How to ask about/say what something is made of*	**È di pelle? No. È di plastica.**
5	*How to ask someone what they prefer*	**Preferisce questo/a o quello/a?**
	How to say what you prefer	**Preferisco questo/a; quello/a.**

Practice

1 *Look at Maria's shopping list and, without mentioning the quantities, write down what she wants to buy. Look up any words you don't know. Start:* **Maria vuol comprare del burro ...**

un etto di burro
due etti di formaggio
due bottiglie di birra
un litro di olio
tre chili di spaghetti
un chilo di zucchero
una scatola di fiammiferi
una bottiglia di acqua minerale gassata

2 *Lisa's likes are marked in the table by one tick, her preferences by two ticks. Make statements about her likes and preferences.*
Esempio: a La birra le piace, ma preferisce il vino. *Be careful with e and f.*

3 *Now imagine that you are Lisa and that somebody else is asking you the questions. Form both questions and answers.*

✔	✔ ✔
a birra	vino
b vino bianco	vino rosso
c cinema	teatro
d Milano	Firenze
e melanzane	peperoni
f libri	riviste

Esempio: Le piace la birra o il vino? La birra mi piace, ma preferisco il vino.

4 *When addressing a man or a woman formally use* **le piace**, *when addressing someone informally use* **ti piace:**
Signora, le piace l'arte moderna? *Do you like modern art, (Madam)?*
Sì. Mi piace./No. Non mi piace. *Yes I do./No I don't.*

Signor Vitti, le piace il cricket? *Do you like cricket, Mr Vitti?*
Sì. Mi piace molto. *Yes, I do, very much.*
Adriano, ti piacciono le lingue straniere? *Adrian, do you like foreign languages?*
Sì. Mi piacciono./No. Non mi piacciono. *Yes, I do./No, I don't.*
Ora tocca a te! *Here you have a choice between* **Mi piace/Mi piacciono (moltissimo)** *and* **Non mi piace/Non mi piacciono (molto).** *Form the complete question, and then answer it yourself.*

   a *(formal)* __ *la cucina italiana?*
   b *(formal)* __ *la musica classica?*
   c *(informal)* __ *lo sport?*
   d *(informal)* __ *il tuo lavoro?*
   e *(informal)* __ *il calcio?*
   f *(formal)* __ *gli animali?*
   g *(informal)* __ *i film americani?*

5 **Le piace + infinitive:** *Do you like ...? This time simply form the questions:*
Ti piace guidare? *Do you like driving?*
Sì. Mi piace molto. *Yes, I do, very much.*

   a *(informal)* __ *viaggiare?*
   b *(informal)* __ *leggere?*
   c *(informal)* __ *studiare?*
   d *(formal)* __ *cucinare?*
   e *(formal)* __ *uscire la sera?*
   f *(informal)* __ *andare al cinema?*
   g *(informal)* __ *ascoltare la radio?*

6 *Answer these questions using* **ne** *in your answers, as in the example:*
Esempio: Quanti biglietti deve fare? (1)
Ne devo fare uno.

   a *Quante sterline deve pagare? (100)*
   b *Quante lettere deve scrivere? (2)*
   c *Quanti amici vuoi invitare? (12)*
   d *Quanti francobolli devi comprare? (9)*
   e *Quante valigie hai? (1)*
   f *Quanti cugini ha? (4)*
   g *Quanti libri leggi? (molti)*

7 *Ask the shop assistant whether she has something bigger,
longer, darker, etc. using* **ne** *in your answer:*
Esempi: Questo impermeabile è troppo corto. __lungo.
Ne ha uno più lungo?
Questa scatola è troppo piccola. Non __ grande.
Non ne ha una più grande?

   a *Questo vestito è troppo lungo.* __ *corto?*
   b *Questa camera è troppo piccola. Non* __ *grande?*
   c *Questo cappello è troppo chiaro. Non* __ *scuro?*
   d *Questa cravatta è troppo scura.* __ *chiara?*
   e *Questo libro è troppo difficile. Non* __ *facile?*

8 *Read the following passage and make comparisons between
the three brothers using* **più grande di …** *or* **più piccolo di …**
Pietro, Paolo e Lino sono tre fratelli. Pietro ha venti anni,
Paolo ne ha dieci e Lino ne ha tre.
Esempio: Paolo __ Lino.
Paolo è più grande di Lino.

   a *Pietro* __ *Paolo.*
   b *Lino* __ *Paolo.*
   c *Lino* __ *Pietro.*
   d *Pietro* __ *Lino.*
   e *Paolo* __ *Pietro.*

Pietro   Paolo   Lino

9 *Using* **più/meno veloce di** + *article …, make comparisons
between the speeds of the following pairs.*
   a *L'aereo* __ *il treno.*
   b *Il treno* __ *l'autobus.*

c *La macchina __ la bicicletta.*

d *La bicicletta __ l'autobus.*

e *L'autobus __ la metropolitana.*

10 *Alfredo is explaining to Gianni what he would like to buy and why.*

Listen to the dialogue and answer the questions on it.

CD 2, TR 3

Alfredo	Vorrei comprare una nuova macchina.
Gianni	Perchè? La sua non va?
Alfredo	Va benissimo. Ma consuma troppa benzina.
Gianni	Ah, ne vuole una più economica!
Alfredo	Sì. Vorrei una macchina più economica e più veloce.
Gianni	Una macchina più piccola allora?
Alfredo	No. Le macchine piccole non mi piacciono.
Gianni	Ma quelle veloci non sono troppo care?
Alfredo	Sì, però non vorrei pagare tanto.

a *What would Alfredo like to buy?*

b *Does Alfredo's car work?*

c *Why does he mention petrol?*

d *Does he want something faster?*

e *Does he want something smaller?*

f *Why? Why not?*

g *Does Gianni think that fast cars are too cheap?*

h *What does Alfredo not want to do?*

11 *Here are some of the foodstuffs sold in* **la salumeria, la macelleria** *and* **la pescheria.** *See if you can group them under the appropriate shop:*

vitello, salame, olio, trota, merluzzo, vino, maiale, olive, prosciutto, agnello, salmone, pasta, manzo, mortadella.

Look at the pictures opposite, then answer the questions.

a *Quanto tempo ci vuole per cuocere le pennette rigate, e quanto tempo ci vuole per cuocere gli spaghetti? (See Unit 5, Section 6.)*

b *Quanti grammi sono le pennette rigate?*

c *Quanti grammi sono i pomodori?*

Markets and shops

I mercati *markets* are still the most popular place for buying provisions in Italy because the food there has the reputation of being fresh and cheap. Many towns have a daily market where a wide range of foodstuffs can be bought.

Before buying anything it is useful to have a look at *all* the stalls; the ones offering the best value are likely to have the longest queues. Don't be surprised to see potential customers handling the produce. Most food markets close around midday: this is when you might well pick up the best bargains.

Below are the names of some of the **negozi** *shops* and what their vendors are called. Very often Italians use the name of the vendor rather than the name of the shop:

Vado dal farmacista or	*I'm going to the chemist or*
Vado in farmacia.	*I'm going to the chemist's*
(shop).	

The words in small letters are the vendors, the ones in capitals are the shops:

panettiere	salumiere	macellaio	pasticciere	pescivendolo
PANETTERIA	SALUMERIA	MACELLERIA	PASTICCERIA	PESCHERIA

For ice cream use the name of the shop: **gelateria**. Going for a walk (**fare la passeggiata**) in the late afternoon or evening is an important feature of Italian life, often used as an excuse to buy ice cream.

For fruit and vegetables use the name of the vendor: **il fruttivendolo**.

TEST YOURSELF

Match the column on the left with the appropriate continuation on the right.

1 Perchè non bevi?

2 Ho fame. C'è una salumeria da queste parti?

3 Perchè non compriamo dei panini e

4 Prendiamo anche un po' di frutta:

5 Ti piacciono le mele?

6 Ecco la salumeria!

7 C'è un ristorante qui vicino?

8 Com'è bello questo vestito!

9 E la borsa? Ti piace?

10 Il golf bianco mi piace molto, è

11 Quale di questi due portafogli preferisci?

12 Quella giacca è troppo chiara.

a un po' di formaggio?

b di pura lana.

c Non ho sete.

d Più avanti c'è una trattoria.

e È difficile ... sono belli tutti e due.

f Piace anche a me. Lo compro subito.

g Ne ha una più scura?

h Buongiorno! Quattro fette di prosciutto e un etto di burro.

i delle mele e dell'uva.

j Sì. A due passi da qui.

k No. Non mi piace tanto. Quella di pelle è più bella.

l Preferisco l'uva. L'uva bianca.

12

....

Cerco casa
I'm looking for accommodation

In this unit you will learn:
- *how to say what type of accommodation you require*
- *how to say what location you prefer*
- *how to express appreciation of the interior*
- *how to ask about the rent.*

---

1 All'agenzia immobiliare
At the estate agency

Roberto is looking for a flat and is speaking to the estate agent
(**l'agente immobiliare**).

From this point onwards the questions will be in Italian; in **Vero o
falso** you should correct any statements that are wrong.

  a **Vero o falso?** *Roberto cerca un appartamento in periferia.*
  b *Quante camere vuole Roberto?*

Ag.imm.	Buongiorno! Desidera?
Roberto	Buongiorno! Cerco un appartamento di quattro camere.
Ag.imm.	Al centro o in periferia?
Roberto	Al centro. Possibilmente da queste parti.
Ag.imm.	Dunque, vediamo un po'… Ah sì! Ce n'è uno proprio vicino al Duomo. È signorile, ammobiliato, ha quattro camere, cucina, ingresso, bagno, balcone.
Roberto	Sì. Va benissimo. Qual è l'indirizzo?
Ag.imm.	Via Mirafiori 12, interno 7.
Roberto	E il numero di telefono?
Ag.imm.	86 84 52.

Ce n'è uno proprio … *There's one just …*
signorile *luxurious*
ammobiliato/a *furnished*
cucina *kitchen*
ingresso *entrance hall*
bagno *bathroom*

2 A chi pago l'affitto?
To whom do I pay the rent?

The estate agent shows **Roberto** round the flat and explains that he should pay the rent to **la padrona di casa** *the landlady*, who lives on the ground floor.

   a Vero o falso? *La padrona di casa abita al secondo piano.*
   b *Che cosa si paga alla padrona di casa?*

Ag.imm.	Ecco l'appartamento. Questo è l'ingresso. Di qua, prego. Da questa parte c'è il salotto.
Roberto	Che bei mobili!
Ag.imm.	Sono tutti moderni. Questa è la camera da letto. Nell'armadio c'è posto anche per le lenzuola e le coperte.
Roberto	Il balcone dà sulla strada?
Ag.imm.	No. Dà sul cortile. Qui c'è la sala da pranzo, e qui il salotto.
Roberto	E questa porta?
Ag.imm.	È la porta della cucina. Avanti, prego!
Roberto	Dopo di lei!
Ag.imm.	Grazie. Come vede, nell'appartamento ci sono tutte le comodità.
Roberto	A chi pago l'affitto?
Ag.imm.	Alla padrona di casa che abita al pianterreno.

QUICK VOCAB

salotto *living/drawing room*
i mobili *furniture*
armadio *wardrobe*
le lenzuola *sheets*
coperta *blanket*
cortile (m) *courtyard*
sala da pranzo *dining-room*
pianterreno *ground floor*

---

3 Un appartamentino
A small flat

The landlord (**il padrone di casa**) shows a woman tenant (**inquilina**) round a small flat. **L'inquilina** first wants to know where to turn the light on.

  a Vero o falso? *La luce si accende vicino al citofono.*
  b *Dove (esattamente) sono la televisione e la lavatrice?*

Inquilina	Dove si accende la luce?
Padrone	Qui, vicino al citofono.
Inquilina	È questo il soggiorno?
Padrone	Sì. Un attimo. Spengo. Guardi, c'è tutto: il divano, le sedie, le poltrone, lo scaffale per i libri, la televisione, il video …
Inquilina	Oh, che bella cucina! Anche il frigorifero è grande! La lavastoviglie …
Padrone	E questo è il bagno. Qui c'è la presa per il rasoio, qui la doccia e lì la lavatrice.

QUICK VOCAB

accendere la luce *to turn on the light*
citofono *entry-phone*
soggiorno *living room*
spegnere (la luce) *to turn off the light (see below)*
divano *settee*
poltrona *armchair*
lo scaffale per i libri *bookshelf*
frigorifero *fridge*
lavastoviglie (f) *dishwasher*
presa per il rasoio *razor socket*
lavatrice (f) *washing machine*

Grammar

1 ACCENDERE *TO TURN ON;* **SPEGNERE** *TO TURN OFF*

These two verbs are also used for turning on/off the radio, television and gas. **Spegnere** is irregular. Here is the present tense:

Present tense **spegnere** *to turn off, extinguish*	
spengo	spegniamo
spegni	spegnete
spegne	spengono

2 CE N'È, CE NE SONO *THERE IS/THERE ARE* + NE

N'è = ne + è. When **ci** precedes **ne** it becomes **ce: ce n'è, ce ne sono.**
In the following examples notice how **uno, una, molti, ecc.** agree
with the noun to which they refer: **ne** substitutes the noun (see Unit
6, Section 6 and Unit 11, Section 8):

Quanti piani ci sono? *Ce n'è uno.* (C'è un piano.)
   How many floors are there? There is one (of them).

Quante camere ci sono? *Ce n'è una.* (C'è una camera.)
   How many rooms are there? There is one (of them).

Quanti negozi ci sono? Ce ne sono molti. (Ci sono molti negozi).
   How many shops are there? There are lots (of them).

Notice also the negative construction:

C'è del latte?	*Is there any milk?*
No. Non *ce n'è.*	*No. There isn't any.*
Ci sono degli sbagli?	*Are there any mistakes?*
No. *Non ce ne* **sono.**	*No. There aren't any.*

3 IL LENZUOLO, LE LENZUOLA *THE SHEET, THE SHEETS*

This is an irregular plural like **le uova, le paia** (see Unit 11, Section
5).

4 *HOW TO USE* DOPO

Although **dopo** is used by itself before a noun, it is used with **di**
before a pronoun:

Il cinema è dopo l'agenzia.	*The cinema is after the agency.*
Dopo di lei!	*After you!*
Ci vediamo dopo.	*See you later.*

5 USES OF DA

Da is also used to describe the purpose of an object:

una sala da pranzo	*a dining-room*
una camera da letto	*a bedroom*
un vestito da sera	*an evening dress*
un bicchiere da vino	*a wine glass*

6 SUFFIXES

It is possible to add suffixes (special endings) to Italian nouns and adjectives in order to emphasize a particular quality or characteristic. Compare English: *statue*, *statuette*; *figure*, *figurine*. Learn these forms as you come across them.

-etto/a and **-ino/a** suggest smallness:

villetta *small villa*	**tazzina** *small cup, espresso cup*
casetta *little house*	**cucchiaino** *coffee/tea-spoon*
	(lit: a little **cucchiaio***)*

carino/a ⎱
bellino/a ⎰ *pretty*

7 CERCARE *TO LOOK FOR*

Notice that **cercare** does not require a preposition to follow it as in English:

Che cosa cerca?	*What are you looking for?*
Non cerco niente.	*I'm not looking for anything.*
Cerco il dizionario.	*I'm looking for the dictionary.*

Insight

You can think of **cercare** as meaning *to seek*, which similarly doesn't need a preposition.

8 VERBS ENDING IN -CARE, -GARE, -SCERE, AND -GERE

Verbs ending in **-care** and **-gare** keep their hard 'c' and 'g' sounds as in 'cat' and 'got' throughout their conjugation. They must therefore add an 'h' before 'i' gio*c*o, gio*ch*i; pago, pag*h*i.

Verbs ending in **-scere** or **-gere**, such as cono*sc*ere and le*gg*ere, do not keep the same hard 'sc' and 'g' sound throughout, i.e. in **conosco** and **conoscono** the 'sc' is pronounced as in '*sc*ore', but elsewhere as in '*sh*ip': **conosci, conosce; leggo** and **leggono** the 'g' sound is pronounced as in '*g*ot', but elsewhere as in '*g*eneral': (**leggi, legge,** ecc.) (see Pronunciation. Unit 10).

Now look at the present tense of **giocare** *to play (a game)* and **pagare** *to pay* and notice where an 'h' has been inserted:

Present tense			
giocare *to play*	**pagare** *to pay*	**conoscere** *to know*	**leggere** *to read*
gioco	pago	conosco	leggo
giochi	paghi	conosci	leggi
gioca	paga	conosce	legge
giochiamo	paghiamo	conosciamo	leggiamo
giocate	pagate	conoscete	leggete
giocano	pagano	conoscono	leggono

Come si dice?
How do you say it?

◄)) **CD 2, TR 5**

1 *How to say that you are looking for a flat and how many rooms you require*

Cerco un appartamento di due/di tre ecc. camere.

2	*How to say what location you prefer*	**Al centro/in periferia/da queste parti.**
3	*How to express appreciation of the interior*	**Che bei mobili! Che bella cucina!**
4	*How to ask who to pay the rent to and answer: to the landlady*	**A chi pago l'affitto? Alla padrona di casa.**

Practice

1 Look at the picture(s) of the rooms below and their contents.

Now look at the following list of fixtures, fittings and furniture, and decide which items belong in which room.

l'acquaio
il bide
la cucina
il comodino
il divano
la doccia
il frigorifero
il lavandino/il lavabo
la lavastoviglie
la lavatrice
il letto
la libreria
l'orologio
la pianta

le poltrone
il quadro
lo scaffale
la scrivania
le sedie
lo specchio
il tappeto
la tavola
il tavolino
le tende
il telefono
la televisione
la vasca da bagno
il water

Group them accordingly under these rooms: il bagno - la cucina - la camera da letto - la sala da pranzo - il salotto - l'ingresso

2 *Look at how many rooms, etc. there are in the homes of* Anna, Maria, *and* i signori Spada.

	stanze*	camere da letto	piani
Anna	4	2	1
Maria	3	1	1
i signori Spada	7	4	2

* In general, you can use either **camera** or **stanza** for *room*, but when you want to distinguish between a bedroom and other rooms use **camera da letto** *for bedroom.*

Answer the questions using Ce n'è *or* Ce ne sono *and the number.*

a *Quanti piani ci sono nella villa dei signori Spada?*
b *Quante camere da letto ci sono nella villa dei signori Spada?*

   c *Quante camere da letto ci sono nell'appartamento di Maria?*

   d *Quante stanze ci sono nell'appartamento di Anna?*

   e *Quante stanze ci sono nella villa dei signori Spada?*

3 *Nel, nella, etc. Link the five objects in the left-hand column with the five most appropriate places for them on the right.*
Esempio: **Le sedie sono nel soggiorno.**

   a presa per il **rasoio**   *salotto*

   b **citofono**   *camera da letto*

   c **frigorifero**   *ingresso*

   d **letto**   *cucina*

   e **divano**   *bagno*

   f **coperte**   *armadio*

4 *Do as in Exercise 3, this time using* **sul, sulla,** *etc.*

   a **sedie a sdraio**   *scaffale*

   b **lenzuola**   *tavolino*

   c **televisione**   *balcone*

   d **libri**   *letto*

5 *Read the following and notice how the information can be extracted from the table below:*

Marco cerca un appartamento di due camere, al centro, vicino al Duomo.

   a *Write a sentence to say what Davide is looking for.*

   b *Write a similar sentence for Bianca.*

   c *Write a similar sentence for Lola e Rita.*

   d *Supposing the estate agent were to ask Lola e Rita what they were looking for, what would they answer?*

	Camere	Centro o periferia?	Dove?
Marco	2	centro	Duomo
Davide	4	periferia	strada principale
Bianca	3	periferia	stazione
Lola e Rita	5	centro	ufficio

6 *In the following questions answer with* **Ce n'è** *(singular) or* **Ce ne sono** *(plural), and a number:*
Esempio: Quanti giorni ci sono nel mese di marzo?

Ce ne sono trentuno.

a *Quanti mesi ci sono in un anno?*
b *Quanti giorni ci sono in una settimana?*
c *Quanti giorni ci sono in un anno?*
d *Quanti minuti ci sono in un'ora?*
e *Quanti anni ci sono in un secolo?*
f *Quanti etti ci sono in un chilo?*
g *Quante lettere ci sono nell'alfabeto italiano?*
h *Quanti mesi ci sono con ventotto giorni?*

7 *Marisa is asking an inhabitant of Rome something about her flat. After listening to the dialogue can you answer the questions on it?*

CD 2, TR 6

Marisa	Abita a Roma, signora?
Signora	Sì. abito vicino al Colosseo.
Marisa	In una casa moderna?
Signora	Beh … non molto moderna.
Marisa	A che piano abita?
Signora	Al quarto.
Marisa	C'è l'ascensore?
Signora	No. L'ascensore non c'è.
Marisa	Quante stanze ha?
Signora	Cinque: tre camere da letto, la sala da pranzo e il salotto. Il bagno è piccolo ma la cucina è bella grande.

a *Near what building does she live?*
b *What is said about the age of the flat?*
c *On what floor does she live?*
d *Is there a lift in the building?*
e *How many rooms does she say she has?*
f *How many bedrooms does she say she has?*
g *Which rooms are not included in her total?*
h *What can you say about these last two rooms?*

8 *The extracts below are from* **piccola pubblicità** *small ads in an Italian newspaper. First look at the* **Houses and flats** *section at the end of this unit, then look carefully at the questions. See if you can understand the advertisements and give the*

*appropriate answers. They are written in 'telegraphic style' –
only the essential words are there.*

a

**Porto Cervo
(Sardegna):
affittasi
appartamento
signorile in zona
turistica.**

b

Milano:
appartamenti
in vendita da 2
a 5 locali.

c

Arona in
zona
residenziale
con parco:
vendesi
appartamento.

d

Milanocase
garantisce
vendita
immediata.

e

*Como: unica
posizione villa
panoramica 2
appartamenti
indipendenti.*

f

La villa che
sognate:
stupenda
costruzione,
fronte mare
Riviera dei Fiori.

g

Cerco in
giugno
appartamento
libero signorile
in costruzione
recente.

h

Studente inglese
cerca alloggio
ammobiliato
con scambio
conversazione.

un locale *room (commercial meaning)*
sognare *to dream (about)*
alloggio *lodgings*

VOCAB

   a *What is being let in Sardinia?*
   b *What are being sold in Milan?*
   c *What is being advertised in Arona?*
   d *What service is the firm Milanocase offering to
prospective sellers?*
   e *Describe the villa in Como.*
   f *What makes the villa at Riviera dei Fiori so desirable?*
   g *What is the advertiser looking for exactly? When for?*
   h *Who is looking for what and what does he want to
exchange?*

Houses and flats

Although strictly speaking **appartamento** means *flat* and **casa** means *house* or *home*, since most Italians live in flats anyway, they do not make any clear distinction between the two, and usually refer to the house or flat they live in as their **casa**. The building itself is called **palazzo** or **condominio**. There is often a caretaker in charge, **il portiere**, but as costs rise, caretakers are becoming rarer, and **il citofono** is used.

In Italian newspaper advertisements you will see the words **vendesi** (from **vendere** *to sell*) and **affittasi** (from **affittare** *to let* or *to rent* – hence **l'affitto** *the rent*). They are a commercial way of saying **si vende** and **si affitta**. *To rent* may also be expressed as **prendere in affitto**. You will also see the expression **doppi servizi** frequently used. This means that the flat has two bathrooms: the second one might have a simpler layout with a toilet, shower and washbasin but not necessarily another bath. Often the washing machine is put in here. Finally, **il box** is *the garage* and **l'attico** *the penthouse*.

As in English, Italian names for reception rooms are subject to regional variations and changes in fashion. Generally speaking, **il salotto** would be a rather formal sitting-room (a larger one would be called **il salone**) and **il soggiorno** would combine the functions of sitting/dining room.

Most flats have balconies. In increasing order of size they are called: **il balcone, il terrazzo, la terrazza**. All three mean a lot to Italians.

Many Italians have **la seconda casa** either in the country or by the sea.

For property on the Internet:
http://www.tecnocasa.it

Now turn to *Test your Italian II*.

TEST YOURSELF

Match columns 1–10 on the left with the appropriate continuation a–j on the right.

A student explains his requirements for a room to the caretaker (a woman) of several apartments. She takes him to view one of them.

1 Siamo tre studenti. Cerchiamo un appartamento ammobiliato.

a Ce ne sono quattro. Tre grandi e una piccola.

2 Preferibilmente al centro.

b Certo. Vuole vedere? Un momento. Ecco: l'accendo e la spengo. Va bene?

3 Non importa. Quante camere da letto ci sono?

c È lì sulla scrivania, vicino alla televisione.

4 C'è la lavatrice?

d Al centro o in periferia?

5 E quanti bagni ci sono?

e Ne abbiamo uno proprio dietro l'università. È al quarto piano. Non è caro, ma non c'è l'ascensore.

6 Quando si paga l'affitto?

f Per la camera piccola non si preoccupi! Conosco io un altro studente che cerca alloggio.

7 Mi scusi, non vedo il telefono. Dov'è?

g No. Mi dispiace, non c'è. Ma c'è una lavanderia a due passi dall'università.

8 La televisione funziona*, vero?

h Ogni mese, al padrone di casa.

*funzionare=to work

(continues overleaf)

9 Sì, sì. Va benissimo. Lo prendiamo per tutto l'anno accademico, ma senza la camera piccola.

i Ce n'è uno solo: il palazzo è vecchio.

10 Grazie mille! Arrivederci!

j Prego. Arrivederci!

13

....

Vita di tutti i giorni
Everyday life

In this unit you will learn how to talk about:
* *what sports you do*
* *how often you do something*
* *the weather*
* *daily routine*
* *putting a relationship on a more informal footing.*

_____

1 Che sport fa?
What sports do you do?

Giulio is talking to a journalist about his sporting activities: tennis, swimming, skiing, jogging and gym.

   a **Vero o falso?** *Lo sport preferito di Giulio è il nuoto.*
   b *Ogni mattina si alza, si lava e si veste.*
   c *Dove va a nuotare d'inverno, e dove va a nuotare d'estate?*

Giorn.	Che sport fa durante le vacanze?
Giulio	Il tennis, il nuoto e lo sci. Palestra quando posso.
Giorn.	Dove va a nuotare? In piscina?
Giulio	D'inverno in piscina, d'estate al lago.
Giorn.	Va a nuotare tutti i giorni?
Giulio	No. Due volte alla settimana.
Giorn.	Ma il suo sport preferito è il jogging, vero?
Giulio	Eh sì. Ogni mattina appena mi alzo, mi lavo, mi vesto e via per un'ora.

durante *during*
le vacanze *holidays*
palestra *gym*
nuotare *to swim*
piscina *swimming pool*
lago *lake*
appena *as soon as*
mi alzo *I get up*
mi lavo *I wash*
mi vesto *I get dressed*
via *away, off I go*

2 Pioggia, neve, vento, sole
Rain, snow, wind, sun

Giulio continues by saying that he goes jogging irrespective of the weather.

a **Vero o falso?** *Quando corre, la pioggia fa una grande differenza per lui.*

b *Giulio corre solo quando fa bel tempo?*

c *Si sente molto stanco dopo il jogging?*

Giorn.	Corre anche quando fa brutto tempo?
Giulio	Pioggia, neve, vento, o sole, non fa nessuna differenza per me.
Giorn.	Si sente stanco dopo un'ora di corsa, immagino!
Giulio	No. Non mi sento affatto stanco. Anzi, per me il jogging è anche un modo per rilassarmi.

correre *to run*
fa brutto tempo *the weather's bad*
si sente stanco? *do you feel tired?*
corsa *running*
non ... affatto *not at all, not in the least*
anzi *on the contrary*
rilassarsi *to relax*

3 Un giorno qualunque
Just an ordinary day

Aldo and **Rita,** a husband and wife who work in their own bookshop, are in the middle of an interview about a typical day of theirs. **Rita** interrupts to offer the journalist a drink.

  a **Vero o falso?** *Rita offre un caffè al giornalista.*
  b *La mattina lei e suo marito si alzano tardi.*
  c *Rita e Aldo si alzano alle dieci?*

Rita	Un bicchiere di vino?
Giorn.	No, grazie. Non bevo. Dunque ... a che ora vi alzate la mattina?
Aldo	Di solito ci alziamo presto: alle sei.
Giorn.	Come mai alle sei? Cosa fate in piedi così presto?
Rita	Prima di tutto facciamo il caffè.
Aldo	Senza un buon caffè non ci svegliamo.
Rita	Mentre facciamo colazione, mettiamo un po' in ordine la casa e ci prepariamo, è già ora di uscire.

QUICK VOCAB

di solito *usually*
far(e) colazione *to have breakfast*
come mai? *how is that?*
in piedi così presto *up so early*
prima di tutto *first of all*
svegliarsi *to wake up*
mettere in ordine *to tidy*
prepararsi *to get ready*
già *already*

4 Lavoriamo insieme
We work together

Aldo explains that he deals with the sales and his wife deals with the book-keeping (**la contabilità**).

a **Vero o falso?** *A mezzogiorno Aldo e sua moglie mangiano a casa.*

b *La sera, cenano presto?*

CD 2, TR 7, 02:26

Giorn.	Lavorate tutti e due?
Rita	Sì. Lavoriamo insieme nella nostra libreria.
Aldo	Io mi occupo della vendita dei libri e mia moglie si occupa della contabilità.
Giorn.	A mezzogiorno mangiate fuori?
Rita	No. Torniamo a casa per il pranzo. Pranziamo verso le due.
Aldo	Dopo pranzo ci riposiamo un po' e poi torniamo insieme al negozio.
Giorn.	E la sera, cenate tardi?
Rita	Sì. Piuttosto tardi. Non ceniamo mai prima delle nove.

Q. VOCAB

libreria *book-shop*
occuparsi *to look after*
riposarsi *to rest*
piuttosto *rather*

5 Diamoci del tu!
Let's use tu

Remo, who is much older than **Rina,** gets acquainted with her and puts the relationship on a more informal footing by suggesting the use of the familiar form **tu** (*you*) instead of the more formal **lei.**

a **Vero o falso?** *Rina studia matematica.*
b *Si laurea a maggio.*
c *Che anno fa all'università Rina?*

Remo	Quindi, è qui per motivi di studio. Che cosa studia?
Rina	Medicina.
Remo	Che anno fa?
Rina	L'ultimo anno. Mi laureo a giugno.
Remo	Ah, c'è tempo per gli esami! Cosa fa di bello stasera?
Rina	Nulla. Resto a casa a studiare.
Remo	Non è stufa di studiare?
Rina	Un po'. E lei, cosa fa?
Remo	Ma, Rina, diamoci del tu!
Rina	E tu, cosa fai?
Remo	Niente d'interessante. Perchè non vieni da me? Possiamo fare quattro chiacchiere, mangiare un piatto di spaghetti, e poi magari andare ad un concerto. Che ne dici?

CD 2, TR 7, 03:13

mi laureo *I'm graduating*
Cosa fa di bello? *Are you doing anything interesting?*
stufo/a di *fed up with*
fare quattro chiacchiere *to have a chat*

QUICK VOCAB

Grammar

1 REFLEXIVE VERBS

In the dictionary, reflexive verbs are recognizable by **-si** (*oneself*) at the end of the infinitive. The final 'e' of the infinitive (**lavare**) is dropped and **lavare** *to wash* becomes **lavarsi** *to wash (oneself)*; (**vestire**) **vestirsi** *to dress oneself, to get dressed*.

The pronouns **mi, ti, si, ci, vi, si,** precede the verb and correspond to *myself, yourself,* etc.

Present tense **lavarsi** *to wash (oneself)*		
(io)	**mi lavo**	*I wash (myself)*
(tu)	**ti lavi**	*you* (inf) *wash (yourself)*
(lei)	**si lava**	*you* (form) *wash (yourself)*
(lui, lei)	**si lava**	*he/she washes (himself/herself)*
(noi)	**ci laviamo**	*we wash (ourselves)*
(voi)	**vi lavate**	*you wash (yourselves)*
(loro)	**si lavano**	*they wash (themselves)*

The other reflexive verbs that have appeared in this unit are: **alzarsi** *to get up*; **laurearsi** *to graduate*; **occuparsi** *to deal with*; **prepararsi** *to prepare*; **rilassarsi** *to relax*; **riposarsi** *to rest*; **sentirsi** *to feel*; **svegliarsi** *to wake up*.

Insight

In English we say 'he washes' whether a person is washing himself or something else. In Italian you must make a distinction: **si lava** (from **lavarsi** reflexive verb) *he washes (himself)*; **lava** (from **lavare**) **la maglietta** *he washes the T shirt*.

2 ANDARE + INFINITIVE (TO GO … -ING)

Andare a + infinitive express the idea of *to go and do something*:

D'estate *va a* nuot*are*. *In summer he goes and swims (i.e. he goes swimming).*

D'inverno *andiamo a* sci*are*. *In winter we go skiing.*

***Vado* a mangi*are*.** *I'll go and eat./ I'm going to eat.*

***Vado a fare* il biglietto.** *I'll go and buy the ticket./I'm going to buy the ticket.*

3 DUE VOLTE AL MESE *TWICE A MONTH*

The idea of frequency is expressed by **a** + definite article:

		mangia (lì)?
	al giorno	prende l'**au**tobus?
Quante volte	*alla* settimana	lavora?
	al mese	viene qui?

			eat (there)?
	day	do you	take a bus?
How many times a	week		work?
	month		come here?

To answer the above, use **una volta** *once*, **due volte** *twice*, **tre volte** *three times*, **molte volte** *many times* etc.

4 OGNI *EVERY*

Ogni, like **tutti** (Unit 11, Section 11), means *every*, but is followed by the singular except when followed by a number:

Ogni giorno; ogni sera.	*Every day; every evening/every night.*
Ogni cinque minuti; ogni due giorni.	*Every five minutes; every two days.*

5 NESSUNO/A *NOT … ANY …/NO ONE, NOT … ANYONE*

Nessuno is always singular, and before a noun is used like **un, uno, una, un'**:

ness*un* libro; ness*uno* sb*a*glio	*no book; no mistake*
***Non* es*e*rcita ness*una* professione.**	*He doesn't practise any profession.*
***Non c'è nessuno* (m or f).**	*There's no one.*

6 SENTIRSI *TO FEEL*

This verb is used (reflexively) to describe how one feels:

Come si sente? Mi sento m*e*glio/bene/male.	*How do you feel? I feel better/well/ill.*

7 THE WEATHER

To ask what the weather is like, the verb **fare** is used in the following expressions:

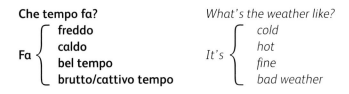

Che tempo fa?

What's the weather like?

Fa
- **freddo**
- **caldo**
- **bel tempo**
- **brutto/cattivo tempo**

It's
- *cold*
- *hot*
- *fine*
- *bad weather*

But notice:

Che tempo fa?
- **C'è il sole**
- **Tira/c'è vento**
- **Piove**
- **Nevica**

It's
- *sunny*
- *windy*
- *raining*
- *snowing*

8 CONTRACTIONS AND EXPANSIONS

Un bicchiere *a glass* can be shortened to **un bicchier** before **di**. You can either say **un bicchiere di vino** or **un bicchier di vino**.

Vorrei un bicchier(e) d'acqua.   *I would like a glass of water.*

E *and*, **a** *at*, *to* can add '**d**' before words beginning with a vowel:

Giorgio e(d) Anna vanno a(d) Amalfi.   *Giorgio and Anna are going to Amalfi.*

9 ANYTHING/NOTHING + DI + ADJECTIVE

A friendly way of asking what people are doing is:

Cosa fa di bello stasera?   *Are you doing anything interesting tonight?*

Note **di** + adjective in parallel positive and negative expressions:

C'è qualcosa di nuovo?   *Is there anything new?*

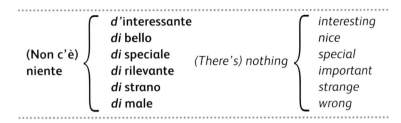

| (Non c'è) niente | d'interessante
di bello
di speciale
di rilevante
di strano
di male | (There's) nothing | interesting
nice
special
important
strange
wrong |

10 DIAMOCI DEL TU *LET'S USE TU*

This expression (lit: *let's give each other tu*) is said when passing from the **lei** form to the more familiar **tu** form. Remember also to use the possessive **tuo/a, ecc.** for *your* and not **suo/a**, etc.

Devi uscire con i tuoi amici?   *Do you have to go out with your friends?*

11 BERE *TO DRINK*

Here is the present tense of the irregular verb **bere** to drink. The only irregularity is the stem: **bev-**. Otherwise it is conjugated like any other **-ere** verb:

bevo, bevi, beve, beviamo, bevete, bevono

12 RILASSARMI *TO RELAX (MYSELF)*

As we have seen in Section 1 above, reflexive verbs add **-si** at the end of the infinitive after taking away the final vowel: **divertirsi** *to enjoy oneself* = **divertire + si**. It can also mean *to enjoy yourself/ himself/herself/themselves*. Similarly, **-mi, -ti, -ci, -vi** can be added to the end of the infinitive: **divertirmi, divertirti, divertirci, divertirvi**. This is often seen with **potere, volere, dovere**, where there is a choice:

Devo lavarmi or **Mi devo lavare.**	*I must/have to wash (myself).*
Vuole divertirsi or **Si vuole divertire.**	*You (form) want to enjoy yourself, he/she wants to enjoys himself/herself.*
Dobbiamo divertirci or **Ci dobbiamo divertire.**	*We must enjoy ourselves.*
Vogliono divertirsi or **Si vogliono divertire.**	*They want to enjoy themselves.*

Come si dice?
How do you say it?

◀) **CD 2, TR 8**

1 *How to ask about and say what sports you do*

Che sport fa? Il nuoto, lo sci, il tennis, il jogging.

2 *How to ask about and say how many times a day, a week, a month, etc.*

Quante volte al giorno, alla settimana, al mese … ? Una volta, due volte al/alla …

3 *How to ask about and describe the weather*

Che tempo fa? Fa bel tempo, fa brutto tempo, c'è il sole, piove, ecc.

4 *How to talk about your daily routine*

La mattina mi sveglio, mi alzo … mi vesto … faccio colazione …

5 *How to put your relationship on a more informal footing*

Diamoci del tu!

Practice

1 **La giornata di Pietro. Che cosa fa?** *Describe what Pietro does in each of the pictures below, using each verb in this list once:* andare a letto, alzarsi, cenare, far(e) colazione, guardare la televisione, lavarsi, leggere il giornale, svegliarsi, tornare a casa, uscire di casa *and give the times.*

2 *Continue these sentences, using the same verb as in the first part, but in the first person, as in the example:*

Esempio: Il mio amico si chiama Roberto, ma io __ Gianni.
Il mio amico si chiama Roberto, ma io mi chiamo Gianni.

a Cesare si riposa la domenica, ma io __ il sabato.
b Lui si diverte a sciare, ma io __ a nuotare.
c Giovanni si sveglia alle otto meno un quarto, ma io __ alle sette.

d *Cesare si alza alle otto, ma io __ alle nove.*

e *Ugo si lava nel bagno, ma io __ in cucina.*

f *Francesca si veste nella camera da letto, ma io __ nel bagno.*

g *Gl'italiani si riposano dopo pranzo, ma noi non __ di pomeriggio.*

3 Gino, *who is described here, has Bohemian habits:*

Gino non si sveglia mai prima delle otto. Non si alza mai presto. Non si lava mai con l'acqua fredda. Non si veste mai prima di mezzogiorno.

Imagine you are Gino *and describe yourself:* **Non mi sveglio mai, ecc.**

4 *Here is a list of reflexive verbs in the infinitive:* **alzarsi** *to get up;* **cambiarsi** *to get changed;* **divertirsi** *to enjoy oneself;* **lagnarsi** *to complain;* **riposarsi** *to rest;* **ubriacarsi** *to get drunk. Select each of them once to complete the following sentences. Make sure that you use the same person of the verb as in the first part of the sentence.*

a *Se siamo stanchi, __*

b *Se non vogliamo andare a teatro con lo stesso vestito, __*

c *Se sono a letto e devo uscire, __*

d *Se bevo troppo vino, __*

e *Se vado a una festa, __*

f *Quando il servizio non è buono, (io) __*

5 *Read the following passage about* **Olga**, *looking up any words you don't know. Then answer the questions on it using* **lo, la, li, le** *or* **l'** *(object pronouns – see Unit 8, Section 5).*

Ogni mattina Olga prende un cappuccino al bar. Poi passa per la salumeria e prende un po' di mortadella e di salame per il pranzo. Al ritorno va prima in panetteria e compra sei panini e infine passa per l'edicola per prendere il giornale e aspettare la sua amica.

a *Dove prende Olga il cappuccino?*

b *Dove prende la mortadella?*

c *Dove compra i panini?*

d *Dove compra il giornale?*

e *Dove aspetta la sua amica?*

6 *What's the weather like?*

Le Alpi

Torino • Milano

Fenomeni
☁ Pioggia
☀ Sole
↳ Vento
☁ Neve

Roma

Napoli

a *Che tempo fa sulle Alpi?*
b *Che tempo fa a Milano e a Torino?*
c *Che tempo fa a Roma?*
d *Che tempo fa a Napoli?*

7 **Ora tocca a te!** *Here, you are a journalist interviewing* **Pina**, *owner of a restaurant.*

CD 2, TR 9

You	*But don't you ever rest, Madam?*
Pina	Beh, con un ristorante è difficile riposarsi. La sera andiamo a letto molto tardi, e la mattina ci alziamo molto presto.
You	*How many hours a day do you work?*
Pina	Dieci, dodici, qualche volta anche quattordici ore.
You	*You work hard!*
Pina	Ma mi riposo durante le vacanze.
You	*How many times a year do you go on holiday?*
Pina	Due volte.
You	*When? In summer?*
Pina	No. D'estate è impossibile. Abbiamo troppi clienti. Andiamo in primavera e in autunno.
You	*Where do you go?*
Pina	Vado in Svizzera con mia figlia. Andiamo a sciare.
You	*Do you like skiing?*
Pina	Sì, molto. Lo sci è il mio sport preferito.

8 **Lo sport: Cosa fanno?** *What are they doing? Give your answers in the singular.*

a   b   c

d   e   f

University life

Most Italian students live at home: they go to the nearest university. **Laurearsi** is to get one's degree **la laurea. Un laureato/una laureata** are, respectively, *a male graduate* and *a female graduate*. Italian universities are open to all who have passed their final secondary school exams. Each student receives **il libretto**, a document which combines a student identity card with a record of all exams taken. It entitles the student to use the university library (**biblioteca**) and canteen (**mensa**). A swipe card (**tessera elettronica**) which contains some of the information electronically is now being used in more and more universities. Normal degree courses last four years, but one or two, such as Engineering and Medicine, take longer. Although graduates may take more than the stipulated time to complete their courses, they have to pay **la tassa di fuoricorso** (a special supplement) to do so. All graduates are entitled to be called **dottore: dottore in legge** *Doctor of Law*, **dottore in medicina, ecc.** *Doctor of Medicine*, etc.

Visit the websites of L'Università Popolare di Roma and of L'Università della Svizzera Italiana:
http://www.upter.it; http://www.unisi.ch

Sport

Italians excel in winter and aquatic sports, fencing, cycling and motor racing, but are probably best known for their prowess in soccer: 2006 saw Italy win the World Cup for the fourth time. The champions, known as **gli azzurri** because of the colour of their shirts, attracted worldwide attention and publicity.

TEST YOURSELF

Unscramble the following to make meaningful sentences.

1 *volte a un settimana fare vado jogging tre alla di po'*

2 *ora a svegli che ti?*

3 *parco spesso nel a mangio un mezzogiorno panino*

4 *per esco alle casa andare mattina otto la a di lavorare*

5 *giornale di l'edicola prendere per per solito passo il*

6 *meglio palestra mi quando sento faccio di po' un*

7 *vento c'è oggi tanto*

8 *di bello cosa stasera fa?*

9 *stasera al vado cinema rilassarmi per*

10 *sono nel mi 2001 laureata*

14

Vorrei un'informazione
I'd like some information

In this unit you will learn:
- *how to ask and give directions*
- *how to ask and say how frequent the buses are*
- *how to give instructions*
- *how to ask and respond to whether one has something.*

1 Come si fa per andare a ...?
How do you get to ...?

Il signor Pozzi is enquiring about the way to the central post office. He asks to go to **Via Garibaldi** and is told to go straight ahead. However …

a Vero o falso? *La Posta Centrale è in Via Garibaldi.*
b *Il signor Pozzi parla con un amico?*

Sig. Pozzi	Scusi, sa dov'è Via Garibaldi?
Passante	Certo, signore. Vada sempre dritto. In fondo a questa strada giri a destra. Che numero cerca?
Sig. Pozzi	Il 122.
Passante	Ah, no. Il numero 122 non esiste. Dove deve andare?
Sig. Pozzi	Alla Posta Centrale.
Passante	Ma la Posta Centrale è in Piazza Garibaldi. Prenda l'autobus fino a Via Roma e poi cambi.

CD 2, TR 10

in fondo a *at the end of*
girare *to turn*
fino a *up to*
esistere *to exist*

---

2 Ogni quanto tempo passano gli autobus?
How often do the buses pass?

The passer-by now tells him how to reach the 48 bus stop.

a Vero o falso? *La fermata del 48 è dopo la stazione.*
b *Cosa deve fare il signor Pozzi al capolinea?*

Sig. Pozzi	Ogni quanto tempo passano gli autobus?
Passante	Per Via Roma ogni dieci minuti circa.
Sig. Pozzi	E che numero devo prendere?
Passante	Il 48. Vada fino all'incrocio. Per attraversare la strada passi per il sottopassaggio. La fermata è dopo il ponte.
Sig. Pozzi	Ho capito. E poi come si fa per andare a Piazza Garibaldi?
Passante	È semplice. A Via Roma prenda il 56 e scenda al capolinea. La posta è a pochi passi dall'ultima fermata.
Sig. Pozzi	Molto gentile, grazie.
Passante	Prego, per carità!

Ogni quanto tempo ...? *How often ...?*
incrocio *crossroads*
attraversare *to cross*
sottopassaggio *underpass*
semplice *simple*
il capolinea *terminus*
per carità *not at all*

3 Alla posta
At the post office

At the post office **il sig. Pozzi** wants to send a registered letter.

a **Vero o falso?** *L'impiegata chiede al sig. Pozzi se vuole la penna.*

b *Qual è l'ultima cosa che il sig. Pozzi vuol sapere dall'impiegata?*

Sig. Pozzi	Vorrei fare una raccomandata.
Impiegata	Sì. Scriva qui nome, cognome e indirizzo del mittente. Vuole la penna?
Sig. Pozzi	No, grazie. Ce l'ho … Ecco fatto! Va bene così?
Impiegata	Sì. Così va bene. Ecco il resto, e questa è la ricevuta. Desidera altro?
Sig. Pozzi	Devo inviare questo pacco. Che sportello?
Impiegata	Per il pacco deve andare all'ufficio pacchi. Vuole spedirlo oggi? Faccia presto perchè chiude.
Sig. Pozzi	Ultima domanda: dov'è la buca delle lettere, per cortesia?
Impiegata	Là, guardi! Là in fondo.

CD 2, TR 10, 01:50

raccomandata *registered letter*
mittente (m) *sender*
Ce l'ho. *I've got one.*
Ecco fatto! *There you are!*
resto *change*
ricevuta *receipt*
pacco; ufficio pacchi *parcel; parcel office*
sportello *counter/window*
spedire, inviare *to post, send*
Faccia presto! *Be quick.*
buca delle lettere *letter box, mail box (US)*

QUICK VOCAB

4 C'è un supermercato ...?
Is there a supermarket ...?

CD 2, TR 10, 02:42

> **A** Mi scusi, c'è un supermercato non troppo lontano da qui?
> **B** Sì. Ce n'è uno subito dopo Piazza della Repubblica, e un altro più grande a cento metri dall'azienda di turismo, prima del cinema. Vada fino alla farmacia, poi dritto, dritto ...
> **A** Grazie, buongiorno.
> **B** Prego, buongiorno.

azienda di turismo *tourist office*
dritto, dritto *keep straight on*

Grammar

1 *IMPERATIVE* **LEI** *FORM*

Scusi, vada, prenda and **giri** are the imperative (**lei** forms) of **scusare, andare, prendere** and **girare,** and are used when telling someone to do something. **Scusi** as we have already seen, is also used to attract attention.

Regular **-are**, **-ere** *and* **-ire** *verbs*
To form the imperative (**lei** form) take off the **-are, -ere** and **-ire** endings of the infinitive and add the following endings:

For verbs ending in	**-are** add **-i**	
Infinitive	Imperative (**lei**)	
aspett-are	aspett-**i**!	*wait!*
guard-are	guard-**i**!	*look!*
attravers-are	attravers-**i**!	*cross!*

For verbs ending in **-iare** (as with the **tu** form; see Unit 3, Section 2) do not double the final -i: **Cambi! Mangi! Cominci! Parcheggi qui!** *Park here* (**parcheggiare** *to park*).

For verbs ending in	**-ere** and **-ire** add **-a**	
pr<u>e</u>nd-ere	prend-**a**!	*take!*
scr<u>i</u>v-ere	scriv-**a**!	*write!*
sc<u>e</u>nd-ere	scend-**a**!	*get off!*
apr-ire	apr-**a**!	*open!*
sent-ire	sent-**a**!	*listen!*

Aspett*i* alla fermata del l'<u>au</u>tobus!	*Wait at the bus stop.*
Scriv*a* il suo nome e cognome!	*Write your first name and surname.*
Apr*a* la porta e chiud*a* la finestra, per favore!	*Open the door and close the window, please.*

To form the negative put **non** before the verb:

Non pass*i* di qua! È pericoloso!	*Don't go this way. It's dangerous.*
Non attravers*i* qui!	*Don't cross here.*

2 IMPERATIVE LEI FORM WITH OBJECT PRONOUNS

Object pronouns (see Unit 8, Section 5) precede the verb in the imperative (**lei** form):

La casa è bella: *la* compri!	*The house is nice: buy it!*
Il vino è <u>o</u>ttimo: *l'*assaggi!	*The wine is excellent: taste it!*

3 IMPERATIVE LEI IRREGULAR FORMS

The stem for the imperative **lei** irregular form is obtained from the first person singular of the present tense. Simply change the -o ending of the 1st person singular into -a.

Infinitive		1st person singular present	Imperative (lei)
andare	*to go*	vad-**o**	vad-**a**!
dire	*to say*	dic-**o**	dic-**a**!
finire	*to finish*	finisc-**o**	finisc-**a**!
leggere	*to read*	legg-**o**	legg-**a**!
salire	*to get on, to go upstairs*	salg-**o**	salg-**a**!
spegnere	*to turn/switch off*	speng-**o**	speng-**a**!

Ora tocca a te! Write down the imperative (**lei**) form of these verbs (you have met the present tense of all of them in previous units): **pulire** *to clean* (like **capire** Unit 5, Section 1), **bere**, **fare**, **uscire**, **venire** (see the Grammar index).

4 *IMPERATIVE OF* **NOI** *AND* **VOI** *FORMS*

The first person plural of the imperative (*let us*) is exactly the same as the first person plural (**noi**) of the present tense (Unit 7, Section 2) but notice that in written Italian the imperative requires an exclamation mark:

***Usciamo** stasera? Sì. **Usciamo**!*	*Are you going out tonight? Yes. **Let's** (go out).*
***Vediamo** un po'!*	***Let's** have a look.*
***Facciamo** così!*	***Let's** do it this way.*

The **voi** (*you* plural) form is also the same as the present tense:

***Aspettate** alla fermata del pullman?*	*Are you waiting at the coach stop?*
***Aspettate** alla fermata del pullman!*	*Wait at the coach stop.*
***Prendete** un gelato!*	*Have an ice cream.*
***Venite** con me!*	*Come with me.*

You will soon learn by the tone of voice (intonation) whether or not an Italian is asking a question.

5 PRIMA DEL CINEMA *BEFORE THE CINEMA*

Like **il cinema,** some nouns ending in **–ma** (Greek origin) are masculine and their plurals end in **-i: il programma** *programme* **i programmi; il tema** *the theme* **i temi; il sistema** *the system* **i sistemi; il problema** *the problem* **i problemi.**

Ci sono molti problemi sociali e politici.	*There are many social and political problems.*
Vuol guardare i programmi italiani?	*Do you want to watch the Italian programmes?*

Il cinema, however, does not change in the plural: **i cinema.**

6 CE L'HO *I'VE GOT IT*

When someone asks you whether you have something or not, the question is **Ce l'ha?** *Have you got it?* When you want to answer *I have/haven't got it*, you use (**Non**) **ce l'ho. Ce** has no meaning.

Ha il mio indirizzo? Sì. *Ce l'ho.*	*Have you got my address? Yes, I have (got it).*
Paolo ha l'internet? No. *Non ce l'ha.*	*Has Paul got/does Paul have the internet? No, he hasn't (got it).*

Present tense **salire** *to go up, get on*	**togliere** *to take off/away*
salgo	tolgo
sali	togli
sale	toglie
saliamo	togliamo
salite	togliete
salgono	tolgono

Come si dice?
How do you say it?

◀ **CD 2, TR 11**

1 *How to ask directions/ ask how to get there*   **Sa dov'è il museo/la posta …? Come si fa per andare al museo/alla posta?**

How to give directions   **Vada/giri/continui/prenda la prima …**

2 *How to ask and say how frequent the buses are*	**Ogni quanto tempo passano gli autobus? Passano ogni cinque/ dieci minuti …**
3 *How to give instructions*	**Scriva nome/cognome/indirizzo. Salga qui/scenda alla prossima fermata …**
4 *How to ask if someone has …*	**Ha la penna/la matita/il dizionario …?**
How to respond	**Sì. Ce l'ho/No. Non ce l'ho.**

Now cover up the right hand side and try to give the Italian; then replace the dots on the right by your own choice of words.

Practice

1 Girare *or* andare? *Using the imperative (***lei*** form) of ***girare*** *or* ***andare**, can you tell a tourist what to do when faced with each of these signs below?*

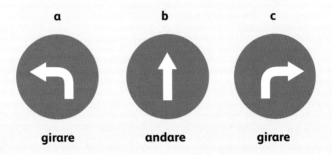

a	**b**	**c**
girare	andare	girare

2 i *Using the example as a model, ask a passer-by how to get*
  a *to the University*
  b *to the museum*
  c *to the bank.*
Es**e**mpio: *(… to the swimming pool)* Scusi! come si fa per andare alla piscina?
ii *Now, using the plan opposite and modelling your answer on the example, explain to a tourist how to get*
  a *to the station*
  b *to the supermarket*
  c *to the Commerical Bank.*
Es**e**mpio: *(… to the swimming pool)* Prenda la

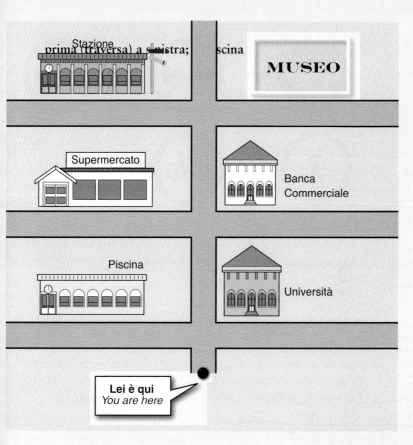

prima (traversa) a sinistra; scina

Stazione

MUSEO

Supermercato

Banca Commerciale

Piscina

Università

Lei è qui
You are here

3 i *All the following signs are surrounded
by a red circle: they are telling you not
to do something, expressed by* **vietato**
(forbidden) and **divieto di** *(lit: prohibition
of). The sign on the right means No
vehicles allowed. Can you match the
following expressions with the road signs?*

Divieto di transito

1 *Transito vietato alle biciclette* ____
2 *Transito vietato ai pedoni* ____
3 *Senso vietato* ____
4 *Divieto di segnalazioni acustiche* ____
5 *Divieto di sorpasso* ____

ii *Here, tell the tourist what not to do when faced with the above signs. Select each expression from the box below once only and again use the* **lei** *form. Take example* **a** *as your model.*

Esempio: a Non entri!

andare in bicicletta – suonare il claxon – passare – sorpassare – entrare

4 i *In the example below ask someone where to cross. Then form similar questions on the same model.*

Esempio: *... where to cross.* **Dove devo attraversare?** *(lit: Where must I cross)*

   a *... where to park.*
   b *... where to book.*
   c *... where to pay.*
   d *... where to get off (from a bus).*

ii *Once you have checked the above, repeat the question and this time give the answer as well, using the imperative (*lei *form).*

Esempio: *... at the traffic light.* **Dove devo attraversare? Attraversi al semaforo!**

   a *... in the square.*
   b *... at the agency.*
   c *... at the cash-desk.*
   d *... at the next stop.*

5 **i** **Ora tocca a te!** *You are going to ask your host if you can do the following …*

Esempio: *…to eat this apple.* **Posso mangiare questa mela?**

   a *… to drink this wine.*

   b *… to open the window.*

   c *… to take this chair.*

   d *… to book the hotel.*

ii *First check the above are correct then play the part of your host who urges you to do so. Remember to use a pronoun in your answer.*

Esempio: **Posso mangiare questa mela? Sì! Sì! La mangi!**

◄)) CD 2, TR 12

6 *Overleaf is a plan of part of the centre of Trento, a town in the mountainous* **Dolomiti** *region of Northern Italy. You are going to hear three sets of instructions given to three different people. Each one is starting from* **Piazza Duomo**, *where the cross is, facing* **Fontana del Nettuno** *(1) the Fountain of Neptune, and is asking how to get to a different place. As you hear the directions given to each person, follow them on the map and find out where each one wants to go. (The circled numbers on the plan correspond to the names of the places listed immediately below it.)*

For your convenience the text is below and not in the Key, but before looking at it, you should try and follow the recording, listening to it two or three times if necessary.

   a *Vada verso Palazzo Cazuffi che è a sinistra e Torre Civica che è a destra. Subito dopo la torre giri a destra. Prenda la prima traversa a sinistra. Dopo pochi passi, a destra, trova la piazza che cerca.*

   b *Vada in Via Cavour. Prenda la prima strada a sinistra e continui fino all'incrocio di Via Prepositura e Via Antonio Rosmini. Il monumento che vuole è davanti a lei.*

   c *Attraversi la piazza. Dopo Torre Civica giri a destra e vada fino in fondo a Via San Vigilio. Poi giri a sinistra e continui lungo Via Santissima Trinità. In fondo alla strada c'è la chiesa che cerca.*

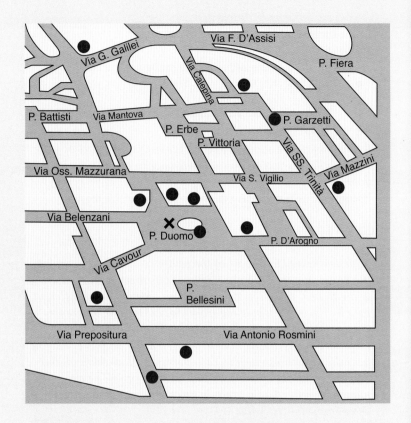

1   Fontana del Nettuno
2   Palazzo Cazuffi
3   Torre Civica
4   Porta Santa Margherita
5   Cattedrale
6   Palazzo Pretorio

7   Torre di Massarelli
8   Chiesa di Santissima Trinità
9   Palazzo Larcher-Fogazzaro
10 Zona Archeologica
11 Palazzo Firmian
12 Basilica di S. Maria Maggiore

Cultural heritage

I beni culturali *the cultural heritage* is the responsibility of a special ministry: **Il Ministero dei Beni Ambientali e Culturali**. Italians take very great pride in their monuments. The majority of them have an audioguide service (**servizio audioguida**) and it is rare to find a town which does not have some work of art or architecture to display. **Trento** is an excellent example of a historically important town.

The Post Office

La Posta (Ufficio Postale) forms part of the Italian state-owned postal system **Poste Italiane**. In recent years many of the buildings and internal layout have undergone a welcome transformation: in the most modern ones you now stand in a single queue and are directed automatically to the next free counter (**sportello**), each one of which will be able to deal with your registered mail, postal orders, stamps, foreign exchange, etc. However, you will probably be asked to go to another section if you wish to send a parcel: **Ufficio Pacchi** Parcel Office. Opening times vary but are generally 8 a.m.– 6.00 p.m. with early closing on Saturdays at about noon. As the normal mail service may still be somewhat erratic, you may choose to send your mail by **posta prioritaria** (designed to reach its destination by the following day) or, (claimed to be faster still), by **posta celere** (aiming at same day delivery within Italy itself). There is always e-mail of course, **posta elettronica**.

The website for the Italian postal service is:
http://www.poste.it

TEST YOURSELF

Match the column on the left with the appropriate continuation on the right.

1 Vorrei fare una raccomandata.

a Giri a sinistra in fondo alla strada.

2 Il 135 va al centro?

b Sì. Prenda la terza strada a destra.

3 Andiamo al cinema stasera?

c No. Si deve prendere o il 25 o il 277.

4 Hai il biglietto?

d Le compri!

5 Quando arriva il prossimo autobus?

e Fra cinque minuti.

6 Come si fa per andare alla banca?

f Sì. Ce l'ho.

7 Scusi. C'è un supermercato da queste parti?

g Arriva per sabato?

8 Venite con me!

h Dove vai?

9 Quali programmi guardi?

i Mi piacciono i documentari e le notizie.

10 Quelle scarpe mi piacciono – sono molto eleganti.

j No, andiamo al bar a prendere una birra.

15

Cos'hai fatto oggi?
What did you do today?

In this unit you will learn:
- *how to ask what someone has done or did*
- *how to ask someone to report information*
- *how to ask what (has) happened*
- *how to answer similar questions.*

---

1 Cos' hai fatto di bello?
Have you done anything interesting?

a Vero o falso? *Elena ha mangiato a casa.*
b *Elena ha bevuto il vino, il liquore o l'acqua minerale?*

CD 2, TR 13

Elena	Hai dormito fino a tardi oggi?
Fabrizio	Eh, sì, perchè stanotte ho dormito male.
Elena	Oh, mi dispiace!
Fabrizio	Ma tu, cos'hai fatto di bello?
Elena	Nel pomeriggio ho fatto una bella passeggiata e stasera ho mangiato in una rosticceria con il mio ragazzo.
Fabrizio	Avete mangiato bene?
Elena	Benissimo! Ed abbiamo bevuto una bottiglia di Barbera.

QUICK VOCAB

hai dormito? (from **dormire**) *did you sleep?*
stanotte *last night*
male *badly*
fare una passeggiata *to go for a walk*
ho mangiato (from **mangiare**) *I ate*
abbiamo bevuto (from **bere**) *we drank*

2 Cos'hai fatto oggi?
What did you do today?

A husband returns home late to find his sick wife worried but feeling better.

  a Vero o falso? *Il marito ha perso il treno.*
  b *Come sta la moglie adesso?*

CD 2, TR 13, 00:36

Moglie	Come mai così tardi? Cos'è successo?
Marito	Non è successo niente. Scusa, cara. Ho perso l'autobus. Ho dovuto aspettare venti minuti alla fermata. Tu, piuttosto, come ti senti?
Moglie	Adesso sto meglio, grazie.
Marito	Cos'hai fatto oggi?
Moglie	Ho dormito quasi tutto il giorno.

QUICK VOCAB

come mai ...? *why, how is that?*
così tardi *so late*
Cos'è successo? (from **succedere**) *What's happened?*
ho perso (from **perdere**) *I missed*
Come ti senti? *How do you feel?*
sto meglio *I'm better*
quasi *almost*

3 Che cosa ti ha detto?
What did he tell you?

She tells her husband what the doctor said: she needs a rest.

a **Vero o falso?** *La moglie ha chiamato il medico.*
b *Il medico ha visitato il marito?*

Marito	Hai visto il medico?
Moglie	Sì. L'ho chiamato stamattina.
Marito	E che cosa ti ha detto?
Moglie	Ha detto che ho bisogno soltanto di un po' di riposo. Nulla di grave.
Marito	Meno male! Ti ha dato delle medicine?
Moglie	No. Non mi ha dato niente.

CD 2, TR 13, 01:13

QUICK VOCAB

Hai visto (from vedere) il medico? *Did you see the doctor?*
l'ho chiamato (from chiamare) *I called him*
stamattina *this morning*
ho bisogno ... di *I need*
soltanto *only*
nulla di grave *nothing serious*
Ti ha dato ...? *Did he give you ...?*
meno male! *thank goodness!*

Grammar

1 PERFECT TENSE

In Italian the perfect tense is used to express something that happened or has happened in the past. It is formed by using the present tense of **essere** or **avere** + past participle. In this unit we shall deal with those verbs which form their perfect tense with **avere**. These constitute most verbs in Italian.

To form the past participle of regular verbs, change the infinitive endings as follows:

Infinitive			Infinitive	Past participle	
parl-**are**	*into*	**-ato**:	**parlare**	**parlato**	*spoken*
v<u>e</u>nd-**ere**	*into*	**-uto**:	**vendere**	**venduto**	*sold*
fin-**ire**	*into*	**-ito**:	**finire**	**finito**	*finished*

Ho parlato $\left\{ \begin{array}{l} I\ spoke \\ I\ have\ spoken \end{array} \right.$ **Ho venduto** $\left\{ \begin{array}{l} I\ sold \\ I\ have\ finished \end{array} \right.$

Ho finito $\left\{ \begin{array}{l} I\ finished \\ I\ have\ sold \end{array} \right.$

Note in the table below that the last vowel of the past participle does not change: **ho parlato** *I spoke/I have spoken*, **ho dormito** *I slept/I have slept*, **abbiamo parlato** *we spoke/we have spoken*, **abbiamo dormito** *we slept/we have slept*.

Perfect tense **parl-are** *to speak*			
(io)	**ho**	**parlato**	*I spoke, I have spoken*
(tu)	**hai**	**parlato**	*you spoke, you have spoken*
(lei)	**ha**	**parlato**	*you* (form), *spoke, you have spoken*
(lui, lei)	**ha**	**parlato**	*he/she spoke, he/she has spoken*
(noi)	**abbiamo**	**parlato**	*we spoke, we have spoken*
(voi)	**avete**	**parlato**	*you spoke, you have spoken*
(loro)	**hanno**	**parlato**	*they spoke, they have spoken*

Perfect tense **v<u>e</u>nd-ere** to sell			
(io)	ho	vend**uto**	*I sold, I have sold*
(tu)	hai	vend**uto**	*you sold, you have sold*
(lei)	ha	vend**uto**	*you* (form) *sold, you have sold*
(lui, lei)	ha	vend**uto**	*he/she sold, he/she has sold*
(noi)	abbiamo	vend**uto**	*we sold, we have sold*
(voi)	avete	vend**uto**	*you sold, you have sold*
(loro)	hanno	vend**uto**	*they sold, they have sold*

Perfect tense **fin-ire** to finish			
(io)	ho	fin**ito**	*I finished, I have finished*
(tu)	hai	fin**ito**	*you finished, you have finished*
(lei)	ha	fin**ito**	*you* (form) *finished, you have finished*
(lui, lei)	ha	fin**ito**	*he/she finished, he/she has finished*
(noi)	abbiamo	fin**ito**	*we finished, we have finished*
(voi)	avete	fin**ito**	*you finished, you have finished*
(loro)	hanno	fin**ito**	*they finished, they have finished*

Insight

Attenzione! Whereas in English we can say *I spoke, I have spoken, I did speak*, in Italian you must use the present tense of **avere** + past participle and say **ho parlato, hai parlato, ecc.** – that is, you must say *I have spoken, I have eaten* and not *I spoke, I ate*, etc.

Hai venduto la m<u>a</u>cchina?	*Did you sell/have you sold your car?*
Non ho potuto venire.	*I couldn't/I haven't been able to come.*
Ho dovuto lavorare.	*I had to/I've had to work.*
Ho venduto la casa.	*I sold/I have sold the house.*

Irregular past participles

Here is a list of some of those most frequently used:

Infinitive		Past participle		Infinitive	Past participle		
accendere	to light	acceso	lit	mettere	to put	messo	put
aprire	to open	aperto	opened	perdere	to lose, miss	perso	lost
bere	to drink	bevuto	drunk	prendere	to take	preso	taken
chiedere	to ask	chiesto	asked	rispondere	to reply	risposto	replied
chiudere	to close	chiuso	closed	rompere	to break	rotto	broken
dire	to say, tell	detto	said, told	scrivere	to write	scritto	written
fare	to do, make	fatto	made, done	togliere	to take off	tolto	taken off
leggere	to read	letto	read	vedere	to see	visto	seen

Cos'ha detto?	*What did you say?*
Ho visto Mirella.	*I saw Mirella.*

Initially, your most important task is to be able to recognize some of these past participles. When you need to use any of them, consult the table above.

2 CON IL MIO RAGAZZO *WITH MY BOYFRIEND*

Notice that **ragazzo**, apart from meaning *boy*, means *boyfriend*. Similarly, **la mia ragazza** is *my girlfriend*.

3 AVER BISOGNO DI *TO NEED*

Need or necessity is expressed by **aver bisogno di** (lit: *to have need of*):

Ho bisogno soltanto di un po' di riposo.	*I only need a bit of rest.*

Siamo contenti così. Non abbiamo bisogno di niente.
We are happy as we are. We don't need anything.

4 THE PERFECT TENSE WITH SOME EXPRESSIONS OF TIME

You will find the expressions below useful when you are talking about the past:

	ieri l'altro ieri*	mattina pomeriggio sera		yesterday the day before yesterday	morning afternoon evening
L'ho visto	la settimana scorsa il mese scorso l'anno scorso		I saw him	last week last month last year	
	molto tempo poco tempo pochi giorni alcune settimane cinque minuti	fa		a long time a short while a few days some weeks five minutes	ago

* It is possible to say **l'altro ieri mattina/pomeriggio/sera** for *the day before yesterday in the/morning/afternoon/evening*.

5 STANOTTE *LAST NIGHT/TONIGHT*

This word means *last night* or *tonight*, depending on the context. If the verb is in the past **stanotte** must be *last night*:

Stanotte non ho chiuso occhio. *Last night I didn't sleep a wink.*

6 OBJECT PRONOUNS

Mi, **ti**, **ci**, **vi** are also object pronouns. Besides meaning *myself*, *yourself*, etc. (see Reflexive verbs, Unit 13, Section 1), they mean *me*, *you*, *us*, and usually precede the verb:

Ida non	mi ti ci vi	capisce	Ida doesn't understand	me. you (inf). us. you (pl).

When object pronouns precede the verb they are called **unstressed** pronouns:

Non *mi* ha dato niente.   *He hasn't given me anything.*

When pronouns are used with prepositions (***con** me, **da** te, ecc.*) they are called **stressed** pronouns.

7 EXPRESSIONS WITH STARE

Expressions with **stare** describing one's state of health:

Come sta? (Sto) bene/ male/   *How are you? I'm well/ ill/better/*
meglio/peggio.   *worse.*

The present tense of **stare** is exactly like that of **dare** (Unit 8, Section 3):

sto   stai   sta   stiamo   state   stanno

Insight

Attenzione! **stare in piedi** *to stand* but **andare a piedi** *to walk* (see Unit 5, Section 8).

8 CHE THAT, WHICH, WHO, WHOM

In English *that/which/who/whom* can sometimes be omitted. In Italian **che** must always be expressed:

Questo è il libro che devo comprare.	*This is the book (that) I have to buy.*
So che non è vero.	*I know (that) it isn't true.*
La ragazza che inviti è fidanzata.	*The girl (whom) you're inviting is engaged.*
Mi ha detto che è disoccupato.	*He told me (that) he is unemployed.*

___

Come si dice?
How do you say it?

◆) **CD 2, TR 14**

1 *How to ask someone what they have done or did (inf)*

How to say what you have done or did

Cos'hai fatto? Ho dormito, ho mangiato, ho bevuto, ho fatto una passeggiata, ecc.

2 *How to ask someone to report information (inf)*

Cosa ti ha detto?

How to give the information

(Mi) ha detto che …

3 *How to ask about what someone gave/has given you (inf)*

Cosa ti ha dato?

How to say what they gave you

Mi ha dato …

4 *How to ask what (has) happened*

Cos'è successo?

Practice

◀)) CD 2, TR 15

1 A, B, C *and* D *are saying how they spent their evening. Can you fill in the gaps by listening to their accounts? (If you do not have the recording, you will find the verbs you need, jumbled up in the box below.)*

A Ho __ alla lettera di mio fratello che vive in America ed __ in ordine la mia camera.

B __ degli amici a casa. __ insieme, poi abbiamo __ tutta la notte.

C Io e il mio ragazzo __ un programma molto interessante in televisione.

D Mio cugino mi __ da Milano. __ un'ora al telefono a parlare con lui e con mio nipote.

··

abbiamo visto - ho passato - ha chiamato - abbiamo bevuto - risposto - ho messo - ho invitato - giocato a bridge

··

2 *Match the words on the right with those on the left:*

i	Hai letto	**a**	la telefonata?
ii	Ho dormito	**b**	un sacco di soldi.
iii	Hai risposto	**c**	il gas?
iv	Hai fatto	**d**	molto bene.
v	Ho rotto	**e**	alle sue domande?
vi	Hai spento	**f**	il giornale?
vii	Ho speso (I spent)	**g**	il bicchiere.

3 *In the following sentences fill the blanks, choosing between* **mi** *and* **ti** *according to the sense. Be careful to distinguish between verbs in the first person, and those in the second person (informal).*

a Dove sei? Non __ vedo.

b Cosa dici? Non __ sento.

c Scusa, chi sei? Non __ conosco.

d Sono qui. Non __ vedi?

e Come? Non __ capisco.

f Quando __ inviti a cena?

g Allora, __ accompagni?

h Va bene. __ aspetto davanti al teatro.

◄ CD 2, TR 15, 00:52

4 *Below are extracts from postcards you have received from friends in Italy. Tell someone you know what each of them has been doing. For instance, a would start:* **Vitt*o*ria ha …**

a

... Ieri ho visto il
Papa in Piazza San
Pietro ...
Saluti da Roma
Vittoria

b

Firenze
...Ho comprato una
villa fra Siena e
Firenze ...
Un caro saluto
Gino

c

Viareggio
... Finalmente ho
aperto un'agenzia
immobiliare! ...
Quando vieni in
Italia?
Ti aspetto!
Roberto

d

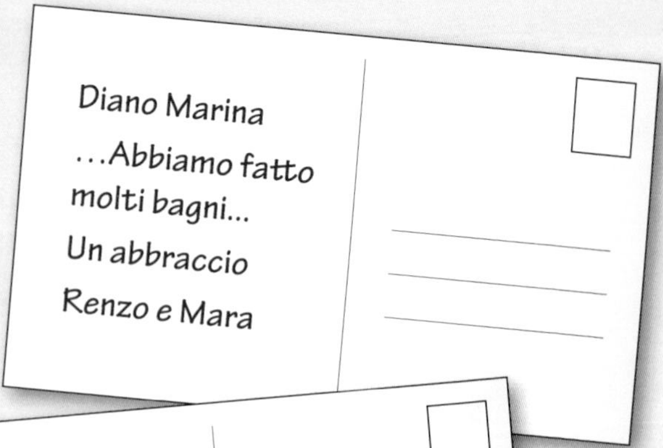

Diano Marina
...Abbiamo fatto
molti bagni...
Un abbraccio
Renzo e Mara

e

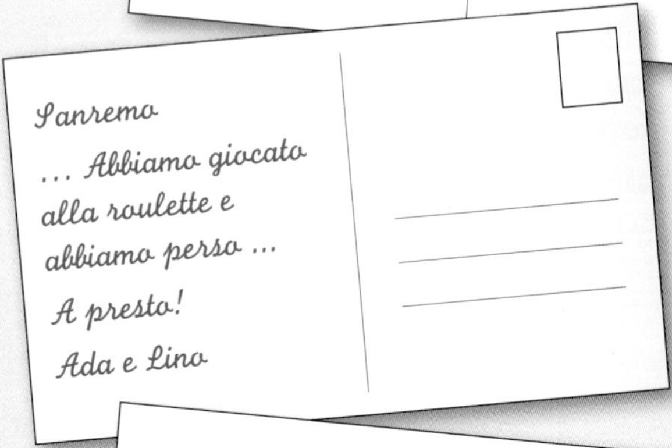

Sanremo
... Abbiamo giocato
alla roulette e
abbiamo perso ...
A presto!
Ada e Lino

f

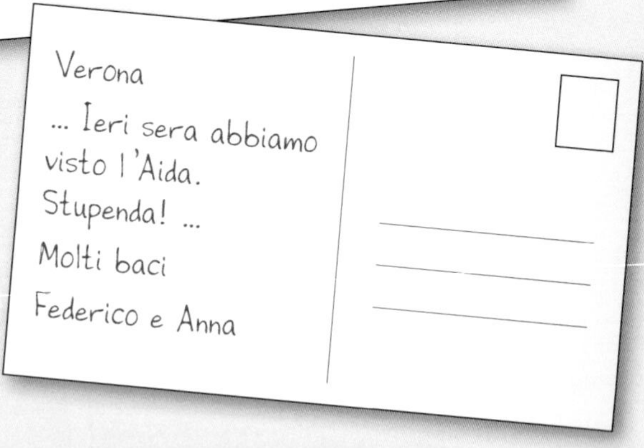

Verona
... Ieri sera abbiamo
visto l'Aida.
Stupenda! ...
Molti baci
Federico e Anna

5 *Ora tocca a te!* Write your own card from Bari:
   'I've seen so many interesting things. Greetings from Bari.'
6 Below you will see what **Mara** decided to do last Monday.
   However, she only managed to do the things that are ticked.
   A cross means that she never got round to doing them. Say in
   Italian what she did and didn't do.

a *pranzare dai suoi genitori* ✔

b *chiamare l'elettricista* ✗

c *guardare il programma 'TV 7 Speciale'* ✔

d *pulire la casa* ✗

e *pagare l'affitto* ✗

f *giocare a tennis con Marco* ✔

g *portare la macchina dal meccanico* ✔

h *scrivere una cartolina a sua zia Maria* ✔

7 *Ora tocca a te!*

You	*Did you do anything interesting today?*	
Olga	Ho lavorato tutto il giorno.	
You	*Didn't you see your boyfriend?*	
Olga	Sì. All'ora di pranzo.	
You	*Did you eat together?*	
Olga	Sì. In una elegante trattoria in Via Manzoni.	
You	*So why aren't you happy?*	
Olga	Perchè ho dovuto pagare io per il pranzo.	

CD 2, TR 15, 01:56

Postcards

When Italians send **cartoline** *postcards* they usually write two or three words only, or simply a greeting, some examples of which are given here: **Affettuosi saluti - Un caro pensiero - Un forte abbraccio - Un bacione**. They are most unlikely to mention the weather.

Regional autonomy and the Northern League

Italy is still a relatively young nation: before 1861 the country consisted of independent states, each dominated by a single regional town. Venice, Florence, Naples and Rome not only had their own governments, but their own languages or dialects too. This has produced a country where even now many feel much greater loyalty to their own particular region than to the nation as a whole. The Northern League, a political party based in the area around Venice, has been able to capitalize on this by disputing the supremacy of Rome. Their aim has been to produce a nation where each region has much more autonomy, the argument being that the highly productive North should no longer subsidize the relatively underdeveloped South. The Prime Minister and leader of the right, **Silvio Berlusconi**, was able to capitalize on this sentiment by enlisting the support of the Northern League in his right wing coalition, and promising a referendum on devolution in return. This took place in 2006, but as the majority of Italians voted against the proposal, central government is set to be firmly in control for the foreseeable future.

Wines

Barbera is a dry red wine from the Piedmont and Lombardy regions in Northern Italy. Other reds include **Bardolino** and **Valpolicella** from the **Veneto** region, and Chianti from Tuscany. **Frascati** from Rome, **Soave** from Veneto and **Orvieto** from **Umbria** are among the better-known white wines. It should be borne in mind that wine, which is relatively cheap and plentiful in Italy, and bread, are essential components of any family meal.

TEST YOURSELF

Fill in the gaps using the words in the box below once only.

1 *Oggi, alla galleria d'arte moderna, ho visto una bella __.*

2 *Lui ha __ perso il treno.*

3 *Vai al ristorante con la __ ragazza?*

4 *Avete bisogno __ qualcosa?*

5 *Ho visto tua moglie pochi giorni __.*

6 *Stasera ho cucinato per i __ amici.*

7 *Mi ha __ che ha comprato una nuova casa.*

8 *Ti ha __ il suo libro?*

9 *(Lei) __ telefonato al medico?*

10 __ *ha visto il medico.*

....

ieri - fa - miei - mostra (*exhibition*) - dato - detto - ha - di - quasi - tua

....

16

....

Le piace viaggiare?

Do you like travelling?

In this unit you will learn:
* *how to ask someone where they have been*
* *how to ask someone whether they have (ever) been to …*
* *how to say where you have lived, worked and were born*
* *how to say how long ago*
* *how to say how long you have been doing something.*

---

1 Quando è venuto in Inghilterra?

When did you come to England?

An interview with an Italian immigrant who came to England 25 years ago.

  a Vero o falso? *L'immigrato ha lavorato prima a Londra.*
  b *Dov'è andato ad abitare dopo tre anni?*

Giornalista	Quando è venuto in Inghilterra?
Immigrato	Venticinque anni fa.
Giornalista	È vissuto sempre a Londra?
Immigrato	No. Quando sono arrivato, sono andato a lavorare a Bedford.
Giornalista	Si trova bene in Inghilterra?
Immigrato	Abbastanza bene. Ma ogni tanto sento la nostalgia dell'Italia.
Giornalista	Quanto tempo è rimasto a Bedford?
Immigrato	Tre anni. Dopo sono venuto ad abitare a Londra.

QUICK VOCAB

È vissuto ...? (from **vivere**) *Have you lived ...?*
trovarsi bene *to be happy*
abbastanza *fairly*
ogni tanto *every now and then*
sento la nostalgia *I feel homesick*
è rimasto ...? (from **rimanere irr**) *did you stay ...?*

2 Le è piaciuta l'Italia?
Did she like Italy?

The immigrant is asked whether he has ever returned to his birthplace.

a **Vero o falso?** *L'immigrato è tornato in Italia molte volte.*
b *Dove spera di ritornare con sua moglie?*

Giornalista	È mai tornato nel suo paese nativo?
Immigrato	Sì. Ci sono tornato con mia moglie molte volte.
Giornalista	Sua moglie è italiana?
Immigrato	È di origine italiana, ma è nata a Liverpool.
Giornalista	Le è piaciuta l'Italia?
Immigrato	Sì. Le è piaciuta molto. Infatti speriamo di ritornarci quest'anno.

paese nativo *birthplace*
sperare di *to hope to*

---

3 Incontro in Sicilia
Meeting in Sicily

Sandro is surprised to meet his friend **Marcello** in Sicily.

  a **Vero o falso?** *Sandro è in Sicilia da una settimana.*
  b *Con quale treno è partito Marcello?*

Sandro	Chi si vede! Che sorpresa!
Marcello	Ciao, Sandro! Da quanto tempo sei qui?
Sandro	Da una settimana. E tu?
Marcello	Sono appena arrivato. Sono partito stamattina col treno delle 10.40 (dieci e quaranta) e sono arrivato un'ora fa.
Sandro	È la prima volta che vieni in Sicilia?
Marcello	No. Ci sono venuto nel '97.
Sandro	Ti piace di più Agrigento o Siracusa?
Marcello	Non sono mai stato nè ad Agrigento, nè a Siracusa.

Chi si vede! *Look who's here!*
Da quanto tempo sei qui? *How long have you been here?*
non sono mai stato nè ... nè ... *I've never been either to ... or ...*

---

4 Sei mai stato in Sardegna?
Have you ever been to Sardinia?

Sandro wants to offer **Marcello** a coffee but his friend has to dash off.

  a **Vero o falso?** *Marcello non è mai stato in Sardegna.*
  b *Perchè Marcello non accetta il caffè?*

Sandro	… E la Sardegna? Sei mai stato in Sardegna?
Marcello	Purtroppo no. Lo so che c'è tanto da vedere anche lì.
Sandro	Posso offrirti un caffè?
Marcello	No, grazie. Devo scappare.
Sandro	Così presto?
Marcello	Purtroppo sì. Mi dispiace.
Sandro	Allora ti accompagno.

QUICK VOCAB

purtroppo *unfortunately*
tanto da vedere *so much to see*
così presto *so soon*
accompagnare *to accompany*

Grammar

1 PERFECT TENSE (CONTINUED FROM UNIT 15, SECTION 1)

In this unit we shall deal with those verbs that form their perfect tense with essere. Use the present of essere (**sono, sei, è, siamo, siete, sono**) + the past participle which is treated as an adjective and must therefore agree with the subject.

Sono tornato.	*I have returned (ms).*
Sono tornata.	*I have returned (fs).*
Siamo tornati.	*We have returned (mpl).*
Siamo tornate.	*We have returned (fpl).*
Roberto è andato in Italia.	*Robert went/has gone to Italy.*
Lucia è andata negli Stati Uniti.	*Lucia went/has gone to the United States.*
I signori Cortese *sono* andati all'estero.	*Mr and Mrs Cortese went/have gone abroad.*
Le ragazze *sono* andate a scuola.	*The girls went/have gone to school.*

Ida non è and_ata_ in Germ_a_nia.   *Ida did not go/has not gone to Germany.*

Perfect tense __essere__ *to be*		
(io)	**sono stato/stata**	*I have been*
(tu)	**sei stato/stata**	*you have been*
(lui, lei)	**è stato/stata**	*he/she has, you have been*
(noi)	**siamo stati/state**	*we have been*
(voi)	**siete stati/state**	*you have been*
(loro)	**sono stati/state**	*they have been*

The past participle of __essere__ *to be* is **stato**.

Note that the past participles of **stare** and __essere__ are the same: **stato**.

The most common verbs which form their perfect tense with __essere__ are listed below:

Regular			
andare	*to go*	**sono andato/a**	*I went, I have been*
arrivare	*to arrive*	**sono arrivato/a**	*I arrived, I have arrived*
entrare	*to enter*	**sono entrato/a**	*I entered, I have entered*
partire	*to leave*	**sono partito/a**	*I left, I have left*
tornare	*to return*	**sono tornato/a**	*I returned, I have returned*
uscire	*to go out*	**sono uscito/a**	*I went out, I have gone out*
Irregular			
__essere__	*to be*	**sono stato/a**	*I have been*
n_a_scere	*to be born*	**sono nato/a**	*I was born*
rimanere	*to stay/ remain*	**sono rimasto/a**	*I (have) stayed/ remained*
venire	*to come*	**sono venuto/a**	*I came, I have come*
v_i_vere*	*to live*	**sono vissuto/a**	*I live, I have lived*

* **V_i_vere** also forms the perfect tense with **avere: ho vissuto.**

In future units, other verbs forming the perfect tense with **essere** will be shown with an asterisk as follows: **salire*** *to go up, to get on* (a bus, train, etc.)

Remember that when you have a masculine and feminine noun together (**Ugo e Maria**) the past participle must be **masculine plural**:

Ugo e Maria *sono* andat*i* al cinema.	*Hugh and Mary went/have gone to the cinema.*

2 ... FA ... *AGO*

Fa expresses the idea of *ago* in English.

Il treno è partito cinque minuti *fa*.	*The train left five minutes ago.*
Siamo arrivati un'ora *fa*.	*We arrived an hour ago.*

3 CI *HERE/THERE/US*

Ci can mean *here, there, us*. The context will make it clear. It behaves like an unstressed pronoun: it comes before the verb or is attached to an infinitive. **Ci + è** is normally contracted to **c'è** (see Unit 6).

È mai stato a Firenze?	*Have you ever been to Florence?*
Sì. Ci sono stato diverse volte.	*Yes, I've been there several times.*
C'è stato il mese scorso.	*He was there last month.*
Spero di andarci l'anno prossimo.	*I hope to go there next year.*

4 È NATA A ... *SHE WAS BORN IN ...*

When someone asks you where you were born, remember to answer with the present tense of **essere**: **Sono nato/a** *I was born* (see Unit 5, Section 10).

5 LE È PIACIUTA L'ITALIA? *DID SHE LIKE ITALY?*

Note that **piacere***, when used impersonally (third person only),
also forms its perfect with **essere** and behaves like an adjective:

Le è piaciuto lo spettacolo?	*Did you like the show?*
Le è piaciuta la mostra?	*Did you like the exhibition?*
Le sono piaciuti i quadri?	*Did you like the pictures (i.e. paintings)?*
No. Non mi sono piaciuti.	*No, I didn't like them.*

6 SPERARE DI + INFINITIVE *TO HOPE TO*

To hope to is expressed by **sperare di + infinitive** in Italian:

Spero di **rivederla al più presto.**	*I hope to see you again as soon as possible.*

7 *USE OF* DA QUANTO TEMPO

Da quanto tempo requires the present tense when the activity
continues into the present; **da** is also required in the answer:

Da quanto tempo *conosci* Marco?	*How long have you known Mark?*
Lo *conosco da* un anno.	*I have known him for a year.*
Da quanto tempo *studia* l'italiano?	*How long have you been studying Italian?*
***Studio* l'italiano *da* tre mesi.**	*I've been studying Italian for three months.*

See also Unit 19, Section 4.

8 *EXPRESSING THE YEAR:* NEL '98 *IN 1998*

In + definite article is used because **anno** *year* is understood. The
'19' is often omitted in speech. But notice **nel 2003** (**duemilatrè**).

9 TI PIACE DI PIÙ ...? *DO YOU PREFER ...?*

Piacere di più can be used instead of **preferire. Di più** (*more* or *most*) is at the end of a phrase instead of **più:**

La musica classica *mi piace di più*.	*I like classical music more.*
È quello che lavora *di più*.	*He is the one who works most.*

10 NÈ ... NÈ *(N)EITHER ... (N)OR*

Note that this expression, like the ones in Unit 7, Section 9, requires the double negative, unless **nè** comes at the beginning of the sentence:

Non vado *nè* a Firenze *nè* a Roma.	*I'm not going either to Florence or Rome.*
Non conosco *nè* lui *nè* lei.	*I know neither him nor her.*
Nè Carlo *nè* Pietro vanno all'università.	*Neither Charles nor Peter goes to university.*

In the last example note that Italian requires a verb in the plural.

11 LO SO ... *I KNOW ...*

Lo is used with **sapere** even when there is no definite object:

Dov'è Carlo? Non *lo so*.	*Where's Carlo? I don't know.*
Sai il mio indirizzo? Sì. *Lo so*.	*Do you know my address? Yes. I do (know it).*
Come *lo sai*?	*How do you know?*

12 CON + ARTICLE

Col = con + il. Coi = con + i. These contractions are optional:

| **Vado a Firenze *col/con il* direttore.** | *I'm going to Florence with the director.* |
| **P<u>a</u>rlano *coi/con i* ragazzi.** | *They are speaking to the boys.* |

Con + article may be used with means of transport instead of in (Unit 5, Section 8):

| **Ci vado *col/con il treno/con la* metropolitana.** | *I'm going there by train/by tube.* |

Come si dice? *How do you say it?*

◄ CD 2, TR 17

1	*How to ask someone where they have been*	**Dov'è stato/stata?**
2	*How to ask someone whether they have (ever) been to … and say where you have been*	**È (mai) stato/a … in Sardegna? … a Roma? Sono stato/a in …/ a …**
3	*How to say where you (have) lived …*	**Ho vissuto/Sono vissuto/a**
4	*How to say where you were born*	**Sono nato/a …**
5	*How to say how long ago something happened*	**È successo due/dieci/venti anni fa**
6	*How to say how long you have been (here)* *How to say how long you have been waiting*	**Sono (qui) da cinque minuti/da un'ora, ecc.** **Aspetto da mezz'ora, ecc.**
7	*How to say you liked something very much*	**Mi è piaciuto/a molt<u>i</u>ssimo.**

Practice

1 *In the left-hand column on the next page you will see what* **Alberto** *generally does every day of the week (see Unit 7, Section 4). Say what he did on that particular day last week, using the words in the right-hand column.*
Es**e**mpio: (Generalmente) il lunedì va al c**i**nema.
(Ma) lunedì scorso è andato a teatro.

Generalmente	La settimana scorsa
a *Il lunedì va al c**i**nema.*	*a teatro*
b *Il martedì cena presto.*	*tardi*
c *Il mercoledì st**u**dia molto.*	*affatto*
d *Il giovedì lavora fino alle sei.*	*dieci*
e *Il venerdì m**a**ngia a casa.*	*fuori*
f *Il s**a**bato gioca a carte.*	*scacchi (chess)*
g *La dom**e**nica dorme fino alle dieci.*	*mezzogiorno*

2 *Imagine you are* **Alberto** *and say what you did last week on Monday, Thursday and Sunday.*

3 *Write about the people in columns* **b, c, d** *and* **e**, *using* **Pietro Rossi** *in column* **a** *as your model.*

a	b	c	d	e
Pietro Rossi	**Paolo Nuzzo**	**Mirella Perrone**	**I signori Caraffi**	**Anna e Silvia**
È nato nel '70.	'79	'67	'68	'71
È stato in Am**e**rica	**A**ustria	Fr**a**ncia	Spagna	Gr**e**cia
per dieci anni.	2	1	12	6
È andato a Boston.	Vienna	Parigi	Barcellona	Atene
Poi è tornato in It**a**lia.	It**a**lia	Sic**i**lia	Sardegna	Roma

4 *Read this passage carefully and answer the questions on it as though you were* **Anna**, *using* **ci** *in every reply. Use the same verbs as in the questions.*
Es**e**mpio: **a** È mai stata all'**e**stero?
          Sì. Ci sono stata molte volte.
*Anna è stata all'**e**stero molte volte. In aprile è andata in It**a**lia*

266

con Marcello. È ritornata a Pisa nel mese di agosto. Poi è
andata a Firenze in macchina con la sua amica Francesca.

   a *È mai stata all'estero?*
   b *Quando è andata in Italia con Marcello?*
   c *Quando è ritornata a Pisa?*
   d *Com'è andata a Firenze?*
   e *C'è andata con sua sorella?*

5 Answer the following questions, using the appropriate
pronouns and the period of time in brackets, as in the
example.
Esempio: Da quanto tempo Lucia aspetta l'autobus? (5 minuti)
L'aspetta da cinque minuti.

   a *Da quanto tempo Sandro non vede sua sorella?*   *(2 anni)*
   b *Da quanto tempo Marcello conosce Sandra?*   *(molti*
     anni)
   c *Da quanto tempo suona il violino Francesca?*   *(9 anni)*
   d *Da quanto tempo Mirella studia l'italiano?*   *(6 mesi)*
   e *Da quanto tempo non vedono Roberto?*   *(molto tempo)*
   f *Da quanto tempo Anna e Roberto aspettano*
     il treno?   *(poco tempo)*

6 Make a statement from the two sentences given, using **fa**, as in
the example.
**Esempio: Sono le dieci. Sandro è andato in banca all nove e un
quarto.**
Sandro è andato in banca tre quarti d'ora fa.

   a *Sono le undici. Mara è andata a fare la spesa alle nove.*
   b *È l'una. Sergio è venuto a pranzo a mezzogiorno.*
   c *Sono le sette e mezza. Mario è tornato dal lavoro alle sei.*
   d *Sono le undici e mezza. Carlo è andato a letto alle undici.*
   e *Sono le cinque e mezza. Filippo è uscito alle cinque e*
     venticinque.

7 *Ora tocca a te!*

*You are being interviewed by a journalist who is asking you
where you have been and what you have done in Italy.*

Giornalista	Va mai in Italia?
You	*Yes, I go there almost every year.*
Giornalista	Dov'è stato l'anno scorso?
You	*I went to Venice and Verona.*
Giornalista	È rimasto molto tempo a Verona?
You	*Two evenings. For the opera.*
Giornalista	È andato con amici?
You	*No. I prefer to travel alone.*
Giornalista	Ma parla benissimo! Sono italiani i suoi genitori?
You	*Yes. And … I studied Italian at university.*
Giornalista	Dove? In Italia?
You	*First in Italy, then at the University of London.*
Giornalista	Quanto tempo fa?
You	*Two years ago.*

8 *In che parte d'Italia si trovano Agrigento, Palermo, Taormina e Siracusa?*

Paese

Italians refer to the place they came from as **il mio paese**.
Generally speaking, **paese** means *village* or *small town* and
has no exact equivalent in English. **Il mio paese nativo** or
natale would be my *native village* or *my birthplace*. **Paese**
may also mean country, but in this case it is often written
with a capital 'P': **L'Italia è un bel Paese**. *Italy is a beautiful
country.*

Emigration and immigration in Italy

Since the unification of Italy in the mid-nineteenth century
right up to the present day, around 28 million have emigrated
from its shores. Even as late as the 1980s, a series of
earthquakes in the **Campania** region led to many Italians
abandoning their homes in search of a new life overseas.
However, the equally disastrous 2009 earthquake in the
Abruzzo region east of Rome found the Italian government
far better prepared, and the prevailing trend has gradually
been reversed over the last quarter of a century, so that it
is now estimated that the immigrant population numbers
almost 3 million. A glance at Italy's coastline will show
how exposed it is to the sea, especially from North Africa
via Sicily and the small islands surrounding it. One such
refuge, the tiny island of **Lampedusa**, has become a reception
centre (**centro di accoglienza**) for emigrants from the coast
of North Africa who risk their lives in thousands hoping to
build a new life in Italy. Albanians, Rumanians and others
from the Balkans also flock to Italy via the Northern route to
provide much needed labour in the large industrial cities of
Lombardy and Piedmont.

Although a good deal of the child and drug-trafficking has
been attributed to this influx of refugees, it must be stressed
that much of Italy's light industry and agriculture depends on
immigrant labour that has settled in Italy through perfectly
legal means. Regular amnesties give ample opportunity for
those already in work to benefit from the rights of Italian

citizenship. The problem lies with an unknown number of **clandestini** (*illegal immigrants*).

A more recent trend, headlined in the magazine *Panorama* as **I clandestini piovono dal cielo** *Illegal immigrants pour down from the sky*, describes how many of them now enter the country by plane, posing as bona fide tourists, then disappearing for ever from official control.

The following web page gives you a list of local web servers on a sensitive map of Italy:
http://www.cilea.it/www-map/nir-map.html

TEST YOURSELF

Try to translate the following sentences into Italian.

1 *How long have you lived in Rome?*

2 *I would like to work in Milan for a year.*

3 *I was born in London but I have lived in Italy for 15 years.*

4 *It's my first time in Berlin.*

5 *Unfortunately I have to leave tomorrow.*

6 *They have been to the United States three times.*

7 *They left two hours ago.*

8 *I hope to see you again next year.*

9 *In 2002 I went to Germany.*

10 *Neither Alessandro nor Maria have read that book.*

17

Tante cose da fare!
So many things to do!

In this unit you will learn:

* *how to say that you have already done something*
* *how to say that you have not yet done it*
* *how to ask someone how much they paid for something*
* *how to say how much you paid for something*
* *how to say where you have put it.*

---

1 Quando vai a fare la spesa?
When are you going to do the shopping?

A mother asks her daughter whether she has bought everything.

  a **Vero o falso?** *Marisa è andata al supermercato con la mamma.*
  b *Dove ha messo il pesce Marisa?*

Mamma	Quando vai a fare la spesa, Marisa?
Marisa	L'ho già fatta, mamma! Sono andata al supermercato con Valeria.
Mamma	Hai preso tutto?
Marisa	Sì. Pane, burro, latte, uova, biscotti ...
Mamma	Ma, hai comprato il pesce per stasera?
Marisa	Sì. L'ho comprato. Ne ho preso mezzo chilo.
Mamma	E dove l'hai messo? Non lo vedo.
Marisa	L'ho messo in frigorifero con l'altra roba.
Mamma	Ah brava, Marisa! Grazie.

QUICK VOCAB

l'ho già fatta (from **fare**) *I've already done it*
l'ho messo (from **mettere**) *I put it*
hai preso ...? (from **prendere**) *did you get ...?*
bravo/a! *well done!*

2 Il regalo per Sandro, l'avete *preso?*
Have you got Sandro's present?

◄) **CD 2, TR 19, 00:43**

Insight

Note that for emphasis, Italians often say both the noun and the pronoun in the same sentence: **Il regalo per Sandro, l'avete preso?**

Franco asks **Sonia** and **Daniele** whether they have done everything that needed doing.

a **Vero o falso?** *Daniele e Sonia hanno comprato un portafoglio per Sandro.*
b *Perchè non hanno prenotato i posti per il concerto?*

274

Franco	Avete comprato le cartoline?
Sonia	Sì. Le abbiamo pure scritte.
Franco	Quante ne avete comprate?
Daniele	Dodici. Ne abbiamo mandata una anche alla vicina di casa.
Franco	Il regalo per Sandro, l'avete preso?
Sonia	Sì. Gli abbiamo comprato una cravatta di seta pura. Eccola qua! Ti piace?
Franco	È veramente elegante! Quanto l'avete pagata?
Daniele	Parecchio.
Franco	I posti per il concerto di domani sera, li avete prenotati?
Sonia	No. Non li abbiamo ancora prenotati. Non abbiamo avuto tempo.

pure *also, as well*
mandare *send*
vicina di casa *neighbour*
gli abbiamo comprato *we have bought (for) him*
parecchio *quite a lot*
prenotare *to book*
non … ancora *not yet*

3 L'ho spento
I've turned it off

🔊 **CD 2, TR 19, 01:32**

Adriano discovers that **Cesare** has pulled the plug out …

a **Vero o falso?** *Cesare ha spento il lettore.*
b *Che cos'ha fatto Cesare per spegnere il lettore?*

oddio! *oh dear!*
Hai rotto (from **rompere**) **il lettore (dvd)?** *Have you broken the DVD player?*
Ho tolto* (from **togliere irr**) **la spina** *I pulled the plug out*
aspirapolvere (m) *vacuum cleaner*
L'ho spento (from **spegnere irr**) *I've turned it off*

*You will also hear **staccare la spina** for **to pull the plug out**

Grammar

1 AGREEMENT OF THE PAST PARTICIPLE

When the perfect tense is formed with **avere,** and is preceded by **lo, la, li, le, l'** (direct object pronouns) or **ne,** the past participle must change its final vowel to agree with them.

Avete comprato *le* cartoline? *Have you bought the postcards?*
Sì. *Le* abbiamo pure scritte. *Yes, we have written them as well.*
… e *ne* abbiamo mandata una … *… and we've sent one …*

As we have seen, **lo** and **la** (i.e. singular only) normally become **l'** before a vowel or 'h' (Unit 8, Section 5). **L'** can therefore be masculine or feminine and in the perfect tense you can tell which it is by the ending of the past participle:

Lo + ho becomes **l'ho. Lo ho letto** therefore becomes **L'ho letto** *I have read it.*

La ho letta therefore becomes **L'ho letta** *I have read it.*

Ha letto il libro? *Have you read the book?/Did you read the book?*

Sì. **L'ho** letto.	*Yes, I've read it/Yes, I read it.*	
Ha letto *la* rivista?	*Have you read the magazine/Did you read the magazine?*	
Sì. **L'ho** letta.	*Yes, I've read it./Yes, I read it.*	
Gino ha letto la lettera.	*Gino (has) read the letter.*	
L'ha letta.	*He (has) read it.*	
Sara ha letto il biglietto.	*Sarah (has) read the note.*	
L'ha letto.	*She (has) read it.*	

The sentences below will make these agreements clearer:

Hai visto	Pietro? Maria? i ragazzi? le ragazze?	Sì.	L'ho visto. L'ho vista. Li ho visti. Le ho viste.	Have you seen	Peter? Mary? the boys? the girls?	Yes, I've seen	him. her. them. them.
Hai chiuso	il cassetto? la valigia? i cassetti? le valigie?	Sì.	L'ho chiuso. L'ho chiusa. Li ho chiusi. Le ho chiuse.	Have you closed	the drawer? the suitcase? the drawers? the suitcases?	Yes, I've closed	it. it. them. them.

When there is no object pronoun, the past participle does not have to agree if the object precedes the verb. In Italian you can say either:

La rivista che ho { comprato. / comprata. } *The magazine that I (have) bought.*

2 LISTS

When you have a list of nouns in Italian you don't need to use the article **pane, burro, latte …**

3 IL REGALO … L'AVETE PRESO? *HAVE YOU GOT THE PRESENT?*

Often, especially in spoken Italian, for the sake of emphasis, both the noun and the pronoun are used as in the example above. Other examples:

I posti … li avete prenotati? *Have you booked the seats?*
L'hai letto **il giornale** di oggi? *Did you read today's paper?*
La carne **l'**ho messa nel *I've put the meat in the freezer.*
  congelatore.

4 *PERFECT OF* DOVERE, POTERE, SAPERE, VOLERE

The perfect of the above verbs may always be formed with **avere**:

ho dovuto, avete voluto, hanno potuto, abbiamo saputo

However, when the verb that follows them has its perfect tense formed with **essere** there is a choice:

Non { **ho** / **sono** } **potuto venire.** *I couldn't come.*

{ **Abbiamo dovuto** / **Siamo dovuti** } **partire.** *We had to leave.*

With **dovere, potere, sapere, volere** there is also a choice of position for unstressed pronouns (see Unit 9, Section 2):

Non ho potuto farlo.
Non l'ho potuto fare. *I couldn't do it.*

Devo alzarmi presto.
Mi devo alzare presto. *I have to get up early.*

5 GIÀ *ALREADY,* NON … ANCORA *NOT … YET*

Notice the position of **già** and **ancora** in the following examples:

Quando fai la spesa?	*When are you doing the shopping?*
L'ho *già* fatta.	*I've already done it.*
Hai fatto la spesa?	*Have you done the shopping?*
Non *l*'ho *ancora* fatta.	*I haven't done it yet.*

6 ECCOLA QUA/QUI *IT'S RIGHT HERE*

Qua/qui *here*, or **là/lì** *there*, may be added to **eccolo, eccola**, ecc. to give more precision: **eccolo qui/là**.

7 TANTO/A, TANTI/E *SO MUCH, SO MANY*

Notice how the above adjectives are used in the singular and plural:

Al mercato c'è tanta frutta!	*There's so much fruit in the market!*
Ho tante cose da fare!	*I've got so many things to do.*

Come si dice? *How do you say it?*

◀) **CD 2, TR 20**

1 *How to say you have already done something* — **L'ho già fatto./L'ho già fatta.**

2 *How to say that you have not yet done it* — **Non l'ho ancora fatto./Non l'ho ancora fatta.**

3 *How to ask someone how much they paid for something* — **Quanto l'ha pagato?/ Quanto l'ha pagata?**

4 *How to say how much you paid for it* — **L'ho pagato/L'ho pagata …**

5 *How to say where you (have) put it* — **L'ho messo qui/lì.** **L'ho messa qui/lì.**

Practice

1 *Imagine the questions below are addressed to you and answer*
  using ne, *making the past participle agree.*
  Esempio: **Quante birre ha preso?** (due)
  Ne ho prese due.
  a *Quanti pacchi ha mandato?* (uno)
  b *Quanti film ha visto?* (molti)
  c *Quante lettere ha spedito?* (sei)
  d *Quante cartoline ha scritto?* (quattro)
  e *Quante gallerie ha visitato?* (una)
  f *Quanti soldi ha speso?* (molti)
  g *Quante sterline ha cambiato?* (poche)
  h *Quanti caffè ha bevuto oggi?* (tre)

2 *You are being asked by your boss when you are going to*
  complete a number of office tasks. With your customary
  efficiency you have already done everything.
  Esempio: **Quando paga il conto?**
  L'ho già pagato.
  a *Quando scrive le lettere?*
  b *Quando compra i francobolli?*
  c *Quando vede i signori Marelli?*
  d *Quando fa le due telefonate a Parigi?*
  e *Quando sbriga la corrispondenza?*
  f *Quando finisce il rapporto?*
  g *Quando prepara i documenti?*
  h *Quando consulta l'agenda?*

3 *You have been working so hard at the office that domestically*
  you have let things slide, and when your flat-mate asks you
  about a series of chores, you have to admit that you haven't
  done them yet.
  Esempio: **Hai preparato la cena?** → **No. Non l'ho ancora**
  preparata.
  a *Hai fatto il letto?*
  b *Hai pulito l'appartamento?*
  c *Hai pagato l'affitto?*
  d *Hai fatto la spesa?*
  e *Hai comprato i giornali?*
  f *Hai riparato la luce?*

4 *Complete the following sentences with a suitable verb in the perfect tense.*

Esempio: Mario ha comprato il gelato e l'__.

Mario ha comprato il gelato e l'ha mangiato.

   a *Ho preso una penna e __ una lettera a Marco.*

   b *Ho comprato il giornale e l'__.*

   c *Ho acceso la radio e l'__.*

   d *Giorgio ha comprato la birra e l'__.*

   e *Anna ha preso il vestito dall'armadio e l'__.*

   f *Sono andati alla stazione ma purtroppo __ il treno.*

5 *Ora tocca a te!*

You are taking on the role of a husband who can't find his passport.

CD 2, TR 21

Moglie	Allora, caro, partiamo?
You	*I'm not ready yet.*
Moglie	Che cosa cerchi?
You	*My passport. Where did I put it? Did you take it?*
Moglie	No. Hai guardato in macchina?
You	*Yes. I've looked. It's not there.*
Moglie	Non l'hai lasciato in banca stamattina quando hai cambiato i soldi?
You	*No. Ah … One moment … Perhaps I put it in the bedroom.*
Moglie	No. Di là non c'è. Ho pulito in tutte le camere e non ho visto niente.
You	*Didn't you by any chance put it with the other documents?*
Moglie	No, no. In borsa ho soltanto i biglietti del treno.
You	*What a nuisance! What do we do now without a passport?*
Moglie	Hai guardato nello studio?
You	*Yes. I've looked everywhere.*
Moglie	Oddio! Ed il treno parte fra mezz'ora!

Eating pasta

Italy produces more than 600 types of **pasta**, which constitutes over 10 per cent of its export trade. **Fusilli, rigatoni** and **fettuccine** are three of the many varieties to be found. A **pasta** dish (the most popular being **spaghetti**) is the typical first course of the average Italian family at lunch which usually takes place at about 1 o'clock. All sorts of **salse** *sauces*, especially those based on tomatoes, are used to go with the **pasta**.

Cirio is one of the well-known tomato purée brands also used for making **salsa**.

TEST YOURSELF

Look at the following questions and choose the right answer, a, b or c.

1 *Avete comprato le cartoline?*
a *Sì. Le abbiamo pure scritte.* **b** *Sì. La abbiamo pure scritte.*
c *Sì. La abbiamo pure scritto.*

2 *Hanno fatto i compiti?*
a *No. Non l'hanno fatte.* **b** *No. Non l'hanno fatto.*
c *No. Non li hanno fatti.*

3 *Avete visto i bambini?*
a *Sì. Lo abbiamo visti.* **b** *Sì. Li abbiamo visti.*
c *Sì. Li abbiamo visto.*

4 *Ti sono piaciuti i fiori?*
a *Sì. Mi sono piaciuto molto.* **b** *Sì. Mi sono piaciuta molto.*
c *Sì. Mi sono piaciuti molto.*

5 *Hai visto lo spettacolo?*
a *Sì. L'ho visto.* **b** *Sì. L'ho vista.* **c** *Sì. L'ho visti.*

Now translate the following sentences into Italian.

6 *We did not want to do it.*

7 *He had to say no.*

8 *Has she already read the article?*

9 *I still haven't seen the film.*

10 *I have the keys. Here they are.*

18

Che cosa regalare?
What present to give?

In this unit you will learn:
- *how to ask what present to give someone*
- *how to suggest what to get for him/her*
- *how to arrange to meet up later.*

1 Il compleanno di Renzo
Renzo's birthday

Beatrice is discussing **Renzo's** birthday present with **Alfredo**.

When you listen to this dialogue notice where **gli** comes before the verb, and when it comes after.

  a **Vero o falso?** *Renzo usa spesso il profumo.*
  b *Perchè Beatrice vuol fare un regalo a Renzo?*

Beatrice	Sabato è il compleanno di Renzo e non so ancora cosa regalargli.
Alfredo	Perchè non gli compri un romanzo?
Beatrice	I romanzi non gli piacciono.
Alfredo	Puoi prendere un profumo. Un bel profumo francese.
Beatrice	Però il profumo non lo usa mai.
Alfredo	Quanto vuoi spendere?
Beatrice	Non troppo. E non posso neanche regalargli delle sigarette perchè non fuma più.

QUICK VOCAB

Non so ancora cosa regalargli *I don't know what to give him (as a present) yet*
gli *(to) him*
romanzo *novel*
non posso neanche … *I can't even …*
non fuma (from **fumare**) **più** *he no longer smokes*

2 Il problema è risolto
The problem is solved

a Vero o falso? *Beatrice prende un nuovo stereo per Renzo.*
b *Cosa vuol fare Alfredo sabato mattina?*

Alfredo	Gli piace la musica?
Beatrice	Mi sembra di sì. So che ha un nuovo stereo.
Alfredo	Allora il problema è risolto. Gli puoi portare un cd o inviargli un SMS.
Beatrice	Buona idea! Gli prendo un cd di musica classica.
Alfredo	Io non gli regalo nulla. Gli mando solamente una cartolina di auguri. Però sabato mattina gli telefono.

mi sembra di sì *I think so*
cd *CD*
inviare un SMS *to send a text message*
non … nulla *nothing*
solamente *only*
auguri *greetings*

---

3 L'onomastico di Carla
Carla's name-day

Sandra decides to get some chocolates from the patisserie, and **Livio** to buy a bunch of roses from the florist's for **Carla's** name-day.

a Vero o falso? *Sandra e Livio devono sbrigarsi perchè sono invitati per l'una.*

b *Cosa devono fare Livio e Sandra all'una?*

Sandra	Dio mio! È già mezzogiorno! Dobbiamo sbrigarci!
Livio	A che ora dobbiamo andare a pranzo da Carla?
Sandra	Siamo invitati per l'una.
Livio	Cosa le portiamo? Dei fiori?
Sandra	Possiamo prenderle dei cioccolatini dal pasticciere qui di fronte. So che i dolci le piacciono molto.
Livio	Ottima idea! Le compriamo una scatola di 'Baci Perugina' ed un bel mazzo di rose.
Sandra	Il guaio è che non abbiamo abbastanza tempo per andare in tutti e due i negozi.
Livio	Allora facciamo così: io vado dal fioraio mentre tu vai dal pasticciere, e poi c'incontriamo sotto il palazzo di Carla.

Dio mio! *good gracious!*
Dobbiamo sbrigarci! *We must hurry!*
da Carla *at Carla's place*
fiore (m) *flower*
scatola *box*
mazzo *bunch*
guaio *trouble*
mentre *while*
fioraio *florist*
poi c'incontriamo *then we'll meet*

Grammar

1 *TO KNOW –* **SAPERE, POTERE** *OR* **CONOSCERE***?*

Sapere, not con<u>o</u>scere, must be used:

▶ *whenever a dependent clause follows:*

So *che* P<u>a</u>olo vive a Taormina. *I know that Paul lives in Taormina.*
Sai *dove* va Ida? *Do you know where Ida is going?*
Sai *se* le piace la cucina cinese? *Do you know whether she likes Chinese cooking?*

▶ *whenever an infinitive follows, in which case it means to know how to (i.e. to be able):*

Sai guidare? *Do you know how to drive?/Can you drive?*
Sai cucinare? *Do you know how to cook?/Can you cook?*

Notice **potere** when contrasted with **sapere**:

So giocare a tennis, ma oggi non *posso* (giocare) perchè non ho la racchetta. *I can play tennis, but can't (play) today because I don't have my racket.*
Senza occhiali non *posso* leggere. *I can't read without glasses.*

288

Non *sa* leggere ancora; è troppo piccolo.   *He can't read yet. He's too young.*

Con*o*scere is mainly used for knowing people, places or languages:

Conosci Carlo? Sì. Lo *conosco*.   *Do you know Charles? Yes. I do.*
Conosce Parigi? Sì. La *conosco*.   *Do you know Paris? Yes. I do.*
Conosce bene lo spagnolo.   *He knows Spanish well.*

Insight

Towns are feminine in Italian: **Parigi è bella.**

2 INDIRECT OBJECT PRONOUNS (UNSTRESSED)

Singular		Plural	
mi	*(to/for) me*	**ci**	*(to/for) us*
ti	*(to/for) you (inf)*	**vi**	*(to/for) you (pl)*
gli	*(to/for) him*	**gli**	⎱ *(to/for) them (m/f)*
le	*(to/for) you/her*	**(a) loro**	⎰ *(see below)*

The pronouns in the box are indirect objects, i.e. where *to/for* are either expressed or understood in English. 'I give him the book' means 'I give the book to him', which in Italian becomes: **Gli do il libro.** To start with it is best to concentrate on **le** and **gli**:

Le ⎱
Gli ⎰ **parlo dopo.** *I'll talk* ⎱ *to you/to her* ⎰ *later/afterwards.*
                                        ⎰ *to him* ⎱

Le porto la valigia.   *I'll carry the suitcase for you/her.*
Gli apro la porta.   *I'll open the door for him/them.*

Like the pronouns in Unit 17, Section 1, they normally precede the verb, but both object and indirect object may come after an infinitive, in which case they are attached to it (**regalargli** stands for **regalare + gli**).

Gli vorrei telefonare.
Vorrei telefonargli. } *I would like to phone him.*

Giorgio { mi ti ci vi gli le } **dà il libro.** *George is giving* { me you us you (pl) him/them her/you } *the book.*

Gli means *to him* or *to them* but in the ***written*** language (and occasionally in the spoken), *to them* is **loro** or **a loro**: it can never precede the verb and can never be attached to the infinitive.

Giorgio dà il libro a loro.
Giorgio dà loro il libro. } *George is giving them the book.*

3 NON ... NEANCHE *NOT ... EVEN*

Neanche is the opposite of **anche**:

anch'io, anche lei; neanch'io, neanche lei.

Vengo *anch'io*.	*I'm coming too.*
(Io) *non* so cosa dire.	*I don't know what to say.*
***Neanch'io*.**	*Neither do I.*
Non ci andate *neanche* voi?	*Aren't you going (there) either?*
Non ci andiamo *neanche* noi.	*We're not going (there) either.*

4 MI SEMBRA/MI PARE ... *IT SEEMS TO ME ...*

Mi sembra is another verb used impersonally in the same way as **mi piace** (Unit 11, Section 7). Both verbs require the indirect object pronoun (Unit 18, Section 2).

Non *mi sembra* il momento adatto.	*It doesn't seem the right moment to me.*
Le *pare* giusto?	*Do you think it's fair?*
Gli *piace* questo cd?	*Does he like this CD?*
I fiori *le piacciono* molto.	*She likes flowers a lot.*
Le *piacciono* i dolci?	*Do you like sweet things?*

When used with **sì** and **no**, **sembra**, like **pensare** and **credere** *to think*, must be followed by **di** and has the same meaning (*to think*).

Mi sembra	di sì.	⎫	*I think*	⎧	*so.*
Penso	di no.	⎭		⎩	*not.*

5 ONLY

Solamente, **solo** and **soltanto** can all be used to mean *only*.

6 DOBBIAMO SBRIGARCI WE MUST HURRY

As this reflexive verb is in the infinitive, the pronoun **ci** is attached to the end of it. **Sbrigarci** (Dialogue 3) is **sbrigare** + **ci** (lit: *to hurry ourselves*).

7 OTTIMO/A, MEGLIO, MIGLIORE EXCELLENT, BETTER

Ottimo/a, an adjective, is another way of saying **buonissimo/a** *very good*, *excellent*. There are two words for *better*: **migliore** (adjective) and **meglio** (adverb):

Fanno degli *ottimi* affari.	*They do excellent business.*
Lei mi dà *ottime* notizie.	*You're giving me very good news.*
Questo libro è *migliore* di quello.	*This book is better than that one.*
Lo so *meglio* di te!	*I know (it) better than you do!*

Il/la migliore means *the best*:

Secondo me *il* periodo *migliore* per visitare l'Italia è la primavera.
In my opinion the best time to visit Italy is spring.

Mario e Paolo sono *i miei migliori* amici.
Mario and Paolo are my best friends.

> **Insight**
>
> **Buono/a, migliore, il/la migliore** mean *good*, *better*, *best*. When *better* is used as an adverb ('He speaks Italian better than I do'), use **meglio**.

8 C'INCONTRIAMO *WE'LL MEET (EACH OTHER)*

Incontrarsi, apparently a reflexive verb, is used reciprocally in this context to express the idea of *each other*. We have already met **ci vediamo** used in this way: it literally means *we'll see each other*.

Here are examples of other verbs being used reciprocally:

Da quanto tempo *si conoscono* Anna e Marcello?
How long have Anna and Marcello known each other?

Paolo e Marisa non *si parlano*.
Paolo and Marisa don't talk to each other.

Gl'italiani *si salutano* molte volte prima di lasciarsi.
Italians say goodbye many times before leaving each other.

Notice how in the last example **gli** (*the*) may be shortened to **gl'** but only before words beginning with i: **gl'italiani; gl'inglesi.**

9 DAL FIORAIO *AT/TO THE FLORIST'S*

When used with people, **da** or **da + article** means *at/to the house of*, *the shop of* or *the place of*:

Vado *dal* tabaccaio.	*I'm going to the tobacconist's.*
Vai *da* Giulia?	*Are you going to Julia's (place)?*
Prima vado *dal* dottore, poi *dal* salumiere.	*First I'll go to the doctor's, then to the grocer's.*
Vado *dalla* mia amica.	*I'm going to my friend's house.*
Perchè non vieni *da* me?	*Why don't you come to my place?*

Come si dice?
How do you say it?

◀)) **CD 2, TR 23**

1 *How to ask what present to give someone* — **Cosa posso regalare a ...?**

2 *How to suggest what to buy him/her* — **Perchè non gli compri ...?** **le compri ...?**

3 *How to suggest what you can get for him/her* — **Posso prendergli .../prenderle ...**

4 *How to say you will meet up later* — **C'incontriamo più tardi/ dopo.**

Practice

1 È il compleanno di Adriano *It's Adrian's birthday. Here is a list of his friends and what they do for the occasion. Write a sentence about each on the pattern of the first example.*
Esempio: **Anna gli dà una cravatta.**

   a *Anna (dare) cravatta.*
   b *Renzo (dare) libro.*
   c *Beatrice (portare) cd.*
   d *Livio (mandare) dvd (m).*
   e *Matteo (regalare) profumo.*
   f *Maria (telefonare) per fargli gli auguri.*

2 *Time is pressing for Rita who is being asked about when she is going to do everything she needs to do: you have to supply her answers using* **gli** *or* **le**.
Esempio: **Quando telefona a Beatrice?** (domani)
         Le telefono domani.

   a *Quando telefona a Giulia?*   (stasera)
   b *Quando telefona a Renzo?*   (più tardi)
   c *Quando telefona a Marco?*   (dopo cena)
   d *Quando scrive a Anna?*   (domani)
   e *Quando scrive a Gina?*   (oggi)
   f *Quando parla a Silvio e Eva?*   (dopo la lezione)

3 *You are being asked to decide which presents should go to each of your friends. Form the question you are being asked, then give your answer, attaching the object pronoun to the infinitive.*
Esempio: **a A chi vuole dare il cd?**
         Voglio darlo a Carla.

   a *Carla:*   *(dare) cd*
   b *Beatrice:*   *(mandare) cartolina di auguri*
   c *Maria:*   *(regalare) borsa di pelle*
   d *Marco:*   *(portare) cioccolatini*
   e *Gino:*   *(dare) portafoglio*

4 *In the following conversation, choose one of the three alternatives which fits the context. Read through the whole conversation before attempting to make your choices.*

Lucia	Hai il *nome/francobollo/biglietto* per la lettera?
Eva	No. Non ce *l'ho/ce l'ha/ce l'hanno*.
Lucia	Perchè non *la/lo/le* compri?
Eva	Perchè la posta è *qui/chiusa/aperta*.
Lucia	Ma il tabaccaio è *aperto/chiuso/nuovo*.
Eva	Sì. Però qui vicino non c'è un *pasticciere/fioraio/tabaccaio* e vorrei spedire questa lettera stasera.
Lucia	Perchè vuoi *spedirlo/spedire/spedirla* stasera?
Eva	Perchè domani è il compleanno di Filippo e devo *mandare/mandarli/mandargli* gli auguri.
Lucia	A chi devi *mandarli/mandargli/mandarle*? Non ho capito.
Eva	A Filippo.

5 **Giorgio** *and* **Pina** *know each other, see each other, etc. Make one statement for each pair as in this example. (There is no need to repeat* **Giorgio e Pina** *every time.)*
Esempio: Giorgio conosce Pina. Pina conosce Giorgio.
(Giorgio e Pina) si conoscono.

   a *Giorgio incontra Pina. Pina incontra Giorgio.*
   b *Giorgio vede Pina. Pina vede Giorgio.*
   c *Giorgio parla con Pina. Pina parla con Giorgio.*
   d *Giorgio saluta Pina. Pina saluta Giorgio.*
   e *Giorgio bacia Pina. Pina bacia Giorgio.*
   f *Giorgio abbraccia Pina. Pina abbraccia Giorgio.*

6 *Ora tocca a te!*

Giorgio	Dove vai, Carla?
You	*First I'm going to the post office, then I'm going to buy a present for Antonio.*
Giorgio	Perchè? È il suo compleanno?
You	*No. It's his name-day.*
Giorgio	Cosa gli compri?
You	*I don't know yet.*
Giorgio	Gli piace leggere?

CD 2, TR 24

You	*I don't think so.*
Giorgio	Quanto vuoi spendere?
You	*Not too much.*
Giorgio	Sai se gli piace la musica?
You	*I know he likes to listen to music when he's driving.*
Giorgio	Puoi comprargli un cd, allora.
You	*Excellent idea!*

7 *Read the section opposite and answer these questions.*

a *È un mazzo di crisantemi?*

b *Quante candeline ci sono sulla torta?*

c *Why do you think the baci are called Perugina?*

d *What is La festa della Mamma?*

'Made in Italy'

As more and more cheap goods from the Balkans and the Far East flood Italian markets, those made in Italy tend to become more and more exclusive.

This artisan culture dating back many centuries still associates Faenza with ceramics, Venice with glass, and the area around Florence with leather goods. The Renaissance tradition of the artisan in his workshop still exists, and will continue to do so as long as the desire for beautifully made objects persists, even though for a very restricted clientele.

As for dress, Milan is renowned as the centre of the fashion industry with such names as Armani, Gucci and Versace. Appealing to a broader market, Italy has no lack of world class designers in furniture, motor vehicles and kitchenware, much of the best being aimed at the export market.

Presents

If invited to a meal it is usual to take your hostess **un mazzo di fiori** *a bunch of flowers*. Beware of taking chrysanthemums, however. They are used only at funerals.

Baci Perugina (originally *made in Perugia*) are a trade mark for chocolates known all over Europe. **I dolci** are literally *'sweet things'* and may therefore refer to sweets, cakes or biscuits. **Il dolce** (see Unit 7) is the *dessert* or *sweet*.

A **pasticceria** sells cakes, pastries and ice cream. Many of these **pasticcerie** are like cafés where you can sit and eat cakes, etc. with a drink.

Here is the Italian version of the song **Tanti auguri a te!** *Happy birthday to you* (lit: *So many greetings to you*):

Tanti auguri a te,
Tanti auguri a te,
Tanti auguri a Renzo, (or any other name, as appropriate)
Tanti auguri a te!

Now turn to *Test your Italian III*.

TEST YOURSELF

Are the following statements true or false? You'll need to re-read the passages in Unit 18 to help you.

1 *Renzo fuma 20 sigarette al giorno.*

2 *Renzo legge i romanzi spesso.*

3 *Alfredo non fa un regalo a Renzo.*

4 *Livio e Sandra portano una borsa e un romanzo a Carla.*

5 *A Carla non piacciono i dolci.*

Now translate the following sentences into Italian.

6 *I can swim, but I can't today because I don't have my swimming costume.*

7 *I know Michael.*

8 *Do you know where Turin is?*

9 *I gave her the flowers.*

10 *Alice sent him a greetings card.*

19

Studio e lavoro
Study and work

In this unit you will learn:
- *how to talk about your studies and your present job*
- *how to talk about the places you have visited and how long you stayed there*
- *how to say that you enjoyed yourself*
- *how to ask others similar questions.*

1 Intervista con una studentessa
Interview with a student

A journalist interviews a woman graduate who has now enrolled for a degree course in languages.

a Vero o falso? *La studentessa è laureata.*
b *(La studentessa) è mai stata in Russia?*

Giornalista	Si laurea quest'anno, signorina?
Studentessa	No. Mi sono già laureata.
Giornalista	E perchè frequenta l'università?
Studentessa	Perchè mi sono iscritta al corso di laurea in lingue. Studio l'inglese e il russo.
Giornalista	È mai stata in Russia?

CD 2, TR 25

> **Studentessa** No. Non ci sono mai stata. Ma sono andata diverse volte in Inghilterra. C'è tanto da vedere!
> **Giornalista** Conosce bene Londra?
> **Studentessa** Abbastanza bene, almeno credo. Ci sono ritornata anche quest'anno.
> **Giornalista** C'è andata da sola?
> **Studentessa** No. Con mio padre e mia madre.

QUICK VOCAB

frequentare *to attend*
mi sono iscritta (from **iscriversi**) *I have enrolled*
diversi/e *several*
almeno *at least*
laurearsi *to graduate*

2 Preferiamo viaggiare per conto nostro
We prefer to travel on our own

When asked whether she and her parents went on a package tour (**viaggio organizzato**), she answers that they prefer to make their own arrangements.

a Vero o falso? *La studentessa e i suoi genitori sono stati a Canterbury solo di passaggio.*
b *Per quanto tempo (la studentessa) è andata in Irlanda?*

> **Giornalista** Avete fatto un viaggio organizzato?
> **Studentessa** No, no. Noi preferiamo viaggiare per conto nostro.
> **Giornalista** Siete stati a Canterbury?
> **Studentessa** Sì. Ma solo di passaggio quando siamo ritornati da Edimburgo.
> **Giornalista** Vi siete fermati parecchio tempo in Scozia?
> **Studentessa** Una settimana solamente. Dopo i miei genitori sono andati a Londra ed io sono partita per l'Irlanda per quattro giorni.

| **Giornalista** | E poi …? |
| **Studentessa** | E poi ci siamo incontrati a Canterbury per fare insieme il viaggio di ritorno. Ci siamo divertiti moltissimo. |

di passaggio	*passing through*
fermarsi	*to stop, stay*
parecchio tempo	*a long time*
incontrarsi	*to meet (each other)*
insieme	*together*
divertirsi	*to enjoy oneself*

3 Un operaio di fabbrica
A factory worker

A factory worker explains that he came to Milan (in Northern Italy) from Messina because there is not enough work for everybody in the South.

a Vero o falso? *Marcello lavora in un negozio.*
b *Come si trova Marcello a Milano?*

Giornalista	Da che parte dell'Italia viene?
Marcello	Da Messina. Sono siciliano.
Giornalista	Quanti anni sono che lavora a Milano?
Marcello	Una quindicina di anni.
Giornalista	Sua sorella mi ha detto che vi trovate bene qui nel nord.
Marcello	È vero. Si guadagna molto. E nella fabbrica in cui lavoriamo noi, gli operai sono trattati veramente bene. Fra poco avremo anche l'aumento.
Giornalista	Come mai vi siete trasferiti qui?
Marcello	Nel sud, purtroppo, è difficile trovare lavoro per tutti.

Quanti anni sono che lavora …? *How many years have you been working …?*
una quindicina di … *about 15 …*
in cui *in which*
fra poco *shortly*
avremo l'aumento *we'll have a rise*
trattare *to treat*
… vi siete trasferiti (from **trasferirsi**)?… *did you move?*

Grammar

1 *PERFECT TENSE OF REFLEXIVE VERBS*

All reflexive verbs (those with infinitives ending in -**si** like **fermarsi**) form their present tense with **essere** (see Unit 16, Section 1)

Sì è divertito **alla festa di Renzo?**	*Did you enjoy yourself at Lawrence's party?*
Sì. *Mi sono divertito* **molto.**	*Yes, I enjoyed myself a lot.*
Ti sei alzata* **tardi stamattina?**	*Did you get up late this morning?*
No. *Mi sono alzata* **presto.**	*No, I got up early.*
Vi siete asciugati?	*Did you dry yourselves?*
Sì. *Ci siamo asciugati* **con l'asciugamano celeste.**	*Yes, we dried ourselves on the blue towel.*

*Alzata the feminine form is used because a woman is being asked the question.

Perfect tense **fermarsi** to stop, stay		
(io)	**mi sono fermato/a**	*I stopped, I have stopped*
(tu)	**ti sei fermato/a**	*you stopped, you have stopped (inf)*
(lui, lei)	**si è fermato/fermata**	*he/she/it/you stopped, he/she has stopped/you have stopped*
(noi)	**ci siamo fermati/e**	*we stopped, we have stopped*

| (voi) | **vi siete fermati/e** | *you stopped, you have stopped* |
| (loro) | **si sono fermati/e** | *they stopped, they have stopped* |

2 PER CONTO NOSTRO *ON OUR OWN*

To express the idea of on one's own, use this expression with the appropriate possessive adjective: **per conto mio** *on my own*, **per conto tuo/suo/vostro** *on your own*, etc.

| **Lavoro per conto mio.** | *I work on my own/for myself.* |
| **Lui lavora per conto suo.** | *He works on his own/for himself.* |

Note too **libero professionista** *freelance*.

In Dialogue 2 **preferiamo viaggiare per conto nostro** is best rendered by *we prefer to make our own arrangements*.

3 INCONTRARSI *OR* CONOSCERSI?

Ci siamo incontrati comes from **incontrarsi** *to meet*. However, if you want to refer to the first time someone met, use **conoscersi**:

| **Si sono conosciuti in Italia, l'anno dopo si sono incontrati a Parigi, e quest'anno si sono sposati.** | *They met (each other) in Italy, the following year they met (again) in Paris, and this year they got married.* |

4 QUANTI ANNI SONO CHE LAVORA ...? *HOW MANY YEARS HAVE YOU BEEN WORKING ...?*

This is another way of expressing: **Da quanti anni lavora?**

Both of these constructions require the present tense in Italian because the activity continues on into the present (see Unit 16, Section 7):

Aspetto da dieci minuti.
Sono dieci minuti che aspetto. $\Big\}$ *I have been waiting for ten minutes.*

If the activity has ceased then **per** is used with the past:

Ho lavorato a Roma per più di dieci anni.   *I worked in Rome for more than ten years.*

5 UNA QUINDICINA *ABOUT 15*

To express approximate quantities, take off the final vowel of the number and add **-ina** preceded by **una** (use for numbers 10, 15, 20, and then in tens up to 90): **una diecina, una quindicina ecc:**

Ha *una ventina* d'anni.   *He's about 20.*
Ci sono *una trentina* di persone.   *There are about 30 people.*
***Una quindicina* di giorni.**   *A fortnight, about two weeks.*

6 *PREPOSITONS WITH* **CHE/CUI**

After prepositions (Unit 4, Section 12) **cui** replaces **che**. Notice the difference between these examples:

La casa *che* ha comprato è modernissima.   *The house that he has bought is very modern.*
La casa *in cui* abita è piccolissima.   *The house in which he lives/he lives in is very small.*
Non capisco la ragione *per cui* non vuoi andarci.   *I don't understand the reason why (lit.: for which) you don't want to go there.*
Questo è l'ingegnere *di cui* ti ho parlato.   *This is the engineer I spoke to you about. (lit.: of whom I spoke …)*

A *che ora* incominci a lavorare la mattina?   *At what time do you start work in the morning? (direct question)*

Non so *a che ora* viene.   *I don't know at what time he's coming. (indirect question)*

7 È DIFFICILE TROVARE LAVORO ... *IT'S DIFFICULT TO FIND WORK* ...

Many other adjectives can be used in this way with the infinitive: **facile** *easy*; **possibile** *possible*; **interessante** *interesting*; **importante** *important*

È facile spendere i soldi.   *It's easy to spend money.*

A quest'ora è difficile trovare un posto.   *At this time it's difficult to find a seat.*

È importante studiare.   *It's important to study.*

Come si dice?
How do you say it?

◀) **CD 2, TR 26**

1 *How to ask when someone is graduating*   **Quando si laurea?**

   How to say you have already graduated   **Mi sono già laureato/a.**

2 *How to say you (have) enrolled on a particular course*   **Mi sono iscritto/a al corso di ...**

3 *How to say that one earns a lot and that the workers are well treated* **Si guadagna molto. Gli operai sono trattati bene.**

4 *How to ask how long someone stayed in …* **Quanto tempo si è fermato/a in/a …?**

How to say how long you stayed **Mi sono fermato/a una settimana, ecc.**

5 *How to ask whether someone had a good time* **Si è divertito? Si è divertita?**

How to say that you had a very good time **Mi sono divertito/a moltissimo.**

Practice

1 Giorgio, Anna, Marco, Carlo *and*
Filippo *all enrolled at various*
universities, and each one
graduated in the subject stated, in
the number of years given in
brackets. Write a statement for each,
modelling it on the one for Giorgio.
Esempio: Giorgio si è iscritto all'università di Milano. Si è
laureato in ingegneria in cinque anni.

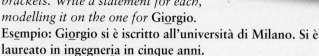

Giorgio	Milano: ingegneria (5)
Marco	Roma: medicina (6)
Anna	Bologna: matematica e fisica (7)
Carlo e Filippo	Napoli: legge* (4)

l'ingegneria *engineering*
la legge *law*

*You can also say **laureato in giurisprudenza**

2 Marco *is being told what he has to do. Read through the*
instructions he is given and then imagine how he would relate
what he has done, as in the example. (The infinitives of the
verbs in bold must be put in the perfect tense.)
Esempio: Mi sono alzato presto ...
Devi **alzarti** *presto. Devi* **vestirti** *subito e* **fare** *colazione. Devi*
comprare *le cartoline dal tabaccaio all'angolo e poi* **telefonare**
a Giulio e **chiedergli** *il nuovo indirizzo. Dopo devi* **andare**
all'ufficio e **dire** *a Marco di non venire sabato. Al ritorno devi*
prendere *i soldi in banca e* **fare** *la spesa.*

3 *Look at* Exercise 5 *in Unit 18, and imagine that you and*
Giorgio *met yesterday:* Io e Giorgio ci siamo incontrati ieri.
Continue, but don't repeat ieri. *Start:* Ci ...

4 Mario *has met his ideal companion, as you will see from what*
he tells his friend about her. Complete his statements using
each of the following prepositions + **cui**, *once only:* **a/con/da/**
di/per

Questa è la ragazza:
  a __ *ti ho scritto.*
  b __ *esco.*
  c __ *ricevo tante telefonate.*
  d __ *non dormo la notte.*
  e __ *scrivo sempre.*

5 *Ora tocca a te!*

You and your partner are on a short summer course at the University of Perugia. You are being interviewed by a journalist and are answering his questions on behalf of both of you.

Giornalista	Siete tedeschi?
You	*No, we're English.*
Giornalista	Da quanto tempo siete qui?
You	*We've been here about a fortnight.*
Giornalista	Siete venuti in aereo?
You	*No, we came by car.*
Giornalista	E perchè siete venuti a Perugia?
You	*Because we've enrolled at the University to study Italian.*
Giornalista	Quanto tempo dura il corso?
You	*It lasts a month.*
Giornalista	Avete visitato altri posti?
You	*Not many. But last Sunday we got up early and went to Assisi.*
Giornalista	Vi siete divertiti?
You	*We enjoyed ourselves very much.*

6 *Read the section below and answer the questions about the* **Accademia Rimini.**

Gli studenti di questa scuola
  a *dove cenano?*
  b *dove vanno il pomeriggio?*
  c *dove fanno la mini-crociera?*

Learning Italian in Italy

Italian language schools flourish in every part of Italy, especially in the resorts, cultural and artistic centres. Students from all over the world attend l'**Università per Stranieri di Perugia**. Below is an example of what is offered at the **Accademia Rimini**.

ACCADEMIA RIMINI

CULTURA E LINGUA ITALIANA, RIMINI ITALIA

MINI-CORSO
CORSO BASE
CORSO GENERALE
CORSO SEMI-INTENSIVO
CORSO INTENSIVO
CORSO INDIVIDUALE
CORSO 'BUSINESS'
CORSI DI CULTURA
CORSI TRIMESTRALI
CORSI 'A CASA DELL' INSEGNANTE'
PROGRAMMI PER GRUPPI
SETTIMANA LINGUISTICA
SEMINARI E STAGE

POMERIGGIO AL PARCO MINICROCIERA SUL MARE ADRIATICO A CENA SULLA SPIAGGIA

Male and female

In the first dialogue **studentessa** is used as the feminine form of **studente**. Many women however would be quite happy to call themselves **studenti,** and this lack of differentiation is most marked in the professional classes. Although **avvocatessa**, **direttrice**, **dottoressa** and **presidentessa** all exist as feminine forms of **avvocato**, **direttore**, **dottore** and **presidente,** a woman lawyer or doctor may well prefer to be addressed as **avvocato** or **dottore.**

At a formal presentation to the head of a leading ballet school, the woman in question was recently addressed as **'signora direttore'**, even though the feminine forms in –ice are in common use (**direttrice, attrice, pittrice**).

2005 saw the first woman to become a pilot in the Italian Airforce, **l'Aeronautica Militare**. She was referred to as **il primo pilota donna**.

In 2006 the first woman to be promoted to warrant officer rank in the **carabinieri** (see the end of Unit 24) was referred to as **il primo maresciallo donna**, (though a joking reference to her as **marescialla** was made on the Internet).

In 2009 the first woman gondolier (**gondoliera**) started working on the Venice canals.

TEST YOURSELF

Unscramble the following to make meaningful sentences.

1 *sono mi iscritta di all'università Napoli*

2 *Francia in ho un organizzato viaggio fatto*

3 *stamattina sono tardi alzato mi*

4 *ci all'aeroporto fermare tre siamo andare volte per dovuti*

5 *quattro ho anni a vissuto per Bologna*

6 *che è la rossa guida macchina*

7 *alla sono mi festa divertita*

8 *Empoli e visitato abbiamo Ancona*

9 *cui parlato la molto di ti è cantante brava ho*

10 *è canta il sempre ragazzo che questo*

20

Come si sente?
How do you feel?

In this unit you will learn:
- *how to say how you feel (well/ unwell)*
- *how to explain what is wrong with you (where it hurts)*
- *how to say when you require something by*
- *how to ask others similar questions.*

1 Non mi sento molto bene
I don't feel very well

Una signorina asks for some aspirin because she doesn't feel very well.

a Vero o falso? *La signorina prende le compresse con l'acqua.*
b *Quante compresse prende la signorina?*

Sig.na	Ha delle aspirine, per favore?
Signore	No. Mi dispiace, non ne ho. Perchè? Si sente male?
Sig.na	Non mi sento molto bene. Ho mal di testa e mal di gola.
Signore	Ha la febbre?
Sig.na	Penso di no. Ma ho anche il raffreddore e un po' di tosse. A che ora apre la farmacia?

CD 2, TR 28

Signore	Fra un'ora. Un attimo … Ho delle compresse per la gola. Le vuole con l'acqua o senz'acqua?
Sig.na	Non importa. Le prendo così, senz'acqua.
Signore	Bastano due?
Sig.na	Ne basta una, grazie. Ah … sto già meglio!

sentirsi male *to feel ill*
mal di testa (m) *headache*
mal di gola (m) *sore throat*
febbre (f) *temperature*
raffreddore (m) *cold*
tosse (f) *cough*
compressa *tablet*

2 Dal medico
At the doctor's

When asked by the doctor where it hurts, **la signora** answers that her head and her legs (**le gambe**) ache. She also has a stomach upset (**disturbi allo stomaco**).

a **Vero o falso?** *La signora ha preso un po' d'insolazione.*
b *Dove deve andare la signora con la ricetta?*

CD 2, TR 28, 00:59

Medico	Dove le fa male?
Signora	Qui e qui: mi fa male la testa e mi fanno male le gambe. Ho anche dei disturbi allo stomaco.
Medico	Respiri profondamente! … Ancora … Va bene. Si rivesta!
Signora	È grave, dottore? Devo andare in ospedale?
Medico	No, no. Stia tranquilla! Non è nulla di grave. Ha preso un po' d'insolazione. Tenga! Vada in farmacia con questa ricetta. Resti a letto per un paio di giorni e prenda queste medicine.

Signora	Quante volte al giorno devo prenderle?
Medico	Tre volte. Le capsule prima dei pasti e le pillole dopo i pasti.
Signora	Grazie, dottore. Quanto le devo per la visita?
Medico	Si rivolga alla mia segretaria.

respirare *to breathe in*
profondamente *deeply*
ancora *again*
rivestirsi *to get dressed again*
Stia tranquilla! *Keep calm!*
insolazione (f) *sunstroke*
tenga! *here you are*
ricetta *prescription*
pasto *meal*
devo (from **dovere**) *I owe*
si rivolga (from **rivolgersi**) *ask, apply*

---

3 Dal dentista
At the dentist's

La signorina tells the dentist she has a toothache (**mal di denti**) and he asks her which tooth (**quale dente**) hurts.

a Vero o falso? *La signorina ha mal di testa.*
b *Che cosa le dà il dentista per lavare i denti?*

Signorina	Buongiorno, dottore.
Dentista	Buongiorno, signorina. Mi dica!
Signorina	Ho mal di denti.
Dentista	Si accomodi! Prego, si segga qui!
Signorina	Grazie.
Dentista	Quale dente le fa male?
Signorina	Questo. Ma che guaio! Proprio ora che ho gli esami!

CD 2, TR 28, 02:10

Mi dica! *What can I do for you?*
si segga! (from **sedersi**) *sit down*
proprio *just*
esame (m) *exam*
cariato/a *decayed*
medicazione (f) *dressing*
piombare *to fill*
spazzolino *toothbrush*

---

4 Dall'ottico
At the optician's

L'avvocato asks the optician if he can repair (**riparare**) his glasses (**gli occhiali**) that are broken. The optician asks if he requires them immediately.

a **Vero o falso?** *L'avvocato non deve telefonare prima di andare a prendere gli occhiali.*
b *Cosa deve riparare l'ottico?*

Avvocato	Si sono rotti gli occhiali. Può ripararli?
Ottico	Vediamo … Sì, sì. È cosa da niente, avvocato. Li lasci qui. Le occorrono subito?
Avvocato	Mi servono per domenica.
Ottico	Ah, fra quattro giorni. Va bene. Saranno pronti senz'altro per domenica.
Avvocato	Devo telefonare prima di venire a prenderli?
Ottico	No, no. Non è necessario.
Avvocato	Grazie mille.
Ottico	Prego. Arrivederla!

cosa da niente *nothing serious*
Le occorrono subito? *Do you need them immediately?*
mi servono (from **servire**) *I need them*
saranno *they will be*
pronto/a *ready*
senz'altro *definitely*
prima di venire *before coming*

Grammar

1 HO LA FEBBRE *I HAVE A TEMPERATURE*

Many expressions to do with health (**la salute**) are formed with
avere + the definite article or **avere** + **mal di**:

Ho
- la febbre.
- la tosse.
- il raffreddore.
- l'influenza.

I have
- a temperature.
- a cough.
- a cold.
- influenza.

Ho mal di
- gola.
- testa.
- stomaco.
- denti.

I have
- a sore throat.
- a headache.
- stomach ache.
- a toothache.

To say to *catch a cold*, use **prendere**:

Ho preso il raffreddore.   *I've caught a cold.*

2 MI FA MALE! *IT HURTS!*

To say something hurts, apart from the
set expressions with **aver mal di** above,
you can also use **far male**, which is much
more general and can refer to all parts
of the body. The indirect object pronoun

(**mi, gli, le, ecc.**: Unit 18, Section 2) is used with the verb **fare** which can be either singular **fa** or plural **fanno**, depending on what hurts. Therefore:

My knee hurts becomes:
Mi fa male il ginocchio.   *(lit: The knee hurts to me.)*

My feet hurt becomes:
Mi fanno male i piedi.   *(lit: The feet hurt to me.)*

Italian does not use the possessive adjective (*my, your*, etc.) with parts of the body or with things that are worn, unless there is ambiguity:

Mi fa male la testa.	*My head hurts, I have a headache.*
Dove ha messo il biglietto?	*Where did you put your ticket?*
L'ho messo in tasca.	*I put it in my pocket.*
Un momento. Prendo il	*One moment. I'll get my coat and*
cappotto e vengo.	*come.*

....

		la bocca		*mouth*	
		il braccio		*arm*	
mi		**il dito**	*my*	*finger*	
ti		**il ginocchio**	*your*	*knee*	
le	**fa male**	**la mano**	*her/your*	*hand*	*hurts*
gli		**il naso**	*his*	*nose*	
		l'occhio destro		*right eye*	
		l'orecchio		*ear*	
		la schiena		*back*	
		lo stomaco		*stomach*	

....

Note the feminine that ends in -o: **la mano**; plural: **le mani**. In the table below note the irregularities in the plural formation of the following parts of the body:

Singular	Plural
il braccio	le braccia
il dito	le dita
il ginocchio	le ginocchia

mi		le braccia	*my*	*arms*	
ti		i denti	*your*	*teeth*	
le	**fanno male**	le ginocchia	*her/your*	*knees*	*hurt*
gli		le mani	*his/their*	*hands*	
		i piedi		*feet*	

3 REFLEXIVE VERBS: IMPERATIVE 2ND PERSON SINGULAR LEI FORM

Reflexive verbs form their imperative (**lei** form) in the same way as other verbs (Unit 14, Section 1), but must be preceded by **si** (*yourself*):

Si vesta! (vestirsi)	*Get dressed!*
Va alla festa? Si diverta! (divertirsi)	*Are you going to the party? Enjoy yourself!*
Mi preparo in due minuti.	*I'll be ready in two minutes.*
Non c'è fretta. Si cambi (cambiarsi) **con calma!**	*There is no hurry. Take your time to get changed. (lit: Change with calm.)*

In this last example, **mi preparo** *I get ready* means literally *I prepare myself*, and **si cambi** *change yourself* (i.e. *get changed*). There are many other instances in Italian of verbs being used reflexively and non-reflexively with slightly different meanings. For instance, **mi chiamo** *my name is* (from **chiamarsi**) literally means *I call myself*, so **chiamare** is used non-reflexively to mean *to call*.

Chiamo il dottore?	*Shall I call the doctor?*
Sì. Lo chiami.	*Yes. Call him.*
No. Non lo chiami.	*No. Don't call him.*

Similarly, **mettere** and **togliere** can become **mettersi** and **togliersi** when referring to things that are worn, thereby avoiding the use of the possessive:

Si metta il **vestito blu!**	*Put your blue suit on!*
Si tolga la **giacca!**	*Take your jacket off!*
Perchè non *ti metti gli* **occhiali?**	*Why don't you put your glasses on?*

To form the negative, put **non** before the verb:

Non **si preoccupi!**	*Don't worry!*
Non **si asciughi con**	*Don't dry yourself on the green*
l'asciugamano verde!	*towel!*

4 QUANTO LE DEVO? *HOW MUCH DO I OWE YOU?*

Another common meaning of **dovere** is *to owe*. In Italian you owe something to someone and an indirect object is therefore required:

Le devo **qualcosa?**	*Do I owe you anything?*

5 PRIMA DI + *INFINITIVE 'BEFORE …'*

Prima di + infinitive expresses the English *before doing …*

Devo telefonare *prima di* **venire?**	*Should I phone before coming?*
Mi lasci l'indirizzo *prima di* **partire.**	*Let me have your address before leaving.*

6 SEDERSI *TO SIT (DOWN)*

Si segga!/Si sieda! *Do sit down!* is the second person singular (**lei** form) imperative of **sedersi**, which is irregular, and, as we have already seen, is formed by changing the first person singular (present tense) ending **-o** to **-a** (Unit 14, Section 1).

Present tense **sedersi** *to sit (down)*	
mi seggo, mi siedo	ci sediamo
ti siedi	vi sedete
si siede	si seggono/si siedono

7 TENGA! *HERE YOU ARE!*

Tenga is the imperative **lei** form of the irregular verb **tenere** *to hold, to keep* (Unit 14, Section 1). In the present it follows the same pattern as **venire** (Unit 8, Section 3).

Present tense **tenere** *to hold, to keep*	
tengo	teniamo
tieni	tenete
tiene	tengono

8 SI SONO ROTTI GLI OCCHIALI *THE GLASSES BROKE*

As **rompere** is a transitive verb and must have an object, the reflexive form **rompersi** must be used in this case (i.e. lit: *the glasses broke themselves*). Therefore, the perfect tense must be formed with **essere** and the past participle must agree with the subject:

Si sono rotti gli occhiali.	*My glasses broke.*
Si è rotta la sedia.	*The chair broke.*

9 NEED

Occorrere and **servire** both express the idea of necessity or need: the verb agrees with the thing needed and the person becomes an indirect object:

Le serve il dizionario?	*Do you need the dictionary?*

Sì. Mi serve.   *Yes, I do (need it).*
***Gli occorre* la scheda telefonica.**   *He needs a phonecard.*

Quando *le* $\begin{cases} \textbf{occ}\underline{\textbf{o}}\textbf{rrono} \\ \quad\textbf{gli occhiali?} \\ \textbf{s}\underline{\textbf{e}}\textbf{rvono} \end{cases}$ *When do you need the glasses? (lit: When are the glasses necessary to you?)*

Mi $\begin{cases} \textbf{occ}\underline{\textbf{o}}\textbf{rrono} \\ \textbf{s}\underline{\textbf{e}}\textbf{rvono} \end{cases}$ **per dom**_**e**_**nica.**   *I need them for Sunday.*

Insight

If the need refers to 'you' in general, **ci vuole/ci vogliono** (lit: *is needed/are needed*: Unit 5, Section 6) may also be used:

Ci vuole la l_**au**_**rea in medicina per fare il medico.**   *You need a degree in medicine to be a doctor.*
Ci v_**o**_**gliono fatti, non parole.**   *You need deeds, not words.*
Ci v_**o**_**gliono più soldi per la ricerca scient**_**i**_**fica.**   *You need more money for scientific research.*

Come si dice?
How do you say it?

◀ŋ **CD 2, TR 29**

1   *How to ask someone how they feel*   **Come si sente?**

    How to say how you feel   **Mi sento bene/male/m**_**e**_**glio, ecc.**

2   *How to say what you are suffering from*   **Ho mal di testa/mal di denti, ecc. Ho la febbre/il raffreddore, ecc.**

3   *How to ask what is wrong (where it hurts)*   **Dove le fa male?**

How to say what is wrong with you	**Mi fa male la testa. Mi fanno male le gambe, ecc.**
4 *How to ask when someone requires something*	**Quando le occorre/le occorrono? Quando le serve/le servono?**
How to say when you require it/ them by	**Mi occorre per … Mi occorrono per … Mi serve per …/Mi servono per …**

Practice

1 *What are these boys and girls saying? Each one is describing what hurts.*
Use **Mi fa male/mi fanno male ...**

Anna **Giorgio** **Alessandro**

Livio **Orazio** **Gina**

2 *First check your answers to Exercise 1, then fit them into the right sentences below, but this time using* **gli/le** *according to the gender (m/f) to describe what hurts* **Anna**, **Giorgio**, *etc.*
  a *Anna non può giocare a tennis perchè ...*
  b *Giorgio non può respirare perchè ...*
  c *Livio non può leggere il giornale perchè ...*
  d *Orazio non può camminare perchè ...*
  e *Gina non può stare in piedi perchè ...*
  f *Alessandro non può giocare a calcio perchè ...*

3 *Complete the following sentences by selecting the most appropriate of these expressions with* **avere**: *il raffreddore, la febbre, mal di denti, mal di testa, mal di gola, mal di stomaco.*
(Use each expression once only.)
  a *Rita non vuole parlare troppo perchè ...*
  b *Non vuole leggere perchè ...*
  c *Vuole prendere delle aspirine, perchè ...*

d *Non vuole mangiare molto perchè ...*

e *Vuole telefonare al dentista perchè ...*

f *Ha bisogno di molti fazzoletti di carta* (tissues) *perchè ...*

4 *Choose the appropriate verb from the following to complete the sentences below. Use each, once only, in the imperative:*
lavarsi, asciugarsi, divertirsi, riposarsi, mettersi.

   a *Si metta sul letto e __.*

   b *Prenda l'asciugamano e __.*

   c *Prenda il dentifricio e lo spazzolino e __i denti.*

   d *Si tolga la giacca e __il cappotto.*

   e *Vada alla festa e __.*

5 *Respond with a negative command and replace the noun with a pronoun.*

   Esempio: Devo accendere la luce? No. Non l'accenda.

   a *Devo prendere le pillole?*

   b *Devo fare i biglietti?*

   c *Devo telefonare a Livio?*

   d *Devo scrivere a Ida?*

   e *Devo aprire la porta?*

   f *Devo chiudere le valigie?*

6 *Ora tocca a te!*

You and **Mara** are out driving: you need a rest.

You	*I don't feel well.*	
Mara	Che hai? Ti fa male la testa?	
You	*No. My eyes hurt.*	
Mara	Perchè non ti metti gli occhiali?	CD 2, TR 30
You	*Unfortunately, they're at the optician's.*	
Mara	Ma posso guidare io se vuoi.	
You	*All right. In that way* I can rest a bit.*	
Mara	Che ne dici di fermarci un momento in farmacia?	
You	*Good idea! And then we can go and have something to drink.*	
Mara	Allora prima ci fermiamo in farmacia e poi andiamo al Bar Quattro Fontane.	
You	*And in that way* I can also phone the doctor.*	

* *in that way* **così**

The Health Service

In Italy, as in Great Britain, there is a **Servizio Sanitario Nazionale** *National Health Service* to which all who are in work pay contributions. Anyone coming from the EU (European Union) who is unlucky enough to fall ill or have an accident is entitled to use it. Central government allocates funds according to the needs of each region. It is then incumbent upon the regions to organize their resources in the best possible way. In theory this should mean that each region is best able to cope with its own particular needs. The result in practice is that there is a great gulf between the most and least efficient services. Perhaps this is one of the reasons why a referendum in 2006 to give the regions more autonomy was rejected. **Il volontariato** *the voluntary sector* and religious institutions also play a significant role. The carers are called **i/le badanti**.

TEST YOURSELF

Match the column on the left with the most appropriate continuation on the right.

1 Come stai?

a Allora, devi bere molto.

2 Hai visto il medico?

b Non ci vado da 10 anni!

3 Ho preso un po' d'insolazione.

c Niente. La visita è gratuita/gratis.

4 Ho mal di denti.

d No, ma ho un appuntamento per domani mattina.

5 Quanto le devo?

e Devi andare dal dentista!

6 Quando le occorre l'appuntamento?

f Va bene. Faccio un appuntamento con la segretaria.

7 Devo telefonare prima di venire?

g Vorrei vedere qualcuno oggi se possibile.

8 Da quando ti senti così?

h Male. Ho mal di testa.

9 Quando è stata l'ultima volta che sei andato dall' ottico?

i Ho la febbre da due giorni.

10 Vorrei rivederla fra una settimana.

j Non c'è bisogno. Può venire senza fare l'appuntamento.

21

Progetti: vacanze, musica, arte
Plans: holidays, music, art

In this unit you will learn:
* *how to say when you will be taking your holidays*
* *how to say who you will be staying with or seeing*
* *how to say when a CD, DVD, book, etc. will come out*
* *how to ask when an exhibition will take place*
* *how to say that you will let someone know.*

1 Progetti per le vacanze
Holiday plans

Massimo, asked whether he has already had his holidays (**le ferie**), answers that he will be having them at the end of July.

a Vero o falso? *Massimo non ha ancora avuto le ferie.*
b *Dove andranno Massimo e sua moglie per le ferie, e da chi andranno?*

Giornalista	Ha già avuto le ferie?
Massimo	No. Le avrò alla fine di luglio.
Giornalista	Dove andrà a passarle? In Calabria?
Massimo	Naturalmente. Andremo dai nostri parenti.
Giornalista	Li andrà a trovare certamente tutti!
Massimo	Eh, no. Sarà impossibile vederli tutti. Ne abbiamo tanti!
Giornalista	E quando partirà?
Massimo	Fra una settimana, ai primi di agosto.

CD 2, TR 31

Dove andrà (from **andare**)? *Where will you go?*
sarà (from **essere**) *it will be …*
Quando partirà (from **partire**)? *When will you leave?*
ai primi di *at the beginning of*

---

2 Non le dà fastidio tanto sole?
Doesn't so much sun bother you?

Massimo explains that they will stay at **Catanzaro** for the Bank Holiday and will then travel around before going back to Milan.

a Vero o falso? *Il sole dà fastidio a Massimo.*
b *Perchè Massimo dovrà essere sul posto di lavoro il venti agosto?*

Giornalista	Nel mese di agosto fa un caldo da morire. Non le dà fastidio tanto sole?
Massimo	Macchè! E poi ci siamo abituati.
Giornalista	Rimarrà per il ferragosto, immagino.
Massimo	Ah, sì. Resteremo a Catanzaro per le feste e poi andremo un po' in giro prima di ritornare a Milano.
Giornalista	Quando ricomincerà a lavorare?
Massimo	Dovrò essere sul posto di lavoro il venti agosto.

un caldo da morire *boiling hot*
macchè! *not at all*
essere abituato/a a *to be used to*
rimarrà (from **rimanere** irr) *you will stay*
ferragosto *August Bank Holiday*
dovrò (from **dovere**) *I'll have to*
sul posto di lavoro *at work (lit: at the place of work)*

3 Una mostra d'arte
An art exhibition

Lucia tells **Claudio** about an important art exhibition she is
working on, and hopes he will come to see it.

a **Vero o falso?** *Lucia dovrà lavorare alla mostra per tutto il
periodo dell'esposizione.*

b *Claudio rivedrà Lucia domenica o sabato?*

Lucia	Senti, Claudio, fra tre giorni ci sarà una mostra di arte moderna.
Claudio	Ci saranno molti quadri?
Lucia	Moltissimi, perchè è un'esposizione importante.
Claudio	Ho sentito dire che vari oggetti verranno dal Museo di Arte Moderna di New York, è vero?
Lucia	Sì, è vero. Verrai anche tu, spero!
Claudio	Si dovrà fare la fila per entrare?
Lucia	Boh ...! Ma penso di sì.
Claudio	Per quanto tempo ci sarà la mostra?
Lucia	Resterà aperta due o tre mesi, credo. Ma non ne sono certa. Te lo farò sapere.
Claudio	E tu lavorerai lì durante tutto il periodo dell'esposizione?
Lucia	Eh, sì. Per forza. Ed ora, scusami Claudio, ma devo andare.
Claudio	Quando ti rivedrò un'altra volta?
Lucia	Dunque ... Fammi pensare ... Sì, domenica, cioè no, meglio sabato.

sentir(e) dire che *to hear that*
te lo farò (from **fare**) **sapere** *I'll let you know*
fare la fila *to queue up*
oggetto *object, thing*
per forza *I must*
verranno (from **venire**) *they will come*
boh ...! *I don't know*
scusami *(you must) excuse me*
rivedrò (from **rivedere**) *I'll see again*
fammi pensare *let me think*
cioè *that is*

4 In un negozio di dischi
In a record shop

Una signorina wants to know when the **Festival di San Remo** song collection (**raccolta di canzoni**) will come out.

a **Vero o falso?** *La signorina vuole consultare la raccolta delle ultime canzoni.*

b *Che cosa deve fare la signorina dopo aver consultato il catalogo?*

Signorina	Scusi, ha il catalogo dei nuovi cd?
Commesso	Sì. Lo vuole consultare? Quando avrà finito, me lo riporti qui per favore. Tenga!
Signorina	Grazie. Quando uscirà la raccolta delle ultime canzoni del Festival di San Remo?
Commesso	Il nuovo cd sarà in vendita dal primo aprile. Glielo metto da parte?
Signorina	Sì, perchè domani parto per le vacanze, e non so se sarò di ritorno in tempo per comprarlo. Immagino che andrà a ruba.
Commesso	Gliene potremo conservare uno, ma deve lasciare un anticipo.
Signorina	Un anticipo? Quanto?
Commesso	Il trenta per cento del prezzo.

quando avrà finito *when you've finished*
in vendita *on sale*
anticipo *deposit*
trenta per cento *30 per cent*
Glielo metto da parte? *Shall I put it aside for you?*
andare a ruba *to sell like hot cakes*
Gliene potremo (from
    potere) **conservare uno**. *We'll be able to put one by for you.*

---

5 Gliele spediranno
They'll send them to you

The shop assistant tells the **Signorina** that she can pay the balance when she comes to collect it.

a Vero o falso? *Il commesso dà una ricevuta alla signorina.*
b *Cosa dovrà fare la signorina se col cd non ci saranno i testi?*

Commesso	Pagherà il resto quando verrà a ritirarlo.
Signorina	Va bene, grazie. Prendo anche questi due dvd. Quanto fa?
Commesso	Le faccio il conto ... Un attimo, signorina, aspetti che le dò la ricevuta per quando ritirerà il cd.
Signorina	Sì, grazie. Un'ultima cosa. Sa se col cd ci saranno i testi delle canzoni? Mi interessano anche le parole.
Commesso	Mi spiace, non saprei. Se non ci saranno, dovrà richiederle direttamente alla casa discografica. Gliele spediranno a casa; o forse potrà trovarle su internet.

ritirerà (from **ritirare**) *you will collect*
testo *text*
mi spiace = **mi dispiace** *I'm sorry*
non saprei (from **sapere**) *I wouldn't know*
richiedere *to ask for, order*
casa discografica *record company*

Grammar

1 FUTURE TENSE: REGULAR FORMATION

Change the infinitive endings **-are** and **-ere** to **-erò, -erai, -erà, -eremo, -erete, -eranno**. For verbs ending in **-ire**, change **-ire** to **-irò, -irai, -irà, -iremo, -irete, -iranno**.

prendere *to take*   **prenderò** *I shall/will take*
finire *to finish*   **finirò** *I shall/will finish*

Insight

Attenzione! Note particularly the final accent on the **io** and **lui/lei** forms as this is where the stress falls.

Future tense **parlare** *to speak* **prendere** *to take* **coprire** *to cover*

parlerò *I shall, will speak, etc.*	**prenderò**	**coprirò**
parlerai	**prenderai**	**coprirai**
parlerà	**prenderà**	**coprirà**
parleremo	**prenderemo**	**copriremo**
parlerete	**prenderete**	**coprirete**
parleranno	**prenderanno**	**copriranno**

For **pagare** and other verbs ending in **-care** and **-gare**, an 'h' is added before 'e' throughout the future to preserve the hard sound of the infinitive (Unit 12, Section 8):

| pagare | pagherò, pagherai, pagherà, ecc. |
| cercare | cercherò, cercherai, cercherà, ecc. |

Verbs ending in **-giare** and **-ciare** omit 'i' in the future tense:

mangiare	mangerò, mangerai, mangerà, ecc.
lasciare	lascerò, lascerai, lascerà, ecc.
cominciare	comincerò, comincerai, comincerà, ecc.

2 FUTURE TENSE: IRREGULAR FORMATION

Future tense **avere** to have	
avrò *I shall have, I will have, etc.*	avremo
avrai	avrete
avrà	avranno

Although the future endings are always the same, the stems of some verbs appear in contracted form. Here is a list of some of the more common ones. Most appear in this unit.

These verbs follow the same pattern as **avere**:

Verbs forming future tense like **avere**		
andare	*to go*	andrò, andrai, andrà, andremo, andrete, andranno
cadere	*to fall*	cadrò, cadrai, cadrà, ecc.
dovere	*to have to*	dovrò, dovrai, dovrà, ecc.
potere	*to be able*	potrò, potrai, potrà, ecc.
sapere	*to know*	saprò, saprai, saprà, ecc.
vedere	*to see*	vedrò, vedrai, vedrà, ecc.
vivere	*to live*	vivrò, vivrai, vivrà, ecc.

The following verbs form the future tense like **fare**:

*Verbs forming future tense like **fare***

fare	*to do, make:*	**farò, farai, farà, faremo, farete, faranno**
dare	*to give:*	**darò, darai, darà, ecc.**
stare	*to stay:*	**starò, starai, starà, ecc.**

The following verbs form the future tense with a double consonant:

Verbs forming future tense with double consonant

bere	*to drink*	**berrò, berrai, berrà, berremo, berrete, berranno**
rimanere	*to remain, stay*	**rimarrò, rimarrai, rimarrà, ecc.**
tenere	*to hold, keep*	**terrò, terrai, terrà, ecc.**
venire	*to come*	**verrò, verrai, verrà, ecc.**
volere	*to wish, want*	**vorrò, vorrai, vorrà, ecc.**

*Future tense **sedersi** to sit (down)*

mi siederò	*I shall, will sit (down) etc.*	**ci siederemo**
ti siederai		**vi siederete**
si siederà		**si siederanno**

*Future tense **essere** to be*

sarò	*I shall, will be etc.*	**saremo**
sarai		**sarete**
sarà		**saranno**

3 FUTURE TENSE: USE

The future tense in Italian is used to express future time:

Verremo a prenderti alla stazione.   *We'll come and collect you from the station.*

Sometimes, as we have seen, the present tense in Italian conveys the idea of something imminent, but whenever it does so, the future may equally be used:

Lo faccio più tardi.⎫
Lo farò più tardi. ⎭ *I'll do it later.*   **Ci penso io.** ⎫
Ci penserò io. ⎭ *I'll see to it.*

Italian also uses the future tense in subordinate clauses introduced by conjunctions of time (*when ... as soon as ...*, etc.) where the future is implied.

Cosa farai *quando sarai* grande?   *What will you do when you grow up?*

***Appena arriverò* sistemerò tutto.**   *As soon as I arrive I'll fix everything.*

Fra, meaning *in*, and **per**, meaning *by*, always refer to something about to happen. They are often used, therefore, with the future tense:

Lo *vedrò fra* una settimana.   *I'll see him in a week's time.*
Lo *finirò per* venerdì.   *I'll finish it by Friday.*

The future is also used to suggest probability or possibility:

Chi *sarà* a quest'ora?   *Who could it be at this time?*
***Sarà* Mirella.**   *It's probably Mirella.*
Chi è quel ragazzo?   *Who's that boy?*
***Sarà* il suo fidanzato.**   *It's probably her fiancé. / Maybe it's her fiancé.*

Che ora è?/Che ore sono?   *What time is it?*
***Saranno* le nove.**   *It will be about nine.*

4 MACCHÈ! *NOT AT ALL*

Macchè is used to contradict or deny what has been said previously:

Funziona bene quest'ascensore? *Does this lift/elevator work properly?*

Macchè! È sempre guasto. *Of course not! It's always out of order.*

Guadagni molto? *Do you earn a lot?*

Macchè! Lo stipendio che prendo non mi basta neanche per vivere. *Certainly not! The salary I get isn't even enough for me to live on.*

Gliel'hanno regalato? *Did they give it to you?*

Macchè regalato! L'ho comprato. *Give it to me! You're joking! I bought it.*

5 SENTIRE *TO HEAR, FEEL*

Sentir(e) means both to *hear* and to *feel*. **Sentir(e) dire** means *to hear that* ... and **sentir(e) parlare** *to hear of* ...

Ho *sentito dire* che questo film è buono. *I hear (lit: heard) this film is good.*

Non ne ho mai *sentito* parlare. *I've never heard of it.*

Senti! (**tu**) and **senta!** (**lei**) are used to attract attention and correspond to the English *Listen!* or *Excuse me!*:

Senti! Perchè non usciamo? *Listen! Why don't we go out?*

Senta per favore! Quando parte il prossimo treno per Verona? *Excuse me! When does the next train leave for Verona?*

6 BOH ....! *I DON'T KNOW!*

This is an exclamation used when the speaker does not know or is not sure of something.

| Chi è quel signore? *Boh ..!* | *Who is that man? I don't know,* |
| | *goodness knows!* |

This renders the idea that something is being done of necessity, whether you like it or not:

Devi lavorare domani?	*Do you have to work tomorrow?*
Sì, *per forza*, altrimenti mi licenziano.	*Yes, I really must, otherwise I'll get the sack. (lit: they dismiss me.)*
Devi già andare?	*Have you got to go already?*
***Per forza*, altrimenti perderò l'aereo.**	*Yes, I've got to, otherwise I'll miss the plane.*
Devo farlo *per forza*.	*I absolutely have to do it.*

8 *DOUBLE PRONOUNS* TE LO FARÒ SAPERE *I'LL LET YOU KNOW*

We have already seen how **ci + ne** becomes **ce ne** in the **expression ce ne sono**. Other combinations of unstressed pronouns may also be found. Here are the principles along which they combine:

Indirect object pronouns **mi** (*to/for me*), **ti** (*to/for you*), **ci** (*to/for us*), **vi** (*to/for you* pl) precede direct object ones **lo, la, li, le,** and also **ne**.

They (**mi, ti, ci, vi**) become **me, te, ce, ve,** before **lo, la, li, le,** and **ne**:

Mi dà *il libro*.	*He gives me the book.*
***Me lo* dà.**	*He gives it to me.*
Ti darò *la ricevuta*.	*I'll give you the receipt.*
***Te la* darò.**	*I'll give it to you.*
***Te lo* farò sapere.**	*I'll let you know (it).*
Vi presenterò *la mia ragazza*.	*I'll introduce my girlfriend to you (pl).*
***Ve la* presenterò.**	*I'll introduce her to you (pl).*

Nino ci presterà *la macchina*. *Nino will lend us his car.*
***Ce la* presterà.** *He will lend it to us.*
***Quante bottiglie di* vino ci** *How many bottles of*
porterài? *wine will you*
bring us?
***Ve ne* porterò due.** *I'll bring you (pl)*
two (of them).

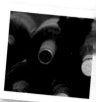

Indirect **gli** and **le** + object pronouns are dealt with
in Unit 24.

Come si dice?
How do you say it?

🔊 **CD 2, TR 32**

1 *How to ask someone when*   **Quando avrai le ferie? Le avrò alla**
they will take their annual   **fine di giugno/fra una**
leave; say when you will have   **settimana/fra un mese, ecc.**
yours

2 *How to ask someone where*   **Dove andrai? Andrò dai miei**
they will be going and say   **genitori/da un mio amico,**
who you will be staying with   **ecc.**
or seeing

3 *How to ask when a book, CD,*   **Quando uscirà il libro, il cd, ecc?**
etc., will come out

How to say when it will do so   **Uscirà il dieci marzo, il quindici**
maggio, ecc.

4 *How to ask someone when an*   **Quando ci sarà la mostra?**
exhibition will take place

How to say you will let them   **Te lo farò sapere.**
know.

340

Practice

1 *Below is a list of things* **Antonella** *has to do next Saturday.*
Imagine you are **Antonella** *and answer in the first person,*
using the future tense, as in the example.

Antonella, cosa farai sabato prossimo?

Esempio: **a** Mi alzerò presto, ecc.

Sabato prossimo Antonella deve:
  a *alzarsi presto*
  b *bere un bicchier(e) di latte*
  c *andare al mercato*
  d *fare i letti*
  e *pulire le camere*
  f *preparare da mangiare*
  g *sparecchiare (to clear) la tavola*
  h *lavare i piatti*
  i *riposarsi un po'*
  j *prendere un po' di sole in terrazza*
  k *andare ad aiutare sua zia nel negozio di elettrodomestici*
    (household appliances)
  l *finire di lavorare verso le otto*
  m *uscire con delle simpaticissime amiche*

2 *Answer these questions with the 3rd person plural of the*
future tense.

Esempio: **Finiscono oggi?** __ fra un paio di settimane.
No. Finiranno fra un paio di settimane.
  a *Escono subito?* __ più tardi.
  b *Restano a pranzo?* __ a cena.
  c *Vengono sabato?* __ domenica.
  d *Possono farlo adesso?* __ domani pomeriggio.
  e *Sono qui alle cinque?* __ per le otto.
  f *Lo fanno stamattina?* __ dopo pranzo.
  g *Arrivano questa settimana?* __ la settimana prossima.
  h *La costruiscono quest'anno?* __ fra tre anni. (**costruire** *to*
    build)

3 *Replace the infinitive (in brackets) by the first person plural of*
the future. Start: **Fra due settimane andremo ...**

Fra due settimane (andare) con i nostri amici in villeggiatura.

(Stare) al mare per una diecina di giorni e poi (trascorrere) una settimana in montagna dove abbiamo una piccola villetta. (Tornare) il quattordici agosto per passare le feste a casa. Il quindici (dare) un grande pranzo all'aperto: (invitare) tutti i nostri parenti. Nel pomeriggio (guardare) la processione dal balcone e poi (andare) un po' in giro per il paese. La sera (sedersi) alla pasticceria 'Roma' dove (prendere) il gelato e (ascoltare) la musica fino a mezzanotte.

andare in villeggiatura *to go on holiday*
villetta *small villa, cottage*
processione *procession*

4 All the questions are addressed to you
   alone or to you and your partner:
   answer with **me** or **ce** + object
   pronoun + verb as in the examples.
   Esempi: Chi le mostrerà le diapositive?
   __ il professore.
   Me le mostrerà il professore.
   Chi vi mostrerà le diapositive? __ il
   professore.
   Ce le mostrerà il professore.

   a *Chi le riparerà la macchina? __ il
      meccanico.*
   b *Chi le cambierà le sterline? __ il cassiere.*
   c *Chi vi prenoterà l'albergo? __ il nostro amico Sandro.*
   d *Chi le farà il quadro? __ un pittore francese.*
   e *Chi vi porterà il vino dall'Italia? __ un nostro collega.*
   f *Chi le disegnerà la casa? __ un architetto italiano.*
   g *Chi le regalerà il dizionario? __ mia sorella.*
   h *Chi vi troverà l'appartamento? __ nostro cugino.*
5 *Ora tocca a te!*

You are in a bookshop and you'd like a book about Italy
(sull'Italia).

You	*I'd like a book about Italy.*
Libraio	Che tipo di libro? Desidera qualcosa sulla politica o sull'economia?
You	*I'm really looking for a book for tourists.*
Libraio	Dunque, è una guida che desidera?
You	*Yes. I'd like to do a tour of the lakes.*
Libraio	Ah! Allora le serve un libro sull'Italia settentrionale!
You	*Exactly. May I see what* you have?*
Libraio	Mi dispiace, ma al momento non abbiamo niente.
You	*How's that?*
Libraio	Purtroppo ho venduto l'ultimo un'ora fa.
You	*Aren't you expecting any others?*
Libraio	Naturalmente! Ma lei quando parte?
You	*I shall be leaving on the first of June.*
Libraio	Bene. Se viene qui alla fine di maggio avrò proprio ciò che desidera.
You	*Can I reserve a copy now?*
Libraio	Senz'altro. Mi lasci il dieci per cento di anticipo e il suo indirizzo. Quando il libro arriverà glielo farò sapere.

*what **ciò che**

6 *Read the following flyer about these summer events* (**manifestazioni**) *and answer the questions.*
Dove si deve andare per vedere:
   a *La Mostra dei mobili antichi?*
   b *La Mostra dei telefilm?*
   c *La festa del lago?*

MANIFESTAZIONI

A Castiglion Fiorentino: **Palio dei rioni** la terza domenica di giugno. A Cortona: **Mostra-mercato nazionale del mobile antico** in agosto-settembre. A Castiglione del Lago: **festa del lago** con sfilata di barche illuminate, in agosto; **mercato dell'antiquariato** il terzo sabato di ogni mese da aprile a settembre. A Montepulciano: **Cantiere internazionale d'arte**, con mostre d'arte e spettacoli de teatro e concerti, in luglio e agosto. A Chianciano Terme: **Mostra internazionale dei telefilm** a maggio-giugno. A Chiusi: **Estate musicale** in luglio.

Le feste *Festivals*

Religious festivals are still celebrated in many Italian towns and villages. Even the smallest villages pay homage to their patron saint and in many towns each district has its own local festival. The celebrations last several days and include processions, music from local bands, sporting events and firework displays. **Le sagre** *food festivals*, celebrate agricultural produce such as **l'uva** *grapes* or **pomodori** *tomatoes*. There are also the festivals that include displays of historical pageantry such as **il Palio di Siena** which dates back to mediaeval times.

Il Ferragosto

This most important national holiday takes place on 15th August. It is particularly special in Italy, where all normal routine is interrupted, and no-one goes to work. Everything is closed down except in tourist resorts where shops remain open for holidaymakers. It is also a period of homecoming for the many Italian emigrants who have sought work abroad and now want to rejoin their families. It coincides with a religious festival, **la Festa dell'Assunta**, *the Feast of the Assumption*, which is celebrated in towns and villages throughout the country, especially in the South, where the local saint is paraded through the streets, accompanied by the local band and a procession, with the festivities often culminating at nightfall in a magnificent firework display.

Il Festival di San Remo *The San Remo Song Festival*

Perhaps because of the Italian dominance throughout Europe in the operatic field during the 18th and 19th centuries, most Italians equate classical music with opera rather than with instrumental music. **The San Remo Song Festival** has had for over half a century the same sort of popularity and standing for Italians today as operatic arias would have had for their forefathers in the past: for almost a week the whole nation sits in judgement of televised performances by the best singers of the latest songs by any composer who is fortunate enough to be included: the winners can count on sales not only in continental Europe, but also abroad, especially in Latin America. Past judges have included **Luciano Pavarotti** (1935–2007), the world famous tenor.

Websites

Film and cinema throughout Italy:
http://www.trovacinema.it/
Art (the **Nuova Accademia delle Belle Arti di Milano**):
http://naba.it

TEST YOURSELF

Translate the following sentences into Italian.

1   *I will go to the Uffizi Gallery on Thursday.*

2   *When will they finish the book?*

3   *Luigi will pay the bill.*

4   *They will come to see us in September.*

5   *I will finish my degree this summer.*

6   *We will have dinner at that new restaurant tonight.*

7   *You will see that it makes sense.*

8   *The park? He will show it to you.*

9   *What time will the show begin?*

10   *When will you (pl) leave for the holidays?*

22

Ieri e oggi
Then and now

In this unit you will learn:
- *how to say where you used to work*
- *how to say whether you liked what you were doing*
- *how to say where you used to live*
- *how to say what you used to do*
- *how to ask others similar questions.*

1 Dove lavoravi?
Where did you use to work?

Filippo asks **Michele** where he used to work before moving to Rome. He answers that he used to be in Turin where he worked for Fiat.

   a **Vero o falso?** *A Torino Michele abitava in periferia.*
   b *La moglie di Michele, quando abitava a Torino, trovava la vita molto interessante?*

Filippo	Dove lavoravi prima di trasferirti a Roma?
Michele	Ero a Torino. Lavoravo alla Fiat.
Filippo	E non ti piaceva stare lì?
Michele	No. La vita di fabbrica non mi andava proprio.
Filippo	Abitavate in centro?
Michele	No. Avevamo un appartamento in periferia; mia moglie trovava la vita molto monotona. Non veniva mai a trovarci nessuno. E tu, cosa fai qui?
Filippo	Adesso sono impiegato in una grande società straniera. Prima lavoravo anch'io in fabbrica.
Michele	Una volta riuscivo a sopportare quel lavoro, adesso non più.

QUICK VOCAB

fabbrica *factory*
non mi andava (from **andare**) *didn't suit me*
avevamo (from **avere**) *we used to have*
sono impiegato *I'm employed*
società *company*
riuscivo (from **riuscire**) **a sopportare** *I managed to put up with/I could bear*

2 Dieci anni dopo
Ten years later

Two men recall when they were bachelors (**scapoli**).

a **Vero o falso?** *Quando Nino e Dario erano scapoli non uscivano mai.*

b *Che cosa dicevano sempre quando erano scapoli?*

Dario	Lo sapevi che abbiamo un altro bambino?
Nino	No. Non lo sapevo. Rallegramenti! Ti ricordi di quando eravamo scapoli? Dicevamo sempre che non volevamo sposarci.
Dario	Eh, come no! Me lo ricordo bene! Si dice sempre così finchè non si incontra la donna ideale.
Nino	Che bei tempi, i tempi del liceo! Uscivamo ogni sera e facevamo sempre tardi. Ti ricordi quella notte in cui ci siamo ubriacati e abbiamo fatto il bagno nel fiume?
Dario	Altroché! Una volta si poteva passare tutta la notte fuori; allora non ci si preoccupava di niente. Si era giovani e spensierati, ma ora con i bambini …
Nino	Hai ragione. E poi c'è l'età. Un tempo bevevo e mangiavo senza problemi. Ora il medico mi ha proibito di bere.
Dario	Purtroppo il tempo passa per tutti, e anche la salute se ne va.

QUICK VOCAB

rallegramenti! *congratulations!*
come no! Me lo ricordo … *of course I remember it …*
finchè non si incontra *until one meets*
ubriacarsi *to get drunk*
fiume (m) *river*
altrochè! *you bet I do!*
spensierato/a *carefree*
far tardi *to stay up late*
un tempo *at one time*
la salute se ne va *our health deteriorates*

---

3 A colloquio per un nuovo posto di lavoro
Interview for a new job

La signora Esposito asks **Eugenio Parisi** how he heard about the new job and he answers that he learnt about it from a newspaper advert (**l'inserzione sul giornale**).

a Vero o falso? *Eugenio Parisi lavorava in una banca.*
b *Perchè non ha fatto gli studi universitari?*

CD 2, TR 34, 01:00

Sig.ra E.	Come ha saputo di questo impiego?
Eugenio P.	Ho visto l'inserzione sul giornale.
Sig.ra E.	Che titolo di studio ha?
Eugenio P.	La maturità classica.
Sig.ra E.	Non ha fatto gli studi universitari?
Eugenio P.	Non ho potuto. Mio padre era gravemente ammalato e non poteva più mantenerci. Così mi sono impiegato in un'azienda agricola.
Sig.ra E.	Che cosa faceva lì?
Eugenio P.	Mi occupavo della produzione.
Sig.ra E.	È stato licenziato?
Eugenio P.	No. Il padrone ha venduto tutto.
Sig.ra E.	Vedrà che ora con la nostra ditta si troverà bene.

QUICK VOCAB

titolo di studio *educational qualifications*
maturità classica *high school leaving certificate*
ammalato/a *ill*
mantenere *to support*
azienda agricola *agricultural firm, farm*
impiegarsi *to get a job*
occuparsi di *to deal with*
licenziato/a *dismissed*
ditta *firm*

---

4 Sa suonare?
Can you play an instrument?

a Vero o falso? *Bruno sa suonare**
il pianoforte.
b *Nel passato anche Antonio*
suonava il pianoforte?

Antonio	Da quanto tempo suona il pianoforte?
Bruno	Da quando ero piccolo. E lei, sa suonare?
Antonio	Una volta suonavo la chitarra. Adesso non suono più.
Bruno	Che tipo di musica suonava?
Antonio	Soprattutto musica rock.
Bruno	Era professionista?
Antonio	No. Ero dilettante.

chitarra *guitar*
una volta ... *once* ...
soprattutto *above all*
il/la professionista *professional*
il/la dilettante *amateur*

*Use **suonare** *to play (an instrument)*, **giocare a** *to play (a game)*.

Grammar

1 *IMPERFECT TENSE (***ANDAVO***): FORMATION*

Take off the -are, -ere and -ire from the infinitive and add the appropriate endings.

parl-are	**parl-avo**	*I was speaking, used to speak, spoke, etc.*
vend-ere	**vend-evo**	*I was selling, used to sell, sold, etc.*
fin-ire	**fin-ivo**	*I was finishing, used to finish, finished, etc.*

Imperfect tense **parlare** *to speak*	**vendere** *to sell*	**finire** *to finish*
parlavo	vendevo	finivo
parlavi	vendevi	finivi
parlava	vendeva	finiva
parlavamo	vendevamo	finivamo
parlavate	vendevate	finivate
parlavano	vendevano	finivano

The stress always falls on the last syllable but one, except in the 3rd person plural where it shifts back to the last syllable but two:

Imperfect tense **andare** to go		
andavo	*I was going, I went, I used to go, etc*	**andavamo**
andavi		**andavate**
andava		**andavano**

Only essere does not conform to this pattern of endings:

Imperfect tense **essere** to be	
ero	*I was, used to be, etc.* **eravamo**
eri	**eravate**
era	**erano**

There are a few other verbs where, although the endings conform to the regular pattern, the stem changes. Here are some of the most important ones:

Infinitive		Imperfect
bere	*to drink*	**bevevo, bevevi, beveva, bevevamo, bevevate, bevevano**
dire	*to say, tell*	**dicevo, dicevi, diceva, dicevamo, dicevate, dicevano**
fare	*to do, make*	**facevo, facevi, faceva, ecc.**
produrre	*to produce*	**producevo, producevi, produceva, ecc.**

2 IMPERFECT TENSE: USE

There is no exact equivalent tense in English. **Parlavo** could mean, according to the context, *I spoke, I used to speak, I was speaking* or *I would speak*. The imperfect expresses continuity or habitual action in the past, whereas the perfect tense emphasizes that the action is completed.

Mentre *aspettavo* l'autobus, è arrivato un tassì.	*While I was waiting for the bus, a taxi arrived.*

In the above example the imperfect **aspettavo** describes what was already happening and could have continued to do so when the taxi arrived.

Mentre *guidavo*, mi sono accorto che non *avevo* più benzina.	*While I was driving I realized I had run out of (lit: had no more) petrol/gasoline.*

Habitual action is often expressed by *used to* or *would*:

***Uscivamo* ogni sera.**	*We used to go out every night.*
***Facevamo* sempre tardi.**	*We would always stay up late.*

Finally, it expresses a state of things in the past:

Ha detto che *abitava* a Venezia.	*He said he lived in Venice.*
In Inghilterra non *conosceva* nessuno.	*He knew nobody in England.*
In quanti *eravate*?	*How many were there of you?*
***Eravamo* in venti, ma ora siamo in dieci.**	*There were 20 of us, but now there are ten.*
Non *sapevo* che *eri* qui.	*I didn't know that you were here.*

It is because such verbs as <u>e</u>ssere and avere are associated with states rather than actions, that they are frequently seen in the imperfect. Other such verbs are: **volevo** (*I wanted*), **pensavo** (*I thought*), **credevo** (*I believed*), and **immaginavo** (*I imagined*).

Giorgio *voleva* sapere dove *andavi*.	*George wanted to know where you were going.*
***Pensavano* solo a divertirsi.**	*They thought only of having a good time.*

Sometimes the tense alters the meaning of the English. Compare the use of **sapere** in the second and third dialogues:

Lo *sapevi* **che ...?** *Did you know that ...?*
Come *ha saputo* **di questo** *How did you hear about this job?*
  posto?

3 FINCHÈ (NON) *UNTIL*

Finchè is frequently followed by **non** even when the sense is not negative:

Finchè non **te lo dico io, non** *You won't go out until I tell you.*
  uscirai.
Lo aspetterò *finchè (non)* *I'll wait (for him) till he comes.*
  verrà.

4 NON CI SI PREOCCUPAVA, SI ERA ... *ONE DIDN'T WORRY, ONE WAS ...*

Here is a summary of points to note when **si** *one* is used impersonally (see also Unit 5, Section 11).

a *The verb used with impersonal* **si** *will be plural if the noun it refers to is plural:*
  In questo istituto *si insegna* *Italian is taught in this institute.*
    l'italiano.
  In questo istituto *si* *Foreign languages are taught in*
    insegnano **le lingue** *this institute.*
    straniere.

b *When impersonal* **si** *is followed by a part of the verb* <u>essere</u> *and an adjective, the verb is always in the singular and the adjective in the plural:*
  Quando *si è giovani, si* *When one is young, one learns*
    impara **presto.** *fast.*

c *When reflexive verbs (**divertirsi**, **lavarsi**, ecc.) are used in the impersonal form, use **ci si** before the verb:*
(lui) si diverte *he enjoys himself*
ci si diverte *one enjoys oneself*
(lei) si lava *she washes (herself)*
ci si lava *one washes (oneself)*

5 PROFESSIONISTA *PROFESSIONAL*

Nouns or adjectives ending in -**ista** may be masculine or feminine. The plural forms end in -**i** when masculine, and -**e** when feminine:

il giornalista *(male journalist)* **i giornalisti**
la giornalista *(female journalist)* **le giornaliste**

Similarly, **il/la: pianista**, **chitarrista**, **violinista**, **farmacista**, **l'artista**, ecc.

6 ANDARSENE *TO BE OFF, TO LEAVE*

Andarsene is formed from the verb **andare** and **si**, which when followed by **ne**, becomes **se**. Similarly, the reflexive pronouns **mi**, **ti**, **ci**, **vi** become **me**, **te**, **ce**, **ve** before **ne**. Here is the present tense of **andarsene** in full:

(io) **me ne vado**	(noi) **ce ne andiamo**
(tu) **te ne vai**	(voi) **ve ne andate**
(lui/lei) **se ne va**	(loro) **se ne vanno**

It is frequently heard in conversation, and one way of rendering **me ne vado** in English would be: *I'm off.*

Me ne devo andare   *I must be off.*
or **devo andarmene.**

Remember that the perfect tense must be formed with **essere**:

Poichè mi annoiavo, *me ne*   *As I was bored, I left.*
   sono andato.

Se *ne sono andati* senza   *They went away without even saying*
   neanche salutarci.   *goodbye.*

Here is the perfect tense illustrated in dialogue form:

Tutti se ne sono andati. *(Everybody's left.)*

A A che ora ***te ne sei andato*** ieri sera?

B ***Me ne sono andato*** a mezzanotte, quando ***se n'è andato Ciro.***

A Io e Luisa invece, ***ce ne siamo andati*** alle dieci.

B Perchè ***ve ne siete andati*** così presto?

A Perchè eravamo stanchi. Anche Ida e Gino ***se ne sono andati*** così tardi?

B No. Loro ***se ne sono andati*** subito dopo che ***ve ne siete andati voi***, perchè stamattina dovevano alzarsi presto.

---

7 CAVARSELA, FARCELA

Cavarsela: a familiar expression meaning *to manage*, *to get off*, *to get away with*, *to pull through*. It behaves like a reflexive verb with the addition of **la**: Me la cavo, te la cavi, se la cava, ce la caviamo, ve la cavate, se la cavano (the **la** never changes).

Non sono stati arrestati: se la   *They weren't arrested: they got off.*
   sono cavata.

Il paziente è grave, ma se la   *The patient is seriously ill, but he will*
   caverà senz' altro.   *certainly pull through.*

Insomma, me la sono cavata   *On the whole I managed fairly well.*
   abbastanza bene.

Farcela means *to cope*, *to go on* or *to make in* the sense of *to manage*. The **ce la** never changes: (**non**) ce la faccio, ce la fai, ce la facciamo.

Sono tanto stanco. Non *ce la faccio* più! *I'm so tired. I can't go on.*

L'aereo parte alla otto. Se andiamo in macchina, *ce la facciamo* sicuramente. *The plane leaves at eight. If we go by car we will be sure to make it.*

Here is the past: ce l'ho fatta, ce l'hai fatta, ce l'ha fatta, ce l'abbiamo fatta, ce l'avete fatta, ce l'hanno fatta.

_____

Come si dice?
How do you say it?

🔊 **CD 2, TR 35**

1 *How to ask someone where they used to work* — **Dove lavorava?**

  How to say where you used to work — **Lavoravo …**

2 *How to ask someone whether they liked what they were doing and answer* — **(Non) le piaceva?** **(Non) mi piaceva.**

3 *How to ask someone where they lived/used to live* — **Dove abitava?**

  How to say where you lived/ used to live — **Abitavo …**

4 *How to ask someone what they used to do* — **Cosa faceva?**

  How to say what you used to do — **Uscivo, bevevo, mangiavo, andavo, suonavo, … ecc.**

Practice

1 Luciano, *in nostalgic mood, notes the differences between life as he saw it in* **Salerno**, *and as he sees it in London. On the left you have to say what he used to do or what happened in* **Salerno** *(imperfect tense), on the right what happens at present.*

Esempio: A Salerno: A Londra:

a *(abitare) in un bell' appartamento in una vecchia casa*

Abitavo in un bell'appartamento. Abito in una vecchia casa.

A Salerno:

	A Londra:
a *(abitare) in un bell'appartamento*	*in una vecchia casa*
b *(fare) così caldo*	*così freddo*
c *(esserci) tanto sole*	*tanta pioggia*
d *(uscire) ogni sera*	*non ... mai*
e *(venire a trovarmi) tante persone*	*non ... nessuno*
f *(andare) ogni domenica alla spiaggia*	*qualche volta in piscina*
g *(parlare) con tanta gente*	*non ... con nessuno*
h *(bere) caffè e vino*	*tè e birra*

2 *Answer these questions, making sure you use the appropriate person of the verb in the imperfect, as in the examples.*

Esempi: Perchè Franca non è uscita ieri? __ (piovere) Perchè pioveva.

Perchè non mi avete scritto? __non (avere) il tuo indirizzo.

Perchè non avevamo il tuo indirizzo.

a *Perchè Franco non l'ha bevuto il caffè? __ (essere) troppo forte.*

b *Perchè sei andato dal dentista? __ mi (far male) un dente.*

c *Perchè avete comprato due biciclette? __ (costare) poco.*

d *Perchè hai cambiato lavoro? __ dove (essere) prima (dovere) lavorare troppo.*

e *Perchè non ha comprato la casa in Via Roma? __ (essere) troppo cara.*

f *Perchè non avete mangiato nulla? __ non (avere) appetito.*

g *Perchè hanno bevuto tutta quell'acqua? __ (avere) sete.*

h *Perchè siete andati a letto così presto? __ (essere) stanchi morti.*

i *Perchè sei andato dal medico? __ non (sentirsi) bene.*

j *Perchè Ida è andata in banca? __ (aver bisogno di) soldi.*

3 Gianfranco *could get no peace: every time he was engaged in a task (imperfect) something happened (perfect).*
   Es**e**mpio: Mentre Gianfranco (*mangiare*), (*r**o**mpersi*) il dente.
   Mentre Gianfranco mangiava si è rotto il dente.

   a *Mentre Gianfranco (r**a**dersi)*, (telefonare) Marco.*
   b *Mentre (scr**i**vere), (r**o**mpersi) la penna.*
   c *Mentre (riparare) la m**a**cchina, (arrivare) Francesca.*
   d *Mentre (cucinare), (scottarsi) la mano.*
   e *Mentre (l**e**ggere), (and**a**rsene) la luce.*
   f *Mentre (guardare) la tv, sua m**o**glie gli (chi**e**dere) di aggiustare la lavatrice.*

ra**dersi to shave (oneself)*

4 *Read the* **p**i**ccoli ann**u**nci (inserzi**o**ni)** *and answer the questions.*

i

> **NEOLAUREATA**
> **offresi come**
> **babysitter di**
> **pomeriggio e di sera.**
> **Abita a Bergamo.**
> **Telefono: 437027**

ii

> Marisa, diplomata in
> ragioneria, si offre
> per mezza giornata
> per lavori d'ufficio.
> Telefonatele nelle ore
> dei pasti al numero
> 64 30 00 6 di Venezia.

iii

> Siamo due giovani
> prossimi alle nozze.
> Vorremmo (we would
> like) prendere in affitto
> un appartamento,
> anche piccolo
> ma confortevole.
> Telefonateci al numero
> 48 93 12 di Pisa.

iv

> Laureato scienze
> politiche, trentenne,
> pluriennale (of many
> years) esperienza
> lavorativa, francese,
> inglese, tedesco,
> esamina proposte
> interessanti.
> Roma 20 14 82.

    i **a** *È laureata da molto tempo?*

        b *Per quale periodo della giornata si offre come baby-sitter?*

        c *Dove vive?*

   ii **a** *Ha il diploma di segretaria o di ragioniera?*

        b *Per quanto tempo vuole lavorare?*

        c *Quando bisogna telefonare?*

  iii **a** *Sono già sposati i due giovani?*

        b *Vogliono comprare l'appartamento?*

        c *L'appartamento deve essere per forza grande?*

   iv **a** *È laureato in scienze economiche e bancarie?*

        b *Quanti anni ha?*

        c *Lavora da poco tempo?*

        d *Quali lingue conosce?*

5 **Tutti se ne vanno** *Everybody's leaving: This dialogue contains all forms of the present tense of andarsene. Fill in the blanks appropriately.*

Esempio: È tardi. __ vado. È tardi. Me ne vado.

A Ma come! Già __ vai?

B Eh, sì. __ devo andare.

A E Bruna? __ va anche lei?

B No. Bruna non __ va ancora. Però Anna e Roberto __ vanno. E voi, quando __ andate?

A Noi __ andiamo più tardi.

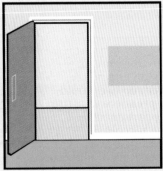

Tutti se ne vanno.   *Tutti se ne sono andati.*

6 *Ora tocca a te!*

You are **il datore di lavoro** (*employer*) interviewing a woman for a job.

You	*Where did you work when you were in Naples?*
Signora	Lavoravo in un'azienda agricola che esportava frutta in tutta Europa.
You	*But you yourself, what did you do exactly?*
Signora	Controllavo la qualità della frutta.
You	*Did you find the work difficult?*
Signora	Sì, perchè bastava un piccolo sbaglio per perdere clienti molto importanti.
You	*How long did you work in that firm?*
Signora	Tre anni e mezzo. Poi ce ne siamo andati a Sorrento, perchè mio padre era stanco di vivere in una grande città.
You	*Is that why you want to change your job?*
Signora	Sì, soprattutto per questo.

7 *A chi puoi rivolgerti se hai bisogno di aiuto per la laurea, il diploma, e che cosa devi fare per avere informazioni gratuite?*

PROBLEMI CON DIPLOMA E LAUREA?

CEPU TI AIUTA A RISOLVERLI

Richiedi informazioni gratuite e senza impegno compilando il form:

Nome* Cognome*

Indirizzo* Città* Cap*

Provincia* ------- seleziona ------- E-Mail*

Telefono* Cellulare

Richiesta* Preparazione esami universitari (CEPU)

INFORMAZIONI IN MATERIA DI PROTEZIONE DEI DATI PERSONALI (art. 13 d. lgs. 196/2003) In relazione all'informativa (PRIVACY POLICY), che dichiaro di aver letto e compreso, esprimo il consenso previsto dall'articolo 23 del CODICE al trattamento dei miei dati personali da parte di CEPU S.R.L. per tutte le finalità ivi descritte.

☑ Autorizzo il trattamento dei dati richiedi informazioni gratuite

Torino *Turin*

Capital of the Piedmont region in Northern Italy, and formerly capital of the whole country (1860–4) **Torino** still retains many vestiges of its former grandeur in its squares and avenues.

During the greater part of the twentieth century most Italians associated it solely with the **Fiat** car industry based there. The transformation came early in 2006 when, having been chosen as the venue for the XX Winter Olympics, it underwent a radical makeover turning it almost overnight into a worldwide attraction. Opinion polls suggest that in future even Italians will consider it as one of the cities worthy of being added to their tourist circuit. The Eurostar high speed rail service (300 km per hour) now connects the city to Milan, Rome and Naples.

Torino also has the distinction of seeing the birth of the **Slow Food Movement**, founded by **Carlo Patrini** in the 1990s as a counter to the fast food industry (**il fast food**) and as a successful protest against the building of a Macdonald's restaurant in nearby **Bra**.

TEST YOURSELF

Unscramble the following to make meaningful sentences.

1 *in di viaggi lavoravo un'agenzia*

2 *una adesso in scuola impiegato sono*

3 *chitarra suonare sai la?*

4 *fa un batteria* anni suonavo la rock in gruppo dieci*

5 *giorno parco andavamo ogni al*

6 *arrivato è cucinavo mentre Pietro*

7 *qui mi non rimarrò vedrà finchè*

8 *aspettato verità non ha la finchè detto gli ha*

9 *devo me andare ne*

10 *Bar a quando bere ogni ero all'Angie's venerdì Firenze qualcosa a andavo*

*batteria = *drums*

23

Senza complimenti!
No need to be polite!

In this unit you will learn:
* *how to invite someone in, informally*
* *how to ask someone what they were saying*
* *how to say that you were about to ...*
* *how to ask someone to do something for you*
* *how to tell someone there's no need to be polite.*

---

1 Stavamo proprio parlando di te
We were just talking about you

Angelo has heard somone ring the bell (**hanno suonato il campanello**) and **Bruna** goes to open the door to let **Gianna** in.

a Vero o falso? *Quando hanno suonato, Angelo è andato ad aprire la porta.*
b *Cos'ha scritto Gianna per Bruna?*

Angelo	Hanno suonato il campanello. Vado ad aprire?
Bruna	No, Angelo, vado io. Dev'essere Gianna. Ciao Gianna! Entra! Stavamo proprio parlando di te.
Gianna	Davvero? E che cosa stavate dicendo?
Bruna	Ah ...
Gianna	Sono venuta a salutarti perchè parto domani mattina presto. Disturbo?
Bruna	No, no, figurati! Vieni, cara, vieni. Entra pure!

CD 2, TR 37

Gianna	Grazie.
Bruna	Ma perchè stai in piedi? Siediti! Faccio il caffè!
Gianna	No, grazie. Me ne devo andare. Ho promesso alla mamma di aiutarla a fare le valigie. Ti lascio il mio indirizzo?
Bruna	Sì, sì. Stavo proprio per chiedertelo. Scrivimelo qui sopra.
Gianna	Ecco, tieni. Ed ora ti saluto.

QUICK VOCAB

Davvero? E che cosa stavate dicendo? *Really? Were you? And what were you saying?*

Sì, sì. Stavo proprio per chiedertelo. *Yes, do. I was just going to ask you for it.*

promettere (pp **promesso**) *to promise*

dev'essere *it must be*

2 Ma dai, siediti!
Come on, sit down

Bruna offers **Gianna** a glass of liqueur.

a **Vero o falso?** *Bruna offre a Gianna un bicchierino di liquore.*
b *Gianna fuma ancora?*

🎧 CD 2, TR 37, 01:09

Bruna	Ma siediti! Cosa posso offrirti? Lo prendi un bicchierino di liquore?
Gianna	No, grazie.
Bruna	Ma dai, siediti! Solo due minuti. Non fare complimenti!
Gianna	Non faccio complimenti. E poi, non bevo più. Ho anche smesso di fumare.
Bruna	Che brava! Ma oggi fa' un'eccezione. Tieni, assaggia questa Sambuca! Vedi com'è buona! Cin cin!
Gianna	Cin cin!

oggi fa' un'eccezione *today make an exception*
smettere di (pp **smesso**) *to stop*
assaggiare *to taste*
Sambuca *a type of liqueur*
cin cin! *cheers!*

---

3 Che cosa facciamo da *mangiare?*
What shall we cook?

Romano suggests they should cook **la pastasciutta** (pasta served with a sauce).

a **Vero o falso?** *Romano chiede a Silvio di prendergli una scatola di pomodori.*
b *A Romano piace l'aglio?*

Romano	Senti, Silvio, facciamo la pasta?
Silvio	D'accordo. Fammi un favore, prendimi una scatola di pomodori!
Romano	Quale? Quella grande?
Silvio	No. Quella che hai in mano. Dammi anche l'apriscatole!
Romano	Dov'è? Lì dentro?
Silvio	Sì. Nel secondo cassetto.
Romano	Non metterci l'aglio nella salsa, però, perchè non mi piace. Falla solo con la cipolla. È cotta la pasta?
Silvio	Penso di sì. Assaggiala! Dimmi se c'è abbastanza sale! Attento! Non scottarti!
Romano	Per me va bene. Se la vuoi al dente, è pronta.

Fammi un favore! *Could you do a me favour?*
falla *make it*
prendimi una scatola *get me a tin*
dammi *give me*
apriscatole (m) *tin-opener*
lì dentro *in(side) there*
aglio, cipolla *garlic, onion*
assaggiala! *try it*
Non scottarti! *Don't burn yourself.*
al dente *slightly underdone (lit: to the tooth)*

Grammar

1 *IMPERATIVE:* **TU, NOI,** *AND* **VOI** *FORMS*

To obtain the **tu** (familiar) form of the imperative of regular **-are** verbs, take off the **-are** from the infinitive and add **-a**:

Ordin-**are** becomes <u>o</u>rdina:

<u>O</u>rdina il secondo piatto!   *Order the second course.*

Paga il conto!   *Pay the bill.*

For most **-ere** and **-ire** verbs, the **tu** form of the imperative is the same as the **tu** form of the present tense:

(tu) prendi …	→	***Prendi* il cappello e l'ombrello!** *Take your hat and umbrella.*	
(tu) chiudi …	→	***Chiudi* (la porta) a chiave!** *Lock the door.*	
(tu) vieni …	→	**Vieni dentro!**	*Come inside!*
(tu) corri …	→	***Corri! Corri!***	*Run! Run!*
(tu) scendi …	→	***Scendi* giù!**	*Come downstairs!*

For the negative of the **tu** form use **non + infinitive**:

Alberto, *non toccare* il quadro!	*Albert! Don't touch the picture.*
Mari̱a, *non parlare* con la bocca piena!	*Mary! Don't talk with your mouth full!*
Non *cambiare* discorso!	*Don't change the subject.*

Insight

As we saw in Unit 14, the **noi** and **voi** forms of the imperative are the same as the present tense. The negative is formed by putting **non** before the verb:

Non parlate tutti insieme! *Don't all speak at once.*

2 IMPERATIVE WITH UNSTRESSED AND REFLEXIVE PRONOUNS

With the **lei** forms, unstressed and reflexive pronouns precede the imperative:

Mi porti una forchetta e un coltello!	*Bring me a knife and fork.*
Si *segga* qui!	*Sit (down) here.*
Non si preoccupi!	*Don't worry.*
Mi scusi tanto, signor Sa̱uri!	*I'm so sorry, Mr Sauri.*

With the other forms of the imperative, the unstressed and the reflexive pronouns follow the verb and are joined to it, except in the negative where there is a choice:

Scu̱sami del ritardo!	*Sorry I'm late! (lit: Excuse me for the lateness.)*
Non dargli la ma̱ncia! *Non gli dare* la ma̱ncia!	*Don't give him a tip.*
Non andarci! *Non ci andare!*	*Don't go there.*

Accompagniamola a casa!   *Let's take her home.*
Sediamoci a tavola!   *Let's sit down to dinner (at the table).*
Sedetevi qui!   *Sit down here.*

3 *IMPERATIVE* **TU** *FORM OF* **FARE, DIRE, STARE, DARE** *AND* **ANDARE:**

> **fa'** *do* **di'** *say* **sta'** *stay* **da'** *give* **va'** *go*

Da' un'occhiata al libro!   *Have a look at the book.*
Sta' attento! Sta' zitto!   *Be careful. Be quiet.*

All the unstressed pronouns (including **ci**, **vi** and **ne**) except **gli**, double their initial consonants when combined with the above verbs (informal **tu**):

fa' + **lo** becomes **fallo**	**Fallo subito!**	*Do it immediately.*
di' + **mi** becomes **dimmi**	**Dimmi la verità!**	*Tell me the truth!*
da' + **le** becomes **dalle**	**Dalle il cucchiaio!**	*Give her the spoon.*
va' + **ci** becomes **vacci**	**Vacci tu!**	*You go there!*
di' + **gli** becomes **digli**	**Digli di venire a pranzo!**	*Tell him to come to lunch.*
sta' + **mi** becomes **stammi**	**Stammi a sentire!**	*Listen to me.*

4 *IMPERATIVE OF* **ESSERE, AVERE** *AND* **STARE**

Imperative **essere** *to be*	**avere** *to have*	**stare** *to be, stay*
sii (tu)!	abbi (tu)!	sta' (tu)!
sia (lei)!	abbia (lei)!	stia (lei)!
siamo (noi)!	abbiamo (noi)!	stiamo (noi)!
siate (voi)!	abbiate (voi)!	state (voi)!

Abbiate pazienza!   *Be patient!*
Siate un po' più generosi!   *Be a bit more generous!*

5 *MEANINGS OF* **PURE**

Pure may be used in the following ways:

a   *To grant permission with more conviction:*

Posso entrare?	*May I come in?*
Entri *pure*!	*Please do.*
Posso fare una telefonata?	*May I make a phone call?*
Sì, prego. Faccia *pure*!	*Certainly, go ahead!*

b   *Like* **anche** *to mean 'also':*

Vieni *pure* tu!	*You come too!*

6 QUELLO, QUELLA, QUELLI, QUELLE *THAT ONE, THOSE ONES*

The above, apart from being adjectives, may also be used as pronouns meaning *the one(s)*, *that(one)*, *those*. They must agree with the noun they refer to:

Questo rasoio non funziona: prendi *quello* del mio compagno.	*This razor doesn't work: take my partner's one.*
Chi è quella donna?	*Who is that woman?*
Quale? *Quella* con gli occhi celesti?	*Which one? The one with the blue eyes?*
Preferisco i quadri moderni a *quelli* antichi.	*I prefer modern paintings to old ones.*

7 WAYS OF SAYING 'WHAT'

In sentences such as the following, **quello che/quel che** means *what*:

Non sa *quello che* vuole.	*He doesn't know what he wants.*

You could equally say:

Non sa *ciò che* vuole, *or* **Non sa *quel che* vuole.**

8 EXPRESSIONS WITH IN

Here are a few more expressions with **in** where Italian uses neither the definite article nor the possessive.

Cos'hai in { **testa?** **tasca?** **mano?** **bocca?** } *What do you have* { *on your head?* *in your pocket?* *in your hand?* *in your mouth?* }

9 COME! *WHAT!*

When used alone **Come!** means *What!* It expresses surprise.

Come! **Questa bottiglia è già vuota?**   *What! Is this bottle already empty?*

10 STARE PER + *INFINITIVE* TO BE ABOUT TO

This construction renders the idea of *to be about to, to be on the point of*. It is used mainly in the present and imperfect:

Lo spettacolo *sta* per finire.   *The performance is about to end.*
Quando siamo usciti, *stava per* piovere.   *When we went out it was just about to rain.*
***Stiamo per* acquistare una nuova casa.**   *We are on the point of buying a new house.*

11 GERUND

Formation of gerund
-are verbs: drop **-are** and add **-ando**
-ere/-ire verbs: drop **-ere/-ire** and add **-endo**

----

pag*are* → **pag*ando***   **pot*ere*** → **pot*endo***   **fin*ire*** → **fin*endo***

Notice, however, these three special forms:

bere → bevendo   fare → facendo   dire → dicendo

Use of gerund

The Italian gerund corresponds to the form of the verb which, in English, ends in *-ing*.

Sbagliando s'impara.   *One learns by making mistakes.*

Sometimes it is best translated by *as*, *since*, *while*:

Dovendo mantenere la   *As he has to support his family, he*
  famiglia, lavora molto.   *works hard.*
Non *avendo* spiccioli, non mi   *Since he didn't have any loose*
  ha dato il resto.   *change, he didn't give me any*
                                        (change).
Andando a teatro, ho   *As I was going to the theatre, I met*
  incontrato Francesca.   *Frances.*

Insight

The Italian gerund can never be preceded by a preposition as in English, and its ending never changes. When object pronouns are used with a gerund, they are attached to the end of it, but when **stare** + gerund is used (see below) they precede **stare**:

Vedendolo arrivare così tardi, ho pensato che …
On seeing him arrive so late, I thought that …

Stare + gerund stresses the time during which the action is happening:

Cosa *stai facendo*?   *What are you doing?*
Di chi *stai parlando*?   *Who are you talking about?*
Stavamo uscendo quando è   *We were just going out when a friend*
  arrivato un nostro amico.   *of ours arrived.*

Ha cambiato i soldi? No, *li* *sta cambiando* adesso. *Has he changed the money? No, he is changing it now.*

It is important to notice that no gerund can refer to the object of a sentence, so that if a sentence has both subject and object, the gerund must refer to the subject: **L'ho visto attraversando la strada** must mean *I saw him as I crossed the road*. To say *I saw him cross(ing) the road* Italian uses the following two ways:

L'ho visto *attraversare* la strada. *I saw him cross the road.*

L'ho visto *che attraversava* la strada. *I saw him crossing the road.*

Come si dice?
How do you say it?

◄) **CD 2, TR 38**

1 *How to invite someone in, informally How to ask them to sit down* **Vieni! Entra (pure)! Siediti!**

2 *How to ask what they were saying How to respond* **Cosa stavi dicendo? Stavo dicendo che …**

3 *How to say that you were about to ask …* **Stavo per chiedere, ecc.**

4 *How to ask someone to do something for you* **Fammi un favore, prendimi, dammi, ecc.**

5 *How to tell someone not to stand on ceremony, there's no need to be polite.* **Senza complimenti!**

Practice

1 *You are* **Vincenzo Alvaro's** *boss. One day, at work, he does not feel very well. Tell him to do the following, using the* **tu** *form of the imperative as in the example.*
Esempio: a Lasciare tutto.
Lascia tutto!

   a *Lasciare tutto.*
   b *Tornare a casa.*
   c *Andare a letto.*
   d *Coprirsi bene.* *
   e *Prendere un paio di aspirine.*
   f *Chiamare il medico.*
   g *Rimanere a casa per qualche giorno.*
   h *Non preoccuparsi di niente.*

*coprirsi bene (like **aprire**) to wrap up well

2 *Turn the following statements into commands or prohibitions according to the sense, using the* **tu** *form.*
Esempi: È vietato entrare. Non entrare!
È meglio telefonare. Telefona!

   a *È vietato fumare.*
   b *È meglio prendere l'aereo.*
   c *È inutile insistere.*
   d *È vietato parcheggiare lì.*
   e *È più conveniente andare in macchina.*
   f *È meglio portare l'ombrello.*
   g *È importante mettere la data su questo modulo.*
   h *È meglio usare la scheda telefonica.*

3 *Prohibitions with the* **tu** *form: You are going to tell someone not to do something. Respond to the following statements by using* **non** + *infinitive* + *direct object pronoun, choosing your verbs from the list below and using each once only.*

> perdere usare prendere attraversare
> pagare firmare comprare bere

Esempio: a Il contratto non mi piace.
Non firmarlo!

a *Il contratto non mi piace.*
b *La macchina è guasta.*
c *Il prosciutto è troppo caro.*
d *Il conto è sbagliato.*
e *L'acqua non è potabile.*
f *Questo treno è troppo lento.*
g *Questa strada è pericolosa.*
h *Questi documenti sono molto importanti.*

contratto *contract*
pericoloso *dangerous*
guasto *out of order*
potabile *drinkable*

4 *Commands and prohibitions (sta', va', di', da', fa'): You are being told to tell individual children to do certain things. Follow the instructions as in the example. Join the pronouns to the imperative. Check Grammar note 3 above for the imperative* **tu** *forms needed here.*
Esempio: Dica ad Alfredo di farle vedere cos'ha in mano.
Alfredo, fammi vedere cos'hai in mano!

a *Dica a Luigi di stare zitto.*
b *Dica ad Alfredo di farle assaggiare il gelato.*
c *Dica ad Elena di andare all'altra tavola.*
d *Dica a Vittorio di darle il bicchiere.*
e *Dica a Maria di darle il sale e il pepe.*
f *Dica a Nina di dirle cosa vuole per secondo piatto.*

5 *Complete as indicated, choosing between the present of* **stare per** *and* **stare** *+ gerund, according to the sense, and using the appropriate person of the verb.*
Esempio: Gli ospiti non si sono ancora messi a tavola?
No__ (chiacchierare) No. Stanno chiacchierando.

a *Posso parlare con Lucia? Mi spiace, ma __ (fare il bagno)*
b *Che buon odore viene dalla cucina! Sì. Mariangela __ (cucinare)*
c *Come sei bagnata Mirella! Sì. __ (piovere)*

d *Vera avrà molto da fare in questi giorni. Perchè? __*
   (sposarsi)

e *Che rumore viene da quella radio! Cosa vuoi! Il gruppo*
   'Ragazzi del Sole'__ (suonare)

f *Perchè fanno le valigie? Perchè __ (partire)*

un odore smell
sposarsi to get married
bagnato/a soaked
un rumore noise

Q. VOCAB

6 *In Column **A** you will see where people are. Match up with what they are doing in Column **B**, and change the infinitives to stare + gerund.*
   Esempio: Sandro è in banca. (cambiare) un assegno (cheque)
   Sandro è in banca. Sta cambiando un assegno.

A

i *Laura è in sala da pranzo.*
ii *Siamo in un negozio di abbigliamento.*
iii *I signori Ricci sono in un supermercato.*
iv *Mirio è in cucina.*
v *Alessandro è in ufficio.*
vi *Gli ospiti sono in salotto.*

B

a *(chiacchierare)*
b *(cucinare)*
c *(fare) la spesa*
d *(lavorare)*
e *(mangiare)*
f *(comprare) delle cravatte*

7 *Ora tocca a te!*

Your mother is surprised to see you up so early, because she had forgotten you had an exam today.

Mamma	Che fai in piedi così presto? Non sono ancora le cinque!
You	*I'd like to study a bit.*
Mamma	A quest'ora? Come mai?
You	*But didn't you know that I've got an exam today?*
Mamma	Ah, me n'ero proprio dimenticata! Ti preparo una tazza di caffè?

CD 2, TR 39

You	*No, thanks. Go back to bed.*
Mamma	Hai ancora molto da fare?
You	*No, not much.*
Mamma	Stai studiando tanto, è vero; fra un paio di anni però, sarai medico!
You	*Yes, but only if I manage to pass this exam. It's one of the most difficult ones.*
Mamma	Ma perchè ti preoccupi tanto?
You	*Because this time I'm not sure of myself.*
Mamma	Non ti preoccupare! Andrà tutto perfettamente, vedrai.

Insight
Senza complimenti!

You will often hear this expression when Italians are eager for you to accept a drink or hospitality. If you don't wish to accept, you in your turn may answer **No, grazie. Senza complimenti!** or **No, grazie. Non faccio complimenti!**

A very polite conversation!

The further south you go, the more likely you are to hear a conversation like this:

A Prende un caffè?	*Will you have a coffee?*
B No, grazie, non si disturbi.	*No thanks. Don't bother.*
A Senza complimenti!	*Go on, have one!*
B Non faccio complimenti!	*No, thanks awfully.*
A Ma su, prenda qualcosa!	*Come on, do have something!*
B Le assicuro: non faccio complimenti.	*Really I won't. But thanks all the same.*
A Allora, prenda un cognac, un dolce... Su, mi faccia contento, accetti qualcosa!	*Well then, have a brandy, a cake... Come on, have something just to please me!*
B Se proprio insiste, prendo del cognac. Grazie.	*Well, if you insist I'll have some brandy. Thanks.*

TEST YOURSELF

Practise the imperative tense by choosing the correct translation of the following sentences. For each one, select a, b or c.

1 *Tell me what you said!* (**tu** form)

    a *Dimmi quello che hai detto!* **b** *Dimmi quello che ha detto!* **c** *Mi dici quello che ha detto!*

2 *Don't touch the flowers!* (**voi** form)

    a *Non tocchi i fiori!* **b** *Non toccare i fiori!*
    c *Non toccate i fiori!*

3 *Don't shout!* (**tu** form)

    a *Non urla!* **b** *Non urlare!* **c** *Non urli!*

4 *Let's go to the party!* (**noi** form)

    a *Andiamo alla festa!* **b** *Andremo alla festa!*
    c *Andremmo alla festa!*

5 *Stay with your sister!* (**tu** form)

    a *Stia con tua sorella!* **b** *Stare con tua sorella!*
    c *Sta' con tua sorella!*

Now translate the following sentences into Italian. (Use the **tu** form.)

6 *I was about to phone you.*

7 *What! Are you here already?*

8 *What are you watching on the television?*

9 *I heard him sing.*

10 *As he has to learn Spanish for his new job, Paul has started a language course.*

24

Ha bisogno di aiuto?
Do you need any help?

In this unit you will learn:
- *how to ask someone to help you or to say that you need help*
- *how to ask someone for advice*
- *how someone's particulars are asked*
- *how to ask someone to hold the line on the phone*
- *how to ask and say whose something is.*

1 Al commissariato
At the police station

Una signora reports the loss of her passport to the police and is told that she has to make a statement (**fare la denuncia**).

a Vero o falso? *La signora è agitata perchè ha perso il passaporto.*

b *Quando si è accorta di non avere più il passaporto?*

Poliziotto	Che cosa posso fare per lei, signora?
Signora	Mi aiuti, per favore! Ho perso il passaporto.
Poliziotto	Non si agiti! Mi dica dove l'ha smarrito.
Signora	Questa mattina sono andata a visitare il Duomo e all'uscita mi sono accorta di non averlo più.
Poliziotto	Ne è sicura? Ha controllato bene?

CD 2, TR 40

Signora	Sì. L'ho cercato dappertutto. Che cosa mi consiglia di fare?
Poliziotto	Deve fare la denuncia.
Signora	Oddio! E come si fa?
Poliziotto	Stia tranquilla! Gliela scriviamo noi. Lei intanto si segga.

2 Mi dia le sue generalità!
Give me your particulars

She gives **il poliziotto** her particulars so that he can write the statement for her.

  a Vero o falso? *La signora deve firmare la denuncia.*
  b *Dov'è nata la signora e in che anno?*

Poliziotto	Di che nazionalità è?
Signora	Sono svizzera.
Poliziotto	Mi dia le sue generalità!
Signora	Franca Pesce, nata a Lugano, il venti luglio 1970, residente a Losanna, Via San Lorenzo numero 14 …
Poliziotto	… e attualmente dimorante …
Signora	… presso mio padre, residente a Roma in Via Giuseppe Verdi, numero 6.
Poliziotto	Ecco. Ho finito. Firmi qui sotto e metta la data.
Signora	Vi mettete voi in contatto con me se lo trovate?
Poliziotto	Sì, sì. Aspetti una nostra comunicazione!

le generalità *details, particulars*
dimorante *staying at*
presso *care of, at*
mettersi in contatto *to get in touch*
aspetti una nostra comunicazione *we will inform you*

Q. VOCAB

---

3 Un incidente
An accident

La signora A asks to use a phone in an emergency.

a Vero o falso? *La signora A telefona all'ospedale perchè suo marito si sente male.*

b *La signora A ha chiesto alla signora B due favori. Quali sono?*

Signora A	Posso usare il suo telefono, per cortesia?
Signora B	Venga, faccia pure! Che cos'è successo?
Signora A	Mio marito si è sentito male per strada.
Signora B	Mi dispiace. Conosce il numero del suo medico?
Signora A	No. Mi aiuti a cercarlo, per favore.
Signora B	Si calmi, signora! Eccolo! Questo è il numero di casa e questo quello dello studio. Ma perchè non telefona all'ospedale? Chiami il pronto soccorso!
Signora A	Sì. Forse è meglio. Pronto! … È l'ospedale? … Come? … Cosa? … Non ho capito! … È caduta la linea? … Alzi la voce! … Ah … Ho sbagliato numero? Mi scusi!

CD 2, TR 40, 01:42

Venga, faccia pure! *Come in! Do by all means!*
sentirsi male *to feel ill*
per strada *in the street*
pronto soccorso *casualty department*
Come? *Pardon?*
È caduta la linea? *Has the line gone dead?*
alzare la voce *to raise one's voice*

Q. VOCAB

4 Attenda in linea!
Hold the line!

La signora A passes the receiver to **la signora B**.

   a **Vero o falso?** *La centralista non capisce subito ciò che le dice la signora B.*

   b *Che cosa ha fatto la signora B per chiamare l'ambulanza?*

Signora B	Dia a me, signora! Faccio io! Pronto? Mi passi il pronto soccorso!
Centralinista	Un attimo. Attenda in linea! ... Parli pure!
Signora B	Un signore sta male. Mandi subito un'ambulanza in Via Pini.
Centralinista	Va bene, ma ripeta l'indirizzo e parli più lentamente, signora.
Signora B	Via dei Pini, 11. Accanto alla pasticceria 'La Perla'.

QV

centralinista (m/f) *operator*
accanto a *by*

5 Una stazione di servizio
A service station

La signora asks **il benzinaio** *pump attendant* to fill up (**fare il pieno**).

   a **Vero o falso?** *La macchina è del benzinaio.*

   b *La signora ha chiesto al benzinaio di controllare l'olio, l'acqua e le gomme?*

Benzinaio	Di chi è questa macchina? È sua, signora?
Signora	Sì. È mia.
Benzinaio	Quanti litri, signora?
Signora	Mi faccia il pieno.
Benzinaio	Benzina o gasolio?
Signora	Gasolio. E controlli l'olio e l'acqua, per piacere.
Benzinaio	Va bene, signora. Ecco fatto! Ho controllato anche le gomme. Tutto a posto.
Signora	Grazie. Quanto le devo? Ho solo questo biglietto da cinquecento.

benzina *petrol/gasoline (US)*
gasolio *diesel*
gomma *tyre*
tutto a posto *everything OK*

Q. VOCAB

Grammar

1 COME? *PARDON? WHAT? SORRY?*

When you do not understand something or cannot hear properly, use either **Come?** or **Prego?**

2 DOUBLE PRONOUNS

◄)) **CD 2, TR 41**

a Le (*to you/for you, to her/for her*) and **gli** (*to him/for him, to them/for them*) both become **glie**, combining with the following pronoun, **lo/la/li/le/ne:**

glielo, gliela, glieli, gliele, gliene.

For other double pronouns see Unit 21.

The examples below illustrate how the double pronouns are used:

Hai dato l'indirizzo a Carla?	*Did you give the address to Carla?*
No. *Glielo* darò domani.	*No. I'll give **it to her** tomorrow.*
Hai dato la chiave a Mario?	*Did you give the key to Mario?*
No. *Gliela* darò più tardi.	*No. I'll give **it to him** later.*
Hai dato i libri a Giulia?	*Did you give the books to Julia?*
No. *Glieli* darò il mese prossimo.	*No. I'll give **them to her** next month.*
Hai dato le diapositive ai tuoi genitori?	*Did you give the slides to your parents?*
***Gliele* darò stasera.**	*I'll give **them to them** this evening.*
***Glielo* farò sapere.**	*I'll let **you** know (**it**).*

b When you use these double pronouns with the perfect tense, remember to make **lo/la/li/le/ne** agree with the past participle. Remember also that **glielo** and **gliela** (singular only) both become **gliel'** before 'h': glielo + ho dato becomes **gliel'ho dato**; gliela + ho data becomes **gliel'ho data**.

Che bell'anello!	*What a lovely ring!*
Chi glie*l'ha* (glie*lo* + *ha*) regalato?	*Who gave **it to you**?*
***Me l'ha* regalato il mio ragazzo.**	*My boyfriend gave **it to me**.*
Che bella casa!	*What a lovely house!*
Chi glie*l'ha* (glie*la* + *ha*) disegnata?	*Who designed **it for you**?*
Che be*i* rega*li*!	*What lovely presents!*
Chi glie*li* ha fatt*i*?	*Who gave **them to you**?*
Che belle rose!	*What lovely roses!*
Chi glie*le* ha regalate?	*Who gave **them to you**?*

Finally, here are two examples with **ne**:

Le ha parlato dei suoi progetti?	*Did he talk to her about his plans?*
Sì. *Gliene ha* parlato ieri.	*Yes, he talked **to her about them** yesterday.*

Quanti dvd *gli* hai comprato?	How many DVDs did you buy for him?
Gliene ho comprati *due*.	I bought **him two (of them)**.

3 PRESSO MIO PADRE *AT MY FATHER'S*

Presso is also used to mean *c/o* (*care of*) when you are writing an address.

4 *OF MINE, OF YOURS, OF OURS*

To say *of mine*, *of yours*, *of ours*, etc., Italian does not translate *of*:

Aspetto *un mio* amico.	I'm waiting for a friend of mine.
Due suoi fratelli lavorano in Germania.	Two of his brothers work in Germany.
Aspetti una nostra comunicazione.	Wait for a message from us (lit: of ours).

5 *IRREGULAR IMPERATIVES*

Note these irregular forms of the imperative 2nd person singular (**lei**):

Infinitive	Imperative **(lei)**
avere	abbia!
dare	dia!
essere	sia!
stare	stia!

Non *abbia* paura!	Don't be afraid!
Dia una buona mancia!	Give a good tip!
Sia puntuale!	Be punctual!
Stia attento!	Be careful!
Stia tranquilla!	Keep calm!

In answer to the question **Di chi è/Di chi sono?** do not use the definite article with the possessive:

	quel cane?	È mio.		*that dog?*	
Di chi è			*Whose is*		*It's mine.*
	quella giacca?	È mia.		*that jacket?*	
	questi guanti?	Sono su<u>oi</u>.		*these gloves?*	*They are*
Di chi sono			*Whose are*		*his/hers/*
	queste scarpe?	Sono sue.		*these shoes?*	*yours.*

Come si dice?
How do you say it?

🔊 **CD 2, TR 42**

1 *How to ask someone to help you*   **Mi aiuti, per favore!**

    How to say that you need help   **Ho bisogno di aiuto.**

2 *How to ask someone for advice*   **Che cosa mi consiglia di fare?**

3 *How someone's particulars are asked*   **Mi dia le sue generalità!**

4 *How to ask someone to hold the line on the phone*   **Attenda in l<u>i</u>nea!**

5 *How to ask/say whose something is*   **Di chi è questo/a? È mio/mia.**

Practice

1 *You are supervising a group of children in a restaurant and telling them what they must and must not do.*
Esempio: Dica loro di: aspettare un attimo. Aspettate un attimo!
Dica loro di:

   a *lavarsi le mani*
   b *aspettare qui*
   c *venire a tavola*
   d *sedersi*
   e *non gridare*
   f *non fare troppo rumore*
   g *non toccare i fiori sulla tavola*
   h *bere piano piano*
   i *non parlare con la bocca piena*

piano piano *slowly*
gridare *to shout*

Q.V.

2 *Each sentence on the right is said in response to one on the left, but they have got mixed up: sort out the correct pairs.*

i	*Dammi le chiavi!*	**a**	*Sì. Gliel'ho detto.*
ii	*Hai dato le riviste a Giulia?*	**b**	*Ma gliene ho già fatte tante!*
iii	*Hai detto a Stefano di venire a pranzo?*	**c**	*Ma te l'ho già detto cento volte!*
iv	*Perchè non me lo dici?*	**d**	*Ma te l'ho già dato!*
v	*Falle una fotografia!*	**e**	*Ma te ne ho già fatte due!*
vi	*Fammi una fotografia!*	**f**	*No. Non gliele ho ancora date.*
vii	*Dammi l'indirizzo!*	**g**	*Gliel'ho già dato.*
viii	*Dagli il caffè!*	**h**	*Glieli ho già dati.*
ix	*Quando gli darai i soldi?*	**i**	*Te le ho già date.*

3 **Ho dimenticato (di ...)** *I have forgotten to ... Here is a list of things you have forgotten to do and which your friend obligingly offers to do for you. Use double pronouns and the present tense as in the example.*

Esempio: **Ho dimenticato di fare la spesa. Non si preoccupi! Gliela faccio io.**

   a *Ho dimenticato di fare i biglietti.*
   b *Ho dimenticato di comprare il pane.*
   c *Ho dimenticato di cambiare i soldi.*
   d *Ho dimenticato di riportare i libri in biblioteca* (library).
   e *Ho dimenticato di imbucare la lettera.*
   f *Ho dimenticato di prendere il giornale.*
   g *Ho dimenticato di chiudere le valigie.*

4 **Di chi è?** *Whose is it?* **Il signor Marchi,** *your boss, is having a big office clean-out, and wants to know to whom various articles belong. Assume they belong to you unless you see (R) by the question, in which case they belong to your senior colleague,* **la signora Renata** *(see Unit 5, Section 9 and Unit 24, Section 6).*

Esempi: **Di chi è questa penna? È mia.**
Di chi è questo libro? (R) È suo.

   a *Di chi è questa fotografia? (R)*
   b *Di chi è questo ombrello? (R)*
   c *Di chi è questo cappello?*
   d *Di chi sono questi occhiali? (R)*
   e *Di chi sono quei documenti?*
   f *Di chi sono quelle chiavi? (R)*
   g *Di chi sono quei giornali? (R)*
   h *Di chi sono queste riviste?*

5 *Now make sure that* **a, b, d, f** *and* **g** *do belong to* **la signora Renata** *by asking her.*

Esempio: **a È sua questa fotografia?**

6 *Ora tocca a te!*

You are asking for advice.

CD 2, TR 43

You	I've *lost my driving licence and I don't know what to do.*
Signorina	Sa dove l'ha smarrita?
You	*I'm not sure. Perhaps I left it in the car. During the night someone got into my car and took everything.*
Signorina	Non si preoccupi! Ci sono buone possibilità di ritrovarla, perchè di solito la spediscono in Questura.
You	*What's the Questura?*
Signorina	È l'ufficio centrale di polizia. Vada lì a denunciare lo smarrimento.
You	*And do you know where it is, please?*
Signorina	Certo. È in Via Mazzini.
You	*Thank you. And meanwhile, what do I do without a licence?*
Signorina	Per il momento può usare una copia della denuncia come documento.

7 *Read the section below and answer the question.*
In caso di emergenza, per un grave incidente stradale per esempio, che numero chiama?

Soccorso pubblico di emergenza
Nell'interesse di tutti, è consigliabile ricorrere a questo numero soltanto in caso di reale e incombente pericolo alle persone o di gravi calamità e qualora non sia possibile chiamare i diversi enti direttamente interessati.

113

Emergenza Sanitaria

118

Soccorso stradale Automobile Club d'Italia **116**

NUMERI DI PUBBLICA UTILITÀ INFORMAZIONI E SERVIZI
PROVINCIA DI ROMA

Servizio ambulanze

Civitavecchia Ambulanze C.R.I.	**3333**
Tivoli Ambulanze USL RM/26	**2439**
Ambulanze C.R.I.	**2008**

La polizia e i carabinieri *The police and carabinieri*
Italian police officers wear various uniforms according to
their role. The most prestigious group are the **carabinieri**
who come under the Ministry of Defence, and are
therefore considered to be part of the army. They deal
with the most serious crime, are highly mobilized, and
recognizable by their dark blue uniforms with a red stripe
down the side of their trousers. Their military discipline
is reflected in the way they are housed: in barracks (**la
caserma**).

La polizia stradale have their head-quarters in the
questura. This is where you would report theft, robbery,
etc.

The **vigili urbani**, conspicuous in summer by their white
helmets, control traffic in urban areas.

Le guardie di finanza, in grey uniforms, are very active
in tracking down money-laundering, smuggling and tax
evasion, a recurrent theme in Italian politics.

TEST YOURSELF

Fill in the gaps in the sentences by using each word in the box below once only.

1   *Hai dato i fiori a Maria? Sì, __ ho dati ieri.*

2   *Hai mandato le lettere a Simone? No, __ spedirò domani mattina.*

3   *L'hai detto a Patrizio? No, ti giuro*, non gliel'ho __ .*

4   *Dove hai comprato quella bella gonna? Me l'ha __ Armando.*

5   *Che begli orecchini! Chi glieli ha __ ?*

6   *Che bel vaso! Chi __ ha dato?*

7   *Jennifer ha capito la storia? No ma __ spiegherò.*

8   *Tre __ amiche vengono.*

9   *Ha perso una __ scarpa.*

10 *Ho visto due __ film.*

* **giurare** = *to swear*

....

regalata - mia - gliel' - gliele - sue - regalati - gliela - su<u>oi</u> - detto - glieli

....

Scambio di opinioni
Exchange of opinions

In this unit you will learn:
* *how to say you could …*
* *how to say you ought to …*
* *how to say you would like to …*
* *how to say it would be necessary to …*
* *how to ask others similar questions.*

1 La stampa italiana
The Italian press

Elsa and **Curzio** are in Italy and are interviewing some passers-by. They see a distinguished-looking man and approach him.

a Vero o falso? *Il Corriere della Sera, La Stampa e La Repubblica sono giornali.*

b *Di dov'è il signor Neri, e qual è il giornale che di solito legge?*

Elsa	Mi scusi, signore. Siamo due studenti della Svizzera italiana e vorremmo farle alcune domande sulla stampa italiana.
Sig. Neri	Sarò lieto di rispondervi.
Curzio	Potrebbe dirci quali sono i quotidiani più diffusi nel suo Paese?

Sig. Neri	Ho appena comprato *Il Corriere della Sera*. Sa, io sono di Milano. *Il Corriere* oltre ad essere il quotidiano della mia città, è anche uno dei più letti in Italia.
Curzio	Potrebbe mostrarmelo?
Sig. Neri	Con piacere. Se non trovo *Il Corriere*, compro *La Stampa* di Torino, o *La Repubblica* di Roma.

QUICK VOCAB

vorremmo *we would like to*
lieto/a di *happy to*
potrebbe dirci *could you tell us*
quotidiano *daily paper*
diffuso/a *widely circulated*
oltre ad essere *besides being*
Potrebbe mostrarmelo? *Could you show it to me?*

2 Potrebbe darci qualche informazione ...?
Could you give us some information ...?

a **Vero o falso?** *Quando il signor Neri è a Napoli e non vuole avere notizie di carattere economico-finanziario, legge* Il Mattino.

b L'Espresso *e* Panorama *escono ogni mese?*

Sig. Neri	Quando sono a Napoli leggo *Il Mattino*. Se poi voglio avere notizie di carattere economico-finanziario compro *Il Sole 24 Ore*.
Elsa	Potrebbe darci qualche informazione sui settimanali più diffusi?
Sig. Neri	I settimanali di carattere politico economico culturale che io compro più frequentemente sono *L'Espresso* e *Panorama*.
Curzio	E che cosa leggono di preferenza le donne della sua famiglia?
Sig. Neri	*Grazia, Panorama,* e più o meno gli stessi giornali.
Elsa	Ci scusi per il disturbo!
Sig. Neri	Ma si figuri!

notizie (f pl) *news*
carattere (m) *character, nature*
settimanale (m) *weekly (paper)*
di preferenza *mostly*
disturbo *inconvenience*

---

3 La televisione: opinioni a confronto
Television: opinions compared

<u>Ezio</u> is asked whether he is satisfied with television programmes.

a Vero o falso? *A <u>E</u>zio e a Bruno non pi<u>a</u>cciono gli stessi programmi.*
b *Secondo <u>E</u>zio, ci dovr<u>e</u>bbero <u>e</u>ssere più film o più documentari?*

Giornalista	È soddisfatto dei programmi televisivi?
<u>E</u>zio	Sì. Ma vedr<u>e</u>i volentieri dei cambiamenti.
Giornalista	Potrebbe suggerirne qualcuno?
<u>E</u>zio	Secondo me ci dovr<u>e</u>bbero <u>e</u>ssere più documentari, più programmi di informazione scient<u>i</u>fica e culturale.
Bruno	Ma che dici! Più film, più sport, più m<u>u</u>sica: ecco cosa ci vorrebbe!
Giornalista	Allora, secondo lei, la televisione dovrebbe divertire il p<u>u</u>bblico?
Bruno	Eh, certamente! Dopo una giornata di lavoro uno vuole distrarsi.

🔊 CD 2, TR 44, 00:52

QUICK VOCAB

vedr_e_i volentieri *I'd love to see*
cambiamento *change*
suggerirne qualcuno *to suggest some*
secondo me *in my opinion*
ci dovr_e_bbero _e_ssere *there ought to be*
ci vorrebbe *one would need*
divertire *to entertain*
distrarsi *to take one's mind off things*

---

4 Non sono affatto d'accordo
I don't agree at all

Bruno is for, **_E_zio** is against, **le televisioni private** *independent television.*

 a Vero o falso? *_E_zio è d'accordo col suo amico sui programmi televisivi.*
 b *Che cosa vorrebbe abolire _E_zio?*

CD 2, TR 44, 01:40

Bruno	Meno male che ci sono le televisioni private!
Giornalista	E lei, che cosa pensa di quello che ha detto il suo amico?
_E_zio	Non sono affatto d'accordo. Bisognerebbe abolirle, queste televisioni private.
Giornalista	Per lei, allora, quale dovrebbe _e_ssere il ruolo della televisione nella società moderna?
_E_zio	Dovrebbe sì divertire, ma prima di tutto informare e offrire diverse visioni del mondo.

Q. VOCAB

abolire *to abolish*
bisognerebbe *one would need to*
ruolo *role*
mondo *world*

Grammar

1 CONDITIONAL: FORMATION

The conditional for all verbs is easily formed by replacing the final
-ò of the future (1st person singular) with the endings in the table
below (in bold italics). There are no exceptions and the endings are
identical for -are, -ere and -ire verbs.

Infinitive	Future	Conditional		
parlare	parlerò	(io)	parler-	-ei
vendere	venderò	(tu)	vender-	-esti
sentire	sentirò	(lui/lei)	sentir-	-ebbe
vedere	vedrò	(noi)	vedr-	-emmo
bere	berrò	(voi)	berr-	-este
avere	avrò	(loro)	avr-	-ebbero

Conditional comprare		essere	
comprerei	I would buy	sarei	I would be
compreresti	you would buy	saresti	you would be
comprerebbe	you/he/she would buy	sarebbe	you/he/she would be
compreremmo	we would buy	saremmo	we would be
comprereste	you would buy	sareste	you would be
comprerebbero	they would buy	sarebbero	they would be

Insight

Note that the ending -**emmo** of the conditional (1st person
plural) has double 'm' and that they must both be clearly
articulated to avoid confusion with the future ending -**emo**
(one 'm').

Here are some examples of irregular verbs to show how easy it is to form the conditional once you know the future tense:

Future	Conditional
avrò:	avr*ei*, avr*esti*, avr*ebbe*, avr*emmo*, avr*este*, avr*ebbero* *I would have, etc.*
andrò:	andr*ei*, andr*esti*, andr*ebbe*, andr*emmo*, andr*este*, andr*ebbero* *I would go, etc.*
vedrò:	vedr*ei*, vedr*esti*, vedr*ebbe*, vedr*emmo*, vedr*este*, vedr*ebbero* *I would see, etc.*
berrò:	berr*ei*, berr*esti*, berr*ebbe*, berr*emmo*, berr*este*, berr*ebbero* *I would drink, etc.*

2 CONDITIONAL: USES

Generally, the conditional renders *should*, *would* or *could* in Italian when these refer to the present or the future.

Prender*ei* volentieri un aperitivo. E tu?	*I'd love to have an aperitif. What about you?*
Che ne *diresti* di una bella passeggiata?	*What would you say to a nice walk?*
A quest'ora *sarebbe* impossibile trovarlo in casa.	*It would be impossible to find him at home at this time.*
Non *saprei* dire perchè.	*I couldn't (lit: wouldn't know) say why.*

Note particularly the meaning of the conditional of **potere**, **dovere** and **volere**:

potrei	*I could (I would be able)*
dovrei	*I should or I ought (I would have to)*
vorrei	*I would like (I would want, wish)*
***Potresti* andare a trovarla.**	*You could go and see her.*
***Dovrebbe* scrivere subito.** {	*You ought to write immediately.* *You should write immediately.*

The conditional of **volere** and **potere** is often used for making polite requests:

Potrebbe farmi un favore?   *Could you do me a favour?*
Vorrei fare una telefonata.   *I'd like to make a phone call.*

A reflexive verb would, of course, have to be preceded by the appropriate reflexive pronoun (**mi, ti, si, ci, vi, si**): **mi divertirei, ti divertiresti, si divertirebbe, ecc.** (*I would enjoy myself* etc.)

To form the perfect conditional simply use the conditional of **essere/avere** + past participle:

avrei comprato *I would have bought*
sarei uscito/a *I would have gone out*

3 ALCUNO/A, QUALCUNO, NESSUNO
ANY, SOMEONE/ANYONE, NO ONE

Alcun, alcuno/a in the singular is used only in a negative sense:

Senza *alcun* dubbio.   *Without a doubt.*

In the plural **alcuni/e** means *some*, *a few*:

***alcuni* mesi fa, *alcuni* giorni fa**   *a few months ago, a few days ago*

It also means *some* when *some, but not all* is implied, i.e. for contrast or emphasis. It may be used with or without a noun:

***Alcune* notizie erano vere,**   *Some news was true, some not*
**   altre false.**   *(lit: false).*

***Alcuni* lo approvano, altri no.**   *Some approve of it, others don't.*

Qualcuno/a *one or two*, *some* is used only in the singular:

Potrebbe suggerirne *qualcuno*? *Could you suggest some?*

Qualcuno is also used in the masculine singular form only and means *someone* or *anyone*:

Cerca *qualcuno*?	*Are you looking for someone?*
No. *Non* cerco *nessuno*.	*No. I'm not looking for anyone.*
Perchè non chiedi a *qualcuno*?	*Why don't you ask someone?*
C'è *qualcuno* che vorrebbe farlo?	*Is there anyone who would like to do it?*

4 NESSUNO/A *NO ONE, ETC.*

Nessuno/a (Unit 13, Section 5) may be used with or without a noun. It can mean *no, none, nobody, no one, not any (one)*. It is used in the singular only and behaves like **un, uno, una**:

***Nessuno* l'avrebbe creduto.**	*No one would have believed it.*
***Nessuno* di noi andrà all'estero quest'anno.**	*None of us will go abroad this year.*
Non ha *nessun* fratello.	*He hasn't any brothers.*

5 WORDS FOR 'DAY'

Giorno is *the day*, considered as a date.

Lunedì è il primo *giorno* della settimana.	*Monday is the first day of the week.*
Che *giorno* è (oggi)?	*What day is it (today)?*

Giornata is used when referring to the duration of the day or to the weather.

Abbiamo passato una bellissima *giornata* a Firenze.	*We spent a very nice day in Florence.*

| Che brutta *giornata*! | *What a horrible day!* |
| Che bella *giornata*! | *What a lovely day!* |

Similarly, **mattina, mattinata** *morning*; **sera, serata** *evening*

6 ADJECTIVES + DI + INFINITIVE/ NOUN/PRONOUN

Some adjectives may be followed by **di** + infinitive:

Sono *stufo di* lavorare.	*I'm fed up with working.*
Sono *stanco di* aspettare.	*I'm tired of waiting.*
Sei *sicuro di* poterlo fare?	*Are you sure you can do it?*
Sono *contento d*i rivederla.	*I'm pleased to see you again.*
Sono *soddisfatto di* lui.	*I'm very pleased with him.*
Sarò *lieto di* rispondervi.	*I'd be happy to answer your questions.*

7 FIGURARSI TO THINK, FANCY, IMAGINE

Figurarsi is mainly used in exclamations:

| *Figurati* che è rimasto senza un centesimo! | *Just think of it! He hasn't a penny left! (lit: he has remained without a cent.)* |

Si figuri! is a polite way of saying *not at all* or *don't mention it.*

La disturbo?	*Am I disturbing you?*
Ma no, *si figuri*!	*No, not at all!*
Molto gentile, grazie!	*That's very kind of you.*
Prego, *si figuri*!	*Don't mention it.*

8 PRIMA, DOPO, POI *FIRST, LATER, THEN*

When referring to time, **prima** means *before, first, earlier*, while **dopo** and **poi** mean *after(wards), later, then*:

Avresti dovuto dirmelo *prima*.	*You ought to have told me before.*
Prima vado in Francia, *poi* in Germania.	*First I'm going to France, then to Germany.*
Vengo a mezzogiorno.	*I'm coming at midday.*
Se vuole, può venire *prima*.	*If you want, you can come earlier.*
È arrivato subito *dopo*.	*He arrived soon afterwards.*
Mangio *dopo*.	*I'm eating later.*

9 POSITION OF UNSTRESSED PRONOUNS

We have already seen that unstressed pronouns have a choice of position when used with **potere/dovere/volere**:

Non posso trovarlo.
Non lo posso trovare.

With impersonal verbs such as **bisognare** *to be necessary*, the object pronouns must be attached to the infinitive if they refer to it:

Bisogna parlar*gli*.	*It is necessary to speak to him.*
Bisogna far*lo* subito.	*It must be done at once.*
Non mi piace far*lo*.	*I don't like doing it.*

> ## Insight
> Attenzione! **Bisognare** is only used in the 3rd person singular: **bisogna, bisognerà, bisognerebbe ecc.** *To need* is **aver bisogno di ...** (Unit 15, Section 3).

Come si dice?
How do you say it?

🔊 **CD 2, TR 45**

1 *How to ask whether someone could tell you, show, give you, do, etc.*
Potrebbe dirmi, mostrarmi, darmi, fare, ecc.?

How to say that you could tell/ show someone, etc.
Potrei dirle/mostrarle, ecc.

2 *How to say someone ought to …*   **Dovrebbe …**

How to say that you ought to …   **Dovrei …**

3 *How to say someone would like to …*   **Vorrebbe …**

How to say that you would like to …   **Vorrei …**

4 *How to say it would be necessary to …*   **Bisognerebbe …**

Practice

1 *Select a verb from the list below once only to complete the responses, using the first person singular of the conditional.*

guardare – mettere – mangiare – bere – ascoltare – prendere

    a *L'acqua? La __ ma non ho sete.*
    b *Gli spaghetti? Li __ ma non ho appetito.*
    c *Il cappotto? Lo __ ma non ho freddo.*
    d *Le aspirine? Le __ ma non ho più mal di testa.*
    e *Il concerto alla radio? L' __ ma non ho tempo.*
    f *Il programma alla tv*? Lo __ ma devo uscire.*
    *pronounced **tivù.**

2 *In the table below you are given details of what Ada, Vittorio, and i signori Miele would do if they had the means.*
    a *Say what Ada would do.* (**Vivrebbe, ecc.**)
    b *Pretend you are Vittorio and say what you would do.*
    c *Say what i signori Miele would do.*

	vivere	comprare	andare	imparare a
Ada	in città	piccolo appartamento	ogni sera a ballare	guidare
Vittorio	al mare	villa	spesso a nuotare	suonare la chitarra
I signori Miele	in montagna	casetta (*small house*)	ogni tanto a sciare	dipingere (*paint*)

3 *Match up the sentences on the left with those on the right.*
    i *Sono tanto stanco!*   **a** *Avresti dovuto assaggiarla prima di comprarla.*
    ii *Perchè non me l'hai ditto che non avevi i soldi?*   **b** *Avresti potuto romperti la testa.*

iii Perchè non sei venuto alla festa di Sandro?	**c** No. Mi dispiace. Non saprei dirglielo.
iv Questo liquore è ottimo!	**d** Ti saresti divertito molto.
v Quest'uva non è buona.	**e** No. Dovrebbe arrivare col treno delle dieci.
vi Meno male che non ti sei fatto niente!	**f** Ne berrei un altro bicchierino.
vii È arrivato tuo nonno?	**g** Avresti dovuto riposarti un po' prima di uscire.
viii Scusi signore, sa dov'è il Consolato Inglese?	**h** Te li avrei prestati io.

4 **Conditional + double pronouns:** *There are several things you would like to do or ought to do. Your friend would love to do them for you but … Use the conditional and the appropriate pronouns in your answer.*

Esempio: Dovrei pagare il conto __ ma sono al verde. *(I'm broke).* **Te lo pagherei io, ma sono al verde.**

a Dovrei portare le valigie alla stazione. __ ma mi fa male la schiena.

b Dovrei portare la macchina dal meccanico. __ ma non ho tempo.

c Non so fare la traduzione. __ ma non ho il dizionario.

d Dovrei pulire l'appartamento. __ ma sono stanco.

e Vorrei cambiare cento euro. __ ma non ho spiccioli.

f Vorrei fare la pizza. __ ma non ho gli ingredienti.

g Dovrei imbucare questa lettera. __ ma non passo per la posta.

5 *Ora tocca a te!*

You are on the phone to Renata and inviting her to your party.

You	Hi, Renata! Can you come to my party this evening?
Renata	Vorrei tanto, ma sono molto impegnata in questo periodo.
You	But what have you got to do that's so important?
Renata	Devo riordinare la casa, devo lavare, ... sono sola e devo pensare a tutto.
You	And couldn't you do all these things at another time?
Renata	Sì, potrei, solo che oggi ritornano i miei genitori da una vacanza all'estero.
You	But weren't they supposed to come back next week?
Renata	Sì, effettivamente, avrebbero voluto fermarsi per altri cinque o sei giorni, ma mia zia ha avuto un bambino e così hanno deciso di rientrare prima.
You	At what time will they arrive?
Renata	Dovrebbero essere all'aeroporto alle sei, e andrò io stessa a prenderli in macchina.
You	Anyway, if you change your mind, you can always let me know. Call me when you like.
Renata	Ti ringrazio. Se posso, verrò volentieri, magari solo per salutarti e farti gli auguri.

6 a *Cos'è la RAI?*
  b *Nel primo dialogo quali sono i quotidiani?*

GRAZIE
AGLI
ABBONATI
RAI

NON È MAI
TROPPO TARDI
PER DIVENTARE
UN NUOVO
ABBONATO

RAI

Italian television

As with the BBC, **Radiotelevisione Italiana** is funded by a licence fee. However, its three channels also depend to some extent on advertising revenue. They are all currently obtainable free of charge via satellite with one proviso: unless you are a subscriber you are unlikely to be able to watch soccer matches (a rich source of dependable revenue) – they will almost certainly be scrambled. All three channels overlap to some extent, but **Rai Uno** is generally considered to have the best news coverage. It also deals with most state, papal and other such ceremonial occasions. **Rai Due** is rather more lightweight and has recently been quick to seize upon the attractions of reality TV. **Rai Tre** deals with more news in depth, has more programmes of a regional nature, and some of the weightier current affairs and discussion programmes. Don't expect to see much except repeats during the summer months. There are in addition many independent channels available of varying quality, though one of them **Rete quattro** was originally supposed to be of a more serious nature.

For more information about Italian radio and tv: http://www.rai.it

For the Italian press: http://www.onlinenewspapers.com/italy.htm

British listeners can tune in to Italian radio. **Spectrum Radio** (MW 558) has an Italian football slot on Sundays, during its Italian programme, 15:00–16:00, and **Vatican Radio** (MW 526) can be received in the evening.

Now turn to *Test your Italian IV*.

TEST YOURSELF

Translate the following sentences into Italian.

1 *I could meet you on Monday.*

2 *I ought to visit my parents this weekend*.*

3 *I would like to see that new German film.*

4 *It would be necessary to book in advance.*

5 *Would you like an ice cream?*

6 *She would have bought that hat.*

7 *They would have left me alone.*

8 *Is there anyone who knows?*

9 *I'm tired of repeating the same thing.*

10 *First I'm going shopping and then I'm going to the cinema.*

***finesettimana** (m) = *weekend*

Taking it further

Acquire a dictionary if you have not yet done so. As there is no standard one on the market your choice will very much depend on your means. Try consulting your local reference library first.

The series offers you another two courses: the first, *Perfect your Italian* (S. Lymbery), will help you develop your language skills still further and aims to give you something more of the flavour of Italy today. The second, *Essential Italian Grammar* (A. Proudfoot), provides you with a 'dip-in' reference guide that can also be worked through. For a wider choice visit the Grant and Cutler website: http://www.grant-c.demon.co.uk

When attempting to read articles from newspapers or magazines, such as those mentioned in Unit 25, it is a good idea to begin with international news where you may be familiar with the subject matter. With radio and television, the easiest to understand initially are quiz programmes and adverts where the same expressions occur over and over again. To start with, listen for no more than a minute or so (you will be amazed at how many words some Italians can pack into 60 seconds).

Website enthusiasts will find that the following two search engines will guide them to any aspect of Italian culture, travel or commerce they care to explore: http://it.yahoo/com and http://www.google.it

We hope you enjoyed working your way through *Complete Italian*. Don't get discouraged. Mastering a new language takes time and perseverance, and sometimes things can seem just too difficult. But then you'll come back to it another day and things will begin to make more sense again.

If you have any queries arising from your study of our book, you are welcome to contact us through Teach Yourself Books, Hodder Headline Ltd, 338 Euston Road, London NWl 3BH. In the meantime, should you decide to visit Italy – **Buon viaggio! Buon divertimento!**

Test your Italian

Test your Italian I (Units 1–6)

Congratulations! You have now completed the first six units, and can test yourself to see how well you have mastered them. Or, if you know some Italian already, use this test to check whether you are ready to start this course at Unit 7. The answers are given in the Key to 'Test your Italian', at the end of the book.

Assess your results according to this chart:

45–60 marks: Congratulations. You are now ready for the next unit.

37–44 marks: Very good, but try and identify your weak areas.

22–36 marks: Quite good: make sure you understand your mistakes.

Below 22: Not bad, but you would probably be wise to revise thoroughly before starting Unit 7.

1 *Can you do the following? Say the answers out loud, then write them down.*
One mark each for correct answers **a** *and* **b**; *two marks each for the rest.*
  a *Attract someone's attention.*
  b *Greet them (daytime) and ask how they are.*
  c *Ask for* **i** *a beer* **ii** *an ice cream.*
  d *Ask where the shops are.*
  e *Ask someone what they are having (in a café).*
  f *Say that you are having a coffee.*
                                                    Marks: __ /10

2 *As above, but this time award yourself two marks per correct answer.*

   a *Ask someone's name* **i** *formally* **ii** *informally.*

   b *Ask what someone's job is* **i** *formally* **ii** *informally.*

   c *Say you are married/not married.*

   d *Say 'goodbye' to your teacher.*

Marks: __ /8

3 *Can you unscramble these sentences? One mark each for* **a–d,** *two marks each for* **e** *and* **f.**

   a *spagnolo vero anche parla?*

   b *è la sinistra a biblioteca.*

   c *la che a signora piano Verdi abita?*

   d *giorno che per parte Parigi?*

   e *usare conosco le vorrei lingue che.*

   f *prendere davanti all' autobus università l' deve.*

Marks: __ /8

4 *Using each contracted preposition in the box below once only, fill the gaps.*
One mark for each correct answer.

   a *Aspetto davanti ___ cinema.*

   b *C'è un treno prima ___ otto?*

   c *Non arriviamo prima ___ una.*

   d *Scendo ___ prossima fermata.*

   e *Deve andare ___ sportello N°8.*

   f *L'ultimo treno parte ___ dieci.*

....

al - alla - alle - allo - delle - dell'

....

Marks: __ /6

5 *Can you find the odd man out in each group?*
One mark for each correct answer.

   a *pasta - posta - pizza - panino.*

   b *giacca - sciopero - vestito - gonna - guanti.*

   c *orario - stazione - saldi - binario - biglietto.*

   d *ragioniere - architetto - granita - dentista.*

Marks: __ /4

6 *Can you say the following in Italian? Two marks for each correct answer.*

a *Ask for a ticket to Venice.*
b *Ask at what time the next train leaves.*
c *Ask at what time it arrives in Venice.*
d *Ask whether it is on time.*

Marks: __ /8

7 *Can you do all this in Italian? Two marks for each correct item and one mark for the final question.*
Say that you would like a pair of black shoes, a white T shirt and a pair of jeans.
Ask how much it is (altogether).

Marks: __ /7

8 *Award yourself two marks each for the following in Italian:*
a *Say where you were born (referring to town).*
b *Say how old you are.*
c *Say whether you are working, a student or unemployed.*
d *Ask: 'How do you say it in Italian?'*

Marks: __ /8

9 *Someone you have helped says Grazie! to you. How do you respond? (one mark)*

Marks: __ /1

Test your Italian II (Units 7–12)

1 *Can you write down how you would say the following in Italian? Two marks for each correct answer.*
a *I've got a passport.*
b *What a nice house!*
c *It doesn't matter.*
d *I'm hungry.*

Marks: __ /8

2 *How would you ask the following? Two marks for each correct answer.*
a *Is there a good restaurant nearby?*
b *Are these seats taken?*
c *Do they live in the centre?*
d *Do they play tennis?*

Marks: __ /8

3 *Carry out this task in Italian. Allow yourself two marks for each section.*

You are at the Hotel Miramare (don't translate the bits in brackets):

a *Say you would like a room with a shower, full board, from 4th to 14th November.*

b *Ask whether the restaurant is open. [You are told it is.]*

c *Ask the waiter what there is to eat.*

d *Ask him where the phone is.*

e *[You are now on the phone.] Ask whether Dr Cortese is in.*

f *[He is out.] Ask whether you can leave a message.*

Marks: __ /12

4 *Choosing each once only, complete each sentence with a suitable form of the verb from the box below:*

a *Non voglio ___ niente oggi!*

b *___ sempre tanti turisti qui?*

c *Tutte le camere ___ sul mare.*

d *Fa molto caldo. (Io) ___ sete.*

e *(Io) non___ aprire la valigia.*

f *Comincio a lavorare alle otto e ___ alle due.*

....

dare - fare - finire - venire - potere - avere

....

Marks: __ /6

5 *You are going shopping. Say in Italian (two marks per item):*

a *What you require: some cheese, some eggs, some ham.*

b *How much of each you require: 400 grams of cheese, six eggs, 100 grams of ham.*

Marks: __ /12

6 *Look at the advertisements in Unit 7, Practice 3. It is midday on Wednesday and your friend wants to go for lunch to 'La Torinese' (al ristorante 'La Torinese') or 'La Bella Napoli' restaurant. Explain to him, in Italian, firstly why he can't go to 'La Torinese', then why he can't go to 'La Bella Napoli'. Give yourself six marks for a correct answer.*

7 *Write down in Italian first what Ida likes (✔) and dislikes (X), then do the same for Renzo, replacing their names by pronouns (e.g. she likes ... he likes ...). Allow two marks for each.*

Ida	Renzo
l'insalata (✔)	la pasta (✔)
i fagiolini (✘)	i funghi (✘)

Marks: __ /4

8 *Look at the picture in Unit 9, Practice 7 and answer each question on it using Ce n'è or Ce ne sono. One mark for each correct answer.*
   a *Quante sedie ci sono?*
   b *Quanti calendari?*
   c *Quante scrivanie?*
   d *Quanti cassetti?*

Marks: __ /4

Check your total score against the ratings at the beginning of this answer key. Are you ready to start Unit 13?

Test your Italian III (Units 13–18)

1 *Can you express the following in Italian? Two marks for each correct answer.*
   a *Ask someone formally what sports they do.*
   b *Ask someone how to get to the University.*
   c *Ask someone informally what they have done today.*
   d *Ask someone informally if they've ever been to Pisa.*
   e *Say that you have already eaten.*
   f *Say that you have not yet paid.*
   g *Say that you will meet up later.*

Marks: __ /14

2 *Choose a suitable contracted preposition (a/da/di/con +
definite article) to complete each of these sentences. One mark
per answer.*

    a *Perchè non esci ___ tuo ragazzo stasera?*
    b *Vengo a prenderti ___ stazione.*
    c *La pensione è lontana ___ mare.*
    d *È stato il più bel viaggio ___ mia vita.*
    e *Mi ha portato ___ fiori bellissimi.*
    f *Mentre tu vai ___ pasticciere, io telefono a Marco.*

Marks: __ /6

3 *In this passage Diana is saying what she did yesterday. Can
you put the bracketed verbs into the perfect tense? After the
asterisk (*) use the first person plural (masc). Remember to
distinguish between verbs whose past is formed with **avere**
and those requiring <u>essere</u>. The first verb is done for you. One
mark for each correct verb.*

*Ieri mattina sono andata a scuola. Dopo pranzo (dormire) un
po'. Alle tre (fare) una bella passeggiata e (prendere) un gelato
al Bar Europa. (comprare) dei regali ma non (spendere) molto.
Quando (tornare) a casa (rispondere) alla lettera di Renzo e
(scrivere) una cartolina a Roberta. Alle otto (uscire) per strada
(incontrare) Giulia e Franco e* (andare) insieme alla trattoria
'Mamma Rosa'. (bere) e (mangiare) molto bene. Verso le
undici (andare) al mare. Sulla spiaggia (vedere) Enrico e l'
(salutare). A mezzanotte (fare) il bagno e poi (tornare) a casa.*

Marks: __ /18

4 *You are at the estate agent's. Fill in your side of the
conversation (allow two marks each for the first two, four
marks each for the last two responses).*

Agente	Desidera?
You	*I'm looking for a flat.*
Agente	Quante camere?
You	*Two are enough.*
Agente	Ne abbiamo uno vicino al Duomo.
You	*Really I prefer it by the sea. I like swimming.*
Agente	Ma questo è vicino a una grande piscina.
You	*I don't like swimming pools. I only like the sea.*

Marks: __ /12

5 *Say that you have already completed these tasks using the appropriate pronoun and making the necessary past participle agreements in your answers. Allow one mark for each correct answer.*

   a *Quando vende la casa?*
   b *Quando cambia i soldi?*
   c *Quando compra le riviste?*
   d *Quando vede Marisa?*
   e *Quando scrive la lettera?*
   f *Quando fa i bagagli?*

Marks: __ /6

6 *Choose between a suitable form (present tense) of* **conoscere**, **potere** *or* **sapere** *in the following sentences (one mark for each correct answer):*

   a *(Io) non ___ bene questa città.*
   b *(Tu) ___ se Gianni è a casa?*
   c *(Tu) ___ il mio amico Paolo?*
   d *Marco non ___ giocare a tennis perchè fa brutto tempo.*

Marks: __ /4

Before starting Unit 19 check your score against the ratings at the beginning of this answer key.

Test your Italian IV (Units 19–25)

1 *Can you express the following in Italian? One mark each for* **a**, **b**, **d** *and* **e**; *two marks each for* **c** *and* **f**.

  a   *Don't worry (formal).*
  b   *Sit down here (formal).*
  c   *Sorry (informal) I'm late.*
  d   *Be careful (informal).*
  e   *Please help me (formal).*
  f   *I enjoyed myself a lot.*

                                                   Marks: __ /8

2 *In the following passage the print has been damaged. Can you complete the words by filling in the gaps? Try guessing the meaning of words you don't know to understand the general sense. One mark for each correctly completed word.*

La piazza rappresenta una parte integrante della vita ital___. Per un caffè, per un appuntamento, per una discussione o per un p___ di musica, un italiano va generalmente in piazza dove c'è spesso un tea___ famoso, un monumento, una statua importante o un ristor___ con un'orchestra. Famosa in tutto il mondo è Piazza San Pietro a Ro___ con il Vaticano e con una fontana a destra e una fontana a sin___ .

A Venezia, Piazza San Marco è veramente stupenda, e a Fir___ Piazzale Michelangelo offre un magnifico panorama di tu___ la città.

                                                 Marks: __ /8

3 *Respond to these questions with the appropriate double pronouns. One mark for each correct answer:*

  a *Me lo farai sapere? Sì, sì. ___ farò sapere senz'altro.*
  b *Mi farai questo favore? Ma certo che___ farò.*
  c *Chi ti ha consigliato l'albergo?___ ha consigliato un mio collega.*
  d *L'hai detto a Carlo?___ dirò domani.*
  e *Ti ha firmato l'assegno? Sì. ___ ha firmato.*
  f *Bambini, chi vi ha regalato i cioccolatini?___ ha regalati il nonno.*
  g *Signora, chi le ha dato queste informazioni?___ ha date il direttore.*

                                                 Marks: __ /7

4 *In sentences* **a, b, c** *explain what Stefano will do before going on holiday with Mara; in* **d, e, f, g** *say what both will do. Use each verb from the box below once only to complete the sentences in the future tense.*
One mark for each correct answer.

   a ___ *alla sua amica, Mara.*
   b *Le chiederà se* ___ *libera.*
   c ___ *i posti.*
   d ___ *i soldi.*
   e ___ *i bagagli.*
   f ___ *i passaporti.*
   g ___ *i loro amici.*

---

salutare – telefonare – cambiare – fare – prenotare – essere – controllare

---

Marks: __ /7

5 *Mario lives in England now. Can you describe in Italian the life he used to live in Taormina? (Use the imperfect tense.) Allow yourself three marks for each correct answer.*

   a *He only spoke Italian.*
   b *He never got bored.*
   c *He was never tired.*
   d *He had lots of friends.*
   e *He saw them every day in the square.*
   f *He used to work from seven o'clock till one.*
   g *He went to the beach every Sunday.*
   h *He ate lots of fresh fruit.*

Marks: __ /24

6 *Using each verb from the box below once only in the conditional, can you complete these sentences? One mark for each correct answer.*

   a *Sono tanto stanco!* ___ *riposarmi prima di uscire.*
   b ___ *andare tu dal tabaccaio? Mi occorrono dei francobolli.*
   c *Ho tanta fame!* ___ *volentieri un bel piatto di spaghetti.*
   d ___ *a prenderlo volentieri all'aeroporto, ma non ho la macchina.*

e *Vuoi uscire stasera? Che ne ___ di un bel film?*
f *Perchè non vai alla festa? ___ molto.*

----

divertirsi – mangiare – andare – volere – dire - potere

Marks: __ /6

Congratulations! You have completed your course, and provided that you are satisfied with your score (see how to asses it by consulting the chart at the beginning of this answer key), you may find it helpful to consult the *Taking it further* section for guidance and suggestions regarding more advanced study.

Bravo! *Well done!*

....

Key to the exercises

Alternative answers are marked / (e.g. **per piacere/per favore**). Words that are not strictly necessary in the answer are put in brackets. With **Vero o falso** statements, a 'V' indicates that the statement is true. Otherwise the corrected version appears.

UNIT 1

Dialogues

1 a Parla inglese? b Parlo inglese e francese. c Non parlo tedesco. d Parlo inglese. Parlo francese. Parlo tedesco. e Non parlo cinese. Non parlo giapponese. Non parlo russo. f Parla italiano? g i Gérard Dupont parla francese. ii Betty Warren parla inglese. iii Anna Muti parla italiano. iv Helga Weil parla tedesco. 2 a Scusi, l'ascensore, per favore? b Grazie. c Scusi, il telefono, per favore? 3 a per piacere. b Mi dispiace. c Scusi, la banca, per piacere/per favore? d Non lo so. e sinistra, stazione, ascensore, grazie, telefono. f La stazione è a destra. g La posta è a sinistra. h V. i La polizia è a destra. j Sempre dritto! k the museum; the police station. 4 Buongiorno, signorina Giulia! Arrivederci, professore! 5 a Un gelato, signorina? b No, grazie. Sì, grazie. c tea; coffee; beer; espresso. d acqua minerale. e Un gelato? Sì, grazie. f Una pasta? No, grazie. g Una limonata? Sì, grazie.

Practice

1 b Anna: Una birra, per favore. c Alfredo: Un gelato, per favore. d Maria: Un tè, per favore. e Roberto: Un cappuccino, per favore. f Rita: Una granita di limone, per favore. g Carlo: Una cioccolata, per favore. h Olga: Una coca-cola, per favore.

2 b La birra è per Anna. c Il gelato è per Alfredo. d Il tè è per Maria. e Il cappuccino è per Roberto. f La granita di limone è per Rita. g La cioccolata è per Carlo. h La coca-cola è per Olga.

3 a Franco parla inglese. b Rita parla francese e spagnolo. c Carlo

parla tedesco e spagnolo. d Carlo parla tedesco, ma non parla francese. e Non parlo spagnolo. f Parla francese? g Parlo inglese, francese e spagnolo; non parlo tedesco.

4	**Turista**	Excuse me!
	You	Sì …? Prego?/Sì …?/Prego?
	Turista	The post office, please.
	You	È lì, a sinistra.
	Turista	And the station?
	You	Sempre dritto!
	Turista	Thank you.
	You	Prego.

Test yourself

1f; 2h; 3j; 4c; 5a; 6i; 7d; 8b; 9e; 10g

UNIT 2

Dialogues

1 a Ecco il Duomo! b il Museo Nazionale; la Banca Commerciale. c Questo è il museo. 2 a Dopo il Consolato Americano b strada; via; principale c Dov'è Piazza Municipio, per favore?/per piacere? d È vicino a Via Roma. e Dove sono i negozi, per favore? 3 a (Io) prendo una pizza e un bicchiere di vino. b Cosa prende? c vino rosso d Un'acqua minerale con gas, per piacere. e Un bicchiere di vino rosso, per piacere. 4 a Altro? b E lo zucchero! c Lo zucchero, per piacere. 5 a 7 beers; 5 sandwiches; 1 ice cream.

Practice

2 b Il Ponte Vecchio: Firenze c Il Palazzo del Parlamento: Londra d La Torre Eiffel: Parigi e La Torre Pendente: Pisa f Il Vesuvio: Napoli g Il Colosseo: Roma h Piazza San Marco: Venezia.

3 Dov'è il Colosseo? A Roma. Dov'è il Vesuvio? A Napoli. Dov'è la Torre Eiffel? A Parigi. La Scala è a Milano. Il Ponte Vecchio è a Firenze. Il Palazzo del Parlamento è a Londra. La Torre Pendente è a Pisa. Piazza San Marco è a Venezia.

4 a Scusi, dov'è il Consolato Americano? (È) a sinistra dopo
la posta. b Scusi, dov'è Piazza Garibaldi? (È) a destra dopo la
stazione. c Scusi, dov'è il Duomo? (È) a destra dopo il Museo
Nazionale. d Scusi, dov'è l'Albergo Miramare? (È) a destra dopo
Piazza Garibaldi. e (Sono) a sinistra dopo la posta.

5 Drinks: la limonata, la birra, l'acqua minerale, l'aranciata, il
tè. Food: la pizza, la pasta, il formaggio, il panino, il prosciutto.
Places: la banca, il Duomo, la piazza, il museo, l'albergo.

6 Marta prende il tè con latte e (con) zucchero. Filippo prende il tè
con limone senza zucchero. Io prendo il tè …

7 Cos'è questo? (Questo) è un espresso. Cos'è questo? (Questo)
è un gelato. Cos'è questa? (Questa) è una pasta. Cos'è questa?
(Questa) è una limonata.

Test yourself
1 sono; 2 dov'è; 3 a; 4 prende; 5 con; 6 buoni; 7 è; 8 bella; 9 a
destra; 10 dove.

UNIT 3

Dialogues
1 a A che piano abitano i signori Nuzzo, (per favore)? 2 a Come
si chiama? Mi chiamo Marco Russo. b Di dov'è? Sono di Napoli.
3 a Come ti chiami? b Io sono di Milano. c Che cosa fai? Sono
segretaria. 4 a Di che nazionalità è, signorina? Sono italiana. b
Anch'io sono italiano. c È greca. 5 a Io sono Massimo. b (E) questa
è Elena. Piacere. c Quanti anni hai? Ho diciotto anni. 6 a Sono
sposata. b Quanti figli ha, signora? c Quanti anni hanno? d La
bambina ha solo quattro anni. e Ha due fratelli e una sorella.

Practice
1 Notice the omission of the letters -i and -a: *venti* + *uno* becomes
ventuno; *quaranta* + *otto* becomes *quarantotto*.

2 a I 12 b IV 47 c I 13 d III 38.

3 a Il professor Russo è architetto. b Carlo Pini è ragioniere. c Olga Fulvi è dentista. d Anna Biondi è giornalista.

4 a Helga è tedesca. b Gérard e Philippe sono francesi. c Juanita è spagnola. d Ivan e Natasha sono russi. e Anna e Pina sono italiane.

5 a Helga è di Bonn. b Gérard e Philippe sono di Nizza. c Juanita è di Barcellona. d Ivan e Natasha sono di Omsk. e Anna e Pina sono di Trento.

6 a Helga abita a Bonn. b Gérard e Philippe abitano a Nizza. c Juanita abita a Barcellona. d Ivan e Natasha abitano a Omsk. e Anna e Pina abitano a Trento.

7 Cara Luisa, ho diciassette anni. Sono di Siena ma abito a Lucca. Mio padre è italiano e mia madre è tedesca. Ho un fratello. Si chiama Luigi e ha diciotto anni./Mio fratello Luigi ha diciotto anni.

Test yourself
1 Anch'io abito a Milano.
2 A che piano abita il signor Marini?
3 Ci vediamo più tardi a Piazza Mazzini.
4 Come si chiama il figlio di Roberto?
5 Questa ragazza greca parla cinese molto bene.
6 E tu, Anna, di dove sei?
7 Non sono qui per lavorare.
8 E tu, come ti chiami?
9 La bambina ha sette anni.
10 Mio padre è italiano e mia madre è tedesca.

UNIT 4

Dialogues
1 a Alle otto. 2 a mattina, sera 3 a €1,23. b Vuole queste? c 3 postcards and 2 papers. d iv e È una cartolina di Roma.
4 a Molto gentile. b 9.00; 8.00 5 a Desidera? b Quanto costa? c La camicetta è troppo cara. 6 a Prendo un paio di sandali marroni. b Che numero?

lunedì, sabato, domenica, aprono, chiudono.

Practice
1 a 9.30–1.00 b 3.00–4.00 c 9.00–2.00 d 9.00–1.30
e 9.00–7.30.

2 a la giacca b la maglietta c la cravatta d la gonna e i jeans f i pantaloni g le scarpe h i sandali i il vestito j la camicetta k i guanti l la camicia.

3 a Quanto costa la maglietta? Diciotto euro e venticinque. b Quanto costano i pantaloni? Settantadue euro e trenta. c Quanto costano le scarpe? Ottantacinque euro e cinquanta.

4 a Carlo compra una maglietta rossa, tre magliette gialle, una cravatta gialla, una cravatta verde, due paia di scarpe nere, un paio di pantaloni gialli e un paio di pantaloni verdi. b Quattrocentoquarantacinque euro e quaranta (€445, 40).

5	**Tabaccaio**	Can I help you?
	You	Due francobolli.
	Tabaccaio	For abroad?
	You	Sì. Per la Francia.
	Tabaccaio	Anything else?
	You	Una cartolina di Roma e questo giornale.
	Tabaccaio	Then …
	You	Nient'altro. Quant'è?
	Tabaccaio	Two euros and ten (cents).
	You	Ecco!

6 a closed; b open; c sales. 7 a 20% discount offer for men's/women's/children's outer wear from 17/10 to 19/11.

Test yourself
1 A che ora chiude questo negozio?
2 Scusi, quanto costano queste scarpe?

3 Di che colore sono i pantaloni?

4 A che ora apre la banca?

5 Quanto costa la gonna nera?

6 Questo vestito è troppo semplice.

7 Un paio di sandali rossi, per piacere.

8 Franco e Roberta abitano a Parigi.

9 Vorrei una cartolina di Torino.

10 Il dottore parte per Venezia domani sera verso le otto.

UNIT 5

Dialogues

1 a Vado a Bologna. b In treno. c Solo per dieci giorni. 2 a Scusi, sa dov'è la fabbrica di scarpe? b Non è lontano. c *una fermata* is a bus stop. 3 a Come si scrive? b Mio marito è svizzero. c Capisco tutto. 4 a Sono nata a Lucca, ma abito a Siena. b Quante lingue parla?

Practice

2 a 76 b 85 c 68 d 79 e 170 f 198 g 177 h 102

3 a ... va in ufficio in bicicletta. b ... va a Parigi in treno. c ... va a Roma in macchina. d ... va a casa a piedi. e ...vanno a scuola in autobus. f ... va a Milano in aereo.

4 – Dove vai, Franco? – Vado a Roma. – Come vai? – In macchina.

– Dove vai, Anna? – Vado a casa. – Come vai? – A piedi.

– Dove vai, Francesca? – Vado a Milano. – Come vai? – In aereo.

5 a Sono le dieci e cinque b È l'una meno un quarto c Sono le tre meno dieci d Sono le tre e venti e Sono le sei meno un quarto f Sono le sei e mezza g È mezzogiorno h È mezzanotte.

6 **Dirigente**	Your name?
You	Pat Brown.
Dirigente	Brown? How do you spell it?
You	B come Bari, R come Roma, O come Ostia/Otranto, W come Washington, N come Napoli.
Dirigente	You're English, aren't you?
You	No. Sono americano/a, ma abito a Londra.
Dirigente	How old are you?
You	Ho trentatrè anni.
Dirigente	What (work) do you do?
You	Lavoro in un'agenzia di viaggi.
Dirigente	Do you speak French and German?
You	Capisco tutto ma non parlo bene.

7 A handbook or guide to professional careers.

Test yourself
1d; 2g; 3i; 4b; 5h; 6j; 7a; 8e; 9f; 10c; 11 la; 12 mie; 13 tua; 14 suoi; 15 mio.

UNIT 6

Dialogues
1 a Alle quindici e venticinque. b Da che binario? 2 a Tre posti per domani mattina. b espresso coffee, fast train; bank note, ticket 3 a È in ritardo di due minuti. b Il treno è in partenza dal binario nove. 4 a Dov'è la fermata del sessantotto? b Alla prossima fermata scendo anch'io. c per favore, per piacere, per cortesia.

Practice
1 a Siena, 1, seconda, 16.20, 3. b Roma, 2, prima, 10.40, 15. c Genova, 1, seconda, 23.55, 7. d Novara, 1, prima, 18.30, 1.

2 a dell' b agli c delle d dello e allo f degli g all' h alle i della j al. 3 i-e ii-i iii-g iv-a v-b vi-c vii-d viii-f ix-h 4 In via Terni ci sono tre alberghi. In Piazza Dante c'è un palazzo. In Piazza Cavour ci sono quattro bar. A Roma ci sono due aeroporti.

5 a Pina va in banca fra un'ora. b Giorgio va al colloquio fra tre ore. c Enrico ritorna a casa fra un quarto d'ora/quindici minuti. d Carlo va alla discoteca fra dieci minuti. e Il treno arriva fra cinque minuti.

6	**Impiegato**	Yes …Can I help you?
	You	Vorrei prenotare tre posti per dopodomani, giovedì.
	Impiegato	Where to?
	You	Firenze.
	Impiegato	Do you want to leave in the morning or evening?
	You	Non c'è un treno diretto alle undici?
	Impiegato	No, but there's a fast train that leaves at midday.
	You	Va bene. Tre posti per giovedì, allora. Seconda classe.

7 a You travel better and you spend less. b Quando vuoi partire? c No. Available only to those resident in Italy.

Test yourself
1 dell'; 2 degli; 3 allo; 4 della; 5 al; 6 di; 7 ai; 8 alla; 9 all'; 10 alle; 11 agli; 12 del; 13 delle; 14 dei; 15 dello.

UNIT 7

Dialogues
1 Aa Bc Cd Da 2 a ottima idea. 3 a Ma oggi è chiuso. b C'è un buon ristorante qui vicino? 4 a Tutti i giorni, eccetto il lunedì. 5 a C'è molta gente oggi. b È una specialità della casa. 6 a Un altro po' di vino? b Per me niente.

Practice
1 Antipasti: antipasto misto, coppa di gamberetti, melone con prosciutto. Primi: lasagne al forno, risotto alla milanese, spaghetti alle vongole. Secondi: bistecca alla griglia, fritto misto di pesce, pollo arrosto, sogliola alla griglia. Contorni: fagiolini, insalata mista, patatine fritte. Frutta – dolci: gelati misti, macedonia di frutta, frutta fresca. Da bere: acqua minerale, vino rosso, vino bianco.

2 i-d ii-h iii-e iv-a v-f vi-g vii-c viii-b

3 i-b & d. ii-d iii-c: because it's a huge park in a wood iv-d: 'You eat well and keep your figure' v-a & c

4 Cameriere	What are you having?
You	(Vorrei) antipasto misto.
Cameriere	And for the first course?
You	Minestrone.
Cameriere	Would you like to order the second course now?
You	Perchè no? Cosa/che cosa mi consiglia?
Cameriere	The fish is very good today.
You	Non mangio pesce. Bistecca alla griglia.
Cameriere	Certainly. And any side dishes?
You	Prendo insalata mista e/con patatine fritte.
Cameriere	And to drink?
You	Mezza bottiglia di vino locale.
Cameriere	Red or white?
You	Meglio il vino rosso con la bistecca.
Cameriere	Straight away.
	…
Cameriere	Everything all right?
You	Sì. Benissimo. Un altro po' di pane, per piacere
Cameriere	Here you are. Anything else?
You	No, grazie. Basta così.

Test yourself
1e; 2g; 3k; 4h; 5f; 6d; 7b; 8c; 9j; 10i; 11l; 12a.

UNIT 8

Dialogues
1 a Singola o doppia? b La colazione è compresa nel prezzo? 2 a Dal ventisei luglio al nove agosto. b (la) colazione, (il) pranzo, (la) cena. 3 a a week. b Abbiamo la patente di guida … eccola! 4 a I bagagli sono nella macchina. b Lo chiamo subito. 5 a Alle sei in punto. b La camera che dà sulla terrazza. 6 a tanti turisti b Comincio alle sei e finisco verso l'una.

5 a Quando compra i libri? Li compro stasera. b Quando compra le riviste? Le compro dopo. c Quando compra la rivista? La compro stamattina. d Quando paga il conto? Lo pago adesso.

Practice

1 a single room, shower, full board, Thursday–Monday.
b double room, bath, full board, 25 June–4 July. c Room with twin beds, shower, half board, 9 May–19 May.

2 a eccolo! b eccola! c eccolo! d eccoli! e eccole! f eccola! g eccolo! h eccolo!

3 a Sì. La conosco molto bene. b Sì. Le conosco abbastanza bene. c La vedo verso le otto. d Lo invito/l'invito oggi. e Li invito spesso. f La guardo dopo cena. g Sì. Lo conosco bene. h No. Lo vedo stasera.

4 a nello studio. b nell'acqua. c sul letto. d sulla spiaggia. e nel bicchiere. f nella borsa. g nelle valigie. h negli spaghetti.

5 a No. Vengo in macchina. b No. Vengo a piedi. c No. Vengo in aereo. d No. Veniamo in metropolitana. e No. Veniamo in bicicletta.

6 a Abito a Terni. Lavoro in un'agenzia di viaggi. La mattina esco alle otto e un quarto. Incomincio a lavorare alle nove. Finisco di lavorare alle sei. Torno a casa alle sette meno un quarto. Il sabato non lavoro. Vado in montagna con mio marito. Abitiamo a Napoli. Lavoriamo in un istituto di lingue. La mattina usciamo alle sette e venti. Incominciamo a lavorare alle otto. Finiamo di lavorare all'una. Torniamo a casa alle due meno venti. Il sabato non lavoriamo. Andiamo in campagna con i nostri genitori.

b Anna lavora in una banca commerciale, ma i signori Spada lavorano in un istituto di lingue. La mattina Anna esce alle otto meno un quarto, ma i signori Spada escono alle sette e venti. Anna incomincia a lavorare alle otto e mezza, ma i signori Spada incominciano a lavorare alle otto. Anna finisce di lavorare alle cinque, ma i signori Spada finiscono di lavorare all'una. Anna torna a casa alle sei meno un quarto, ma i signori Spada tornano a casa alle due meno venti. Il sabato Anna va al mare con sua sorella, ma i signori Spada vanno in campagna con i loro genitori.

7	**Direttore**	Good morning.
	You	Buongiorno! Ha due camere per dieci giorni?
	Direttore	For how many?
	You	Per quattro persone.
	Direttore	We have two rooms on the third floor.
	You	Con bagno?
	Direttore	One with a private bath, the other with a shower.
	You	Sì. Va benissimo. C'è il ristorante in questo albergo?
	Direttore	No. There's only a bar.
	You	C'è un ristorante qui vicino?
	Direttore	There's the 'Trattoria Monti' in the square.

8 a Accettazione carta di credito. b Si accettano piccoli animali domestici. c (Un) campo da tennis. d No vacancies. e Dry cleaning.

Test yourself
1 preoccupi; 2 il; 3 tutto; 4 ne; 5 due, terzo; 6 al; 7 vengono, tanti; 8 ma; 9 un; 10 esco; 11 pago; 12 spiaggia.

UNIT 9

Dialogues
1 a Ha un appuntamento? b Le passo il dottor Fini. 2 a Avanti! b Posso offrirle un caffè? 3 a Mi dispiace, non c'è. b Un attimo. La chiamo. c Sono io.

Practice
1 a Out. b He asks whether she can call back later. c She says she will call back in half an hour. d 10 June. e His name.

2 Dove lo posso contattare? La chiamo io ... Le do... La richiamo io ... La ringrazio.

3 i-b ii-g iii-d iv-f v-c vi-h vii-a viii-e

4 a Vuole telefonare ad Anna. b Vuole vedere un film. c Vuole uscire con Carla. d Deve lavorare fino a tardi. e Deve uscire con i suoi genitori. f Deve scrivere una lettera a suo zio. g Non può fumare. h Non può comprare un altro vestito. i Non può venire a pranzo con noi.

5 a Puoi aspettare qui? b Puoi telefonare per me? c Puoi passare il sale e il pepe? d Puoi prenotare un'altra camera? e Puoi aprire la porta, per piacere?

6 **Segretaria**	Hello!
You	Pronto! Posso parlare con Lisa, per piacere?
Segretaria	Lisa is in a meeting.
You	Posso lasciare un messaggio?
Segretaria	Certainly. Who's speaking?
You	Pat Iles.
Segretaria	How do you spell it?
You	P come Palermo, A come Ancona, T come Torino, I come Imola, L come Livorno, E come Empoli, S come Salerno.
Segretaria	And what's the message?
You	Pat Iles non può andare alla riunione domani.

8 Costa €55,78 (cinquantacinque euro e settantotto) ed è garantita per sei mesi.

9 È per i bambini. Non costa niente./È gratuito.

Test yourself

1 Pronto. Chi parla?; 2 Mi dispiace. Ho sbagliato numero.; 3 Posso parlare con Pietro?; 4 Mi dispiace. Non c'è.; 5 Vorrei vedere la segretaria.; 6 Devo partire domani mattina.; 7 Posso lasciare un messaggio per il dottor Bini?; 8 Può aspettare un momento/attimo, per piacere?; 9 Non è qui. Lo chiamo.; 10 Devo andare a una conferenza.

UNIT 10

Dialogues

1 a Vivo e lavoro a Napoli. b Gioco a tennis. 2 a Sono i suoi genitori? b E questi qui sono i miei nonni.

Practice

1 a quel signore b quell'orologio c quella camicia d quell'istituto e quello studente f quegli appartamenti g quei libri h quei pomodori i quelle cartoline j quei bicchieri.

2 a bella macchina b bello studio c bel posto d bei bambini e bell'albero f bella spiaggia g belle camere h begli uccelli.

3 a ... rimango a casa e guardo ... b ... vado a ballare ... c ... vado al cinema ... d ... resto a casa a giocare a bridge. e ... gioco a tennis ... f ... esco di casa ... g ... mangio ...

4 i-b ii-d iii-a iv-c

5 Guido: Vado al cinema, leggo, ascolto la radio.

Carla: Guardo la televisione, gioco a tennis, vado a ballare.

Adamo e Ida: Andiamo al cinema, leggiamo, andiamo a teatro, ascoltiamo la radio.

Enzo e Rina: Guardiamo la televisione, giochiamo a tennis, leggiamo, andiamo a ballare.

6 I c Enzo è mio figlio. d Isabella è mia figlia. e Teresa è mia sorella. f Filippo è mio fratello. g Rina è mia nipote. h Pietro è mio nipote. i Guido e Elena sono i miei genitori.

II b Anna è nostra madre. c/d Noi siamo i loro figli. e Teresa è nostra zia. f Filippo è nostro zio. g Rina è nostra cugina. h Pietro è nostro cugino. i Guido e Elena sono i nostri nonni. 7 Cara Laura, grazie della tua lettera. Ho diciassette anni e un giorno vorrei lavorare in Italia. Quest'anno studio l'italiano ed il francese. Sono due lingue molto interessanti. Abito/Vivo in un paesino/piccolo paese vicino a Brighton che non è troppo lontano da Londra. Mio padre è elettricista e mia madre lavora a casa per un'agenzia pubblicitaria. Ho un fratello che lavora a Londra e una piccola sorella che ha sette anni. Si chiama Sandra e passa molto tempo a giocare con il nostro cane Rover. Vorrei venire in Italia a luglio. A presto. Un caro saluto. Gloria.

8 **Angelo**	Hi, Isa!
You	Ciao!
Angelo	Would you like to come out with me?
You	Dove?
Angelo	Dancing.
You	Quando? Adesso?
Angelo	This evening, at nine.
You	No. Stasera non posso. Devo andare al cinema con un amico/un'amica.
Angelo	Can you come tomorrow? Or have you got to go out tomorrow too?
You	Domani sera devo andare a teatro con i miei genitori.
Angelo	Pity! Sunday at eight?
You	Domenica va benissimo. Ma non posso venire prima delle nove.
Angelo	Nine o'clock is fine. Goodbye then!
You	Ciao!

Test yourself

1 a; 2 periferia, lavorano; 3 leggono; 4 rimango; 5 bel; 6 vogliono; 7 quella, dello; 8 bello; 9 mie; 10 ascoltiamo.

UNIT 11

Dialogues

1 a (Io) ho fame. b Vorrei mangiare qualcosa. 2 a Vorrei dei panini. b Mezzo chilo di spaghetti. 3 a Com'è bella questa borsa! b Non

mi piace. 4 a Mi piacciono moltissimo. b Allora li compro tutti e
due. c Non ho più soldi!

Practice

1 Maria vuol comprare del burro, del formaggio, della birra,
dell'olio, degli spaghetti, dello zucchero, dei fiammiferi, dell'acqua
minerale gassata/con gas.

2 b Il vino bianco le piace, ma preferisce il vino rosso. c Il cinema
le piace, ma preferisce il teatro. d Milano le piace, ma preferisce
Firenze. e Le melanzane le piacciono, ma preferisce i peperoni. f I
libri le piacciono, ma preferisce le riviste.

3 b Le piace il vino bianco o il vino rosso? Il vino bianco mi
piace, ma preferisco il vino rosso. c Le piace il cinema o il teatro?
Il cinema mi piace, ma preferisco il teatro. d Le piace Milano o
Firenze? Milano mi piace, ma preferisco Firenze. e Le piacciono le
melanzane o i peperoni? Le melanzane mi piacciono, ma preferisco
i peperoni. f Le piacciono i libri o le riviste? I libri mi piacciono, ma
preferisco le riviste.

4 a Le piace …? b Le piace …? c Ti piace …? d Ti piace …? e Ti
piace …? f Le piacciono …? g Ti piacciono …?

5 a, b, c, f, g Ti piace? d, e Le piace?

6 a Ne devo pagare cento. b Ne devo scrivere due. c Ne voglio
invitare dodici. d Ne devo comprare nove. e Ne ho una. f Ne ho
quattro. g Ne leggo molti.

7 a Ne ha uno più corto? b Non ne ha una più grande? c Non ne
ha uno più scuro? d Ne ha una più chiara? e Non ne ha uno più
facile?

8 a Pietro è più grande di Paolo. b Lino è più piccolo di Paolo. c
Lino è più piccolo di Pietro. d Pietro è più grande di Lino. e Paolo è
più piccolo di Pietro.

9 a L'aereo è più veloce del treno. b Il treno è più veloce dell'autobus. c La macchina è più veloce della bicicletta. d La bicicletta è meno veloce dell'autobus. e L'autobus è meno veloce della metropolitana.

10 a A new car. b Yes, very well. c Because his car uses too much petrol. d Yes. e No. f He doesn't like small cars. g No. He thinks they are too expensive. h He does not want to pay all that much.

11 Salumeria: salame, olio, vino, olive, prosciutto, pasta, mortadella.

Macelleria: vitello, maiale, agnello, manzo.

Pescheria: trota, merluzzo, salmone.

12a Ci vogliono cinque minuti per (cuocere) le pennette rigate, e undici minuti per gli spaghetti. b Sono cinquecento grammi. c Sono quattrocento grammi.

Test yourself
1c; 2j; 3a; 4i; 5l; 6h; 7d; 8f; 9k; 10b; 11e; 12g.

UNIT 12

Dialogues
1 a Roberto cerca un appartamento al centro. b Ne vuole quattro. 2 a La padrona di casa abita al pianterreno. b Si paga l'affitto. 3 a V. b La televisione è nel soggiorno, e la lavatrice è nel bagno.

Practice
1 Bagno: il bidè, la doccia, la vasca da bagno, il water, il lavandino/lavabo.

Cucina: la cucina, il frigorifero, la lavastoviglie, la lavatrice, l'acquaio.

Camera da letto: il letto, il comodino, lo scaffale.

Sala da pranzo: le tende, le sedie, la tavola.

Salotto: il divano, la libreria, le poltrone, il quadro, la scrivania, il tappeto, la televisione.

Ingresso: il telefono, il tavolino, la pianta, lo specchio, l'orologio.

2 a Ce ne sono due. b Ce ne sono quattro. c Ce n'è una. d Ce ne sono quattro. e Ce ne sono sette.

3 a La presa per il rasoio è nel bagno. b Il citofono è nell'ingresso. c Il frigorifero è nella cucina. d Il letto è nella camera da letto. e Il divano è nel salotto. f Le coperte sono nell'armadio.

4 a Le sedie a sdraio sono sul balcone. b Le lenzuola sono sul letto. c La televisione è sul tavolino. d I libri sono sullo scaffale.

5 a Davide cerca un appartamento di quattro camere, in periferia, vicino alla strada principale. b Bianca cerca un appartamento di tre camere, in periferia, vicino alla stazione. c Lola e Rita cercano un appartamento di cinque camere, al centro, vicino all'ufficio. d Cerchiamo un appartamento di cinque camere, al centro, vicino all'ufficio.

6 a Ce ne sono dodici. b Ce ne sono sette. c Ce ne sono trecentosessantacinque. d Ce ne sono sessanta. e Ce ne sono cento. f Ce ne sono dieci. g Ce ne sono ventuno. h Ce n'è uno.

7 a The Coliseum. b It's not very modern. c On the fourth. d No. e Five. f Three. g Bathroom and kitchen. h The bathroom is small but the kitchen is nice and big.

8 a A luxury flat in a tourist district. b Two- to five-room flats. c A flat in a residential district with park. d Immediate sale. e A villa with a scenic view built as two separate flats, in a unique position. f It's a superbly built dream villa, and on the seafront. g He's looking for a luxury flat in a modern block that is free in June. h An English student is looking for furnished accommodation in exchange for conversation.

UNIT 13

Dialogues

1 a Lo sport preferito di Giulio è il jogging. b V. c D'inverno va a nuotare in piscina, d'estate (va a nuotare) al lago. 2 a Quando corre, la pioggia non fa nessuna differenza per lui. b No. Corre anche quando fa brutto tempo. c No. Non si sente affatto stanco. 3 a Rita offre un bicchiere di vino al giornalista. b La mattina lei e suo marito si alzano presto. c No. Si alzano alle sei. 4 a V. b No. Cenano piuttosto tardi. 5 a Rina studia medicina. b Si laurea a giugno. c Fa l'ultimo anno.

Practice

1 a Si sveglia alle sei e mezza. b Si alza alle sette. c Si lava. d Fa colazione alle otto. e Legge il giornale. f Esce di casa alle otto e mezza. g Torna a casa alle sei. h Cena alle otto. i Guarda la televisione. j Va a letto alle undici.

2 a ... io mi riposo ... b ... io mi diverto ... c ... io mi sveglio ... d ... io mi alzo ... e ... io mi lavo ... f ... io mi vesto ...g ... noi non ci riposiamo ...

3 Non mi sveglio mai ... Non mi alzo mai ... Non mi lavo mai ... Non mi vesto mai prima ...

4 a ... ci riposiamo. b ... ci cambiamo. c ... mi alzo. d ... mi ubriaco. e ... mi diverto. f ... mi lagno.

5 a Lo prende al bar. b La prende in salumeria. c Li compra in panetteria. d Lo compra all'edicola. e L'aspetta all'edicola.

6 a Nevica. b Piove. c C'è il sole/fa bel tempo. d Tira vento/c'è vento.

7	You	Ma non si riposa mai, signora?
	Pina	Well, with a restaurant it's difficult to rest. We go to bed very late at night, and in the morning we get up very early.
	You	Quante ore al giorno lavora?
	Pina	Ten, 12, sometimes even 14 hours.
	You	Lavora duro!
	Pina	But I rest during the holidays.
	You	Quante volte all'anno va in vacanza?
	Pina	Twice.
	You	Quando? D'estate?
	Pina	No. In summer it's impossible. We have too many customers. We go in spring and autumn.
	You	Dove va?
	Pina	I go to Switzerland with my daughter. We go skiing.
	You	Le piace sciare?
	Pina	Yes, a lot. Skiing is my favourite sport.

8 a Scia. b Nuota. c Fa il jogging. d Gioca a calcio. e Gioca a carte. f Gioca a tennis.

Test yourself

1 Vado a fare un po' di jogging tre volte alla settimana.
2 A che ora ti svegli?
3 Spesso a mezzogiorno mangio un panino nel parco.
4 La mattina esco di casa alle otto per andare a lavorare.
5 Di solito passo per l'edicola per prendere il giornale.
6 Mi sento meglio quando faccio un po' di palestra.
7 C'è tanto vento oggi./Oggi c'è tanto vento.
8 Cosa fa di bello stasera?
9 Stasera vado al cinema per rilassarmi.
10 Mi sono laureata nel 2001.

UNIT 14

Dialogues

1 a La Posta Centrale è in Piazza Garibaldi. b No. Parla con un passante. 2 a La fermata del 48 è dopo il ponte. b Deve scendere. 3 a V. b Vuole sapere dov'è la buca delle lettere.

Grammar

3 pulisca, beva, faccia, esca, venga.

Practice

1 a Giri a sinistra. b Vada sempre dritto/dritto dritto. c Giri a destra. 2i Scusi come si fa per andare … a all'università? b al museo? c alla banca? ii a Prenda la terza traversa a sinistra; la stazione è a destra. b Prenda la seconda traversa a sinistra; il supermercato è a destra. c Prenda la seconda a destra; la banca commerciale è a sinistra. 3i 1e; 2d; 3a; 4b; 5c. ii b Non suoni il claxon! c Non sorpassi! d Non passi (di qua!) e Non vada in bicicletta!

4i a Dove devo parcheggiare? b Dove devo prenotare? c Dove devo pagare? d Dove devo scendere? ii a Parcheggi in piazza! b Prenoti all'agenzia! c Paghi alla cassa! d Scenda alla prossima fermata!

5i a Posso bere questo vino? b Posso aprire la finestra? c Posso prendere questa sedia? d Posso prenotare l'albergo? ii a Sì. Sì. Lo beva! b Sì. Sì. L'apra! c Sì, Sì. La prenda! d Sì. Sì. Lo prenoti!

6 a Piazza Vittoria. b Porta Santa Margherita. c Chiesa di SS. (Santissima) Trinità.

Test yourself

1g; 2c; 3j; 4f; 5e; 6a; 7b; 8h; 9i; 10d.

Dialogues

1 a Elena ha mangiato in una rosticceria. b Ha bevuto il vino. 2 a
Il marito ha perso l'autobus. b Sta meglio. 3 a V. b No. Ha visitato
la moglie.

Practice

1 A ... risposto ... ho messo in ordine ... B Ho invitato ...
Abbiamo bevuto ... giocato a bridge ... C ... abbiamo visto ... D
... ha chiamato ... Ho passato ...

2 i-f ii-d iii-e iv-a v-g vi-c vii-b

3 a Non ti vedo. b Non ti sento. c Non ti conosco. d Non mi vedi?
e Non ti capisco. f Quando m'inviti? g Allora, mi accompagni? h Ti
aspetto ...

4 a Vittoria ha visto il Papa in Piazza San Pietro. b Gino ha
comprato una villa fra Siena e Firenze. c Roberto ha (finalmente)
aperto un'agenzia immobiliare. d Renzo e Mara hanno fatto
molti bagni. e Ada e Lino hanno giocato alla roulette e hanno
perso. f Federico e Anna hanno visto l'Aida. 5 Ho visto tante cose
interessanti. Saluti da Bari.

6 a Ha pranzato dai suoi genitori. b Non ha chiamato l'elettricista.
c Ha guardato il programma TV 7 speciale. d Non ha pulito la
casa. e Non ha pagato l'affitto. f Ha giocato a tennis con Marco. g
Ha portato la macchina dal meccanico. h Ha scritto una cartolina a
sua zia Maria.

7 **You**	Cos'hai fatto di bello oggi?	
Olga	I worked all day.	
You	Non hai visto il tuo ragazzo?	
Olga	Yes. At lunchtime.	
You	Avete mangiato insieme?	
Olga	Yes. At a smart trattoria in Via Manzoni.	
You	Perchè non sei contenta allora?	
Olga	Because I had to pay for the lunch.	

Test yourself

1 mostra; 2 quasi; 3 tua; 4 di; 5 fa; 6 miei; 7 detto; 8 dato; 9 ha; 10 ieri.

UNIT 16

Dialogues

1 a L'immigrato ha lavorato prima a Bedford. b È andato ad abitare a Londra. 2 a V. b Spera di ritornare in Italia. 3 a V. b È partito col/con il treno delle dieci e quaranta. 4 a V. b (Non l'accetta) perchè deve scappare.

Practice

1 (a)… lunedì scorso è andato a teatro. b … martedì scorso ha cenato tardi. c … mercoledì scorso non ha studiato affatto. d … giovedì scorso ha lavorato fino alle dieci. e … venerdì scorso ha mangiato fuori. f … sabato scorso ha giocato a scacchi. g … domenica scorsa ha dormito fino a mezzogiorno. 2 Lunedì scorso sono andato a teatro. Giovedì scorso ho lavorato fino alle dieci. Domenica scorsa ho dormito fino a mezzogiorno.

3 b Paolo Nuzzo è nato nel '79. È stato in Austria per due anni. È andato a Vienna. Poi è tornato in Italia. c Mirella Perrone è nata nel '67. È stata in Francia per un anno. È andata a Parigi. Poi è tornata in Sicilia. d I signori Caraffi sono nati nel '68. Sono stati in Spagna per dodici anni. Sono andati a Barcellona. Poi sono tornati in Sardegna. e Anna e Silvia sono nate nel '71. Sono state in Grecia per sei anni. Sono andate ad Atene. Poi sono tornate a Roma.

4 b Ci sono andata in aprile. c Ci sono ritornata nel mese di agosto. d Ci sono andata in macchina. e No. Ci sono andata con la mia amica Francesca.

5 a Non la vede da due anni. b La conosce da molti anni. c Lo suona da nove anni. d Lo studia da sei mesi. e Non lo vedono da molto tempo. f L'aspettano da poco tempo.

6 a Mara è andata a fare la spesa due ore fa. b Sergio è venuto a pranzo un'ora fa. c Mario è tornato dal lavoro un'ora e mezza fa. d Carlo è andato a letto mezz'ora fa. e Filippo è uscito cinque minuti fa.

7	**Giornalista**	Do you ever go to Italy?
	You	Sì. Ci vado quasi ogni anno.
	Giornalista	Where did you go last year?
	You	Sono andato a Venezia e a Verona.
	Giornalista	Did you stay long in Verona?
	You	Due sere/notti. Per l'opera.
	Giornalista	Did you go with friends?
	You	No. Preferisco viaggiare da solo.
	Giornalista	(But) you speak very well! Are your parents Italian?
	You	Sì. E … Ho studiato l'italiano all'università.
	Giornalista	Where? In Italy?
	You	Prima in Italia, poi all'università di Londra.
	Giornalista	How long ago?
	You	Due anni fa.

8 Si trovano in Sicilia.

Test yourself

1 Da quanto tempo vive a Roma?
2 Vorrei lavorare a Milano per un anno.
3 Sono nato/a a Londra ma vivo in Italia da 15 anni.
4 È la mia prima volta a Berlino.
5 Purtroppo devo partire domani.

6 Sono stati negli Stati Uniti tre volte.

7 Sono partiti due ore fa.

8 Spero di rivederla l'anno prossimo.

9 Nel 2002 sono andato(a) in Germania.

10 Nè Alessandro nè Maria hanno letto quel libro.

Dialogues

1 a Marisa è andata al supermercato con Valeria. b (L'ha messo) in frigorifero. 2 a Daniele e Sonia hanno comprato una cravatta di seta pura per Sandro. b (Non li hanno prenotati) perchè non hanno avuto tempo. 3 a V. b Ha tolto/staccato la spina.

Practice

1 a Ne ho mandato uno. b Ne ho visti molti. c Ne ho spedite sei. d Ne ho scritte quattro. e Ne ho visitata una. f Ne ho spesi molti. g Ne ho cambiate poche. h Ne ho bevuti tre.

2 a Le ho già scritte. b Li ho già comprati. c Li ho già visti. d Le ho già fatte. e L'ho già sbrigata. f L'ho già finito. g Li ho già preparati. h L'ho già consultata.

3 a No. Non l'ho ancora fatto. b No. Non l'ho ancora pulito. c No. Non l'ho ancora pagato. d No. Non l'ho ancora fatta. e No. Non li ho ancora comprati. f No. Non l'ho ancora riparata.

4 a … ho scritto … b … l'ho letto. c … l'ho ascoltata. d … l'ha bevuta. e … l'ha messo. f … hanno perso il treno.

5	**Moglie**	Are we leaving then, dear?
	You	Non sono ancora pronto.
	Moglie	What are you looking for?
	You	Il passaporto. Ma dove l'ho messo? L'hai preso tu?*
	Moglie	No. Have you looked in the car?
	You	Sì. Ho guardato. Non c'è.
	Moglie	Didn't you leave it in the bank this morning when you changed your money?
	You	No. Ah … Un momento … Forse l'ho messo in camera da letto.
	Moglie	No. It's not there. I've cleaned (in) every room and I haven't seen anything.
	You	Non l'hai mica messo con gli altri documenti?
	Moglie	No, no. I've only got the train tickets in my bag.
	You	Che guaio! Come facciamo ora senza passaporto?
	Moglie	Have you looked in the study?
	You	Sì. Ho guardato dappertutto.
	Moglie	My goodness! And the train leaves in half an hour!

*The personal pronoun *tu* is added at the end of the question for emphasis. Compare Unit 3, Section 7.

Test yourself
1a; 2c; 3b; 4c; 5a.
6 Non abbiamo voluto farlo.
7 Ha dovuto dire di no.
8 Ha già letto l'articolo?
9 Non ho ancora visto il film.
10 Ho le chiavi. Eccole qui/qua.

Dialogues

1 a Renzo non usa mai il profumo./Renzo il profumo non lo usa
mai. b Perchè è il suo compleanno. 2 a Beatrice prende un cd di
musica classica per Renzo. b Vuole telefonare a Renzo. 3 a V. b
Devono andare a pranzo da Carla.

Practice

1 a Anna gli dà una cravatta. b Renzo gli dà un libro. c Beatrice
gli porta un cd. d Livio gli manda un dvd. e Matteo gli regala un
profumo. f Maria gli telefona per fargli gli auguri.

2 a Le telefono stasera. b Gli telefono più tardi. c Gli telefono dopo
cena. d Le scrivo domani. e Le scrivo oggi. f Gli parlo dopo la
lezione./Parlo loro dopo la lezione.

3 b A chi vuole mandare la cartolina di auguri? Voglio mandarla a
Beatrice. c A chi vuole regalare la borsa di pelle? Voglio regalarla
a Maria. d A chi vuole portare i cioccolatini? Voglio portarli a
Marco. e A chi vuole dare il portafoglio? Voglio darlo a Gino.

4 il francobollo – Non ce l'ho. – non lo compri? – la posta è chiusa
– il tabaccaio è aperto – non c'è un tabaccaio – vuoi spedirla – devo
mandargli – devi mandarli?

5 a S'incontrano. b Si vedono. c Si parlano. d Si salutano. e Si
baciano. f Si abbracciano.

6	Giorgio	Where are you going, Carla?
	You	Prima vado alla posta, poi vado a comprare il regalo per Antonio.
	Giorgio	Why? Is it his birthday?
	You	No. È il suo onomastico.
	Giorgio	What are you buying him?
	You	Non lo so ancora.
	Giorgio	Does he like reading?
	You	Mi sembra di no.
	Giorgio	How much do you want to spend?
	You	Non troppo.
	Giorgio	Do you know whether he likes music?
	You	So che gli piace ascoltare la musica quando guida.
	Giorgio	You can buy him a CD then.
	You	Ottima idea!

7 a No. È un mazzo di rose. b Ce ne sono quindici. c They originated in Perugia. d Mother's day.

Test yourself
1F; 2F; 3T; 4F; 5F.

6 So nuotare, ma oggi non posso nuotare perchè non ho il costume da bagno.
7 Conosco Michele.
8 Sai/sa dov'è Torino?
9 Le ho dato i fiori.
10 (Per il suo compleanno) Alice gli ha mandato una cartolina di auguri.

Dialogues

1 a V. b No. Non c'è mai stata. 2 a V. b (C'è andata) per quattro giorni. 3 a Marcello lavora in una fabbrica. b Si trova bene.

Practice

1 Marco si è iscritto all'università di Roma. Si è laureato in medicina in sei anni. Anna si è iscritta all'università di Bologna. Si è laureata in matematica e fisica in sette anni. Carlo e Filippo si sono iscritti all'università di Napoli. Si sono laureati in legge in quattro anni.

2 Mi sono vestito … ho fatto colazione … ho comprato … ho telefonato … gli ho chiesto … sono andato … ho detto … ho preso … ho fatto …

3 b Ci siamo visti. c Ci siamo parlati. d Ci siamo salutati. e Ci siamo baciati. f Ci siamo abbracciati.

4 a di cui b con cui c da cui d per cui e a cui.

5	**Giornalista**	Are you German?
	You	No. Siamo inglesi.
	Giornalista	How long have you been here?
	You	Siamo qui da una quindicina di giorni.
	Giornalista	Did you come by air?
	You	No. Siamo venuti in macchina.
	Giornalista	And why did you come to Perugia?
	You	Perchè ci siamo iscritti all'università per studiare l'italiano.
	Giornalista	How long does the course last?
	You	Dura un mese.
	Giornalista	Have you visited any other places?
	You	Non molti. Ma/però domenica scorsa ci siamo alzati presto e siamo andati ad Assisi.
	Giornalista	Did you enjoy yourselves?
	You	Ci siamo divertiti moltissimo.

6 a Cenano sulla spiaggia. b Il pomeriggio vanno al parco. c La fanno sul Mare Adriatico.

1 Mi sono iscritta all'università di Napoli.
2 Ho fatto un viaggio organizzato in Francia.
3 Mi sono alzato tardi stamattina./Stamattina mi sono alzato tardi.
4 Ci siamo dovuti fermare tre volte per andare all'aeroporto.
5 Ho vissuto a Bologna per quattro anni.
6 La macchina che guida è rossa.
7 Alla festa mi sono divertita.
8 Abbiamo visitato Ancona e Empoli.
9 La cantante di cui ti ho parlato è molto brava.
10 Questo è il ragazzo che canta sempre.

UNIT 20

Dialogues
1 a La signorina prende le compresse senz'acqua. b Ne prende una.
2 a V. b Deve andare in farmacia. 3 a La signorina ha mal di denti.
b Le dà uno spazzolino e un dentifricio speciali. 4 a V. b Deve riparare gli occhiali dell'avvocato.

Practice
1 Anna: Mi fa male il braccio. Giorgio: Mi fa male il naso.
Alessandro: Mi fa male il ginocchio. Livio: Mi fanno male gli occhi. Orazio: Mi fanno male i piedi. Gina: Mi fanno male le gambe.

2 a … le fa male il braccio. b … gli fa male il naso. c … gli fanno male gli occhi. d … gli fanno male i piedi. e …le fanno male le gambe. f … gli fa male il ginocchio.

3 a … ha mal di gola. b … ha mal di testa. c … ha la febbre.
d … ha mal di stomaco. e … ha mal di denti. f … ha il raffreddore.

4 a ... si riposi! b ...si asciughi! c ... si lavi i denti! d ... si metta il cappotto! e ... si diverta!

5 a Non le prenda! b ... Non li faccia! c ... Non gli telefoni! d ... Non le scriva! e ... Non l'apra! f ... Non le chiuda!

5	**You**	Non mi sento bene.
	Mara	What's the matter? Have you got a headache?
	You	No. Mi fanno male gli occhi.
	Mara	Why don't you put your glasses on?
	You	Purtroppo sono dall'ottico.
	Mara	But I can drive if you like.
	You	Va bene. Così mi riposo un po'.
	Mara	How about stopping a moment at the chemist's?
	You	Buon'idea! E poi possiamo andare a prendere qualcosa da bere.
	Mara	So first we'll stop at the chemist's and then we'll go to the Quattro Fontane Bar.
	You	E così posso anche telefonare al medico.

Test yourself
1h; 2d; 3a; 4e; 5c; 6g; 7j; 8i; 9b; 10f.

UNIT 21

Dialogues
1 a V. b Andranno in Calabria dai loro parenti. 2 a Il sole non dà fastidio a Massimo. b Perchè dovrà ricominciare a lavorare. 3 a V. b La rivedrà sabato. 4 a La signorina vuole consultare il catalogo dei nuovi cd. b Deve riportarlo/Lo deve riportare al commesso. 5 a V. b Dovrà richiederli/Li dovrà richiedere alla casa discografica.

Practice
1 b Berrò ... c Andrò ... d Farò ... e Pulirò ... f Preparerò ... g Sparecchierò ... h Laverò ... i Mi riposerò ... j Prenderò ... k Andrò ... l Finirò ... m Uscirò ...

452

2 a … Usciranno … b … Resteranno … c … Verranno … d
… Potranno farlo … e Saranno qui … f … Lo faranno … g …
Arriveranno … h … La costruiranno …

3 … andremo … … staremo … trascorreremo … torneremo …
daremo … inviteremo … guarderemo … andremo … ci siederemo
… prenderemo … ascolteremo …

4 a Me la riparerà il meccanico. b Me le cambierà il cassiere. c
Ce lo prenoterà il nostro amico Sandro. d Me lo farà un pittore
francese. e Ce lo porterà un nostro collega. f Me la disegnerà un
architetto italiano. g Me lo regalerà mia sorella. h Ce lo troverà
nostro cugino.

5	You	Vorrei un libro sull'Italia.
	Libraio	What type of book? Do you want something on politics or economics?
	You	Veramente cerco un libro per turisti.
	Libraio	So it's a guide you are after?
	You	Sì. Vorrei fare il giro dei laghi.
	Libraio	Ah! Then you need a book on Northern Italy.
	You	Esattamente! Posso vedere ciò che ha?
	Libraio	I'm sorry, but at the moment we haven't got anything.
	You	Come mai?
	Libraio	Unfortunately I sold the last one an hour ago.
	You	Non ne aspetta altri?
	Libraio	Of course. But when are you leaving?
	You	Partirò il primo giugno.
	Libraio	Good. If you come here at the end of May I'll have just what you want.
	You	Posso prenotarne una copia adesso?
	Libraio	Of course. Leave me 10 per cent deposit and your address. When the book arrives I'll let you know.

6 a Per vedere la Mostra dei mobili antichi si deve andare a
Cortona. b Per vedere la Mostra (internazionale) dei telefilm si deve

andare a Chianciano Terme. c Per vedere la Festa del lago si deve andare a Castiglione del Lago.

1 Andrò alla Galleria degli Uffizi giovedì.
2 Quando finiranno il libro?
3 Luigi paga/pagherà il conto.
4 Verranno a trovarci in/a settembre.
5 Finirò la laurea quest'estate.
6 Stasera ceneremo a quel ristorante nuovo.
7 Vedrai che ha senso.
8 Il parco? Te lo/glielo mostrerà lui.
9 A che ora comincia/comincerà lo spettacolo?
10 Quando partirete per le vacanze?

UNIT 22

Dialogues
1 a V. b No. La trovava molto monotona. 2 a Quando Nino e Dario erano scapoli uscivano ogni sera. b Dicevano sempre che non volevano sposarsi. 3 a Eugenio Parisi lavorava in un'azienda agricola. b Perchè non ha potuto./Perchè suo padre era gravemente ammalato e non poteva più mantenerlo. 4 a V. b No. Suonava la chitarra.

Practice
1 b Faceva così caldo; fa così freddo. c C'era tanto sole; c'è tanta pioggia. d Uscivo ogni sera; non esco mai. e Venivano a trovarmi tante persone; non viene a trovarmi nessuno. f Andavo ogni domenica alla spiaggia; vado qualche volta in piscina. g Parlavo con tanta gente; non parlo con nessuno. h Bevevo caffè e vino; bevo tè e birra.

2 a Perchè era troppo forte. b Perchè mi faceva male un dente. c Perchè costavano poco. d Perchè dov'ero prima dovevo lavorare troppo. e Perchè era troppo cara. f Perchè non avevamo appetito. g Perchè avevano sete. h Perchè eravamo stanchi morti. i Perchè non mi sentivo bene. j Perchè aveva bisogno di soldi.

3 a ... si radeva, ha telefonato ... b ... scriveva, si è rotta ... c ... riparava, è arrivata ... d ... cucinava, si è scottato ... e ... leggeva, se n'è andata ... f ... guardava ... gli ha chiesto ...

4 i a No. È laureata da poco tempo. b Si offre come baby-sitter di pomeriggio e di sera. c Vive a Bergamo. ii a Ha il diploma di ragioniera. b Vuole lavorare per mezza giornata. c Bisogna telefonarle nelle ore dei pasti. iii a No. Sono prossimi alle nozze. b No. Vogliono prenderlo in affitto. c No. Può essere anche piccolo. iv a No. È laureato in scienze politiche. b Ha trent'anni./Ne ha trenta. c No. Lavora da molto tempo. d Conosce il francese, l'inglese e il tedesco.

5 A Ma come! Già te ne vai? B Eh, sì. Me ne devo andare. A E Bruna, se ne va anche lei? B No. Bruna non se ne va ancora. Però Anna e Roberto se ne vanno. E voi quando ve ne andate? A Noi ce ne andiamo più tardi.

6 You	Dove lavorava, signora, quando era a Napoli?
Signora	I worked in an agricultural firm which exported fruit all over Europe.
You	Ma lei, che faceva di preciso?
Signora	I checked the quality of the fruit.
You	Trovava il lavoro difficile?
Signora	Yes. Because a minor error was enough to lose very important customers.
You	Quanto tempo ha lavorato in quell'azienda?
Signora	Three and a half years. Then we went to Sorrento because my father was tired of living in a big town.
You	È per questo che vuol cambiare lavoro?
Signora	Yes, mainly because of that.

7 (Mi rivolgo) a CEPU./Se ho bisogno di aiuto per la laurea o il diploma, posso rivolgermi/mi posso rivolgere a CEPU, e per avere informazioni gratuite, devo compilare il modulo (form).

Test yourself

1 Lavoravo in un'agenzia di viaggi.
2 Adesso sono impiegato in una scuola.
3 Sai suonare la chitarra?
4 Dieci anni fa suonavo la batteria in un gruppo rock.
5 Andavamo al parco ogni giorno/Ogni giorno andavamo al parco.
6 Mentre cucinavo, è arrivato Pietro.
7 Rimarrò qui finchè non mi vedrà.
8 Ha aspettato finchè non gli ha detto la verità.
9 Me ne devo andare/Devo andarmene.
10 Quando ero a Firenze, ogni venerdì andavo a bere qualcosa
all' 'Angie's Bar'.

UNIT 23

Dialogues

1 a Quando hanno suonato, Bruna è andata ad aprire la porta. b
Le ha scritto il suo indirizzo. 2 a V. b No. (Gianna) ha smesso di
fumare./Non fuma più. 3 a V. b No. Non gli piace.

Practice

1 b Torna ...! c Va' ...! d Copriti ...! e Prendi ...! f Chiama ...! g
Rimani ...! h Non preoccuparti di ...!

2 a Non fumare! b Prendi l'aereo! c Non insistere! d Non
parcheggiare lì! e Va' in macchina! f Porta l'ombrello! g Metti la
data ...! h Usa la scheda telefonica!

3 b Non usarla! c Non comprarlo! d Non pagarlo! e Non berla! f
Non prenderlo! g Non attraversarla! h Non perderli!

4 a Luigi, sta' zitto! b Alfredo, fammi assaggiare il gelato! c Elena,
va' all'altra tavola! d Vittorio, dammi il bicchiere! e Maria, dammi
il sale e il pepe! f Nina, dimmi cosa vuoi per secondo piatto!

5 a ... sta facendo il bagno. b ... sta cucinando. c ...sta piovendo. d
... sta per sposarsi. e ... sta suonando. f ... stanno per partire.

6 i-e Sta mangiando. ii-f Stiamo comprando … iii-c Stanno facendo … iv-b Sta cucinando. v-d Sta lavorando. vi-a Stanno chiacchierando.

7	**Mamma**	What are you doing up so early? It's not yet 5 o'clock!
	You	Vorrei studiare un po'.
	Mamma	At this time? How's that?
	You	Ma non sapevi che oggi ho un esame?
	Mamma	Oh! I'd completely forgotten. Shall I make you a cup of coffee?
	You	No grazie. Ritorna a letto.
	Mamma	Have you still got a lot to do?
	You	No. Non molto.
	Mamma	You're studying so much, it's true; but in a couple of years' time you'll be a doctor.
	You	Sì. Ma solo se riesco a superare questo esame. È uno dei più difficili.
	Mamma	But why are you so worried?
	You	Perchè questa volta non sono sicuro/a di me.
	Mamma	Don't worry. Everything will be fine. You'll see.

Test yourself
1a; 2c; 3b; 4a; 5c
6 Stavo per telefonarti.
7 Come! Sei già quì?
8 Che cosa stai guardando alla televisione?
9 L'ho sentito cantare.
10 Dovendo/poichè deve/dato che deve imparare lo spagnolo per il nuovo impiego, Paolo ha cominciato un corso di lingua.

UNIT 24

Dialogues
1 a V. b (Se n'è accorta) quando è uscita dal Duomo. 2 a V. b È nata a Lugano nel '70. 3a V. b di usare il suo telefono; di aiutarla a cercare il numero telefonico del suo medico. 4a V. b Ha telefonato

al pronto soccorso. 5a La macchina è della signora. b No. Gli ha
chiesto di controllare (solo) l'olio e l'acqua.

Practice

1 a Lavatevi le mani! b Aspettate qui! c Venite a tavola!
d Sedetevi! e Non gridate! f Non fate troppo rumore! g Non
toccate i fiori sulla tavola! h Bevete piano piano! i Non parlate con
la bocca piena!

2 i-i ii-f iii-a iv-c v-b vi-e vii-d viii-g ix-h.

3 a … Glieli faccio io. b …Glielo compro io. c … Glieli cambio io.
d … Glieli riporto io. e …Gliela imbuco io. f … Glielo prendo io. g
… Gliele chiudo io.

4 a È sua. b È suo. c È mio. d Sono suoi. e Sono miei. f Sono sue. g
Sono suoi. h Sono mie.

5 b È suo quest'ombrello? d Sono suoi questi occhiali? f Sono sue
quelle chiavi? g Sono suoi quei giornali?

6	**You**	Ho perso la patente di guida e non so (che) cosa fare.
	Signorina	Do you know where you lost it?
	You	Non ne sono certo. Forse l'ho lasciata in macchina. Durante la notte qualcuno è entrato nella mia auto e ha preso tutto.
	Signorina	Don't worry. There's a good chance of recovering it, because usually they send it to the 'Questura'.
	You	Che cos'è la Questura?
	Signorina	It's the police headquarters. Go there and report the loss.
	You	E sa dov'è, per cortesia?
	Signorina	Certainly. It's in Via Mazzini.
	You	Grazie. Intanto come faccio senza patente?
	Signorina	For the moment you can use a copy of the statement as a document.

7 Il 113.

Test yourself
1 glieli; 2 gliele; 3 detto; 4 regalata; 5 regalati; 6 gliel'; 7 gliela; 8 sue; 9 mia; 10 su_oi.

UNIT 25

Dialogues
1 a V. b È di Milano ed il giornale che di s_olito legge è Il Corriere della Sera. 2 a V. b No. _Escono ogni settimana. 3 a V. b Secondo lui ci dovr_ebbero _essere più documentari. 4 a Ezio non è d'accordo col suo amico sui programmi televisivi. b Vorrebbe abolire le televisioni private.

Practice
1 a La berr_ei ... b Li manger_ei ... c Lo metter_ei ... d Le prender_ei ... e L'ascolter_ei ... f Lo guarder_ei ...

2 a Ada vivrebbe in città. Comprerebbe un p_iccolo appartamento. Andrebbe ogni sera a ballare. Imparerebbe a guidare. b Vivr_ei al mare. Comprer_ei una villa. Andr_ei spesso a nuotare. Imparer_ei a suonare la chitarra. c I signori Mi_ele vivr_ebbero in montagna. Comprer_ebbero una casetta. Andr_ebbero ogni tanto a sciare. Imparer_ebbero a dip_ingere.

3 i-g ii-h iii-d iv-f v-a vi-b vii-e viii-c.

4a Te le porter_ei io ... b Te la porter_ei io ... c Te la far_ei io ... d Te lo pulir_ei io ... e Te li cambier_ei io ... f Te la far_ei io ... g Te la imbucher_ei io ...

5	You	Ciao Renata! Puoi venire alla mia festa stasera?
	Renata	I'd love to, but I'm very busy at the moment.
	You	Ma cos'hai di così importante da fare?
	Renata	I've got to tidy up the house, I've got to do some washing, I'm on my own and I have to think of everything.
	You	E non potresti fare tutte queste cose in un altro momento?
	Renata	Yes, I could, only that my parents are coming back from their holiday abroad today.
	You	Ma non dovevano ritornare la settimana prossima?
	Renata	Yes. In fact they would have liked to stay for five or six days longer, but my aunt has had a baby and so they decided to come back early.
	You	A che ora arriveranno?
	Renata	They should be at the airport at six. I'll go and collect them myself by car.
	You	Comunque, se cambi idea, puoi sempre farmelo sapere. Chiamami quando vuoi.
	Renata	Thank you. If I can, I'd love to come, if it's only to greet you and give you my best wishes.

6 a RAI: Radio Televisione Italiana. b La Stampa, La Repubblica e (il) Corriere della Sera.

Test yourself
1 Potrei incontrarti/la lunedì.
2 Dovrei andare dai miei genitori questo finesettimana.
3 Vorrei vedere quel nuovo film tedesco.
4 Sarebbe necessario prenotare prima./Si dovrebbe prenotare prima.
5 Ti piacerebbe un/il gelato?/Vuoi un/il gelato?
6 Avrebbe comprato quel cappello.
7 Mi avrebbero lasciato solo.
8 C'è qualcuno che lo sa?
9 Sono stanco di ripetere la stessa cosa.
10 Prima faccio la spesa e poi vado al cinema./Prima vado a fare la spesa e poi vado al cinema.

Key to 'Test your Italian'

Alternative answers are shown thus: un gelato/un caffè. Words in brackets are optional.

TEST YOUR ITALIAN I (UNITS 1–6)

1a Scusi! b Buongiorno, come sta? c i Una birra, per piacere/per favore. ii Un gelato, per piacere/per favore. d Dove sono i negozi? e Cosa prende? f (Prendo) un caffè. 2a i Come si chiama? ii Come ti chiami? b i (Che) cosa fa? ii (Che) cosa fai? c Sono sposato/ sposata or Non sono sposato/sposata/Sono single. d Arrivederci, professore. 3a Parla anche spagnolo, vero? b La biblioteca è a sinistra. c A che piano abita la signora Verdi? d Che giorno parte per Parigi? e Vorrei usare le lingue che conosco. f Deve prendere l'autobus davanti all'università. 4a ... davanti al cinema. b prima delle otto. c ... prima dell'una. d ... alla prossima ... e ... allo sportello ... f ... alle dieci. 5a posta b sciopero c saldi d granita 6a (Vorrei) un biglietto per Venezia. b A che ora parte il prossimo treno? c A che ora arriva a Venezia? d È in orario? 7 Vorrei un paio di scarpe nere, una maglietta bianca e un paio di jeans. Quant'è (in tutto)? 8a Sono nato/nata a ... b Ho ... anni. c Lavoro/sono studente/ studentessa/sono disoccupato/disoccupata. d Come si dice in italiano? 9 Prego!

TEST YOUR ITALIAN II (UNITS 7–12)

1a Ho il passaporto. b Che bella casa! c Non importa/non fa niente. d Ho fame. 2a C'è un buon ristorante qui vicino? b (Scusi,) sono occupati questi posti? c Abitano al centro? d Giocano a tennis? 3a Vorrei una camera con doccia, pensione completa, dal quattro al quattordici novembre. b Il ristorante è aperto?/È aperto il ristorante? c (Che) cosa c'è da mangiare? d Dov'è il telefono? e C'è il dottor Cortese? f Posso lasciare un messaggio? 4a ... fare ... b Vengono ... c ... danno ... d ... ho ... e ... posso... f ... finisco ... 5a del formaggio, delle uova, del prosciutto. b quattro etti di formaggio, sei uova, un etto di prosciutto. 6 Non puoi andare al ristorante 'La Torinese' perchè è chiuso il mercoledì, e non puoi andare al ristorante 'La Bella Napoli' perchè è aperto solo la sera. 7 Le piace l'insalata, (ma) non le piacciono i fagiolini; gli piace la pasta (ma) non gli piacciono i funghi. 8a Ce n'è una. b Ce n'è uno. c Ce n'è una. d Ce ne sono tre.

TEST YOUR ITALIAN III (UNITS 13–18)

1a Che sport fa? b Come si fa per andare all'università?/Sa dov'è l'università? c (Che) cos'hai fatto oggi? d Sei mai stato/a a Pisa? e Ho già mangiato. f Non ho ancora pagato. g C'incontriamo più tardi. 2a col b alla c dal d della e dei f dal 3 ho dormito – ho fatto – ho preso – ho comprato – ho speso – sono tornata – ho risposto – ho scritto – sono uscita – ho incontrato – siamo andati – abbiamo bevuto e (abbiamo) mangiato – siamo andati – abbiamo visto – l'abbiamo salutato – abbiamo fatto – siamo tornati. 4 Cerco un appartamento ... Due bastano/due sono abbastanza ... Veramente lo preferisco vicino al mare ... Mi piace nuotare ... Non mi piacciono le piscine/le piscine non mi piacciono ... Mi piace solo il mare. 5a L'ho già venduta. b Li ho già cambiati. c Le ho già comprate. d L'ho già vista. e L'ho già scritta. f Li ho già fatti. 6a conosco ... b sai ... c conosci ... d può ...

TEST YOUR ITALIAN IV (UNITS 19–25)

1a Non si preoccupi! b Si segga qui!/Si accomodi qui! c Scusa(mi) del ritardo! d Sta' attento!/Fa' attenzione! e Mi aiuti, (per piacere)! f Mi sono divertito/a molto. 2 italiana – po' – teatro – ristorante – Roma – sinistra – Firenze – tutta. 3a ... te lo b te lo c Me l' d Glielo e Me l' f Ce li g Me le 4a Telefonerà b (se) sarà c Prenoterà d Cambieranno e Faranno f Controlleranno g Saluteranno 5a Parlava solo italiano. b Non si annoiava mai. c Non era mai stanco. d Aveva molti amici. e Li vedeva ogni giorno in/nella piazza. f Lavorava dalle sette all'una. g Andava alla spiaggia ogni domenica/ tutte le domeniche. h Mangiava molta frutta fresca. 6a Vorrei b Potresti c Mangerei d Andrei e diresti f Ti divertiresti ...

Glossary of grammatical terms

Adjectives Adjectives give more information about nouns: The *new* house is *comfortable*. La casa *nuova* è *comoda*. This year the prices are *high*. Quest'anno i prezzi sono *alti*.

Adverbs Adverbs tend to give more information about verbs: You'll *certainly* find it. Lo troverai *certamente*. I go there *regularly*. Ci vado *regolarmente*. They can also provide more information about adjectives: It's a *really* beautiful film. È un film *veramente* bello. In English, adverbs often (but not always) end in *-ly*. The equivalent of this in Italian is -**mente**.

Articles There are two types of articles: definite and indefinite. In English the definite article is *the* and in Italian it is **il/lo/la/l'/i/gli/le**. The English indefinite article *a/an* becomes **un/uno/una/un'** in Italian.

Gender see **masculine/feminine**

Imperative The imperative is the form of the verb used to give instructions, orders or commands: *Sign* here! **Firmi qui!** *Turn* right! **Giri a destra!** *Be* quiet! **Sta' zitto!**

Indirect object see **object**

Infinitive The infinitive is the basic form of the verb, the form found in dictionaries. In English the infinitive is usually accompanied by the word *to*; in Italian infinitives end in -**are**, -**ere**, or -**ire**: *to speak* **parlare**, *to see* **vedere**, *to finish* **finire**.

Intransitive verbs Italian verbs that cannot be followed by a direct object, that is, where a preposition is required after the verb, are called *intransitive*. They usually form the perfect tense with **essere**: Maria *went to the* market. **Maria è andata al mercato.** She did not *stay at* home. **Non è rimasta a casa.**

Irregular verbs Life would be considerably simpler if all verbs behaved in a regular fashion. Unfortunately, Italian, like other European languages, has verbs which do not behave according to a set pattern and which are commonly referred to as irregular verbs. Three of the most common ones in

Italian are *to go* **andare**, *to have* **avere** and *to be* **essere**, but there are many others.

Masculine/feminine In English, gender is usually linked to male and female persons or animals, so, for example, we refer to a man as *he* and to a woman as *she*. Objects and beings of an indeterminate sex are referred to as having neuter gender. So, for instance, we refer to a table as it. In Italian, nouns referring to female persons are feminine and those referring to male persons are masculine. But all nouns are either masculine or feminine. This has nothing to do with sex: *the butter* **il burro**, *the tea* **il tè**, are masculine in Italian, while *the table* **la tavola** and **la lezione** *the lesson* are feminine. You will find some rules to help you but the best way of mastering gender is to learn the nouns with the appropriate article.

Nouns Nouns are words like *door* **porta** and *bread* **pane**. They are often called 'naming words'. A useful test is whether you can put *the* in front of them: *the door* **la porta**, *the bread* **il pane**.

Object: direct/indirect The term 'object' expresses the 'receiving end' relationship between a noun and a verb. So, for instance, 'the patient' is said to be at the receiving end of the examining in this sentence: The doctor examined *the patient*. **Il medico ha visitato** *il malato*. *The patient* is therefore said to be the *object* of the sentence. In sentences such as My mother gave *my wife an expensive ring*, **Mia madre ha regalato** *a mia moglie un anello molto caro* the phrase *an expensive ring* is said to be the *direct object*, because the ring is what the mother actually gave, and the phrase *my wife* is said to be the *indirect object* because *my wife* is the recipient of the giving. See also **subject**.

Plural see **singular**

Possessives Words like *my*, *mine* **mio**, *your*, yours **tuo**, *his*, hers **suo**, *our*, ours **nostro**, etc. are called possessives.

Prepositions Words like *in* in, *on* **su**, *between* **fra**, *for* **per** are called *prepositions*. Prepositions often tell us about the position of something. They are normally followed by a noun or pronoun: The consulate is *between* the bank and the church. **Il consolato è *fra* la banca e la chiesa.** This present is *for* you. **Questo regalo è *per* te.**

Pronouns Pronouns fulfil a similar function to nouns and often stand in the place of nouns which have already been mentioned. When pronouns refer to people they are called *personal pronouns*.

	singular	plural
first person	**io** *I*	**noi** *we*
second person	**tu** (informal), **lei** (formal) *you*	**voi** *you*
third person	**lui, lei** *he, she*	**loro** *they*

As you can see, the first person plural pronoun is *we* **noi**; *we speak noi* **parl*iamo*** or simply **parl*iamo*** is therefore the first person plural of the verb **parl*are*** *to speak*.

Reflexive pronouns Words such as *myself* **mi**, *yourself* **ti, si,** *ourselves* **ci** are called reflexive pronouns.

Reflexive verbs When the subject and the object of a verb are one and the same, the verb is said to be *reflexive*: *I washed (myself)* before going out. **Mi sono lavato prima di uscire.** *We enjoyed ourselves* very much. **Ci siamo divertiti molto.**

Singular The terms *singular* and *plural* are used to make the contrast between 'one' and 'more than one': *market/markets* **mercato/mercati.**

Subject The term *subject* expresses a relationship between a noun and a verb. So, for instance, in the sentence, *The doctor* examined the patient **Il medico ha visitato il paziente,** because it is the doctor who did the examining, the doctor is said to be the subject of the verb to *examine*.

Tense Most languages use changes of the verb to indicate an aspect of time. These changes in the verb are traditionally referred to as tense, and the tenses may be *present*, *past* or *future*:

Present *Today I am* very busy. **Oggi *sono* molto occupato.**
Past *Yesterday I worked* till midnight. **Ieri *ho lavorato* fino a mezzanotte.**

Future *Tomorrow I won't do anything.* **Domani non *farò* nulla.**

Verbs Verbs often communicate actions, states and sensations: action: *to play* **giocare**; state: *to exist* **esistere**; sensation: *to hear, feel* **sentire**.

....

Abbreviations

adj	adjective
adv	adverb
f	feminine
f pl	feminine plural
form	formal
inf	informal
infin	infinitive
irr	irregular
lit	literally
m	masculine
m/f	masculine or feminine
m pl	masculine plural
n	noun
pl	plural
pp	past participle
QV	Quick Vocab
s	singular
US	American usage
vb	verb

Italian–English vocabulary

For numbers, days of the week, months and seasons consult the *Grammar Index*. Unless indicated otherwise with (m) or (f), nouns ending in **-o** are masculine, and in **-a** feminine. Irregular or doubtful stress is shown by underlining: **accendere**.

a, ad *at, to, in, on*
abbastanza *enough, fairly*
abbigliamento *clothing, clothes shop*
abbonato/a *subscriber*
abbracciare *to embrace, hug*
abbraccio *embrace, hug*
abitante (m/f) *inhabitant*
abitare *to live*
abituato/a *used to*
abolire *to abolish*
accanto *a near, next to*
accendere *to light, turn on*
acceso *from* **accendere**
accettare *to accept*
acciuga *anchovy*
accomodarsi *to sit down;* **si accomodi!** *take a seat!*
accompagnare *to accompany*
accordo: essere d'accordo *to agree*
accorgersi (pp accorto) *to notice, realize*
aceto *vinegar*
acqua *water;* **– minerale** *mineral water;* **– gassata**/*non sparkling/still*
acquaio *sink*
acquistare *to acquire, purchase*

adesso *now*
aereo *aeroplane*
aeroporto *airport*
affare (m): gli affari *business*
affatto (non) *not at all*
affettuoso/a *affectionate*
affittare *to let, rent;* **affitto** *rent*
agenda *diary*
agente (m/f) immobiliare *estate agent, realtor (US)*
agenzia di viaggi *travel agency*
agenzia immobiliare *(real) estate agency*
agitarsi *to get upset, excited*
agli = a + gli
aglio *garlic*
agnello *lamb*
ai = a + i
aiutare *to help;* **aiuto** *help*
al = a + il
albergo *hotel*
albero *tree*
alcuni/e *a few, some, several*
all' = a + l'
alla = a + la
alle = a + le
allo = a + lo
alloggio *lodging*
allora *so, then*

alto/a *tall*

altrettanto! grazie – *the same to you*

altrimenti *otherwise, or else*

altro ieri (l') *the day before yesterday*

altro/a *other;* **senz'altro** *certainly* **altro?** *anything else?* **un altro po'?** *a bit more?*

altroché! *you bet I do! certainly*

alzare la voce *to raise one's voice*

alzarsi *to get up*

amaro/a *bitter*

ambulanza, autoambulanza *ambulance*

americano/a *American*

amico/a *friend (m/f)*

ammalato/a *ill, sick*

ammobiliato/a *furnished*

anche *also, too;* **anch'io** *me too*

ancora *still, yet, again, more*

andare irr *to go, suit, fit*

andarsene irr *to go away, be off*

andata *single, one way ticket (US)*

andata e ritorno *return, round-trip ticket (US)*

anello *ring*

angolo *angle, corner*

animale (m) *animal*

anno *year*

annoiarsi *to be/get bored*

anticipo *deposit;* **in –** *early*

antico/a *ancient, old*

antipasto *starter(s), hors d'oeuvre*

anzi *as a matter of fact, and even, on the contrary*

aperto/a *open;* **all'aperto** *in the open*

appartamento *flat, apartment (US)*

appena *as soon as, just, barely*

appetito *appetite*

approvare *to approve of*

appuntamento *appointment, date, rendez-vous*

aprire (pp aperto) *to open*

apriscatole (m) *tin-opener*

aranciata *orangeade*

architetto (m/f) *architect*

argento *silver*

armadio *wardrobe*

arrivare *to arrive;* **arrivo** *arrival*

arrivederci, arrivederla *goodbye*

arrosto *roast*

arte (f) *art;* **arte culinaria** *cookery*

artista (m/f) *artist*

ascensore (m) *lift, elevator (US)*

asciugamano *towel*

asciugarsi *to get dry, wipe oneself*

ascoltare *to listen to*

aspettare *to wait for*

aspettarsi *to expect*

aspirapolvere (m) *vacuum cleaner*

aspirina *aspirin*

assaggiare *to taste, try*

assegno *cheque*

attendere (pp atteso) *to wait* **– in linea** *to hold the line*

attenzione! *be careful!*

attento/a *attentive*

attimo *moment*

attività *activity*
attraversare *to cross*
attraverso *across, through, by means of*
attuale *present, current*
attualmente *at present*
auguri (m pl) *best wishes, greetings*
aumento *rise, increase*
australiano/a *Australian*
auto (f) *car*
autobus (m) *bus*
autostrada *motorway, freeway (US)*
avanti! *forward! come in!*
avere (irr) *to have*
avvicinarsi *to approach*
avvocato *lawyer*
azienda *business, firm;* – **agricola** *agricultural firm, farm*
azzurro/a *blue*
baciare *to kiss*
bacio *kiss;* **bacione (m)** *big kiss*
bagagli (m pl) *luggage;* **un bagaglio** *an item of luggage*
bagnato/a *soaked, wet*
bagno *bath, bathroom, toilet (US)*
balcone (m) *balcony*
ballare *to dance*
bambina *little girl, child, baby (girl)*
bambino *little boy, child, baby (boy)*
banana *banana*
banca *bank;* **bancario/a** *banking*
bar (m) *bar, café*

basta *enough;* **basta così** *that's enough*
be', beh *well*
beato/a *lucky;* **beata lei!** *lucky you!*
bei *from* **bello/a**
bel *from* **bello;** **bel tempo** *fine weather*
bellino/a *pretty*
bello/a *beautiful, nice, handsome, lovely*
bene *well*
benissimo! *great! very well*
benzina *petrol, gasoline (US)*
benzinaio *(petrol) pump attendant*
bere irr (pp bevuto) *to drink*
bevuto/a *from* **bere**
bianco/a *white*
biblioteca *library*
bicchier(e) (m) *glass*
bicchierino *small glass*
bicicletta *bicycle*
bidè (m) *bidet*
biglietteria *ticket office*
biglietto *(bank)note, ticket*
binario *platform*
birra *beer*
biscotto *biscuit, cookie (US)*
bisognare *to need, be necessary*
bisogno di; aver – *to need*
bistecca *steak*
blu *navy blue*
bocca *mouth*
boh! *I don't know*
bollente *boiling*
borsa *bag, handbag*
bosco *wood*

bottiglia *bottle*
box (m) *garage*
bracciale (m) *bracelet*
braccio *arm*
bravo/a *good, clever, well done!*
breve *brief, short*
brutto tempo *bad weather*
buca delle lettere *letter-box, mail-box (US)*
buonanotte *good night*
buonasera *good evening*
buongiorno *good morning*
buono/a *good;* **buon = buono**
burro *butter*
busta *envelope*
cadere *to fall*
caffè (m) *coffee*
calamari (m pl) *squid*
calcio *football, soccer (US)*
caldo/a *hot;* **fa caldo** *it's warm/ hot*
calendario *calendar*
calmarsi *to grow calm, calm down*
calzino *sock*
cambiamento *change*
cambiare *to change*
cambiare discorso *to change the subject*
cambiare idea *to change one's mind*
cambiarsi *to get changed*
cambio *exchange (rate)*
camera (da letto) *(bed) room*
cameriera *waitress, maid*
cameriere (m) *waiter*
camicetta *blouse*
camicia *shirt*

camminare *to walk*
campagna *country(side)*
campanello *(door)bell*
campeggio *camping, campsite*
campo da tennis *tennis court*
candelina *little candle*
cane (m) *dog*
canzone (f) *song*
capire *to understand;* **ho capito** *I understand/understood*
capolinea (m) *terminus, end of the line*
cappello *hat*
cappotto *coat*
capsula *capsule*
carattere (m) *character*
caratteristico/a *characteristic*
carciofo *artichoke*
cariato/a *decayed*
carino/a *pretty*
carne (f) *meat*
caro/a *expensive, dear, darling*
carriera *career*
carta *paper, card;* **alla –** *à la carte*
carta bollata *stamped paper*
carta di credito *credit card*
carte (f pl) *playing-cards*
cartolina *postcard*
casa *house, home;* **casetta** *small house*
caso *chance;* **per –** *by chance*
cassetto *drawer;* **cassettone (m)** *chest of drawers*
cassiere (m) *cashier*
castello *castle*
catalogo *catalogue*
cattedrale (f) *cathedral*
cattivo tempo *bad weather*

c'è *there is, it's there, he's in, she's in*
celeste *light blue*
cellulare (m) *mobile phone*
cena *dinner, supper*
cenare *to have dinner, dine*
cento *hundred;* **per –** *per cent*
centrale *central*
centralinista (m/f) *phone operator*
centralino *phone exchange*
centro *centre;* **– storico** *old town*
centro città *town centre*
cercare *to look for*
certamente, certo *certainly*
certo/a *certain, sure*
che *that, which, who(m)*
che? che cosa? *what?*
che ora/ore ..? *what time ..?*
che cos'è? *what is it?*
chi *who, whom*
chi si vede! *look who's here!*
chiacchierare *to talk, chat*
chiamare *to call*
chiamarsi *to be called*
chiaro/a *clear, light*
chiave (f) *key*
chiedere (pp chiesto) *to ask*
chiesa *church*
chiesto *from* **chiedere**
chilo *kilo*
chitarra *guitar*
chitarrista (m/f) *guitarist*
chiudere (pp chiuso) *to close*
chiuso/a *closed;* **chiusura** *closure*
ci *here, there; us, ourselves, each other*
ci vediamo! *see you!*

ci vuole, ci vogliono *it takes*
ciao! *hello, hi! goodbye*
cin cin! *cheers!*
cinema (m) *cinema*
cinese *Chinese*
ciò che *what*
cioccolata *(drinking) chocolate*
cioccolatino *small chocolate*
cioccolato *chocolate*
cioè *that is*
cipolla *onion*
circa *about*
citofono *entry-phone*
città *town, city*
civico *civic*
classe (f) *class*
classico/a *classical, classic*
cliente (m/f) *customer*
cognome (m) *surname*
colazione (f) *breakfast;* **far –** *to have breakfast*
collega (m/f) *colleague*
colloquio *interview*
colore (m) *colour*
coltello *knife*
come *sorry? pardon? how, what, as*
come no! *of course*
come si dice in italiano? *how do you say (it) in Italian?*
come sta? (form)/come stai? (inf) *how are you?*
cominciare a *to begin to, start to*
commerciale *commercial*
commesso/a *shop assistant*
commissariato *police station*
comodino *bedside table*
comodità *comfort, convenience*

comodo/a *comfortable*

compagno/a *partner*

compleanno *birthday*

completo/a *full, no vacancies*

complimenti! (m pl)
congratulations! **senza –!** *no need to be polite*

comprare *to buy*

compreso/a *included*

compressa *tablet*

comunicazione (f)
communication

comunità *community*

comunque *anyway, however*

con *with*

concerto *concert*

condire *to season*

conferenza *lecture, conference*

confortevole *comforting, comfortable*

confronto *comparison;* **a –** *compared*

congelatore (m) *freezer*

conoscere *to know*

conseguire *to obtain*

conservare *to keep*

consigliare *to advise*

consolato *consulate*

consultare *to consult*

comsumare *to use*

contabilità *book-keeping*

contattare *to contact*

contatto *contact;* **mettersi in –** *to contact*

contento/a *pleased, happy*

continuare a *to continue to*

conto, per – mio *personally, on my own, by myself*

conto *bill;* **fare il –** *to make out the bill*

contorno *side-dish*

contratto *contract*

controllare *to check*

conveniente *convenient*

convento *convent*

conversazione (f) *conversation*

coperta *blanket*

coperto *cover (charge)*

coppa di gamberetti *prawn cocktail*

coprire (pp coperto) *to cover*

correre (pp corso) *to run*

corrispondenza *correspondence*

corsa *run, race*

corso *from* **correre**

corso *course, avenue*

cortesia, per – *please*

cortile (m) *courtyard*

corto/a *short*

cosa *thing;* **– da niente** *nothing*

cosa? che –? *what?;* **cos'è?** *what is it?*

cosa sono? *what are (they)?*

cos'è? *what is (it)?*

così *as, so, like this;* **basta –** *that's enough*

costare *to cost*

costruire *to build*

costruzione (f) *building*

costume (m) (da bagno) *swimsuit*

cotoletta *cutlet, escalope*

cotone (m) *cotton*

cotto/a *(from* **cuocere***) cooked*

cottura *cooking time*

cravatta *tie*

creare *to create*
credere *to think, believe*
crisantemo *chrysanthemum*
cristallo *crystal*
crudo/a *raw, uncooked*
cucchiaino *tea/coffee spoon*
cucchiaio *spoon*
cucina *kitchen, cooker, cooking*
cucinare *to cook*
cugino/a *cousin*
cui *whom, which;* **il/la –** *whose*
culturale *cultural*
cuocere (pp cotto) *to cook*
cuoio *leather*
da *from, at, to, by, for, as, like, since*
da bere *to drink;* **qualcosa da bere** *something to drink*
da questa parte *this way, over here*
d'accordo *agreed, all right;* **essere –** *to agree*
dappertutto *everywhere*
dare *to give*
dare fastidio *to bother, annoy, disturb*
dare su *to look out over, to give onto*
data *date*
datore (m) di lavoro *employer*
davanti a *in front of*
decimo/a *tenth*
dei = di + i
della = di + la
dente (m) *tooth;* **al –** *slightly underdone*
dentifricio *toothpaste*
dentista (m/f) *dentist*

dentro *inside, in*
denuncia *statement*
deposito *deposit*
desidera? *can I help you?*
desiderare *to desire, want, wish*
destro/a *right;* **a destra** *on the –*
detto *from* **dire**
devo *from* **dovere**
di dove sono? *where are they from?*
di dov'è? *where are you from?/ where is he/she from?*
di fronte *opposite, in front of*
dialogo *dialogue*
diamoci del tu *(from* **dare**) *let's use* **tu**
diapositiva *slide, colour transparency*
dica! (from dire) *yes? tell me! can I help you?*
dietro/indietro *behind*
differenza *difference*
difficile *difficult*
diffuso/a *widely circulated, popular*
dilettante (m/f) *amateur*
dipendere (pp dipeso) *to depend*
dipingere (pp dipinto) *to paint*
diploma (m) diploma, *high school leaving certificate*
dire irr (pp detto) *to say, tell*
diretto/a *direct, through*
direttore (m/f) *director*
dirigente (m/f) *manager*
disco *record, CD*
discoteca *discotheque*
discretamente *reasonably well*
disegnare *to draw, design*

disoccupato/a *unemployed*

distinto/a *distinguished*

distrarsi (pp distratto) *to take one's mind off things*

disturbare *to disturb, bother*

disturbo *disturbance, inconvenience*

disturbo allo stomaco *stomach upset*

dito *finger*

ditta *firm, business*

divano *sofa, settee*

diventare *to become*

diversi/e (pl) *several*

diverso/a *different*

divertimento *entertainment*

divertire *to amuse, entertain*

divertirsi *to enjoy oneself, have a good time*

dizionario *dictionary*

do *from* **dare**

doccia *shower*

documentario *documentary*

documento *document*

dolce (m) *dessert, sweet* **dolci** *cakes, sweets*

dollaro *dollar*

domanda *question, request*

domani *tomorrow*

domenica *Sunday*

domestico/a *domestic*

donna *woman*

dopo *later, after(wards), then, beyond*

dopodomani *the day after tomorrow*

doppio/a *double*

dormire *to sleep*

dottore dott. (m/f) *doctor*

dove *where*

dov'è? *where is (he/she/it)?*

dovere irr *to have to, owe, be supposed to*

dritto dritto *keep straight on*

dunque *well, where was I?*

Duomo *cathedral*

durante *during*

durare *to last*

duro/a *hard, solid*

è *is, it's, you are, is it? etc.*

e, ed *and*

ecc. *etc.*

eccetto *except*

eccezione (f) *exception*

ecco! *here is, here are; look!*

ecco fatto! *there you are*

economico/a *economic, economical*

edicola *news-stand*

edificio *building*

effettivamente *actually, really*

elegante *smart, elegant*

elettricista (m/f) *electrician*

elettrodomestici (m pl) *household appliances*

entrare *to enter*

entrata *entrance*

entro *within, on or before*

ero *from* **essere**

esame (m) *examination*

esaminare *to examine, consider*

esatto/a *exact(ly)*

esco *from* **uscire**

esempio *example*

esistere (pp esistito) *to exist*

esperienza *experience*
esportare *to export*
esposizione (f) *exhibition*
espressione (f) *expression*
espresso *express/fast train*
espresso *espresso (coffee)*
essere (irr) *to be*
esterno/a *outer, external*
estero *foreign;* all'- *abroad*
età *age*
etto *100 grams*
europeo/a *European*
evidente *evident*
fabbrica *factory*
facile *easy*
fagiolino *green bean*
fai *(from* fare*) you do*
falso/a *false*
fame (f) *hunger;* aver – *to be hungry*
famiglia *family*
far male *to hurt*
far sapere *to inform*
far(e) complimenti *to pay compliments*
fare irr (pp fatto) *to do, make*
fare i bagagli *to pack*
fare il bagno *to have a bath, to swim*
fare il biglietto *to buy a ticket*
fare il pieno *to fill up with petrol/ gas (US)*
fare una domanda *to ask a question*
farmacia *chemist's shop, drugstore (US)*
farmacista (m/f) *chemist, druggist (US)*

fastidio *trouble, bother*
fatto *from* fare
favore (m) *favour;* per – *please*
fazzoletto *handkerchief*
febbre (f) *temperature, fever*
felicità *happiness, joy*
ferie (f pl) *holidays, leave*
fermarsi *to stop (oneself), stay*
fermata *(bus) stop*
ferragosto *August bank holiday*
ferri: ai ferri *grilled*
ferrovia *railway, railroad (US)*
Ferrovie dello Stato *State Railways*
festa *fete, party, public holiday, fair*
fetta *slice*
fiammifero *match*
fidanzato/a *engaged, boyfriend/ girlfriend*
figli (m/f pl) *children*
figlio/a *son/daughter*
figurarsi *to imagine, fancy*
figuri; si figuri! *not at all!*
fila *queue;* fare la fila *to queue up*
film (m) *film*
finanziario/a *financial*
finchè (non) *till, until*
fine (f) *end*
finestra *window*
finire *to finish*
finito/a *finished*
fino *a until, up to*
fioraio/a *florist;* fiore (m) *flower*
Firenze (f) *Florence*
firma *signature;* firmare *to sign*
fisica *physics*

fisso/a *fixed*
fiume (m) *river*
foglio *sheet*
fondo *end, bottom;* **là in fondo** *down there*
fontana *fountain*
forchetta *fork*
formaggio *cheese*
forno *oven;* **al –** *baked*
forte *strong, loud*
fotografia *photograph*
fra *in, among, between*
fra poco *soon*
fra un'ora *in an hour's time*
francese *French;* **Francia** *France*
francobollo *stamp*
fratello *brother*
freddo/a *cold*
frequentare *to attend, go to*
frequente *frequent, often*
fresco/a *fresh, cool*
frigorifero *fridge*
fritto/a *fried*
frutta *fruit*
fruttivendolo *fruiterer, greengrocer*
fuori *out, outside*
gabinetti (m pl) *toilets, comfort station (US)*
gamba *leg*
garantire *to guarantee*
garanzia *guarantee*
gas (m) *gas;* **con –** *sparkling;* **senza gas** *still (water)*
gasolio *diesel*
gatto *cat*
gelateria *ice-cream parlour*
gelato *ice cream*

generale *general*
generalità (f pl) *particulars*
generi (m pl) alimentari *groceries*
generoso/a *generous*
genitore (m) *parent*
Genova *Genoa*
gente (f) *people*
gentile *kind*
Germania *Germany*
ghiaccio *ice*
già *already; yes, of course*
giacca *jacket*
giallo/a *yellow*
giapponese *Japanese*
giardino *garden, yard (US);* **– pubblico** *park*
ginocchio *knee*
giocare a *to play (game)*
giornale (m) *newspaper*
giornalista (m/f) *journalist*
giornata *day;* **che bella –** *what a nice day!*
giorno *day*
gioventù (f) *youth*
girare *to turn*
giù *down, downstairs*
giurisprudenza *law*
gli *the* **(pl)** *(to) him*
glielo = gli + lo
gola *throat*
gomma *tyre; rubber, eraser (US)*
gonna *skirt*
grammo *gram*
gran *big large;* **in – parte** *to a great extent*
grande *big, large, grown up*
granita di caffè *crushed ice with coffee*

granita di limone *crushed ice with lemon*
gratuito/a *free of charge*
grave *serious, seriously ill*
grazie (mille) *(many) thanks, thank you*
greco/a *Greek*
gridare *to shout*
grigio/a *grey*
griglia: alla griglia *grilled*
gruppo *group*
guadagnare *to earn*
guaio *trouble, problem;* il – è *the trouble is;* che – *what a nuisance!*
guanto *glove*
guardare *to look at, watch*
guasto/a *out of order, broken down*
guida (f) *guide*
guidare *to drive*
ha, hai, hanno *(from* avere*) s/he, you, they has/have*
ho *(from* avere*) I have*
ho capito *(from* capire*) I understand, understood*
i (m pl) *the*
ideale *ideal*
ieri *yesterday*
il (m s) *the*
imbucare *to post*
immaginare *to imagine*
immediato/a *immediate*
immigrato/a *immigrant*
imparare *to learn*
impegnato/a *busy, engaged*
impiegarsi *to get a job*
impiegato *clerk;* impiego *job*

importa *it matters;* non – *it doesn't matter*
importante *important*
impossibile *impossible*
in *in, inside, to, at, into*
in giro *out and about*
incidente (m) *accident;* – stradale *road accident*
incominciare a = cominciare a
incontrare *to meet*
incontrarsi *to meet each other*
incrocio *crossroads*
indirizzo *address*
infatti *indeed, in fact*
infine *finally*
influenza *influence, influenza*
informare *to inform*
informatica *computer science*
informazione (f) *(piece of) information*
ingegnere (m/f) *engineer*
ingegneria *engineering*
Inghilterra *England*
inglese *English*
ingrediente (m) *ingredient*
ingresso *entrance, entrance hall*
insalata *salad*
insegnante (m/f) *teacher*
insegnare *to teach*
inserzione (f) *advertisement*
insieme *together*
insolazione (f) *sunstroke*
intanto *meanwhile, to begin with*
intelligente *intelligent*
interessante *interesting*
interessare *to interest*
interno *flat number*
intervista *interview*

intervistare *to interview*
invece *on the other hand, instead, but, on the contrary*
inviare *to send*
invitare *to invite*
io *I, me*
Irlanda *Ireland*
iscriversi (pp iscritto) *to enrol, register*
istituto *institute*
Italia *Italy;* **italiano/a** *Italian*
jeans (m pl) *jeans*
jogging (m) *jogging*
là/lì *(over) there*
lagnarsi *to complain*
lago *lake*
lana *wool*
lasagne al forno *baked lasagne*
lasciare *to leave, let*
latte (m) *milk*
laurea *degree*
laurearsi *to graduate*
laureato/a *graduate*
lavabo *washbasin*
lavanderia *laundry;* **– a secco** *dry cleaning*
lavandino *washbasin*
lavare *to wash, clean*
lavarsi *to get washed, clean*
lavastoviglie (f) *dishwasher*
lavatrice (f) *washing machine*
lavorare *to work*
lavoro *work, job*
le (m/f) *to you;* **(f pl)** *the*
legge (f) *law*
leggere (pp letto) *to read*
lei *she, her, you*
lenzuolo (pl lenzuola) *sheet*

lettera *letter*
letto *bed*
letto *(from* **leggere***)*
lettore (dvd) (m) *DVD player*
lezione (f) *lesson*
lì/là *(over) there*
libero/a *free*
libreria *bookshop, bookcase*
libro *book*
licenziare *to dismiss, sack*
liceo *secondary school, high school (US)*
lieto/a *happy, glad, delighted*
limonata *lemonade*
limone (m) *lemon*
linea *line, figure*
lingua *language*
liquore (m) *liqueur*
litro *litre*
lo *the; it*
locale (m) *room;* **(adj)** *local*
Londra *London*
lontano *far;* **– da** *far from*
loro *(to) them, they, their, theirs*
luce (f) *light*
lui *he, him*
lungo/a *long;* **lungomare (m)** *promenade, seafront*
ma *but*
macchè! *not at all, of course not*
macchina *car*
macedonia (di frutta) *fruit salad*
macellaio *butcher*
macelleria *butcher's shop*
madre (f) *mother*
magari *maybe, I wish I could, I'd love to*
magazzino *store*

maglietta *T shirt, vest; undershirt (US)*

mai *never, ever*

maiale (m) *pork, pig*

mal (m) di denti *toothache*

mal (m) di gola *sore throat*

mal (m) di testa *headache*

male *badly, bad;* **non c'è male** *not bad*

mamma *mother, mum, mummy, mom (US)*

mancia *tip*

mandare *to send*

mangiare *to eat*

mano (f) *hand*

mantenere irr *to retain, maintain, keep*

manzo *beef*

marche da bollo *revenue stamps*

mare (m) *sea*

marinaro/a *sea- (adj)*

marito *husband*

marmellata *jam*

marrone *brown*

matematica *mathematics*

matita *pencil*

matrimoniale: camera – *room with a double bed*

mattina *morning*

maturità classica *high school leaving cert. in classics*

mazzo *bunch*

me *(to/for) me*

meccanico *mechanic*

medicazione (f) *dressing, treatment*

medicina *medicine*

medico (m/f) *doctor*

meglio *better*

mela *apple*

melanzana *aubergine*

melone (m) *melon*

meno *less*

meno male *thank goodness, a good job that*

mentre *while*

menù (m) *menu*

mercato *market*

merluzzo *cod*

mese (m) *month*

messaggio *message*

messicano/a *Mexican*

messo (pp) *from* **mettere**

metro *metre*

metro(politana) *underground, subway (US)*

mettere (pp messo) *to put*

mettere da parte *to put aside*

mettere in ordine *to tidy up*

mettersi *to put on, wear*

mettersi in contatto con *to contact*

mezza pensione *half-board*

mezzanotte (f) *midnight*

mezzi (m pl) *means*

mezzi di comunicazione (di massa) *mass media*

mezzo/a *half;* **mezzogiorno** *midday*

mi *(to/for) me, myself*

mi dispiace *I'm sorry*

mica: non ... mica *not really, by any chance*

migliore *better, best*

mila *thousands*

milione (m) *million*

mille _a/one thousand_
minerale _mineral_
minestra _soup_
minestrone (m) _vegetable soup_
minicrociera _mini-cruise_
minuto _minute_
mio/a _my, mine_
misto/a _mixed_
mittente (m) _sender_
mobili (m pl) _furniture_
moderno/a _modern_
modo _manner_
modulo _form_
moglie (f) _wife_
molti/e _many_
molto _very, very much_
molto/a _much_
momento _moment_
mondo _world_
monotono/a _monotonous_
montagna _mountain_
monumento _monument_
morire irr (pp morto) _to die_
mortadella _Bologna sausage_
morto/a _dead_
mostra _exhibition_
mostrare to _show_
municipio _town hall_
museo _museum_
musica _music_
Napoli (f) _Naples_
naso _nose_
Natale (m) _Christmas_
nativo/a _native_
nato/a _born_
natura _nature_
naturalmente _naturally_
nazionale _national_

nazionalità _nationality_; **di che – ?** _what nationality?_
nè ... nè _neither ... nor_
neanche _not even, neither_
necessario/a _necessary_
necessità (f) _necessity_
negozio _shop_
nei = in + i _in the_
nel, nell', nella, nei, negli, ecc. _in the_
nero/a _black_
nessuno/a _no, not any, no-one_
neve (f) _snow_
nevicare _to snow_
niente _nothing_
nipote (m/f) _nephew, niece, grandchild_
Nizza _Nice_
no _no_; **no, grazie** _no thank you_
noi _we_
nome (m) _forename, name_
non _not_; **non ... ancora** _not yet_
non c'è male _not too bad_
non fa niente _it doesn't matter_
non lo so _I don't know_
non ... proprio _not at all_
nonno/a _grandfather/ grandmother_
nono/a _ninth_
nostalgia _nostalgia_; **sentire la –** _to feel homesick, to miss_
nostro/a _our, ours_
notizia _(piece of) news_
notte (f) _night_
nulla _anything, nothing_
numero _number, size_
nuotare _to swim_; **nuoto** _swimming_

nuovo/a *new*
o *or*
obbligatorio/a *compulsory*
occhiali (m pl) *glasses*
occhiata *glance, look*
occhio *eye*
occorrere (pp occorso) *to be necessary, to need*
occuparsi di *to deal with, look after*
occupato/a *engaged, busy, taken*
oddio! *my goodness!*
odore (m) *smell*
offrire (pp offerto) *to offer*
oggetto *object*
oggi *today*
ogni *every, all, any*
ogni tanto *now and then*
olimpico/a *Olympic*
olio *oil*
oliva *olive*
oltre a *besides, apart from*
ombrello *umbrella*
ombrellone (m) *beach umbrella*
onomastico *name-day*
operaio *worker, employee*
opinione (f) *opinion*
opinioni a confronto *opinions compared*
oppure *or, or else*
ora *hour, o'clock*
ora *now*
orario *timetable,* **in –** *on time*
ordinare *to order*
ordine (m) *order*
orecchio *ear*
organizzare *to organize*
origine (f) *origin*

oro *gold;* **d'oro** *golden*
orologio *watch, clock*
ospedale (m) *hospital*
ospitalità *hospitality*
ospite (m/f) *guest*
ostello *hostel*
ottavo/a *eighth*
ottico *optician*
ottimo/a *excellent*
pacco *parcel*
padre (m) *father*
padrona di casa *landlady*
padrone (m) *owner, landlord*
Paese (m) *country*
paese (m) *village, small town*
paesino *small village*
pagare *to pay*
paio *couple, pair*
palazzo *palace, (apartment) building (US)*
pallone (m) *ball*
pane (m) *bread;* **panino** *roll*
panetteria *baker's*
panettiere (m) *baker*
pantaloni (m pl) *trousers; pants (US)*
Papa (m) *Pope*
pappagallo *parrot*
parcheggiare *to park*
parcheggio *car-park, parking lot (US)*
parco *park*
parecchio tempo *quite a time*
parecchio/a *quite a lot, several*
parente (m/f) *relative, relation*
parere *to appear, seem*
Parigi (f) *Paris*
parla? *do you speak?*

parlare *to speak*
parlarsi *to speak to each other*
parola *word*
parrucchiere (m) *hairdresser*
parte (f) *side, part;* **a –** *not included*
partenza *departure*
parti: da queste – *in/to these parts*
partire *to leave*
passaggio: di – *passing through*
passante (m/f) *passer-by*
passaporto *passport*
passare *to pass, spend*
passato *past*
passeggero *passenger*
passeggiata *walk;* **fare una –** *to go for a walk*
passo *step*
passo: a due passi da ... *very near ...*
pasta *pasta, cake*
pasticceria *patisserie*
pasticciere (m) *pastrycook, confectioner*
pasto *meal*
patata *potato;* **patatine fritte** *chips, french fries (US)*
patente (f) di guida *driving licence*
paura: aver – *to be afraid*
pazienza! *never mind*
peccato: (che) –! *what a pity!*
pelle (f) *leather*
pendente *leaning*
penna *pen*
pennette rigate (f pl) *pasta quills*

pensare *to think, believe*
pensiero *thought*
pensione (f) *guest house, pension*
pensione completa *full board*
pepe (m) *pepper*
peperone (m) *pepper (veg)*
per *in order to, for, through, by, about, round*
per carità! *not at all*
per favore/piacere *please*
per forza *at all costs, necessarily*
per terra *on the floor*
pera *pear;* **– avocado** *avocado pear*
percentuale (f) *percentage*
perchè *why, because*
perdere (pp perso) *to lose, miss*
pericoloso/a *dangerous*
periferia *outskirts, suburbs*
periodo *period*
permesso! *excuse me! may I come in?*
però *however, but*
perso *from* **perdere**
persona *person*
personale (m) *personnel, personal*
personalmente *personally*
pesca *peach*
pesce (m) *fish*
pescheria *fishmonger's*
pescivendolo *fishmonger*
piacciono *from* **piacere**
piace (di) più *from* **piacere** *to prefer*
piace: mi piace *I like (it)*
piacere (m) *pleasure, favour*

piacere irr *to please, to like*
piacere! *pleased to meet you, how do you do?*
pianista (m/f) *pianist*
piano *quietly, slowly*
piano *floor*
piano(forte) (m) *piano*
pianta *plan, plant, map*
pianterreno *ground floor; first floor (US)*
piatto *plate, dish, course*
piazza *square*
piccolo/a *small, little*
piede (m) *foot;* **a piedi** *on foot;* **in piedi** *standing*
pieno/a *full*
pigiama (m) *pyjamas*
pillola *pill*
pioggia *rain*
piombare *to fill (of teeth)*
piovere *to rain*
piscina *swimming pool*
pittore (m) *painter*
più *more, most;* **più tardi** *later*
più avanti *further on*
più presto (al) *as soon as possible*
piuttosto *rather*
pizza *pizza;* **pizzeria** *pizza house*
plastica *plastic*
po': un po' di *a bit of, a little*
poco a poco *little by little*
poco/a *a few, little*
poi *then, after*
politica *politics*
politico/a *political*
polizia *police*
pollo *chicken*

poltrona *armchair*
pomeriggio *afternoon*
pomodoro *tomato*
ponte (m) *bridge*
porta *door, gate*
portafoglio *wallet*
portare *to take, bring, wear, carry*
portiere (m) *porter*
portoghese *Portuguese*
possibile *possible*
possibilità *possibility, chance*
posso *(from* **potere***) I can*
posta *post office*
posto *place, seat, job, space*
posto di lavoro *place of work*
potabile *drinkable*
potere irr *to be able*
povero/a *poor*
pranzo *lunch;* **pranzare** *to lunch*
pratico/a *practical*
preferenza *preference*
preferenza: di – *mostly, preferably*
preferibilmente *preferably*
preferire *to prefer*
preferito/a *favourite*
prego *don't mention it, can I help you?, you're welcome*
prende *has, have, take(s)*
prendere (pp preso) *to have, take, get, buy*
prendo *I take, have*
prenotare *to book*
prenotazione (f) *booking*
preoccuparsi *to worry*
preparare *to prepare*
presa *socket*
preso *from* **prendere**

presso *care of, at*

prestare *to lend, borrow*

presto *early, soon;* **far –** *to be quick, hurry up;* **a –** *see you soon*

prezzo *price*

prima *at first;* **– di** *before*

prima di tutto *first of all*

primi: i – di agosto *early August*

primo/a *first;* **– (piatto)** *first course*

principale *main, principal*

privato/a *private*

problema (m) *problem*

processione (f) *procession*

produrre irr (pp prodotto) *to produce*

produzione (f) *production*

prof. = *professor(e)*

professionista (m/f) *professional, expert*

professor(e) (m/f) *teacher, professor*

profondo/a *deep, thorough*

profumo *perfume*

progetto *project, plan*

programma (m) *programme*

promettere (pp promesso) *to promise*

pronto soccorso *casualty, first aid*

pronto/a *ready:* **pronto***? hello! (telephone)*

pronuncia *pronunciation*

proposta *proposal, proposition*

proprio *just, really*

proprio/a *one's own, real*

prosciutto *ham;* **– crudo** *Parma ham*

prossimo/a *near, next*

provare *to try (on), taste*

pubblico/a *public*

pulire *to clean*

pullman (m) *coach, intercity bus (US)*

punto: in – *punctually*

puntuale *punctual*

può *from* **potere**

pure *too, also, by all means*

puro/a *pure*

purtroppo *unfortunately*

qua *here;* **di qua** *this way*

quadro *picture*

qual = quale *which, what*

qualche *some, one or two*

qualche volta *sometimes*

qualcosa *something*

qualcuno *someone, anyone, one or two*

qualunque *any, whatever, ordinary*

quando *when*

quant'è? *how much is it?*

quanti/quante? *how many?*

quanto fa? *how much does it come to?*

quarto/a *fourth, quarter*

quasi *almost, nearly*

quattro chiacchiere: fare – *to have a chat*

quegli *(from* **quel***) those*

quel/quello/a *that (one)*

questo/a *this (one)*

questura *police station (HQ)*

qui *here;* **– vicino** *near here*

quindi *so, well, therefore*

quindicina: una – *about fifteen; fortnight*

quinto/a *fifth*

quotidiano/a *daily;* **quotidiano** *daily paper*

racchetta *tennis racket*

raccolta *collection*

raccomandata *registered letter*

radersi *to shave*

radio (f) *radio*

raffreddore (m) *cold*

ragazza *girl, girlfriend*

ragazzo *boy, boyfriend*

ragione (f) *reason;* **aver –** *to be right*

ragioneria *book-keeping, accountancy*

ragioniera/e (f/m) *accountant*

rallegramenti! *congratulations!*

rapido *high-speed train*

rapporto *report, link, relationship*

rasoio *razor*

ravioli (m pl) *ravioli (pasta)*

recente *recent*

regalare *to give as a present*

regalo *present*

regolare *regular*

reparto *department*

repubblica *republic*

residente *resident*

residenziale *residential*

respirare *to breathe*

restare *to remain, stay*

resto *change, balance*

ricetta *prescription*

ricevere *to receive;* **ricevuta** *receipt*

richiamare *to call back*

richiedere *to ask for, order*

ricordarsi *to remember*

rientrare *to come back, re-enter*

rilassarsi *to relax*

rilevante *important, relevant*

rimanere irr (pp rimasto) *to remain, stay*

rimasto *from* **rimanere**

ringraziare *to thank*

riordinare *to tidy up*

riparare *to repair*

ripetere *to repeat*

riportare *to bring back*

riposarsi *to (have a) rest*

riposo *rest*

risolto (from risolvere) *solved*

risotto *risotto (rice)*

rispondere (pp risposto) *to answer, reply*

risposta *answer*

ristorante (m) *restaurant*

ritardo *lateness, delay;* **essere in – ** *to be late*

ritirare *to collect, get back*

ritornare *to return*

ritorno *return, way back*

ritrovare *to recover, find (again)*

riunione (f) *meeting*

riuscire irr (pp riuscito) *to manage, succeed (like* **uscire***)*

rivestirsi *to get dressed again*

rivista *magazine*

rivolgersi *to ask, apply*

roba *things, stuff*

romanzo *novel*

rompere (pp rotto) *to break*

rosa *rose, pink*

rosso/a *red*

rosticceria *take-away, carry-out (US)*

rotto *from* **rompere**

ruba: andare a – *to sell like hot cakes*

rumore (m) *noise*

ruolo *role*

Russia *Russia* **russo/a** *Russian*

sa *from* **sapere**

sacco *sack;* **un – di soldi** *pots of money*

sala da pranzo *dining room*

salame (m) *salami sausage*

saldi (m pl) *sale(s)*

sale (m) *salt*

salire irr *to go up, get on*

salmone (m) *salmon*

salone (m) *large sitting room*

salotto *sitting room*

salsa *sauce*

salumeria *grocery, delicatessen*

salumiere (m) *grocer*

salutare *to greet, say hello, goodbye*

salutarsi *to greet each other*

salute (f) *health;* **alla –!** *cheers!*

saluto *greeting*

San Marco *St Mark*

San Pietro *St Peter*

sandalo *sandal*

sanitario/a *of health, sanitary*

sanno *from* **sapere**

sapere irr *to know*

sarete *you will be, from* **essere**

sbagliato/a *wrong*

sbaglio *mistake*

sbrigare *to deal with*

sbrigarsi *to hurry (up)*

scacchi (m pl) *chess*

scaffale (m) *bookshelf*

scambio di ospitalità *exchange*

scambio *exchange*

scapolo *bachelor*

scappare *to dash off*

scarpa *shoe*

scatola *tin, box*

scelta *choice*

scendere (pp sceso) giù *to go/come down(stairs), to get off*

scheda telefonica *phonecard*

schiena *back*

sci (m) *skiing;* **sciare** *to ski*

scientifico/a *scientific*

scienza *science*

scienze economiche *economics*

sciopero *strike*

sconto *discount*

scontrino *ticket, receipt*

scorso/a *last*

scottarsi *to get burnt*

scritto *from* **scrivere**

scrivania *desk*

scrivere (pp scritto) *to write*

scuola *school*

scuro/a *dark*

scusare *to excuse;* **scusi!** *excuse me*

se *if*

secco/a *dry*

secolo *century*

secondo *according to*

secondo/a *second*

sede (f) centrale *head office*

sedere, sedersi irr *to sit (down)*

sedia (a sdraio) *(deck) chair*

seduto/a seated

segnale (m) acustico (sound) signal, tone

segretaria secretary

segreteria telefonica answerphone

sei (from **essere)** you are

semaforo traffic lights

sembrare to seem, appear

semola di grano duro durum wheat

semplice simple

sempre always; **– dritto** straight ahead

sentir dire to hear of; **senti!** listen!

sentire to hear, feel

sentirsi male/bene to feel ill/well

senza without

senz'altro! of course, certainly

separato/a separated

sera evening

servire to serve; need

servirsi da soli to help oneself

servizio service

sesto/a sixth

seta silk

sete (f) thirst; **aver –** to be thirsty

settentrionale northern, north

settimana week

settimanale weekly

settimo/a seventh

si one, oneself, you (impersonal)

si dice one says (it)

si figuri! not at all, it's no trouble

si prega di please

sì yes (I do)

sì, grazie yes please

Sicilia Sicily

sicuro/a sure, safe

sig. = sign**o**r(e)

sig.na = signorina

sig.ra = signora

sigaretta cigarette

signora lady, woman, Madam, Mrs

signore (m) (gentle)man, Mr, Sir

signorile: appartamento – luxury flat

signorina young lady, woman, Miss

simpatico/a nice, pleasant

singolo/a single

sinistro/a left; **a sinistra** on the left

sistema (m) system

sistemare to fix, arrange

sistemarsi to get settled

smarrimento loss

smarrire to lose, mislay

smettere (pp smesso) to stop

so from **sapere; non lo so** I don't know

soccorso assistance, help

sociale social

società company, society

soddisfatto/a satisfied, happy

soggiorno living room

sogliola sole

sognare to dream

solamente/solo/soltanto only

soldi (m pl) money

sole (m) sun

solito; di solito usually

solo/a alone; **da –** on one's own

sono (from **essere**) *I am; they are*

sono io *it's me*

sopportare *to bear*

sopra *up, upstairs*

soprattutto *above all*

sorella *sister*

sorpassare *to overtake, pass (US);* **sorpasso** *overtaking*

sorpreso/a *surprised*

sotto *under, underneath, by*

sottopassaggio *underpass*

spaghetti (m pl) *spaghetti*

Spagna *Spain;* **spagnolo/a** *Spanish*

sparecchiare *to clear the table*

spazzolino *toothbrush*

specchio *mirror*

speciale *special*

specialità *speciality*

spedire *to post, despatch, send*

spegnere irr (pp spento) *to turn off, switch off*

spendere (pp speso) *to spend*

spensierato/a *carefree*

spento *from* **spegnere**

sperare di *to hope to*

spesa *shopping*

speso *from* **spendere**

spesso *often*

spettacolo *show*

spiacere = dispiacere

spiaggia *beach*

spiccioli (m pl) *small change*

spiegazione (f) *explanation*

spina *plug;* **staccare la** – *to pull the plug out*

sport (m) *sport*

sportello *counter, window counter*

sposarsi *to get married*

sposato/a *married*

sposo/sposa *bridegroom/bride*

sta (form)/stai (inf): Come –? *How are you?*

stadio *stadium*

stagione (f) *season*

stamattina *this morning*

stampa *press*

stanco/a *tired*

stanotte *tonight, last night*

stanza *room*

stare irr *to be, stay*

star(e) + gerund *to be doing*

star(e) attento/a *to be careful*

star(e) male/bene *to be/feel unwell/well*

star(e) meglio/peggio *to be/feel better/ worse*

star(e) per *to be about to*

stasera *this evening, tonight*

Stato *State;* **gli Stati Uniti** *USA*

stato *from* **essere** *or* **stare**

statua *statue*

stazione (f) *station*

stazione (f) di servizio *service station*

sterlina *£ sterling*

stesso/a *same;* **io** – *I myself*

stesso: lo – *all the same*

stia tranquillo/a! *don't worry!*

stipendio *salary, wages*

stomaco *stomach*

strada *street, road;* **per** – *in the street*

straniero/a *foreign*

strano/a *strange, odd, funny*
studente (m) *student*
studentessa *(female) student*
studiare *to study*
studio *office;* **– legale** *lawyer's office*
stufo/a (di) *fed up (with)*
su *on*
subito *straight away, immediately*
succedere (pp successo) *to happen*
successo *from* **succedere**
sud (m) *south*
sugo *sauce*
suo/a *his, your(s), her(s)*
suonare *to play (an instrument), ring, sound*
superare *to pass (an exam)*
supermercato *supermarket*
supplemento *supplement*
svegliare *to wake someone up*
svegliarsi *to wake up*
Svizzera *Switzerland*
svizzero/a *Swiss*
tabaccaio, tabaccheria *tobacconist's*
tabacco *tobacco*
taglia *size*
tagliatelle *pasta strips*
taglio *cut*
tanto da vedere *so much to see*
tanto/a, tanti/e *so much/so many*
tappeto *carpet*
tardi *late;* **far –** *to be late*
tasca *pocket*
tassì (m) *taxi*

tastiera *keyboard*
tavola/o *table*
tavolino *small table*
tazza/tazzina *cup/small cup*
tè (m) *tea*
teatro *theatre*
tecnico/a *technical, technician*
tedesco/a *German*
telefonare *to phone, call (US)*
telefonata *phone call*
telefonino *mobile phone*
telefono *telephone*
televisione (f) *television*
televisivo/a *television (adj)*
tema (m) *theme*
tempio *temple*
tempo *time, weather*
tenda *curtain*
tenere irr *to keep, hold*
terrazza/o *terrace, balcony*
terzo/a *third*
testa *head*
testo *text, words*
ti *(to/for) you (inf), (to/for) yourself*
tipo *type, kind*
tirare *to pull;* **– vento** *to be windy*
titolo di studio *qualification(s)*
tocca a te! *it's your turn*
toccare *to touch*
togliere irr (pp tolto) *to take off/ away, remove, pull out*
tolto (pp) *from* **togliere**
Torino (f) *Turin*
tornare = ritornare
torre (f) *tower*
torto (aver) *to be wrong*
tosse (f) *cough*

tovagliolo *serviette, table napkin*
tra = **fra**
traduzione (f) *translation*
tramezzino *sandwich*
tranquillo/a *quiet, calm*
trascorrere (pp trascorso) *to spend (time)*
trasferirsi *to move*
trasporto *transport*
trattare *to treat, deal with*
trattoria *modest or trendy restaurant*
traversa *turning*
treno *train*
trentenne *thirty-year-old*
trentina: una – *about thirty*
trimestre (m) *term*
troppo (adv) *too, too much*
troppo/a (adj) *too much*
trota *trout*
trovare *to find, see, visit*
trovarsi *to be; –* **bene** *to be happy*
tu *you (inf)*
tuo/a *your(s) (inf)*
turismo *tourism*
turista (m/f) *tourist*
tutti e due/tutte e due *both (of them)*
tutto a posto *everything in order*
tutto *all, everything*
tutto/a *all, whole, every*
tv *private independent tv*
ubriacarsi *to get drunk*
uccello *bird*
ufficio *office*
ultimo/a *last*
un un', uno, una *a, an, one*
università *university*

universitario/a *(adj) (of the) university*
uno/a *one;* **è l'una** *it's one o'clock*
uomo (pl uomini) *man*
uovo (pl uova) *egg*
urgente *urgent*
usare *to use*
uscire (irr) *to go out, leave*
uscita *exit, way out*
utile *useful*
uva (s) *grapes*
va bene *all right, it fits*
va/vado *from* **andare**
vacanza *holiday*
vaglia (m) *postal order*
vasca da bagno *bathtub*
vasto/a *huge*
vecchio/a *old*
vedere (pp visto) *to see*
vediamo un po' *let's have a look*
vegetariano/a *vegetarian*
veloce *fast*
vendere *to sell*
vendita *sale*
Venezia *Venice*
venire irr (pp venuto) *to come*
ventina: una – *about twenty*
vento *wind*
venuto *from* **venire**
verde *green;* **al –** *broke*
verità *truth*
vero/a true; vero? *isn't it? don't you? etc.*
versare *to pour*
verso *at, about, towards*
vestirsi *to get dressed*
vestito *suit, dress; –* **da sera** *evening dress*

Vesuvio *Vesuvius*
vetrina *shop window*
vi/ve (to/for) *you, yourselves*
via *street, road, away*
viaggiare *to travel;* **il –** *travelling*
viaggiatore (m) *traveller*
viaggio *journey*
vicino *near; –* **a** *next to*
vicino/a di casa *neighbour*
vietato/a *forbidden, prohibited*
villa *villa;* **villetta** *small villa*
villeggiatura *holiday*
vino *wine*
violinista (m/f) *violinist*
violino *violin*
visione (f) *vision*
visitare *to visit, examine*
vissuto *from* **vivere**
visto *from* **vedere**
vita *life*
vitello *calf, veal*
vittoria *victory*

vivere (pp vissuto) *to live*
voce (f) *voice*
vogliamo *from* **volere**
voi *you (pl)*
volentieri *willingly*
volere (irr) *to wish, want*
volta: una – *once;* **due volte**
    twice; **tre –** *three times;* **molte**
    – *many times*
vongola *clam*
vorrei *I would like*
vostro/a *your, yours*
vuole *from* **volere; ci vuole,**
    ci vogliono *it takes*
vuoto/a *empty*
water (m) *w.c.*
zero *nought, zero*
zia /zio *aunt/uncle*
zitto/a *quiet*
zona *zone*
zucchero *sugar*
zucchino/zucchina *courgette*

English–Italian vocabulary

This is not an exhaustive vocabulary list; it is provided to help you with exercises in the *Practice* sections of the book.

able: to be – **potere**
about **circa**; *a book – Italy* **un libro sull'Italia**
about a fortnight **una quindicina di giorni**
abroad **all'estero**; *for –* **per l'estero**
after **dopo**
age **età**
agency **agenzia**
ago **fa**
agree **(vb) essere d'accordo**
agricultural **agricolo/a**
ah **ah!**
all **tutto/a**
all right **va bene**
almost **quasi**
alone **da solo/a**
already **già**
also **anche, pure**
always **sempre**
ambulance **(auto)ambulanza**
America **l'America**; *American* **americano/a**
among **fra**
and **e, ed**
another **un altro, un'altra**
another time **in un altro momento**
any **ne**
anyone **qualcuno**

anything **qualcosa**; *– else?* **altro?**
anyway **comunque**
appetizers; a selection of – **antipasto misto**
apple **mela**
are: they – **sono**
arm **braccio**
arrive **(vb) arrivare**
as **come**
as soon as possible **al più presto**
at **a**; *– your house* **da te**; *at what time?* **a che ora?**
at about (of time) **verso**
at first **prima**
bank **banca**
be **(vb) essere (pp stato)**
beach **spiaggia**
beautiful **bello/a**
because **perchè**
bed **letto**; *to go back to –* **ritornare a letto**
bedroom **camera (da letto)**
been: have you – to ...? **sei (inf)/è (form) stato/stata a ...?**
beer **birra**
before **prima di**; *– nine* **prima delle nove**
begin **(vb) (in)cominciare**
better **(adv) meglio**
bicycle **bicicletta**
big **grande**

bill **conto**

bit: a – **un po'** ; *a – more …* **un altro po' di …**

black **nero/a**

blue **azzurro/a;** *light –* **celeste**

book **(n) libro; (vb) prenotare**

bored: to get – **annoiarsi**

born: I was – **sono nato/a**

bottle **bottiglia**

boy **ragazzo;** *– friend* **ragazzo**

bread **pane (m)**

bridge **ponte (m)**

brother **fratello**

brown **marrone**

but **ma, però, invece**

buy **(vb) comprare, prendere**

by **vicino a;** *– car* **in macchina**

cake **pasta, torta**

call **(vb) chiamare**

can I? **posso?**

can't you …? – **non puoi (inf)/ può (form) …?**

cannot: he cannot/can't **non può**

car **macchina, auto (f);** *by/into/ in the –* **in macchina**

cards **carte (f pl)**

careful: be – ! **sta' (inf)/stia (form) attento!**

car park **parcheggio**

cash-desk **cassa**

cathedral **Duomo**

cent **centesimo**

centre: in the – **al/nel centro**

certain **certo/a, sicuro/a**

chair **sedia**

chance; not by any – **non … mica**

change **(vb) cambiare;** *– one's job* **cambiare lavoro;** *– one's*

mind **cambiare idea**

cheese **formaggio**

child **bambino/a;** *children* **figli**

chips **patatine fritte**

cinema **cinema (m)**

class **classe (f)**

coffee **caffè (m)**

Coliseum **Colosseo**

come **(vb) venire (pp venuto)**

come back **(vb) ritornare**

copy **copia**

could you …? **potresti (inf) …?**

couldn't you …? **non potresti (inf)…?**

day **giorno;** *the – after tomorrow* **dopodomani**

difficult **difficile**

dinner **cena**

dislike **(vb) non piacere**

do **(vb) fare (pp fatto)**

do a tour **(vb) fare il giro**

doctor **medico, dottor(e) (m/f)**

document **documento**

doesn't **non;** *he – speak* **non parla**

dog **cane (m)**

don't **non;** *I – speak* **non parlo;** *– mention it* **prego;** *don't you?* **vero?**

door **porta**

drink **(vb) bere (pp bevuto)**

drive **(vb) guidare** *driving licence* **patente (f)**

during **durante**

early **presto**

easy **facile**

eat **(vb) mangiare**

egg **uovo;** *eggs* **le uova**

England l'**Inghilterra;** *English* **inglese (m/f)**

enjoy oneself **(vb) divertirsi**

enough **abbastanza;** *to be –* **bastare;** *(that's) –* **! basta (così)!**

enrol **(vb) iscriversi (pp iscritto)**

evening **sera**

ever **mai**

every **ogni**

everything **tutto**

everywhere **dappertutto**

exactly **esattamente, di preciso**

exam(ination) **esame (m)**

excellent **ottimo/a**

excuse me! **(mi) scusi! (form)**

expect **(vb) aspettare**

eye **occhio;** *my eyes hurt* **mi fanno male gli occhi**

fairly **abbastanza**

family **famiglia**

far from **lontano da**

father **padre (m)**

feel **(vb) sentirsi**

find **(vb) trovare**

fine **benissimo;** *it's –* **va benissimo**

firm **azienda;** *agricultural –* **azienda agricola**

first **(adv),** *at first* **prima;** *on the – of June* **il primo giugno**

fish **pesce (m)**

flat **appartamento**

foot **piede (m)**

football **calcio**

for **per, da;** *we have been here –* **siamo qui da**

fortnight; about a – **una quindicina di giorni**

four **quattro**

France **la Francia;** *French* **francese**

french fries **patatine fritte**

friend **amico, amici (pl); amica, amiche (pl)**

from **da**

from: I come/am – Pisa **sono di Pisa**

full board **pensione completa**

Germany **la Germania;** *German* **tedesco/a**

get **(vb) prendere (pp preso)**

get into **(vb) entrare**

get off **(vb) scendere**

get on **(vb) salire**

get up **(vb) alzarsi**

give **(vb) dare**

go **(vb) andare;** *to – and have ...* **andare a prendere ...**

go back to **(vb) ritornare a**

go on holiday **(vb) andare in vacanza**

go out **(vb) uscire**

going; I'm – to buy **vado a comprare**

good **buono/a;** *– morning* **buongiorno**

goodbye **arrivederci! ciao (inf)!**

got: I have got **ho**

gram **grammo;** *100 grams* **un etto**

Greece **la Grecia;** *Greek* **greco/a**

green **verde**

greetings **saluti**

grey **grigio/a**

grilled **alla griglia**

gymnasium **palestra**

half **mezzo/a;** *– board* **mezza pensione**

ham **prosciutto;** *Parma* **ham prosciutto crudo**

happy **contento/a**

hard **duro/a;** *to work* **– lavorare molto/duro**

have **(vb) avere, prendere;** *I'll –* **prendo**

have to **(vb) dovere**

hello **ciao!;** *(phone)* **pronto!**

help **(vb) aiutare;** *– me!* **aiutami! (inf), mi aiuti! (form)**

her/his name is **si chiama**

here **qui**

here you are **ecco!**

hi!/hello! **ciao!**

his/her **(il) suo, (la) sua, i suoi, le sue**

holiday: on – **in vacanza**

home: at – **a casa**

hope **(vb) sperare**

hotel **albergo**

hour **ora;** *two hours a day* **due ore al giorno**

house **casa**

how are you? **come stai (inf)/sta (form)?**

how do you say it in Italian? **come si dice in italiano?**

how does one get to ...? **come si fa per andare a ...?/sa dov'è ...?**

how long ...? **quanto tempo ...?**

how many? **quanti/e?;** *– times a year?* **quante volte all'anno?**

how many hours a day? **quante ore al giorno?**

how much (does it come to altogether)? **quant'è?**

how old are you? **quanti anni hai (inf)/ha (form)?**

how's that? **come mai?**

hungry: to be – **aver fame**

hurt **(vb) far male**

husband **marito**

I **io**

I am/I'm **sono**

I'd like **vorrei**

ice cream **gelato**

idea **idea**

if **se**

important **importante;** *(that's) so –* **di così importante**

in **in, a**

interesting **interessante;** *did you do anything – ?* **cos'hai (inf) fatto di bello?**

is, it is **è;** *– there?* **c'è?**

it **(object) lo/la**

Italy **l'Italia;** *Italian* **italiano/a**

jeans **jeans (m pl)**

job **lavoro;** *what (job) do you do?* **che cosa fai (inf)?/fa (form)?**

jogging: to go – **fare il jogging**

July: in – **a luglio**

kind **gentile**

knee **ginocchio**

know **(vb) sapere;** *I don't –* **non lo so;** *to – that* **sapere che**

lake **lago**

language **lingua**

large **grande, vasto/a**

last **(vb) durare;** *it lasts* **dura**

last **scorso/a**; *– year* **l'anno scorso**

last: the – one **l'ultimo**

later **più tardi, dopo**

leave **(vb) lasciare, partire, andar via**

left **(adj) sinistro/a**; *on the –* **a sinistra**

leg **gamba**

let **(vb) lasciare**; *you can let me know* **puoi (inf) farmelo sapere**

library **biblioteca**

like **(vb)** *(to want)* **volere**

like: he likes **gli piace**; *she –* **le piace**; *do you -?* **ti (inf)/le (form) piace?**

like; I would – **vorrei, mi piacerebbe**

listen to **(vb) ascoltare**

little **piccolo/a**

live **(vb) abitare, vivere**

local **locale**

London **Londra**

look **(vb) guardare**; *– for* **cercare**

lose **(vb) perdere, smarrire**

lot: a – **molto**; *a – of time* **molto tempo**; *lots of* **molti/e**

love (letter ending) **un caro saluto**

Madam **signora**

manage **(vb) riuscire**

many **molti/e**

married **sposato/a**

matter: it doesn't matter **non importa/non fa niente**

may I ....? **permesso?/posso?**

maybe **forse**

me **io, mi**; *– too* **anch'io**

meal **pasto**

meanwhile **intanto**

meet up **(vb) incontrarsi**; *we'll meet up* **c'incontriamo, ci vediamo**

meeting **riunione (f)**

message **messaggio**

Milan **Milano (f)**

mind: to change one's – **cambiare idea**

miss **(vb) perdere**

mixed **misto/a**; *– salad* **insalata mista**

moment: one – **un momento! un attimo!**

month **mese (m)**

most **il/la più**

mother **madre (f), la mamma**

much **molto**; *not much* **non molto**

museum **museo**

music **musica**

must: I must **devo**

my **(il) mio, (la) mia, le mie, i miei**

myself: of – **di me**

name **nome (m)** *what's your name?* **come ti chiami (inf)/si chiama (form)?**

name: her/his – is **si chiama**

name-day **onomastico**

Naples **Napoli (f)**

navy blue **blu**

near (next to) **vicino a ...**

near **vicino**; *-by* **qui vicino**

nearly **quasi**

never **mai, non... mai...**

newspaper **giornale (m)**

next **(adj) prossimo/a;** – *to*
  vicino a

nice **bello/a, simpatico/a;** *what*
  a – picture! **che bel quadro!**

night **notte (f)**

no **no;** *no thank you* **no, grazie**

nose **naso**

not **non;** *not ... yet* **non ... ancora**

nothing **niente, nulla;** – *else*
  nient'altro

November **novembre**

now **adesso, ora**

nuisance **guaio**

o'clock: from seven – **dalle sette**

of **di**

often **spesso**

old **vecchio/a**

old: I am 18 years – **ho diciotto
  anni**

on **su;** – *time* **in orario**

once **una volta**

one **si, un, una, uno**

one day **un giorno**

only **solo**

open **(vb) aprire (pp aperto);**
  aperto/a (adj)

opera **opera**

optician **ottico;** *at the optician's*
  dall'ottico

other **altro/a**

our **(il) nostro, (la) nostra, i
  nostri, le nostre**

over there **lì;** – *by ...* **lì, vicino a ...**

pair **paio; due paia (irr)** *two pairs*

parents **genitori (m pl)**

park **(vb) parcheggiare**

Parliament: the Houses of – **il**

Palazzo del Parlamento

party **festa**

pass **(vb) passare;** *(an exam)*
  superare

passport **passaporto**

pay **(vb) pagare**

people **gente (f s);** *four* – **quattro
  persone**

pepper **pepe (m)**

perhaps **forse**

phone **(vb) telefonare; (n)
  telefono**

play **(vb) giocare a**

please **per piacere, per favore,
  per cortesia**

post office **posta**

postcard **cartolina**

prefer **(vb) preferire**

present (gift) **regalo**

price **prezzo**

private bath: with – **con bagno**

put **(vb) mettere (pp messo)**

put on **(vb) mettere, mettersi**

read **(vb) leggere (pp letto)**

ready **pronto/a**

really **veramente**

recommend **(vb) consigliare**

red **rosso/a**

reserve **(vb) prenotare, riservare**

rest **(vb) riposarsi;** *I can* – **mi
  riposo**

restaurant **ristorante (m),
  trattoria**

right: all – **va bene**

Rome **Roma**

room **camera;** *(space)* **posto**

rose **rosa**

salt **sale (m)**

sea **mare (m)**
seat **posto**
second **secondo/a**
see **(vb) vedere (pp visto)**
see you soon **a presto**
seem **(vb) sembrare, parere**
selection of appetizers **antipasto misto**
sell **(vb) vendere**
shoe **scarpa**
shop **negozio**
shower **doccia**
single **single**; – *room* **camera singola**
sister **sorella**
sit **(vb) sedersi**; *sit down!* **siediti! (inf)/si segga (form)!**
ski **(vb) sciare**
skiing: I like skiing **mi piace sciare**
so **allora, quindi, dunque**
so many **tanti/tante**
soccer **calcio**
some **del, della, ecc.**
some, someone **qualcuno**
something **qualcosa**; – *to drink* **qualcosa da bere**
sorry: – I'm late **scusami (inf)/mi scusi (form) del ritardo**
Spanish **spagnolo/a**
speak **(vb) parlare**; *I –* **parlo**; *to – to* **parlare con/a**
spend **(vb)** *a lot of time playing with …* **passare molto tempo a giocare con**
sport: what sport(s) do you do? **che sport fa?**
square **piazza**

St Mark's Square **Piazza San Marco**
stamp **francobollo**
steak **bistecca**; *grilled –* **bistecca alla griglia**
stop **(vb) fermare**; *bus –* **fermata**
straight ahead **sempre dritto**
student **studente (m), studentessa (f)**
study **(vb) studiare**
summer **estate (f)**; *in –* **d'estate**
Sunday **domenica**
supposed to: they were – **dovevano**
sure **certo/a**; *– of myself* **sicuro di me**
swim **(vb) nuotare**; *I like swimming* **mi piace nuotare**
swimming pool **piscina**
T shirt **maglietta**
take **(vb) prendere (pp preso)**
taken **occupato/a**
teacher **professor(e) (m/f), professoressa (f)**
tennis **tennis (m)**
thank you **grazie**; *– for …* **grazie di/per**
that **che**
that (one) **quello/a**; *that's fine* **va benissimo**
the **il, lo, la, l', i, gli, le**
theatre **teatro**; *to the –* **a teatro**
them **(direct object) li/le**
then **poi, allora, dunque**
there **lì, là, ci** ; *it's not –* **non c'è**
there is **c'è**; *– are* **ci sono**
they are **sono**
thing **cosa**

think (vb) **pensare;** *I don't – so* **mi sembra di no**

thirsty: to be – **aver sete**

this evening **stasera**

this, this one **questo/a;** *these* **questi/queste**

through **per; –** *train* **treno diretto**

Thursday **giovedì**

ticket **biglietto;** *– office* **biglietteria**

till **a, fino a**

time **tempo;** *on –* **in orario;** *have a good -!* **buon divertimento!**

time (by the clock) **ora;** *at what – ?* **a che ora?**

time: this – **questa volta;** *at another –* **in un altro momento**

timetable **orario**

tired **stanco/a**

to **a, ad, da;** *in order to* **per**

to: – me **mi;** *– him* **gli; –** *her* **le; –** *you* **ti (inf)/le (form);** *– you* (pl) **vi; –** *them* **(a) loro/gli**

today **oggi**

together **insieme**

tomorrow **domani**

too **anche, pure;** (adv) **troppo**

too many **troppi/e;** *too much* **troppo**

tourist **turista (m/f)**

towel **asciugamano**

tower **torre (f);** *the Leaning Tower* **la Torre Pendente**

town **città; –** *centre* **centrocittà;** *old –* **centro storico**

town hall **municipio**

traffic lights **semaforo**

train **treno;** *by –* **in/col treno**

travel (vb) **viaggiare**

travel agency **agenzia di viaggi**

twice **due volte**

two **due**

understand (vb) **capire**

unemployed **disoccupato/a**

unfortunately **purtroppo**

university **università;** *at –* **all'università**

vegetable soup **minestrone (m)**

Venice **Venezia**

Verona **Verona**

very **molto; –** *kind of you* **molto gentile**

very much **moltissimo**

Vesuvius **il Vesuvio**

village **(piccolo) paese (m), paesino**

wear (vb) **portare, mettere, mettersi**

wait (vb) **aspettare**

want (vb) **volere**

we're, we are **siamo**

we've been here since/for … **siamo qui da …**

week **settimana**

well **bene;** *to feel –* **sentirsi bene**

went: he went **è andato/andava**

what **(che) cosa?** *at – time?* **a che ora?**

what a nuisance! **che guaio!**

what a nice house! **che bella casa!**

what do I do? **come faccio?/cosa faccio?**

what do we do? **come facciamo?**

what have you got to do? **cos'hai (inf) da fare?**

what is there to eat? **cosa c'è da mangiare?**

what time is it? **che ora è?/che ore sono?** *at what time?* **a che ora?**

when **quando;** *– you like* **quando vuoi**

where **dove**

whether **se**

which **che**

white **bianco/a**

who **che;** *who?* **chi?**

why? **perchè? come mai?** *is that why ...?* **è per questo che ...?**

why not? **perchè no?**

window **finestra**

wine **vino**

with **con**

without **senza**

woman **donna, signora;** *young –* **signorina**

work (n) **lavoro;** *to –* **lavorare, funzionare**

worry (vb) **preoccuparsi;** *don't –!* **non preoccuparti (inf)/non si preoccupi (form)!**

write **(vb) scrivere (pp scritto)**

wrong: to be – **aver torto**

year **anno**

yellow **giallo**

yes **sì;** *– please* **sì, grazie;** *yes?* **prego?**

yesterday **ieri;** *the day before –* **l'altro ieri**

yet: not yet **non ancora**

you **tu, lei, voi;** *– yourself* **lei;** *to –* **le (form), ti (inf), vi (pl)**

you were **eri (inf)/era (form)**

your (form) **(il) suo, (la) sua, i suoi, le sue**

your (inf) **(il) tuo, (la) tua, i tuoi, le tue**

your (pl) **(il) vostro, (la) vostra, i vostri, le vostre**

Grammar index

Numbers in bold refer to unit number and subsequent number refers to Grammar, i.e. **2.6** = Unit 2, Grammar 6.

Credits